The AMERICAN HERITAGE *History of the* Confident Years

By the Editors of
AMERICAN HERITAGE
The Magazine of History

Editor in Charge
Ralph K. Andrist

Narrative
Francis Russell

Pictorial Commentary
Michael Harwood

Published By
American Heritage Publishing Co., Inc.,
New York

American Heritage Book Division

EDITORIAL DIRECTOR
Richard M. Ketchum

GENERAL EDITOR
Alvin M. Josephy, Jr.

Staff for this Book

EDITOR
Ralph K. Andrist

ASSOCIATE EDITOR
Michael Harwood

ART DIRECTOR
Chester Prosinski

COPY EDITOR
Joan Rehe Wilkinson

PICTURE EDITOR
Linda Silvestri Sykes
Assistant: Carla Davidson

ASSISTANT EDITOR
Susan H. Baker

EDITORIAL ASSISTANT
Nancy F. Oakes

CONTRIBUTING EDITOR
Margaret Christ

EUROPEAN BUREAU
Gertrudis Feliu, *Chief*

American Heritage
Publishing Co., Inc.

PRESIDENT
James Parton

CHAIRMAN, EDITORIAL COMMITTEE
Joseph J. Thorndike

EDITOR, AMERICAN HERITAGE MAGAZINE
Oliver Jensen

SENIOR ART DIRECTOR
Irwin Glusker

PUBLISHER, AMERICAN HERITAGE MAGAZINE
Darby Perry

Picture Credits. Pages 2-3: Collection of Mr. and Mrs. J. William II; Front Endsheet: I. N. P. Stokes Collection, New York Public Library; Back Endsheet: Eno Collection, New York Public Library

J. WELLS CHAMPNEY, *THE BICYCLIST*, COLLECTION OF MR. AND MRS. HENRY N. FLYNT

Contents

Narrative   *Portfolios*

Introduction   7

Trial of a President   9

Grant in the White House   37

                                               65   Rebels and Reconstructors

The Politics of Boodle   81

                                              107   Faces of the West

An Era of Expansion   119

                                              145   In Rural America

Rise of the Tycoons   161

                                              187   A Time for Sports

The Return of the Democrats   199

                                              225   Builders and Doers

Unrest in the Farm Lands   241

                                              267   Avenue and Alley

Free Silver and Expansionism   279

                                              305   In the Melting Pot

War with Spain   321

                                              347   Horseless Carriage Days

America Enters into the Twentieth Century   359

                                              383   Twilight on Elm Street

Acknowledgments and Index   392

*A summer afternoon in the early 1900's beside the Atlantic
Ocean at Seabreeze, Florida, then a recently developed resort.
Now long gone are both Seabreeze, incorporated into the city
of Daytona Beach, and the leisurely way of life pictured here.*

Introduction

At the end of the Civil War the nation was emotionally exhausted, but except for the ruined South, its economic health was excellent. Industry had flourished under the spur of war production. New opportunities had opened for the ambitious, the talented, and the shrewd, and many a young man who in less favorable times might have lived out a comfortable small-town existence was drawn to the city to achieve success in factory, money market, or the murky world of ward politics.

Unhappily, public moral standards turned shoddy and crass. Men whose chief attributes were acquisitiveness and ruthlessness were applauded simply because they had become wealthy and powerful. But integrity was not dead; men opposed injustice and corruption and marched behind banners whose devices proclaimed that there were wrongs to be righted. Meanwhile the tide of immigration from Europe continued, a flood of humans whose eagerness testified that the United States, whatever its faults might be, was still the land of opportunity.

It was a period of exuberant growth, in population, industry, and world prestige. As the twentieth century opened, American political pundits were convinced that the nation was on an ascending spiral of progress that could end only in something approaching perfection. Even those who saw the inequity between the bright world of privilege and the gray fact of poverty were quite sure that a time was very near when no one would go cold or hungry or ill clothed. These were indeed the Confident Years.

The assurance that the United States was the best of all possible nations in a rational world came to an end with the outbreak of the First World War. Disorder and confusion replaced the neat and nicely organized scheme of things. Today we are still trying to recapture at least a small part of what we lost more than fifty years ago: the sense of security that comes with the belief that one lives in a safe and well-ordered world.

The Editors

RESPECTFULLY DEDICATED
TO THE
PEOPLE OF THE UNITED STATES.

PRESIDENT LINCOLN'S FUNERAL MARCH
COMPOSED BY
E. MACK.
Philadelphia LEE & WALKER. 722 Chestnut St

Trial of a President

$\mathcal{T}$he floor of the crimson and gilt Senate Chamber filled quickly as the senators and representatives took their places to hear Congressman Ben Butler of Massachusetts present the case against President Andrew Johnson. Twenty-five days earlier, on March 5, 1868, the President's trial had formally opened with Chief Justice Salmon P. Chase presiding over the fifty-three senators who sat as a court of impeachment. One hundred and ninety-two members of the House of Representatives, having already voted to impeach Johnson for "high crimes and misdemeanors in office," were present as accusers. On March 3 the representatives had adopted eleven articles of impeachment, the most notorious, Article X, having been written by Butler himself. In it he had accused Johnson of bringing Congress into disgrace by "inflammatory and scandalous harangues" and of degrading his office "to the great scandal of all good citizens." That ailing but most savagely vindictive Radical Republican leader Thaddeus Stevens had taken the occasion to warn the President: "Unfortunate, unhappy man, behold your doom!"

The trial of the President of the United States and the attempt to remove him from office filled Washington with crowds of inaugural proportions. Diplomats and ministers of foreign countries in all the formal glitter of their gold-trimmed uniforms, newsmen and favored politicians, jammed the Senate's galleries. The Capital's most fashionable women, along with the less elegantly dressed wives of congressmen, occupied the ladies' gallery. Every seat could have been filled ten times over by the time Ben Butler, the ringmaster of the Radicals, took the floor. A *Harper's Weekly* correspondent described him as "a man whose large pudgy body seemed literally bursting out of his extraordinary swallow tail coat, exposing a broad expanse of not too immaculate linen, and whose massive bald head with its little fringe of oily curls was probably familiar to every occupant of the galleries, for Benjamin F. Butler had not hidden his light under a bushel. There was power in the man's coarse, big-featured face, force and aggressiveness in every line, but his curiously ill-mated eyes with their half-closed lids, his hard mouth and small, drooping moustache, all combined to create an un-

The responsibility of leading a divided nation, which Andrew Johnson now assumed, had aged his assassinated predecessor far more than the portrait on this sheet music cover would have it.

comfortable impression of cunning and insincerity. . . ."

He was indeed an extraordinary man, self-made, a Democrat turned Radical Republican, one of the ablest lawyers—perhaps the ablest criminal lawyer—in the United States, and one of the most inept of the Civil War's political generals. In 1864 as a prominent Unionist Democrat he had been offered the vice-presidential place on Lincoln's National Union ticket, although Lincoln privately considered him "as full of poison gas as a dead dog." As military governor of conquered New Orleans he had achieved the nickname Beast Butler by his general order that any female showing contempt for an officer or soldier of the United States should be treated as "a woman of the town plying her avoca-

tion." He had even been accused of taking away a coffin filled with stolen silver spoons on his leaving New Orleans. Spoons Butler, the Southerners called him, as well as Beast, and in the next decade they applied his puffy features to the bottoms of chamber pots in the cabins of Mississippi side-wheelers. His soldiers and his political enemies called him Old Cock-Eye.

In preparing his opening argument, Butler had slept only nine hours in the previous three days. Yet, for all his allegations, he and everyone else present knew that Johnson's crime was that he had opposed the will of the dominant Radical Republicans. They, in turn, had designed the Tenure of Office Act of March, 1867, an unconstitutional measure, which provided that the Pres-

In the painting at left by Thomas Nast—best known for his Harper's Weekly *cartoons—a vanguard of General William T. Sherman's huge force takes possession of a Georgia plantation in the autumn of 1864. The aloof, defiant ladies on the veranda would no doubt have had advance word of the Yankees' freewheeling destruction and looting. (Above is Nast's study for one of the figures.) Union troops and hangers-on cut a broad charred trail from Atlanta to Savannah and, that winter, through South Carolina. Southern bitterness was the legacy. "One could track the line of Sherman's march . . . by the fires on the horizon," an ex-Rebel general said. "He stripped our people of everything. He deserves to be called the great robber of the nineteenth century."*

ident could not remove any civil officer or a member of his Cabinet without the "advice and consent" of the Senate. Earlier attempts at impeachment had failed. But when Johnson suspended his patently disloyal Secretary of War, Edwin M. Stanton, and Stanton refused to leave office, the President's congressional enemies seized the opportunity to bring forward impeachment proceedings. Johnson was denounced on the floor of the House as an "ungrateful, despicable, besotted, traitorous man," an accidental President, an American Nero, his career marked "by a degree of perfidy and treachery and turpitude unheard of in the history of the rulers of a free people. . . ."

Butler had a gift for extemporized invective and a voice like a bullwhip, yet this time he read from a carefully prepared text; and since he was not a good reader, much of his native dynamic power was lost. Wearing evening clothes and a white tie, although it was afternoon, he went through the articles of impeachment one by one. The President, he said, had removed his Secretary of War contrary to an act of Congress. Even though the act was passed over his veto, "he and all others must execute the law, whether in fact constitutional or not." He failed to do so "at his peril; but that peril" is impeachment. As Butler continued his charges, the galleries grew restless, the senators torpid. Only at the end of his three-hour speech did they come to life again with his perorating invective. "This man," he told them, "by murder most foul succeeded to the Presidency, and is the elect of an assassin to that high office, and not of the people. . . . We are about to remove him from the office he has disgraced by the sure, safe, and constitutional means of impeachment."

Johnson had followed a turbulent, descending road from that high moment of April 15, 1865, when Chief Justice Chase had sworn him in as the seventeenth President of the United States and then, extending his hand, had declared: "You are President. May God support, guide and bless you in your administration." The upward road had also been notable, for Johnson, like his predecessor, had been born into obscurity. The son of a tavern handy man in Raleigh, North Carolina, the boy Andy never attended school a day in his life. When he was three his father died, and his mother supported him and his older brother, William, by weaving and taking in washing. At fourteen he was apprenticed to a tailor for the traditional seven years, but after two years he ran away. For a time he plied his trade in South

Carolina, and then made his way across the Smokies to Tennessee. After working some months in Rutledge, Tennessee, he set up his own tailoring shop at Greeneville. There in May, 1827, at the age of eighteen he married Eliza McCardle, the daughter of a Scottish shoemaker, an attractive young woman who had supported herself since her father's death—the record is now confused as to her vocation. At the time of his marriage he could read after a fashion, but it was Eliza who taught him to write and cipher.

The young couple lived in a single room behind the plank-sided tailor shop on Greeneville's Main Street. Andy was a skilled workman, and he worked hard. The tailoring business prospered. Before many years he was hiring his own apprentices and bought a fine new shop. But his mind expanded beyond his confining trade. He joined two debating societies, one at Greeneville College, and once a week walked four miles to the college to attend its meetings. He now read voraciously, as if he were making up for lost time. Finally he started his own Saturday-night debating club in his shop. At twenty-one he ran for the town council and was elected. Two years later the best people of Greeneville were surprised to find the tailor Johnson their mayor. By the time he was twenty-seven, campaigning as the candidate of the common people, he had beaten the Greeneville candidate of wealth and position for state legislator.

Defeated in the following election, Johnson succeeded subsequently in being re-elected. Andrew Jackson was his proclaimed idol, and in Greene County Johnson seemed to many a local model of "Old Hickory." The tailor-turned-politician became a compelling public speaker, with a ringing voice that carried even in the open air. In 1841 he was elected to the state Senate, and two years later ran for Congress in a strong Whig district, carrying the day for his own emphatic brand of Jacksonian Democracy.

As a congressman he found the social world of Washington of little concern or interest, and spent his free time in the Library of Congress. He became a clamorous advocate of homestead legislation, of giving the nation's Western holdings without cost to the mudsills— the landless white settlers—as "free land for free labor." Ten years he spent in the House of Representatives, creditably if not with outstanding distinction, until the Whigs gained control of Tennessee and redistricted the state to gerrymander him out of his seat. But the Whig

For this lady He Returns No More. *Reconstruction America fed on such tragic sentiment. "Love and tears for the Blue," went a popular song, "Tears and love for the Gray."*

politicians were not as clever as they had thought, for Johnson, on returning home, ran for governor and managed to defeat his Whig opponent. As governor he was concerned much more with state than national affairs, showing himself particularly interested in expanding aid to education. As a follower of Old Hickory's, he continued to find in the common man the source of his political strength. Know-Nothings unsuccessfully opposed his re-election. At the end of his second term, in 1856, the by-then Democratic legislature elected him to the United States Senate.

In Washington the patricians and would-be patricians of the South looked down on the tailor-made senator from Tennessee, and he in turn nursed his resentments against aristocrats. Jefferson Davis later accused him of "the pride of having no pride." As senator, he reintroduced his homestead bill, seeing it through both houses of Congress only to have it vetoed by the Southern-minded Buchanan. Paradoxically Johnson,

12

COLLECTION OF EDGAR WILLIAM AND BERNICE CHRYSLER GARBISCH

who—to the applause of the North and West—advocated giving land to settlers, was himself a small slaveholder. But he, Old Hickory's shoot, continued to move further and further away from his alignment with the leaders of the slave states.

After the Democratic split of 1860, which made Lincoln's election inevitable, Johnson, out of what he felt was party loyalty, supported the Southern Democratic ticket of Breckinridge and Lane. But after Lincoln's election, while the Stars and Stripes was being hauled down in the South as the slave states prepared to secede, Johnson came to the support of the President-elect. "I voted against him," he said in a Senate speech as the crisis deepened. "I spoke against him; I spent my money to defeat him; but still I love my country; I love the Constitution: I intend to insist upon its guarantees." And he begged every man who called himself a patriot to "rally around the altar of our common country . . . that the Constitution shall be saved and the Union preserved." Such a speech by a Southern Democrat gained thousands of Southerners for the Union and made Johnson one of the most popular men in the North, although secessionists in Tennessee burned him in effigy. Throughout the eastern part of his state he defended the Union successfully, but was overwhelmed by the secessionists elsewhere, who were directed by their governor in Nashville. In danger of assassination, Johnson was finally forced to leave Tennessee for Washington, a senator without a state.

Through the following winter the exiled senator begged the President in vain to aid loyal Union men in East Tennessee. Then in 1862 General Grant's capture of Forts Henry and Donelson forced the Confederates to abandon Nashville and the central section of the state. In an attempt to restore Unionist control there, Lincoln sent Johnson to the state capital as military governor of Tennessee with the rank of brigadier general. Nashville, still controlled by pugnacious secessionists, received him as a "vile wretch, this traitor to the State," and threatened him with tar and feathers, and even death. At first the new governor tried to conciliate his opponents in office, but the Nashville municipal authorities remained belligerently Southern, refusing to take the oath to the Union and continuing their expressions of contempt. Faced with such recalcitrance, Johnson removed all those of dubious allegiance from office, replacing them with "unconditionally loyal Union men." By September,

1862, the military governor's own position grew shaky following the sweep of Braxton Bragg's Confederate forces into Tennessee. The timid Union General Don Carlos Buell prepared to abandon Nashville. Only Johnson's dogged determination during a siege of two months kept the state capital from falling.

Not until January, 1864, was federal occupation of Tennessee considered complete enough for establishing a civil government. Johnson then called for an election in March, with the condition that each voter must swear to support the Constitution as "a true and faithful citizen of the United States" who "ardently desires the suppression of the present insurrections and rebellions." Conservative Unionists were indignant at having their loyalty questioned; secessionist sympathizers were all for taking the oath and disregarding it. In the midst of the turmoil, Johnson received word that Lincoln was considering him as a vice-presidential candidate, a Unionist Democrat who would balance the National Union ticket in the November election, which Lincoln felt far from sure of winning.

Unionism in the end carried the day in Nashville— if not throughout the state—and huge crowds, invigorated by brass bands, serenaded Johnson at his nomination. "I am a Democrat in the strictest meaning of the term," the old Jacksonian told his cheering supporters. "I am for putting down the rebellion, because it is a war against democracy." Slavery, the old slaveowner announced, was dead, killed by those who had wished to save it. Speaking from the steps of the state capitol in Nashville just before the election, he said, "I, Andrew Johnson, do hereby proclaim freedom, full, broad and unconditional, to every man in Tennessee. . . . This damnable aristocracy should be pulled down. No longer should the wives and daughters of the colored men of Tennessee be dragged into a concubinage compared to which polygamy was a virtue."

In spite of the incursions of Hood's army and Forrest's cavalry into Tennessee, most of the polling places were able to open, and Lincoln and Johnson carried the state. Lincoln, though elected by only a 400,000 majority out of a total of 4,010,000 votes, carried nineteen of the twenty-two eligible states. The solid, erect figure of the Vice President-elect, though of medium height, gave the impression of strength and power. In young manhood his sensitive face with its dark luminous eyes had seemed almost wistful. In middle age his eyes retained their intensity, but his face had grown harder, the chin more combative; the mouth now turned down at the corners, and the brows were knit in a slight but permanent frown.

A raw, drizzling Inauguration Day found Johnson still recovering from an attack of typhoid fever. That March day turned out to be the most unfortunate and humiliating one of his life. In the Vice President's room at the Capitol he complained that he felt "very weak and enervated" and asked for whiskey. Vice President Hannibal Hamlin offered a bottle, and Johnson "drank a good potation." Then, before going into the Senate Chamber, he downed still another stiff drink, telling Hamlin, "I need all the strength for the occasion I can have." By the time he reached the rostrum of the overheated chamber he was pugnaciously drunk. In the

HARPER'S WEEKLY, APRIL 11, 1874

presence of the President—the noble second inaugural address still to be delivered—the Cabinet, the justices of the Supreme Court, members of the diplomatic corps, and assembled senators, Johnson harangued at random, as though still smarting from his earlier rebuffs. A "plebian boy," he proclaimed himself, denouncing the "fine feathers" of the diplomatic corps and all those who put themselves above "the people" and, as one reporter present wrote, "bellowing and ranting and shaking his fists at Judges, Cabinet and Diplomats, and making a fool of himself to such a degree that indignation is almost compelled to pity." The dismayed Lincoln stared at the floor. Several senators hid their heads in their hands; some of those present left. Hamlin edged forward to pull Johnson's coattail, whispering, "Stop! Johnson, stop!" For days after the incident, Washington was in a ferment, the whole country was shocked, and Johnson's enemies were delighted. "He made a bad slip the other day," Lincoln observed, "but I have known Andy a great many years and he ain't no drunkard."

Seven weeks later General Lee had surrendered his Confederate forces to General Grant, Lincoln had been murdered, and the tailor from Greeneville had succeeded to the Presidency.

The first modern war, the first fought with the tools and weapons of the industrial age, had left the South in ruins. What had at the beginning seemed to Southerners a romantic adventure had in four years become a relentless contest of attrition. In Georgia, Virginia, Mississippi, the Carolinas, wherever the armies had passed, the land lay weed-grown and abandoned, marked by gaunt black chimneys, which became known as Sherman's sentinels. The rich Shenandoah Valley had been systematically laid waste by General Sheridan, who carried out Grant's instructions to ravage the land so completely that a crow, in flying across it, would have to carry his own rations. Railroads, factories, cotton gins, farms, everything of possible use to the enemy had been destroyed. The air itself was rancid with the odor of dead farm animals and smoldering grain. Many of the tree-lined and gracious cities had been burned—

"The Cradle of Liberty in Danger," warned the 1874 Harper's Weekly *caption. The looks and shenanigans of Ben Butler (then running for the Massachusetts governorship) made him an ideal target for such cartoonists as Thomas Nast.*

Jackson, Charleston, Mobile, Richmond, Atlanta, Savannah. Across the desolate landscape the pathetic, rootless ex-slaves wandered, sometimes searching for relatives, more often merely moving because they were at last free to move.

How could the South restore herself? Not through the ex-slaves, their minds as well as their bodies so long in bondage. Not through the aristocrats, who had arrogantly led the South to disaster. Restoration would come, in President Johnson's opinion, through the efforts of the common man, the plain "Andy Jackson" Democrat who had carried Old Hickory triumphantly to the White House, who had elected Andy Johnson to offices, from mayor of Greeneville to senator from Tennessee, over the opposition of the Whig patricians.

On becoming President, Johnson the Unionist saw himself as the inheritor of the conciliatory policy of his Republican predecessor. The noble phrases of Lincoln's second inaugural address — "with malice toward none; with charity for all" — which would become clichés in their heedless repetition, meant, when freshly minted, exactly what Lincoln said. Only a magnanimous peace, Lincoln had felt, could heal the wounds of a fratricidal war. In his opinion no state had seceded from the Union because no state *could* secede. Already in December, 1863, the President had offered a general pardon to Southerners willing to lay down their arms and return to their old allegiance. In the same proclamation he had offered to recognize any state government organized by citizens who had taken an oath of allegiance and whose numbers were at least equal to 10 per cent of the voters of the 1860 election.

After his re-election, Lincoln pressed on with his restoration plans. When Congress convened in December, 1864, Louisiana became the test state. Some twelve thousand of its citizens had reorganized under Lincoln's plan — had taken the prescribed oath, adopted a new constitution, held an election, and installed a loyal government. The new Louisiana legislature had elected two United States senators, and these appeared with the state's quota of congressmen at the Capitol. The following February, Senator Lyman Trumbull of Illinois offered a joint resolution to recognize the Louisiana delegation. The resolution would have passed quickly and overwhelmingly but for Senator Charles Sumner of Massachusetts, who, as spokesman of the Radicals in the Senate, objected that under its provisions the Negro would not be allowed to vote. Congress was then little concerned with this issue, which would later loom so large. Sumner's objections were doctrinaire, for though as the hero of the abolitionists he held uncompromisingly to the dogma of Negro equality, the actual Negro left him cold and indifferent.

Fenced in by his aloof egotism, Sumner had become a walking abstraction. The man who sat in Daniel Webster's old seat in the Senate seemed to have sea water in his veins. "I long since ceased to take any interest in individuals," he once told Julia Ward Howe. Handsome, theatrical, and pedantic, disliked by his colleagues North and South, he saw himself as an eagle soaring high and alone in the sky. Some of his Massachusetts associates considered him insane. When he spoke, he larded his speeches with quotations from four languages; yet for all his Harvard learning, his speeches were pompous and second-rate. His bleak complacency could even irritate Grant to a witticism. Once when someone remarked in the General's presence that Sumner did not believe in the Bible, Grant replied: "Why should he? He didn't write it."

Although Trumbull's resolution had Lincoln's backing, Sumner used every parliamentary trick to obstruct its passage, finally resorting to a filibuster to keep it from coming to a vote. As the end of the session neared, vital Army and Navy appropriations bills were being held up by Sumner's obstinacy. Finally the administration yielded, and the Senate dropped the resolution. Though no one sensed it at the time, Sumner's triumph marked the end of the policy of reconstructing the South through reconciliation.

On Lincoln's death, Secretary Stanton informed his Cabinet colleagues that they must place their resignations in the new President's hands. But Johnson, directly after he had taken his oath of office, asked Lincoln's whole Cabinet to stay with him in this difficult period. To the Radical Republicans with their abolitionist roots, Johnson's accession was a relief. They had never trusted Lincoln's pragmatic approach to the South. If the Radicals had dared, they would have turned openly against Lincoln. They had worked privately against his nomination, and at one point had even been considering Ben Butler as their choice for the Presidency in 1864. "Treason must be made infamous and traitors must be impoverished," Johnson had thundered the day after Lincoln died. These were pleasantly consistent words from the man who had in Congress referred to the Jefferson Davis clique as a

Above is Mathew Brady's photograph of Richmond after the Rebels had set fire to it as they withdrew. Reporter John Trowbridge, who saw the Confederate capital's business district in September, 1865, described acres of "cellars half filled with bricks and rubbish . . . impassable streets deluged with debris . . . the iron fragments of crushed machinery."

"bastard, scrub aristocracy," and who as military governor of Tennessee had moved against the Tennessee secessionists with a ruthlessness unhampered by legal restraint. "Johnson, we have faith in you," Radical Senator Ben Wade of Ohio remarked after visiting the new President just before Lincoln's burial. "By the gods, there will be no trouble now in running the government."

In the shocked anger following Lincoln's death, his successor seemed at first glimpse a Southern intruder in the White House. But, benefiting from the initial good will that Americans bear their Presidents, Johnson in a few months achieved a popularity that must have been surprising even to himself. Practically, the war had ended April 9 with Lee's surrender at Appomattox —although the last Confederate army, under General Edmund Kirby-Smith, did not surrender until the end of May. Three days before this, on May 23, 1865, the triumphant grand review of the Union armies under Grant and Sherman had begun in Washington, helping to assuage the bitterness of Lincoln's murder. Spectators watched with pride and a new sense of unity as the endless lines of men in blue, the long columns of cavalry, the rumbling guns and caissons of the artillery, moved down Pennsylvania Avenue in the spring sunlight for two days in their final review.

In early June the President moved into the White House; his family came from Nashville to join him in August. After the tense wartime atmosphere under Lincoln, with the official family limited to the shrewish Mary Lincoln and the spoiled, speech-impeded Tad, the Mansion suddenly became gay and sunny with the influx of Johnson's household: his gracious, plain-mannered wife; his married daughter, Martha Patterson, who took over the role of mistress of the White House; his widowed daughter, Mary Stover; his other children; his son-in-law, Senator David Patterson of Tennessee; and his five grandchildren. To official Washington the change seemed a promise of better times. The sharp consciousness of Lincoln's assassination had been to a degree blunted by the grand review. Then, on a sweltering July afternoon in the court-yard of the Arsenal Penitentiary, the hanging of four of the conspirators associated with the assassin, John Wilkes Booth, gave a vicarious release to pent-up emotions of vengeance.

In the evanescent bright months following his succession, Johnson was able briefly to appear all things to all men. To the Radicals, long alienated by Lincoln's practical moderation, the plebian from Tennessee who had just issued a proclamation offering a reward of a hundred thousand dollars for the arrest of Jefferson Davis seemed much more amenable to their goal of vengeance on the aristocratic South. The majority of moderate Republicans saw the new President as Lincoln's successor, intent on following the dead President's policy of conciliation and reunion. Northern Democrats rejoiced in another leader of their own party occupying the White House. Southerners, from their war-torn and exhausted homeland still occupied by federal troops, looked to a fellow Southerner for sympathy and assistance. Only the irreconcilables—the remnants of Northern Copperheads and Southern secessionists—remained beyond approbation.

Preferring the term "restoration" to "reconstruction," Johnson, like Lincoln, took the position that the Southern states had never been "out of the Union." With Congress in recess until December, in May the President issued an amnesty proclamation by which all but former leaders of the Confederacy received "amnesty and pardon, with restoration of all rights of property, except as to slaves." On that same day he issued a second proclamation appointing a provisional governor for North Carolina to construct a government there. Shortly afterward, Johnson issued similar proclamations for Mississippi, Georgia, Texas, Alabama, South Carolina, and Florida. The four other states of the Confederacy—Arkansas, Louisiana, Tennessee, and Virginia—he considered far enough ahead in the process of restoration not to need provisional governors. With most of the former Confederacy still controlled by federal bayonets, Johnson set out the informal terms for restoration. The seceded states must call a convention of "loyal" citizens to make an end to slavery in each state, to declare the acts of secession null and void, to repudiate all debts incurred by them during the rebellion, and to arrange an election of governors, state legislators, and national congressmen. The new state governments would then ratify the Thirteenth Amendment, abolishing slavery nationally.

By the time Congress convened in December, all the former secessionist states but Texas had held their conventions and had gone on to elect legislators, governors, and members of Congress. Johnson's policy was to retire each provisional governor in favor of the elected governor as soon as a state had ratified the Thirteenth Amendment. All did so, with the exception of uncompromising Mississippi. The opening of Congress found the newly elected Southern representatives gathered in Washington. The restored states had named four Confederate generals as congressmen with several times as many colonels and ex-members of the Confederate Congress, while Georgia had even elected the former Confederate vice president, Alexander H. Stephens, to the Senate.

To see these ex-Confederates knocking jauntily on the doors of the Capitol gave many in the North the uneasy feeling that the South had never really sur-

A black couple is married by a Freedmen's Bureau chaplain, above. Such ceremonies between slaves had been proscribed, since legal recognition of the sanctity of the black family as a unit would have put a decided crimp in the slave trade.

rendered. What the North had expected, an emotional repudiation of the Confederacy, was not forthcoming. Though Southerners could admit that slavery was a thing of the past, they still hoped to be compensated for their lost "property." They still looked on their war-incurred debts as a moral obligation. Upper-class Southerners refused to fraternize with federal officers. Although only six Northern states allowed the Negro to vote, Northerners in their victory expected at least a token form of Negro suffrage in the South. Johnson, like Lincoln, favored extending the vote to literate Negroes and to those who owned property or had served in the Army—a very small number. Instead Southern legislatures, led by Mississippi, reacted with the so-called Black Codes. To the problem of almost four mil-

lion liberated slaves, most of them illiterate field hands, wandering uncontrolled and aimlessly across the countryside, the South responded with control by peonage. There would be no Negro access to the ballot, not even for literate town Negroes or ex-soldiers. According to the Mississippi Black Code, every Negro under eighteen had to be apprenticed to a white person, preferably a former owner, who must treat him well, provide an elementary education, and take care of any medical needs. Negroes not employed by January, 1866, would be jailed as vagrants and "hired out" by the sheriff. Each Negro must have a lawful home and carry a certificate to prove it. Although similar laws against vagrancy had long existed in the North, in the South they were grist for the mill of Radicalism. Even moderate Republicans were disturbed by such Southern intractability.

Southern congressmen- and senators-elect, seeking admission to the Capitol, found their way was barred by the cadaverous, club-footed Radical from Pennsylvania, Thaddeus Stevens. As chairman of the Ways and Means Committee, "Old Thad" had become one of the most powerful men in Congress. Seventy-three years old, grotesquely crippled, fox-featured, his baldness disguised if not concealed by a chestnut-colored wig, with a harsh hollow voice and a truculent permanent pout, he was for all his age and frailty the South's most implacable congressional enemy and Johnson's most redoubtable opponent. Unlike the dogmatic Sumner, Stevens was a pragmatist in the hatred that seemed to be bound up in his nature. He had in the preceding half century hated Andrew Jackson, the Democratic party (above all else), Freemasonry, slavery, the Compromise of 1850, the Irish and other immigrant groups, and finally Andrew Johnson. He had been an Antimason, a Whig, an abolitionist, a Know-Nothing, and finally a Republican and a Radical. According to Sumner's theory, the seceding states had committed suicide. Stevens held to the simpler view that they were a defeated nation. "We must conquer the Southern States," he said in one wartime speech, "and hold them as conquered provinces." The war was for him a "radical revolution," a means to "remodel our institutions." In September, 1865, he called for the confiscation of the estates of "70,000 proud, bloated and defiant rebels"; he wanted forty acres to be given to each ex-slave, and the remaining land sold for the profit of the federal government.

A rich man, an economic conservative, owner of lands and ironworks, counsel and favorite of railroads, banks, and Northern industry, Stevens followed the pattern of many a self-made young American lawyer in the burgeoning nineteenth century. Born in the frontier region of Vermont in Washington's first administration, a sickly, crippled child, he found himself further handicapped by a ne'er-do-well father. His hard-working mother scrimped to give the boy an education. Eventually he went to Dartmouth, and graduated in 1814. For two years he taught school, first in Vermont, then in York, Pennsylvania, meanwhile studying law by candlelight in his spare time. By the time he became of age he was a lawyer. He settled in Gettysburg, Pennsylvania, and won his first fame by defending a murderer even though he was unable to save his client's neck. As fees came in, he invested in real estate until in a dozen years he became Gettysburg's largest taxpayer and an accepted member of the town's ruling elite.

Jacksonian democracy had little appeal for this

self-made lawyer with one eye on the main chance and the other on politics. Expediency drew him to the crusade against Freemasonry. Exploiting the common man's distrust of exclusive secret societies, he became a state political figure through this issue, keeping Antimasonry alive in Pennsylvania long after it had disappeared in the other states. In 1833 he was elected to the Pennsylvania legislature and became a spokesman of the Jackson-haters. Though despising Clay, he advocated the latter's American System: internal improvements, a protective tariff, a national bank. Never had he shown any strong feeling against the South's "peculiar institution"; in one of his first cases he had even defended a property owner's right to his slave. But as Antimasonry faded, he turned toward antislavery, and with his galling tongue soon became the hero of the abolitionists. John Quincy Adams, meeting him at about this period in Stevens' career, noted in his diary: ". . . a remarkable man, likely hereafter to figure in the history of this Union."

In 1848 he was elected to Congress as a Whig, and was quickly recognized as a potential leader. In 1854 he secretly joined the Know-Nothings; then in 1855, after the Republican party had emerged in the turmoil following the Kansas-Nebraska Act, he became a Republican. In 1858 he ran for Congress again and won. Outside his own congressional district his influence was still small, although his bizarre appearance and his dubious habits gave him a certain notoriety, which he enjoyed. He was an avid patron of Washington's gambling dens. A bachelor, he kept a mulatto housekeeper, whom most people assumed to be his mistress. Yet for all his repellent manner and corrosive speech, he was often privately kind and generous and, in his solicitude for the Negro, sincere.

The war brought him into his own. In 1861, in his seventieth year, he became chairman of the Ways and Means Committee, the most important standing committee of the House of Representatives. Toward the South, toward slavery—which he now equated with the Democrats—he was merciless. For him there would be no bargaining or negotiating with Southern states. "I would rather, sir," he declared, "reduce them to a condition where their whole country is to be repeopled by a band of freemen." As conservative and radical Republicans divided, Stevens became the leader of the Radicals in the House, with Ben Wade heading the Senate's Radical Committee on the Conduct of the War,

while Stanton and Chase represented the Radicals in Lincoln's Cabinet.

Every political figure in Washington sensed that when Congress convened on December 4, 1865—the first session since Lincoln's death—it would mark the hour of decision between Johnson and the Radicals. The President, determined to have the Southern representatives admitted, was confident that through pressure and patronage he could hold a majority of the Republicans in line. Stevens, equally determined to bar the Southerners—twenty senators and fifty-eight representatives, all Democrats—relied on the intricacies of parliamentary maneuvering. Two years earlier Old Thad had made his friend Edward McPherson chief clerk of the House of Representatives. He now arranged with McPherson to omit the names of the elected Southerners from the House roll. Then he planned a resolution appointing a Joint Committee on Reconstruction—six senators and nine representatives—to deal with the admission of Southern members and with Reconstruction questions. To avoid a presidential veto, he prepared a concurrent rather than a joint resolution, one that would not require the President's approval. At a preliminary caucus the iron-willed old man had prevailed upon his fellow Republicans, many of them new to Congress, to accept his Reconstruction program. "He is radical throughout," Congressman Rutherford B. Hayes wrote his wife, "except, I am told, he don't believe in hanging. He is leader."

The December day on which Congress met was as warm and mild as May. From the visitors' galleries a "brilliant and fashionable" crowd looked down on the newly decorated Hall of Representatives, resplendent in "a new Brussels carpet of tasteful pattern and in cheerful colors." There was a tense hush as the clerk began to call the roll. Johnson had arranged that Congressman Horace Maynard of Tennessee, a staunch Unionist, would appear to challenge the omission of the Southern names. McPherson passed over Maynard's name with those of the other Southerners. Livid with rage, shaking his credentials in his hand, Maynard demanded that he be recognized. When McPherson offered to explain why he could not do so, Stevens cut him short with: "It is not necessary. We know all." And when Maynard appealed personally to Stevens to grant him the floor, he replied: "I cannot yield to any gentleman who does not belong to this body—who is an outsider." While Maynard continued to appeal, Old

Thad dismissed him with "a Podsnappian wave of the hand," to the laughter of the galleries. After the election of officers the gaunt old cripple took charge. Stifling all debate, he forced through the concurrent resolution for his Joint Committee on Reconstruction by a vote of 133 to 36. Then, after the motion to adjourn that he had earlier throttled was finally passed, "the old war horse leaned back squarely and gloriously triumphant."

The Radicals and the President clashed again in February over the Freedmen's Bureau. The Bureau of Refugees, Freedmen, and Abandoned Lands had been established with Lincoln's approval in March, 1865, to assist refugees and newly freed slaves for a year after the war with food, clothing, and shelter, and to aid

them in settling on abandoned land during the same period. In February, 1866, Congress passed a bill continuing the Freedmen's Bureau indefinitely while expanding its functions to protect certain legal and civil rights of the Negro. Johnson vetoed the measure as both unnecessary and unconstitutional: unnecessary, because the freedmen could best make their way "through their own merits and exertions"; unconstitutional, since the states chiefly affected by the law were not represented in Congress. The President stated again that in his judgment the seceded states had already been fully restored to the Union. Though Congress was not able to override his veto—the bill, however, would be passed later in another form—even the moderates in the

In late May, 1865, the victorious Grand Army of the Republic was reviewed in Washington by President Johnson and General Grant: for two days the troops marched by. Above is a romanticized depiction of the event by James Walker.

OVERLEAF: Skaters crowd a pond in New York's Central Park. Then being landscaped, the 776-acre park would be finished in 1876. Boosted by the business of war and infused with the blood of its returned soldiers, the North was flourishing.

North resented the veto. The reading of the veto message in the Senate was repeatedly interrupted by hisses—with a counterpoint of applause—from the galleries. The Joint Committee on Reconstruction, meeting the following day, adopted a concurrent resolution, prepared by Stevens, forbidding the admission of any senator or representative from the eleven Southern states "until Congress shall have declared such state entitled to such representation." The resolution was later adopted by the House and the Senate.

On the evening of Washington's Birthday a crowd of Johnson's supporters—Copperheads, the Radicals called them—marched behind a band to the White House to serenade the President and endorse his veto. After they had massed on the White House lawn, the solid, pugnacious figure of the President appeared on the terrace just above them. With a guttering candle for illumination, he began to read the speech he had prepared. Stimulated by their approving shouts, carried away by the moment, Johnson again became the tailor

from Tennessee, boasting of his humble origins, accusing the Radicals of fomenting a new rebellion "to overthrow the Constitution and revolutionize the government." There were men of the North, he told his listeners in the darkness, as treasonable as any of the Confederates had been. "Give us the names!" a voice in the crowd called out. "A gentleman calls for their names," Johnson replied. "Well, suppose I should give them . . . I say Thaddeus Stevens, of Pennsylvania —(tremendous applause)—I say Charles Sumner— (great applause)—I say Wendell Phillips and others of the same stripe among them."

He concluded with his old identification with the common man: "I am your instrument. Who is there I have not toiled and labored for? . . . They say that man Johnson is a lucky man, that no man can defeat me. I will tell you what constitutes luck. It is due to right and being for the people. . . . So far I have not deserted the people, and I believe they will not desert me."

Johnson's new harangue caused almost as much dis-

Eastman Johnson's gentle but patronizing Labor Question in the South *capsulized the Reconstruction dilemma: largely uneducated, unprepared, and thought of as generically inferior, blacks had suddenly been freed to shift for themselves.*

may to his friends as had his vice-presidential inaugural address. A friend wrote to John Sherman, the Union Republican senator from Ohio, asking if the President had been drunk again, and mean rumors circulated in Washington that he had been intoxicated for a week. Public feeling in the North reacted sharply. "I think," said Sherman, "there is no true friend of Andrew Johnson who would not be willing to wipe out that speech from the pages of history."

Even at this tense moment, a degree of confidence and cooperation might have been established between the President and those majority Republicans who had earlier been willing to endorse him. The critical measure was the moderate-supported Civil Rights Bill, intended to reinforce the Thirteenth Amendment. That bill granted citizenship to all those born in the United States, with a guarantee, backed by federal district courts and attorneys, of "full and equal benefit of all laws and proceedings for the security of person and property. . . ." Senator Sherman was convinced that Johnson would sign it. So was a future Republican President, Congressman James Garfield. "If he signs," wrote Congressman Rutherford Hayes, "the chances are that a complete rupture will be avoided. Otherwise, otherwise."

But to the old Jacksonian Democrat in the White House, the bill would destroy "our federative system of limited powers." Veto it he must. "I know I am right," he told his secretary in private, "and I am damned if I do not adhere to it." In his veto message he declared that even if it were necessary to grant Negroes citizenship, he did not consider such a measure "sound policy" while eleven states were still unrepresented in Congress. Nor should federal law enact equality in an area where it had "frequently been thought expedient to discriminate between the two races." The bill was unconstitutional. It would establish "for the security of the colored race safeguards which go infinitely beyond any that the General Government has ever provided for the white race." It would break down the rights of the states, rights guaranteed to them by the Constitution, to make and execute laws in all matters within their jurisdiction.

Amidst much applause and turmoil in the galleries, the Senate overrode the Civil Rights Bill veto by a single vote. Johnson in the eyes of the North was now no longer a Unionist but a Democrat. Reconstruction was in the hands of Congress.

While attention focused on the President and Congress, the Joint Committee on Reconstruction moved behind the scenes, holding hearings and taking testimony about Southern iniquities preparatory to evolving its own Reconstruction policy. Yet its recommendations, which were finally released in April, 1866, were less punitive than might have been expected. Radicals like Stevens had found a countervailing influence in intellectual conservatives like William Pitt Fessenden of Maine, the chairman of the Senate Finance Committee, who had once expressed the irate wish that he could cut Sumner's throat. Sumner's insistence on instant and universal Negro adult male suffrage was sidetracked. Even Stevens considered it at the time inadvisable politically to run counter to so much ingrained opposition in the North and the West. Caring little about votes for Negroes, he aimed at the cutting down of Southern political power by disfranchising as many former Confederates as possible.

In its detailed plan for Reconstruction, presented on April 30, the committee skirted the issue of Negro suffrage. Before the war, representation in Congress had been based on the white population plus three-fifths of the slave population. Now the committee proposed a constitutional amendment that would base the number of congressmen on the adult male population, and reduce that number proportionately whenever any segment of the population was denied the vote. The amendment would further guarantee to all citizens the rights of life, liberty, and property. Until July 4, 1870, those who had voluntarily adhered to the Confederacy would be denied the right to vote in federal elections. No state would be allowed to assume any debt incurred during the rebellion. Finally, Congress would have the power to enforce these provisions. The committee concluded with a proposed enabling act by which any Southern state ratifying the new amendment would then have its senators and representatives admitted to Congress.

The committee's plan, revised on the basis of debates in Congress and submitted again to Congress in May, became substantially the Fourteenth Amendment. Senator Fessenden, heading a committee of five, was responsible for the final version, in which citizens were specifically defined as all persons born or naturalized in the United States. In this revision there were no longer restrictions on who might vote, but those who had taken the oath of allegiance to the United States and who subsequently supported the Confederacy were declared ineligible for federal office—a disability that might be removed only by a two-thirds vote of Congress. The other provisions remained the same.

Recognized as a compromise, the amendment was received by the country with little enthusiasm; however, many of Johnson's friends considered the terms not unreasonable. Henry J. Raymond, the President's chief supporter in the House, voted for the measure, calling it a move "in the direction of harmony and conciliation." Johnson remained adamant. During the committee's work on the amendment, he had refused to use any of his presidential influence to modify it more to his liking. In a June message to Congress he stated again that no amendment to the Constitution ought to be proposed "until after the admission of such loyal Senators and Representatives of the now unrepresented states as have been, or may hereafter be, chosen. . . ." He advised the Southern states that they had no obligation to ratify the amendment, and later in the month he sent out a call for a National Union convention, the basis—he hoped—of the party to help him wage his campaign in the fall elections against all Republican candidates who opposed his policies. Congress, by neglecting any enabling bill at all in that election year, still left the Southern states with no guideline as to how they might be readmitted to participation in the national government.

Only Tennessee, of the eleven Southern states, was willing to ratify the Fourteenth Amendment. The others, supported by Johnson and seeing the restrictive clause as barring their best men from office, refused. Tennessee, however, was a special case, the most Union-influenced of all the seceding states. As soon as Congress had passed the Fourteenth Amendment, Tennessee's Governor William G. Brownlow, "the Fighting Parson," called a special session of the General Assembly. A former Whig, a former slaveholder, a preacher and pistol-carrying Unionist of East Tennessee, he had succeeded Johnson as governor and had once called him an atheist and a bastard—Brownlow had become the delight of the Radicals. By force and guile he proceeded to dragoon his state legislators into ratifying the amendment, then telegraphed "the good news" to Congress: "We have fought the battle and won it. We have ratified the Constitutional amendment . . . two of Andrew Johnson's tools not voting. Give my respects to the dead dog of the White House."

When Andrew Johnson was named to run with Lincoln in 1864, the New York World *lamented that "the age of rail splitters and tailors, of buffoons, boors and fanatics has succeeded. . . ."*

By his refusal to come to terms with moderate Republicans over the provisions of the Civil Rights Act and the Fourteenth Amendment, Johnson alienated the moderates who wished to act with rather than against him and impelled them toward the Radical camp. Meanwhile tension was rising in the South in the wake of the Black Codes and the counteractivities of the Freedmen's Bureau. A rumor had spread like a forest fire through the Negro cabins at Christmas, 1865, that each adult male ex-slave would receive forty acres and a mule from the government. Many Northerners were migrating southward—some of them predators of social convulsion, others merely clergymen, educators sympathetic to ex-slaves, and Union veterans attracted to that milder climate—to take their place in Southern legend as carpetbaggers, shabby adventurers arriving with nothing more than a carpetbag and a determination to enrich themselves. Out of the political chaos some Southerners, respectable and otherwise, revived the cause of Unionism and espoused Radicalism, to become stereotyped in the legend as scalawags, Confederate deserters. From the ruined countryside, former slaves flocked to the cities, where they remained workless and potentially explosive. At the end of April a race riot broke out in Memphis after Irish policemen and Negro soldiers had engaged in a street brawl. The white mob then attacked the Negro population, killing forty-six. An even more savage riot occurred in New Orleans three months later in which many were killed or wounded. To many in the North, Memphis and New Orleans became warnings and watchwords.

So important did the 1866 mid-term elections seem in the growing Reconstruction crisis that four political conventions were held that year. The National Union convention, organized by supporters of Johnson, was held in Philadelphia in August. The Arm-in-Arm Convention, it was called, conjuring up the image of loyal Southern Democrats and Union Republicans from the North linked arm in arm in support of the President and his Reconstruction policies. A Massachusetts politician and a former Confederate senator were actually seen walking together, and the band in the vast jerry-built hall where the convention was held even alternated conscientiously between "The Star-Spangled Banner" and "Dixie." Congressman Henry Raymond, editor of *The New York Times,* gave the keynote address, in which he demanded immediate and unqualified admission of the South to participation in the federal government. Unfortunately for the intended Union image, the bulk of the convention's support came from Democrats and they in turn refused to weed out of their ranks even such notorious Copperheads as Fernando Wood and Clement Vallandigham, although these two were forced by general antagonism to leave the convention. As far as national union was concerned, Johnson's party was stillborn. In answer to the Arm-in-Arm Convention, the Radicals summoned a convention of their own—called sneeringly by the Democrats the Black and Tan Convention after the Negro abolitionist delegate Frederick Douglass appeared arm in arm with the white Radical Theodore Tilton. This was followed by an ex-servicemen's convention in support of the President. Among the military leaders present were former Major General George A. Custer, then reduced to the

postwar rank of lieutenant colonel, and the oldest major general in the Army, General John E. Wool. The Radicals again countered with a second soldiers' convention, which featured Major General Ben Butler, "the Hero of Fort Fisher."

One of Johnson's beliefs, amounting to a superstition, was that everything in the universe moves in a "magic circle," from planets in their orbits to political problems. In preparation for the 1866 elections, he conceived the idea of a tour, a "swing round the circle," in which he could carry his fight for "one country, one flag and a union of equal states" to the people. The official reason for the journey that he undertook in late August was to assist at the dedication of the Stephen A. Douglas monument in Chicago, but his real purpose was to speak along the way in defense of his policy. Traveling with his large party in the special presidential railroad cars were General Grant, Admiral Farragut, Secretary of State William H. Seward, and the reluctant Gideon Welles, Secretary of the Navy.

The response to Johnson's swing round the circle seemed at first a hopeful augury. A hundred thousand supporters greeted him enthusiastically as he rode through Baltimore with Grant and Farragut along the flag-decked street from the station to Fort McHenry amidst the booms of cannon. Huge crowds gathered in Philadelphia, and in New York a half million flocked to see him. A great dinner was held in his honor at Delmonico's, and in the evening he was serenaded. Yet for all the crowds and the receptions, Republican leaders were notably absent wherever he went. The Republican governors of Indiana, Ohio, Pennsylvania, Illinois, Missouri, and Michigan all dodged him.

Worried by the initial enthusiasm for Johnson, the Radicals rallied the opposition, denouncing the applause as a Copperhead subterfuge. Stevens crawled from his sickbed to make a speech, in which he called Johnson and Seward the two clowns of a traveling circus. "Parson" Brownlow organized a countertour "to wipe out the moccasin tracks of Andrew Johnson and William H. Seward." Johnson spoke at countless small towns, on station platforms or from the back of the train, repeating over and over his uniform declaration: "I leave in your hands the Constitution and the Union, and the glorious flag of your country, not with twenty-five but with thirty-six stars."

Conservative Republicans were dismayed by the numbers of Copperhead Democrats who everywhere thronged to hear the President and hail him as their own. Grant was so troubled that he left the official party after St. Louis, confiding to a friend that he did not "care to accompany a man who was deliberately digging his own grave." And as the President moved westward, the public mood turned increasingly hostile. Threatening crowds greeted him in Michigan and Illinois. Heckling began in Cleveland, the home of Ben Wade, and Johnson—flaring up at the scornful voices and unmindful of his office—lashed out at his anonymous deriders. Although the Chicago reception itself was "magnificent," Radicals sent bands through the streets playing the *Dead March,* and Lincoln's widow fled the city to avoid her husband's successor. In St. Louis, speaking extemporaneously from the balcony of the Southern Hotel, Johnson was interrupted with shouts of "Traitor!" and became almost incoherent with anger. In Indianapolis there was a riot in the lobby of his hotel in which several men were killed or wounded. From that time on hecklers took to interrupting him whenever he spoke with shouts of "Judas!" "New Orleans!" "Three Cheers for Congress!" and "Don't get mad, Andy!" and he would be roused to reply in furious gutter language. "I do not care about my dignity," he shouted to one crowd—at which a newspaperman observed that this was much to be regretted. Radicals revived the old canard of drunkenness, although Grant was the only member of the party who had indulged. Only in the South—in Kentucky and Maryland—as Johnson neared the end of his trip, was the enthusiasm for him general and sustained. He returned to Washington, riding down Pennsylvania Avenue under a banner inscribed: "The Constitution and Andrew Johnson Now and Forever."

Welles thought that the swing round the circle had been on the whole a success, but the Secretary of the Navy had optimistically assumed that interest in seeing the President meant support of him. There were several reasons for the failure of the tour. Copperheads and former Rebels were his most numerous and ardent supporters in his audiences. The Radical newspapers gave biased and even completely false reports of events, such as the accounts of the President's drunkenness. The Memphis and New Orleans riots just before the trip did Johnson no good. And Johnson's Tennessee stump techniques, including delivering the same set speech at every stop, were not effective before more sophisticated audiences. As a result, by the time John-

son returned, opposition to his National Union party had solidified. Moderates, like Fessenden and Garfield, who feared the death of the Republican party, were moving toward old abolitionists, like Henry Ward Beecher and Horace Greeley; Radicals, like Wade and Stevens; and instant-rights advocates, like Sumner. Weeks before the election it was clear that "Andy Johnsonism" was in eclipse. Sensing the shifting mood, the two great Johnson-Unionist papers, *The New York Times* and James Gordon Bennett's supersensational New York *Herald,* switched their support from the President to Congress.

The early Maine election barometer portended a Republican sweep. In the North and the West every state legislature as well as every contested governorship was carried by the Republicans. Although nationally the Republicans did not gain in the Senate and—with 143 seats to the Democrats' 49—actually lost 6 seats in the House, the proportion as well as the spirits of Radicals in the new Congress rose. Newcomers like Ben Butler were replacing the conservatives.

At the opening of the last session of the Thirty-ninth Congress in December, legislators reflected a mood, which was intensified by stories drifting north of Southern intimidation of Unionists and of atrocities against Negroes. "I was a Conservative in the last session of this Congress," said Stevens, to the laughter of the House, "but I mean to be a Radical henceforth."

By the end of 1866 the Fourteenth Amendment had come to represent Congress' terms to the South. Conservatives, men like Senator John Sherman of Ohio, expected that once the South accepted the amendment, "its Senators and Representatives should take their seats by our side." Most moderates hoped, as did Sherman, that Johnson and the South would make this concession, and many Southerners were coming around to their point of view. But the President, in his second annual message, remained unwaveringly opposed. Privately Johnson advised Southern legislators to reject the amendment, fortifying their resolve.

Congress, divided into three factions, seemed deadlocked. The moderate Republicans demanded that the Southern states ratify the Fourteenth Amendment as the price of their readmission. The Radicals, led by Stevens and Sumner, wanted to replace all state governments in the South—except for Tennessee's—by direct federal rule "under the guardianship of loyal men" and to enforce disfranchisement of ex-Confederates and universal Negro suffrage at the point of a bayonet. The Democrats maintained that the Southern states could not be punished for refusing to ratify an amendment. They also felt that harsh measures by the Republicans against the South would alienate moderate public opinion. What they were unable to see was that Southern persistence in rejecting the Fourteenth Amendment would bring the two wings of the Republican party together. In endeavoring to perpetuate the political deadlock, Democrats voted by turns with the moderates and with the Radicals, with the result that many measures that would have made Reconstruction far easier for the South were blocked.

Although still unwilling to yield to Stevens' vindictive policies, the Republican moderates by the end of the session had become willing to accept direct military rule for the South as an alternative to the obduracy of the Southern states, although the waning Thirty-ninth Congress would probably have settled for a temporary occupation merely to keep the Southern states out of the Union until after the 1868 presidential election. To a bill proposing to extend military rule throughout the South, James G. Blaine offered an amendment to allow the states to regain representation on ratifying the Fourteenth Amendment and guaranteeing Negro suffrage. Indignantly Stevens objected that this "universal amnesty and universal Andy-Johnsonism" would let in "a vast number of rebels" and exclude no one. Finally Congressman Samuel Shellabarger of Ohio introduced an amendment that all state governments in the South should be considered "provisional only, and in all respects subject to the paramount authority of the United States at any time, to abolish, modify, control, or supersede the same. . . ." Congress passed the bill overwhelmingly through the combined votes of moderates and Radicals, and when Johnson vetoed it, immediately passed it over his veto.

The Reconstruction Act of March 2, 1867, established military government in the ten Southern states on the grounds of there being "no legal State governments or adequate protection for life or property." The states were divided into five military districts, each commanded by a general who would maintain order and would try and punish offenders. The Blaine-Sherman

COLLECTION OF FELIX H. KUNTZ

For many years after the war, despite the rapid growth of railroads, the broad and frequently treacherous Mississippi swarmed with a lively traffic of river packets and barges, showboats and rafts. Above, a stern-wheeler takes on wood.

amendment provided for readmitting the states after
they had ratified the Fourteenth Amendment and
agreed to universal Negro suffrage, while another
amendment severely restricted the suffrage of ex-
Confederates. Shellabarger's amendment was retained
intact. For better or—more probably—for worse, a
Reconstruction policy had at last emerged from the
deadlock.

It was soon clear to members of the new Fortieth
Congress that the Reconstruction Act would be no more
than a scrap of paper unless means were provided to
enforce it. On March 23 the Republican majority
passed an enabling act that soon sent swarms of federal
officials to the South as supervisors: drifters, failures,
opportunists for the most part—in Southern terms
"carpetbaggers." A supplementary Reconstruction act
was passed at the same time, regulating the register-
ing of voters and holding of constitutional conventions. A third Reconstruction act passed in July. As the
law required the new state constitutions to be voted
on by at least half the registered voters, Southerners
were able to repudiate their carpetbag governments
merely by staying away from the polls. Congress passed
a fourth and final act in March establishing that a
majority of the *voters* would suffice for ratification.
Arkansas, in June, 1868—over Johnson's veto—was the
first to be readmitted to the Union under these terms;
not until July, 1870, did Georgia, as the last of the
Confederate states, submit.

At the same time that Congress had passed the First
Reconstruction Act, it passed two other measures to
limit the powers of the President: the Army Appropriation Act, one section of which required the President
thenceforth to issue all his military orders through the
general of the Army; and the fateful Tenure of Office
Act. This last measure, a retaliation for Johnson's pre-
election purge of officeholders, laid down that the
President could not remove those appointed by the
President and confirmed by the Senate without permission of the Senate, although when the Senate was not
in session, the President might suspend an officer if he
reported his reasons to the Senate within twenty days
after its convening. The act, it was generally believed,
would encompass all appointed and commissioned
government personnel, including Army and Navy officers. It further laid down that Cabinet officers "shall
hold their offices . . . during the term of the President
by whom they may have been appointed, and for one

month thereafter, subject to removal by and with the advice and consent of the Senate." This latter clause was planned by Republican congressmen as a shield for the Radical spokesman in Johnson's Cabinet, Secretary of War Stanton.

It was a shield that Stanton did not at the time want, since he saw the act as tying his hands in the removal of incompetent Army officers and War Department subordinates. For all his personal dislike of Johnson, he advised the President to defend his power against usurpation by vetoing the measure. Johnson, with a certain amount of malice, asked his War Secretary to prepare the veto. Stanton begged off, pleading rheumatism and lack of time, but finally assisted Seward, who actually wrote it. Like the military Reconstruction measures, the Tenure of Office Act was promptly passed over the President's veto. The tenure act would result in open warfare between the President and his Secretary of War and lead in the end to Johnson's impeachment trial.

When Stanton, the Ohio lawyer and former Attorney General in the last days of the Buchanan administration, had joined Lincoln's Cabinet in 1862 as Secretary of War, he was still a Democrat. Lincoln had accepted a man he hardly knew on the recommendation of Treasury Secretary Salmon Chase, with the argument that such a man would rally Democratic support to the administration. In the 1860 presidential election Stanton had supported Breckinridge, and after the election, had scorned Lincoln as the "gorilla" in the White House. Yet, in the course of three years, Secretary Stanton would become the President's confidant and companion, his closest and most trusted collaborator in the conduct of the war. As Secretary of War, Stanton achieved greatness, inheriting a department that was in chaos and reorganizing it into an efficient military machine. Without his dynamic energy, a Union victory might not have been possible. Lincoln compared him to a Methodist preacher who conducted himself so vigorously in the pulpit that his parishioners wanted to put bricks in his pocket to hold him down. Arrogant in manner, fierce-looking behind his narrow-gold-rimmed spectacles,

Though emancipation of the slaves upset considerably the Southern agricultural system, the division of labor on plantations remained much the same. In this detail from a painting by Winslow Homer, Negro women harvest the cotton crop.

with black hair and a coarse black beard, Stanton was nicknamed the Black Bull by unsympathetic colleagues. Not long after Lincoln's death, he contemplated resigning from the Cabinet. His disaffection with Johnson came gradually as he found himself increasingly troubled over the President's states' rights attitude to Reconstruction and his indiscriminate pardoning of Confederate leaders.

Stanton, as he grew apart from Johnson, drew closer to Sumner and the Radicals. Eventually Stanton alone would be in opposition to the President in the Cabinet. Johnson did obey the letter of the Military Reconstruction Act by appointing five Army commanders for the Southern districts, but he made it clear that he viewed the troops and their commanding officers as under his direction, independent of his untrustworthy Secretary of War and of his commander of the Army,

General Grant, whom he no longer trusted. Stanton joined with Grant in asserting that the commanders in the South were answerable only to Congress and its laws, and he announced this to Johnson's face in a Cabinet meeting. Johnson came to believe that Stanton had conspired against him, that he had secretly been trying to undermine his whole Reconstruction program, that he had helped write the Third Reconstruction Act, and that one of his subordinates might even have tried to implicate Johnson in Lincoln's assassination. The President hinted broadly that he would accept a resignation; the Secretary did not take the hint.

Stanton had once told Welles that "any man who would retain his seat in the cabinet as an adviser when his advice was not wanted was unfit for the place." Nevertheless, the Secretary of War continued to remain at his post for months after he knew that the

New Orleans fell to Northern troops in the spring of 1862, and when journalist Whitelaw Reid saw it in June, 1865, he found that it "showed no traces of war." Above is the Treme Market as viewed in 1863 by local artist Richard Clague.

President wanted him to resign, feeling that to protect his own Reconstruction policies he must keep his office. On August 5, 1867, came Johnson's anticipated demand that Stanton resign. Stanton refused. A week later Johnson sent for Grant, and despite their differences on Reconstruction, offered him an interim appointment as Secretary of War, which the General accepted, saying he would obey orders. The next morning Stanton received a letter from the President ordering him to transfer all records to Grant. Stanton, while denying Johnson's right to suspend him without the approval of the Senate, replied that he had no alternative but to submit under protest to superior force.

Under the terms of the Tenure of Office Act, the suspension would last until Congress met in November. Johnson further enraged the Republicans and Northern public opinion by removing all but one of the Stanton-approved district military commanders in the South, creating the greatest uproar by removing Phil Sheridan from command of the Louisiana-Texas district after Sheridan himself had removed the mayor of New Orleans, the governor of Louisiana, and several other local officials. For some time there had been loose talk in Washington of impeaching the President, whose popularity continued to sink. When in January, 1867, Johnson had rejected Sumner's District of Columbia Negro suffrage bill, a crackpot congressman from Ohio, James M. Ashley, presented to the House a resolution to investigate the actions and conduct of President Johnson. It was passed without being taken seriously. Ashley, who believed that all American Presidents who had died in office had been victims of vice-presidential foul play, then accused Johnson, before the investigating Judiciary Committee, of bribery, drunkenness on his tour, treason, and conspiring with Booth to kill Lincoln. Such accusations were so without basis in fact that the disgusted chairman and the majority of the committee soon voted that no evidence of high crimes and misdemeanors existed. After Sheridan's removal, however, the Judiciary Committee in November, 1867, voted 5 to 4 to impeach the President on the grounds of "usurpation of power." Impeachment failed in a House vote, since whatever their hostility, the Republicans were forced to realize that they had no shadow of a case.

Just before the Christmas holidays, Johnson submitted to the Senate his reasons for suspending Stanton. Congressmen and senators returned to Washington aft-er Christmas in a sullen anti-Johnson mood. On January 10, 1868, the Senate Committee on Military Affairs released a report exonerating Stanton, and three days later the Senate refused to approve his suspension. Grant, his slow-moving mind now aware—probably through Stanton—that anyone violating the tenure act might find himself with a ten-thousand-dollar fine and a five-year prison term, asked on January 11 to be relieved of his temporary appointment. Johnson tried to persuade his reluctant general to stay, but after the Senate's action, Grant bolted from his new office to his old Army headquarters, explaining lamely that he had not expected the senators to act so quickly. The President, in his anger, accused the commanding general of having deceived him, and their differences developed into an embittered quarrel, which would eventually align Grant with Stanton and the Radicals.

No sooner had Grant left his interim office than Stanton arrived at his old quarters and demanded the office key, which Grant's adjutant delivered with a mock present arms. Grant then formally resigned his temporary appointment. It seems unlikely that Stanton intended to take up his post for more than a few days, but Republican members of Congress bolstered his resolve and insisted on his remaining. Meanwhile, Johnson was equally insistent on getting rid of him. Candidates for the unvacated vacancy were, however, hard to come by. A friend of General William T. Sherman's remarked that it was amusing to see how everyone was afraid of the War Office. Faced with the prospect of Cabinet honors, brave generals fled. Sherman himself hastily left the Capital, and when Johnson tried to bring him back with a brevet general's commission, appealed to his senator brother to have the Senate reject the appointment. General George Thomas—"the Rock of Chickamauga"—and General Thomas Ewing also took evasive action. Even the chief clerk at the War Department, John Potts, balked at such a glittering promotion. Finally Johnson recalled the semiretired General Lorenzo Thomas, a tippling dandy who had seen no active duty since the Mexican War. Thomas agreed to "support the Constitution and the laws" by accepting the interim appointment, whereupon Johnson dispatched him to the War Department with two orders, one commanding Stanton to vacate the office, the other appointing Thomas interim Secretary of War. "I want some little time for reflection," Stanton told the general. "I don't know whether I shall obey your orders or not." Thomas, assuming that he would, left to celebrate. That evening he attended a masked ball, waltzing and toasting away the hours while he boasted of how he was going to oust Stanton—by force if necessary—the following morning. "The eyes of Delaware are upon you!" Thomas' home state announced proudly.

While Thomas waltzed, Stanton was fortifying himself in his office, posting guards at the doors, and announcing that he would stay there night and day until the issue was resolved. Congressmen and senators hurried up Pennsylvania Avenue with words of encouragement. Sumner sent a famous one-word message, "Stick!" Heartened by such support, which now included that of Grant, Stanton had an order made out for Thomas' arrest for planning to remove the Secretary of War forcibly. The next morning, his head still spinning, Thomas was hauled out of bed by a district marshal, who brought him breakfastless before a judge to be charged with violating the tenure law. Released on bail, still without breakfast, he scurried to the White House, where Johnson again sent him to eject Stanton. This time Stanton, surrounded by his supporters, flatly refused to budge. Finally the Secretary of War broke the tension by taking his challenger to a side office and opening a bottle of whiskey. Between drinks the conversation mellowed. As Thomas left about noon for the White House, glowing with defeat, he thought that on the whole it had been a rather pleasant day.

Stanton, in his office-fortress, defiantly prepared for a siege. He sent home for food, clothing, and blankets, but his wife was so irate over the imbroglio that she refused to comply. "This ridiculous conduct," wrote Welles, "makes Stanton a laughing stock. He eats, sleeps, and stays cooped up in his entrenched and fortified establishment—scarcely daring to look out of the window."

At a special Friday night session, at the same time that Thomas was waltzing at the masked ball, the Senate had approved a resolution that Johnson could not legally oust Stanton or replace him by Thomas. On Sunday the President wrote a message protesting this resolution, but events had already taken a more ominous turn, for on Saturday morning the House Reconstruction Committee, through its spokesman, Old Thad, had presented a formal resolution for impeachment, which, after floods of oratory, was passed by the House on Monday, February 24, two days after Washington's Birthday. Seven impeachment managers, including

Butler and Stevens, were selected. The Radicals spitefully ordered the House clock set back to Saturday so that officially the thirteenth President might be impeached on the birthday of the first. Of the eleven articles of impeachment, the first eight had to do with Johnson's "plot" to violate the Tenure of Office Act by his "illegal" dismissal of Stanton. Butler's malice was distilled in the tenth article, while the eleventh was an omnibus indictment. Johnson had become the figure on whom all the postwar resentments could be concentrated. Even those politicians who supported him would have been happy to see the last of him.

At the trial's opening the sergeant at arms cried out his formal proclamation: "Hear ye! Hear ye! Andrew Johnson, Andrew Johnson!" But Johnson, on the advice of his lawyers, never put in an appearance. Stevens was now so feeble that throughout the trial he had to be carried to his seat each morning by two Negro boys. Grimly Old Thad fortified himself with sips of brandy, smacking his lips over the coming downfall of his enemy. For all the aroused passion, there was very little real evidence offered against the President; the trial came down to the basic question of whether he was guilty of "high crimes and misdemeanors" in removing Stanton and appointing Thomas. The defense—ably managed by Henry Stanbery, who had resigned his office as Attorney General to aid the President—pointed out that Stanton was not protected by the Tenure of Office Act, since he had been appointed by Lincoln. And, in any case, Johnson's removal of Stanton was not a criminal act but a test of the legality of a law that was probably unconstitutional. In the arguments pro and con, Johnson had all the advantages of logic and dignity, his enemies those of prejudice and invective. Stevens, too weak to take the floor himself, had Butler read his manuscript, in which he described Johnson as "this offspring of assassination." Any senator, he warned, who votes to acquit would be "tortured on the gibbet of everlasting obloquy."

While the trial went into mid-May of 1868 Stanton remained holed up in his War Department office and Johnson lived quietly in the White House. As the proceedings neared their end, it was clear that the outcome would be close. Thirty-six Senate votes would be necessary to convict the President out of a total of 54. Six Republicans, including Fessenden, were already known as being "wrong," that is, for acquittal. Only one more would be required to add to the votes of

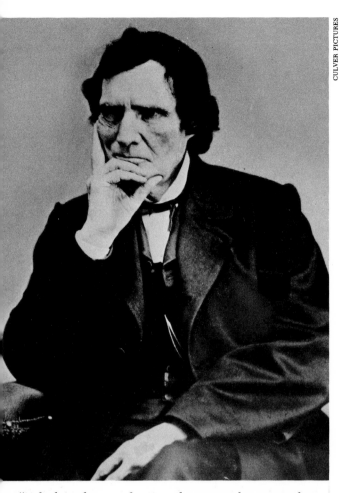

"Nobody said more in fewer words or gave to language a sharper bite," said Charles Sumner of his fellow Radical Thad Stevens (above). "Speech was with him at times a cat-o-nine-tails and woe to the victim on whom the terrible lash descended."

nine Democrats and three "Johnson Conservatives"—Republicans who supported the President—to make conviction impossible. Radicals were doing their frantic best to whip any waverers into line. Ben Wade, who as president of the Senate was the next in line to replace Johnson, felt confident enough to start planning his Cabinet, which was to include Ben Butler as Secretary of State. "It hangs in almost an even balance," Garfield wrote two hours before the senators began voting. "There is an intensity of anxiety here, greater than I ever saw during the war." The balance had come to hang on the young Radical senator from Kansas, Edmund G. Ross, who, in spite of all the pressures from fellow Radicals and telegrams from Kansas, refused to announce how he would vote.

May 16 came as the day of decision in the Senate Chamber. With tickets of admission hawked at fantastic prices, with the galleries packed and police stationed throughout the Capitol, the Senate prepared to decide Andrew Johnson's fate. Just before the session, Ross was warned by his Kansas colleague, in Old Thad's presence, that a vote for acquittal would be political death. James W. Grimes of Iowa, who, though an enemy of Johnson's, had recorded himself for acquittal, had had a stroke two days earlier, and Radicals had high hopes for his absence. At the last minute, pale and shrunken, he was helped to his seat by four men. The Senate, sitting as a court, agreed to take up Article XI first. The secretary then read the article, and Chief Justice Chase asked: "Is the respondent, Andrew Johnson, President of the United States, guilty or not guilty of a high misdemeanor as charged in this article?"

Under the flaring gas jets, in an atmosphere of silent, almost unendurable tension punctuated only by the clerk's drone and the responding voices of the senators, the voting proceeded. By the time Ross's name was called, twenty-four senators had voted for conviction. Ross's voice was low and wavering—he said so himself—as he replied: "Not guilty!" Everyone present, from the managers and the senators and congressmen to the diplomats and people of fashion in the galleries, knew then that the thrust at the President had failed, that the final vote would be 35 to 19, one vote short of the necessary two-thirds majority. "I almost literally looked down into my open grave," Ross said afterward of that climactic moment. "Friendships, position, fortune, everything that makes life desirable . . . were about to be swept away by the breath of my mouth. . . ."

In the public mind, and for all practical purposes, the defeat of Article XI marked the end of the trial, although the impeachment managers planned to continue and secured a ten-day adjournment because of the Republican National Convention in Chicago. Johnson's trial was a great turning point in the evolution of American government. His removal from office would have established the precedent and principle that the President of the United States is subject to the will of Congress, that he is, in effect, a Prime Minister—as in England—dependent on a congressional majority for his survival in office. Old Thad, defeated and now dying, saw this clearly. No Chief Executive, he observed with sour regret, "will . . . be again removed by peaceful means."

Grant in the
White House

The opening of the impeachment trial had found Johnson troubled and anxious, but his anxiety soon gave way to a quiet serenity. He steadily refused to fight the Radicals with their own political weapons. "I had rather be convicted than resort to fraud, bribery or corruption of any kind," he told an acquaintance. For consolation during the trial weeks he read Addison's *Cato* and works on immortality. Each evening when a messenger arrived to report on what had occurred during the session in the Senate, he would ask, "Well, what are the signs of the zodiac today?"

When the Senate clerk announced the verdict, Stanbery and another of Johnson's lawyers, T. A. R. Nelson, dashed to a carriage and drove headlong to the White House. They found a beaming Johnson in his study, for the President had already received a vote-by-vote tally over a private telegraph wire from the Capitol. Seward arrived soon after from the State Department with his congratulations, to be followed by hundreds of callers, who stopped to leave their cards. By evening the White House had become "as hilarious as a royal palace after a coronation."

During the ten-day adjournment interlude the Radicals struggled to rally their forces, the managers doing their best to intimidate the seven Republican recusants. They threatened to bring charges of bribery against Ross. His constituents telegraphed: "Kansas repudiates you as she does all perjurers and skunks." In a practical political sense Ross's vision of his open grave came true, for none of the Republican senators who had voted to acquit Johnson were ever elected to national office again. For all the manipulations of the managers, the trial's resumption proved an anticlimax. By the same vote of 19 to 35 the Senate rejected Articles II and III, and then adjourned for an indefinite period.

While President Johnson's reputation sank, General Grant's soared. By the time of the Republican National Convention, the General was easily the most popular man in the country. Wherever he went, long lines of veterans formed to shake his hand, and at his appearance bands broke out so frequently with "Hail to the Chief" that even the tone-deaf Grant came to recognize the tune. Colleges offered him their honorary

In the lithograph by Thure de Thulstrup the Grant portrait is set off by sketches of the General's military career—from West Point to the Mexican War and through the Civil War to Lee's surrender.

degrees. Gifts poured in on him—boxes of cigars, ceremonial swords, horses, large sums of money. Admirers presented Mrs. Grant with a handsome house in Philadelphia and later gave Grant an extensive library. All this bounty he received with mute gratitude —in contrast, it was noted by the more acute, to Johnson, who always refused all presents.

To the public, Grant appeared to have neither political awareness nor ambitions. Earlier, over the searingly divisive issue of slavery, he had expressed no opinions, although he had always been against secession. In 1856 he had voted for Buchanan. Democrats still claimed him for their own. They would have been happy to nominate him as their presidential candidate in 1868 if his quarrel with Johnson had not tended to make him their adversary. The Republicans were even more happy to claim him. To preserve the war-created tariff, Eastern industrialists were willing to join with the Radicals in keeping the party in power through Northern bayonets and black ballots. The Democratic surge in the off-year elections of 1867 had been a warning, and Republicans of every stripe, even the reluctant Radicals, had come to see the general of the armies as

The trim readiness of Tammany Hall belied the sweaty struggles that awaited the 1868 Democratic conventioneers. In weather "too hot for the warm work," they maneuvered through twenty-two roll calls to the nomination of Horatio Seymour.

their only hope in 1868. Months before their convention Republicans were forming Grant clubs. The New York political boss and manipulator Thurlow Weed, in drawing the Astors, Vanderbilt, "Uncle Daniel" Drew, and other Eastern magnates to Grant's candidacy, let it be known that if Grant would make no speeches and write no letters, he, Weed, would nominate and elect him. Ben Butler, who privately considered Grant "America's greatest humbug"—the "Galena Tanner's Pup"—felt obliged to endorse publicly the general who had relieved him of command during the war.

When the Republican convention opened in Chicago in Crosby's Opera House, Grant the silent had by attrition eliminated all other candidates. The Convention of Soldiers and Sailors, meeting in the city at the same time, heard three Union generals endorse the General and denounce the seven Republican senators who had voted for Johnson's acquittal, while at mention of the President, the band played the "Rogues March." There was no need for speeches at the regular convention. The six hundred and fifty delegates nominated Grant by acclamation, to the accompaniment of cheers from the balconies and the bewildered circling of released doves. Speaker of the House of Representatives Schuyler Colfax was picked as candidate for Vice President on the sixth ballot. Smiler, they called the amiable, chin-whiskered Speaker, "a good-tempered, chirping, warbling, real canary bird"; he was said never to have lost a friend or made an enemy.

Overshadowed by the personality of Grant, the Republican platform called for "equal suffrage to all loyal men [in] the South," but then hedged by declaring that the solution to the suffrage problem "belongs to the people of those states." In the generalized language of political platforms, it called for a reduction in the national debt "over a fair period" and for repayment of the bonds issued during the Civil War in specie rather than in the depreciated greenback currency. The eighth plank regretted "the accession to the presidency of Andrew Johnson, who has acted treacherously to the people who elected him and the cause he was pledged to support. . . ."

During the convention Grant had remained at Army Headquarters in Washington, outwardly indifferent to the course of events in Chicago. Even when Stanton bustled in with the news of the nomination, he made no comment. After later being officially notified, Grant replied in a formal letter of acceptance, concluding with the epigrammatic phrase "Let us have peace," which would become a campaign slogan.

If Grant's nomination had been a foregone conclusion for the Republicans, the Democrats, meeting in New York's newly completed Tammany Hall, seemed headed for no conclusion at all. Forty-seven possible candidates preened themselves, among them the erstwhile Radical Republican Chief Justice Chase. Ever since 1860 the will-o'-the-wisp of the Presidency had bewitched Chase and now in 1868, after being scorned by his old Radical associates, he was ready to throw in his lot with the Democrats on a platform of "suffrage for all, amnesty for all; good money for all; security for all citizens at home and abroad against governmental invasion." "Gentleman George" H. Pendleton, a former congressman from Ohio, mustered the largest number of convention delegates. Gentleman George advocated

paying off the war bonds in greenbacks, and his followers wore five-dollar-bill badges. The third leading candidate, Johnson's friend General Francis P. Blair of Missouri, favored declaring the Reconstruction acts null and void and compelling the Army to "disperse the carpetbag State governments." President Johnson still remained a possible candidate, and among the other possibilities were Pennsylvania's favorite son, General Winfield Scott Hancock; Indiana Senator Thomas A. Hendricks; and the convention's chairman, the former governor of New York Horatio Seymour.

While the delegates in Tammany Hall sweltered through the torrid July days, party leaders backstage were evolving a platform. Hard-money Easterners were forced to yield to the greenbackers' cry of one currency for all debts. Beyond that, the platform denounced the Reconstruction acts as unconstitutional and demanded a general amnesty with "immediate restoration of all States to their rights in the Union." The first ballot put Gentleman George in the lead with 105 votes, President Johnson following him with 65, Sanford Church, New York's favorite son, with 34, and Hancock with 33½. Johnson was eliminated early in the balloting, and the struggle narrowed down to a contest between Pendleton, Hendricks, and Hancock. On the fourth ballot North Carolina gave its 9 votes to Seymour, who announced: "I must not be nominated by this convention. I could not accept the nomination if tendered, which I do not expect."

During the morning of the third day of balloting it became increasingly clear that neither Pendleton nor Hancock could win. To prevent a swing to Hendricks, the Ohio Copperhead Clement Vallandigham proposed, with the secret support of Tammany, to give the Ohio vote to Seymour. Although the chairman still refused to consider himself a candidate, Vallandigham nevertheless presented his name on the next ballot as "a man whom the Presidency has sought and who has not sought the Presidency." Seymour shed unsought tears, but in spite of them the convention swung to him on the twenty-second ballot. After more tears and more hesitation, he accepted—to become known as the Great Decliner. Without discussion the sweat-soaked delegates nominated Missouri's Blair for Vice President. Chosen without enthusiasm, Seymour seemed a loser from the start. Gideon Welles thought his nomination a piece of trickery that had cost the Democrats any chance of winning they might have had with Johnson or Hancock. Johnson thought the Great Decliner about the worst choice that could have been made.

Even as the conventions met, voter registration, directed by the military governors and executed under the bayonets of twenty thousand regulars and a number of Negro militia units, was proceeding smoothly in the "Sinful Ten" states of the South. In Alabama, Florida, Louisiana, South Carolina, and Mississippi the newly enfranchised freedmen formed a majority of the voters, and in the whole Sinful Ten 703,000 Negro voters registered to only 627,000 whites. Congressman George W. Julian of Indiana, a member of the powerful Committee on the Conduct of the War and an advocate of a "hard" peace, made one of the ablest defenses of such immediate suffrage when he declared: "If you wish to teach the ignorant man, black or white, how to vote, you must grant him the *right* to vote." Other men saw the mass Negro vote in terms of their own personal or political gains. By June of 1868 the Carolinas, Florida, Alabama, Louisiana, and Georgia, all under Radical control, had followed Arkansas in adopting federally approved constitutions and ratifying the Fourteenth Amendment, and their delegations were readmitted to Congress. The following month the amendment became part of the federal Constitution. But Georgia in a short time was returned to military rule after the carpetbaggers and scalawags in the legislature had combined with the old Democrats to expel the Negro members. However, the loss of Georgia would not come until after November, and the readmission of all but three of the Southern states in their reconstructed form was for the Republicans an assurance of victory in the coming presidential election.

Both candidates conducted quiet campaigns. Seymour spent most of the period at his dairy farm near Utica, New York. Grant, after presenting the diplomas at West Point's graduation, told his managers that he would take no further part in election politics. He made a Western trip with Generals Sherman and Sheridan, visible but silent. But his plain manner, above all his reluctance to speak, increased his popularity, made him seem a simple soldier ready to assume the additional burden of the Presidency with the same sense of duty that Washington had once shown. To the Boys in Blue, looking back on the war years through a haze of increasingly fond memories, their general seemed a father figure. They paraded with oilskin capes and torches behind "Grant bands," tramping the streets in chorus to:

Oh! God was kind and heaven was true
When it gave us a man like U—
—lysses Grant
When it gave us a man like you!

To rank-and-file Republicans, Democrats were no more than Rebels under the skin. Conservative Republican financial circles blanched at the thought of paying war debts in depreciated greenbacks. As in 1866, atrocity stories from the South, swelled in volume now by the activities of the increasingly aggressive Ku-Klux Klan, filled the Radical press.

Democrats tried to counter Republican propaganda by denouncing Grant as a "soaker behind the door and in the dark," a liar, a puppet, and a butcher, and warned that if the "man on horseback" was elected, he would rule from the White House like another Napoleon. But when the early September elections in Vermont and Maine showed a Republican swing far greater than

HARPER'S WEEKLY, NOVEMBER 2, 1872

In art, in print, and on the minstrel stage, the Negro of Reconstruction America was regularly portrayed as a charmingly simple or colorfully venal clown—a caricature of Man. R. N. Brooke's Canvassing for Votes, *above, is an example.*

that in 1864, and when a month later supposedly Democratic Ohio and Pennsylvania—the "October states"—went Republican, the Democrats panicked. The New York *World* begged Seymour to withdraw in favor of Chase or Johnson, while members of the Democratic National Committee even considered drafting Johnson. The Great Decliner, however, refused to decline any more. Instead, prodded by Johnson, he left his farm for the last few weeks of the campaign to make a series of inconsequential stump speeches.

In the Electoral College Grant overwhelmed Seymour by 214 votes to 80, carrying twenty-six states to the Democrats' eight, with unreconstructed Mississippi, Texas, and Virginia excluded. Yet in the popular balloting Grant received only 3,012,833 votes to Seymour's 2,703,249, and but for the 450,000 Negro votes in the South, would have been—even though elected—a minority President.

Grant spent the election night at his small house in Galena, Illinois. During the early evening he had visited a friend who had had a telegraph instrument installed to catch the returns. When it became clear that the General had won, he received his neighbors' congratulations without comment, then walked up the hill in the darkness to his house. A hundred or so townspeople had gathered before his door. Standing on his porch, he thanked them briefly and promised to conduct himself according to the people's will.

The laconic man, standing on his porch in the darkness before his neighbors, had come a long way in a short time. Eight years earlier he had been a middle-aged tanner's clerk, failure bending his shoulders. Now he was the hero of the War of the Rebellion, Unconditional Surrender Grant, general of the armies, President-elect of the United States of America, and father figure to whom his countrymen had turned for guidance in their postwar confusion.

Hiram Ulysses Grant, he had been born in southern Ohio in 1822, and there seemed nothing to indicate talent or ambition either in the child or the man until he was almost forty. "Useless," his schoolmates had called this inconspicuous, reticent son of a bombastic tanner father. Friendless as a boy, cautious, mediocre and lackadaisical in his schoolwork, he showed a certain knack at managing horses and early drove a team. Beyond that he had no apparent abilities. His future was uncertain when his father called his attention to a West Point vacancy caused by a dropout cadet from his Ohio district. Ulysses asked for the appointment—the sole applicant. The congressman who casually appointed him sent his name to the War Department as Ulysses Simpson Grant, and so it remained.

Neither Ulysses nor any of his Ohio neighbors expected that he would pass the West Point entrance examinations, but somehow he did. As a cadet he continued an indifferent student, less than diligent, intellectually stagnant. At the end of every examination period he expected to be dropped; yet in the end he graduated, standing twenty-first among the thirty-nine members of the class of 1843, generally considered the sorriest class ever turned out at West Point. No martial dreams inspired young Second Lieutenant Grant on graduation. For him the Academy had been a means to a free education rather than to a military career, and he planned to leave the Army as soon as he could.

As a junior lieutenant stationed at Jefferson Barracks in St. Louis, he found the peacetime routine of Army life little different from that of a cadet. While off duty, he courted Julia Dent, the sister of a West Point classmate. Though neither especially intelligent nor attractive, and with her appearance marred by a cast in her left eye, Julia was a warmhearted and enduring girl, and would bear with her husband through years of adversity. They were married when Grant returned from the Mexican War, wearing a spade beard and the bars of a full lieutenant.

It took five more years for Grant to reach the rank of captain. Assigned to the Pacific Coast, bored and lonely, with his wife and family forced for financial reasons to stay in the East, he took to drink. His colonel, who had long disliked him, ordered him to put away the bottle or leave the Army. Grant resigned. That year, 1853, was a milepost on his downward path. His father-in-law gave him a farm, but the crops turned out badly. So did Grant's other ventures. He grew stooped and ragged. In 1858 he had to pawn his watch to buy Christmas presents for his family. The next year he sold his farm and moved to Galena, Illinois, where he worked as a clerk in his brothers' leather store for fifty dollars a month. Silent, dressed in a faded blue Army overcoat, and usually smoking a clay pipe, the reticent tippler with his dowdy, plodding wife and four children was scarcely noticed in the neighborhood.

The cannon flashes at Fort Sumter that ushered in the war came as unexpected rays of hope for the middle-aged clerk. Eager now to resume his abandoned military career, he applied for duty to Generals John C. Frémont and George B. McClellan, and when his approaches were rejected, wrote directly to Secretary of War Simon Cameron asking for a commission. Cameron did not reply. Finally Grant found a job as a civilian clerk in the office of the Illinois adjutant general, where his knowledge of military affairs and his unsuspected organizing ability soon brought him to the attention of Governor Richard Yates. The governor was faced with the problem of the Twenty-first Illinois Volunteers, whose colonel, though elected, had driven his regiment to a state of near mutiny by his incompetence. Yates, searching for a man with a Regular Army background, replaced him with Grant. Once in command, the old West Pointer soon showed himself an able disciplinarian, bringing the Twenty-first to such a state of efficiency in a month that he was able to take the field in Missouri against Confederate irregulars.

When Lincoln called on the Illinois congressional delegation to nominate a new group of brigadier generals, Grant was chosen because he was the only colonel from his district who was also a professional military man. As a brigadier general surrounded by his staff, the unsuccessful soldier, the tanner's clerk, had at last achieved a position of authority. The one-star general emerged a hero to a country thirsty for heroes after his capture of Forts Henry and Donelson, in which he first employed the phrase that would be applied to his initials: Unconditional Surrender. In Unconditional Surrender Grant, the Union had finally found a general who could win, a taciturn, stern-faced leader who fought rather than talked. Congress hastened to vote him its thanks, and for the first time in his life Grant tasted acclaim. Less than two months later his near defeat at Shiloh rubbed some of the gilt off his epaulets and taught him how undependable is public favor. But, given command of the District of West Tennessee and constantly expanding his command, he succeeded on July 4, 1863, in capturing Vicksburg and opening the Mississippi to Union commerce. The general in the untidy uniform, monosyllabic, a cigar always clamped in his mouth, became overnight a folk hero. Lincoln raised him to a major general in the Regular Army, and after his success in the Battle of Chattanooga, Congress revived the rank of lieutenant general for him—a rank that had not been held since Washington's day.

In 1864 Grant took command as general in chief of all the Union armies. Attaching his command to the Army of the Potomac, he made the defeat of Lee his main objective. "I propose to fight it out on this line if it takes all summer," Grant announced during the five days of fighting at Spotsylvania Court House, the second battle of the campaign; he pursued Lee through Virginia from the Rapidan to Cold Harbor with a Prussian disregard for casualties that shocked the country. In a coordinated campaign during that same summer of 1864, Sherman advanced on Atlanta, captured the city, devastated the landscape by the year's end from Atlanta to Savannah and the sea, and then made his smoking way north toward Virginia. Grant, after a nine-month siege of Petersburg, captured Richmond on April 2, 1865, and forced Lee's surrender at Appomattox a week later. The shy, uncommunicative Grant—a full general after 1866, and again the first man since Washington to hold the rank—with his "reticence, modesty and unostentatious simplicity" became the champion of the North. To the South he seemed—in his generous terms to Lee—a worthy adversary. Even before Johnson's trial it appeared increasingly clear that the general of the armies was on his way to becoming the next President of the United States.

On New Year's Day, 1869, Johnson held one of his last formal public receptions. The President, in good health and spirits, received his guests in the Blue Room. More than five thousand visitors flocked to the White House in the rain to bring their good wishes. Grant had left Washington to avoid having to call on the man he had come to detest. The most startling sight at the reception was Ben Butler's bald head in the long line of Cabinet officers, judges, diplomats, and politicians. Johnson shook hands with his droop-eyed adversary, greeting him with apparent geniality and chatting for several minutes. "A very pleasant and cordial meeting," said Butler afterward. "My unpleasantness was political, not personal. I don't believe in carrying political disputes into social life."

Other important events of Johnson's last year had been overshadowed by the impeachment trial and the turmoil over Reconstruction. "Hot denunciation and defense of Andrew Johnson through leafy June and dusty dog days," wrote Seward in his diary, "and press and public give cursory attention to foreign affairs which engross the Secretary of State." There was, early in Seward's Secretaryship, the dilemma of Mexico. Napoleon III, taking advantage of the preoccupation

of the United States with an internal war, had landed troops in the turbulent land south of the Texas border. The French forces quickly captured Mexico City. Napoleon, after a managed plebiscite that came out in favor of a monarchy, dispatched the Austrian Archduke Ferdinand Maximilian and his wife, Carlota, overseas to become Emperor and Empress of Mexico. Seward protested this violation of the Monroe Doctrine, and but for his country's own conflict would have favored declaring war on France. After Lee's surrender, such war talk flared up. General Sherman was sent to Mexico to consult with Benito Juárez—the Indian President of the Republic of Mexico, who was waging guerrilla war against Maximilian and the French—but failed to find the Mexican leader. General Philip Sheridan was sent to the border with fifty thousand troops; later Sheridan even considered recruiting an independent expeditionary force to aid Juárez. The dilemma was resolved in 1867, when Napoleon, faced with grave internal difficulties, the rising external threat of Prussia, and a request by Seward—amounting to an ultimatum—for the withdrawal of French troops, called his soldiers home. Maximilian, loyal to the few Mexican aristocrats who had supported him, refused to leave and was seized by Juárez' men in May, 1867, and shot.

Seward had observed during the war that the Navy was hampered by its lack of coaling stations in the West Indies. After the war he arranged to purchase the island of St. Thomas from Denmark, but his already-signed agreement was blocked by the Senate. His other expansionist efforts to acquire island footholds in the Caribbean and the Pacific were equally unsuccessful, although he did manage to secure the Midway Islands far to the west of Hawaii. But he was brilliantly successful with the half million square miles of Alaska, in Russian possession since the Empress Catherine's day. One evening in the spring of 1867 the Czar's minister Baron Edward de Stoeckl unexpectedly called on Seward and informed him that the Czar wished to dispose of his Alaska colony. The Secretary of State suggested an immediate discussion, and within two hours had gathered his staff together. By four the

Albert Graefle portrayed the Emperor Maximilian and the Empress Carlota in 1865, at the height of France's Mexican adventure. Soon Carlota would go mad, to live insane for sixty years, and her husband would die before a firing squad.

43

"One does nothing here," Edgar Degas complained in a letter from New Orleans. *"It's in the climate, so much cotton, one lives for and by cotton."* Even so, in 1873 he returned to France with studies for Portraits dans un bureau, Nouvelle-Orléans, *above,* of his two brothers' cotton brokerage office.

next morning he had a treaty drawn and executed and ready to go to the Senate. Stoeckl's asking price for Alaska was ten million dollars. Seward countered by offering half that; the baron proposed to split the difference. When the American held out for seven million dollars, the Russian agreed if two hundred thousand dollars more could be added to liquidate the claims of the Russian Fur Company. The Secretary did not spend any further time in quibbling.

It fell to Senator Sumner, as chairman of the Committee on Foreign Affairs, to present the treaty to his colleagues. For all his animus against the administration, in regard to Alaska the senator was for once in agreement with Johnson and his Secretary of State. Sumner was less concerned about the wealth of fish and fur that the northern region might contain than about dismissing "one more monarch from this continent." The Senate promptly ratified the treaty, but less expansionist-minded Republicans in the House refused at first to vote the money. The Radical press started an outcry against "Johnson's polar bear garden," and hostile congressmen claimed that Alaska was a land inhabited only by criminals, where it rained three hundred days a year. Cartoonist Thomas Nast caricatured Johnson as King Andy being anointed by Seward with Russian oil.

Johnson did not wait for the dilatory House to vote the money for "Seward's Folly," but sent American forces north to take immediate possession. In October, 1867, at the Russian capital of Sitka, before parading detachments of Russian and American soldiers, the white-blue-red flag of Russia was lowered and the Stars and Stripes hoisted in its place. In spite of Republican ire, and charges of bribery and fraud in the transaction, the House finally appropriated the funds for the Alaska purchase the following July.

A thorny international problem was the Fenian agitation, with hot-headed Irish-Americans plotting to seize Canada from the hated English. In May, 1866, a band of fifteen hundred well-armed Fenians from New York crossed the Niagara River, seized Fort Erie, and raised their green flag. Canadian troops soon counterattacked. The skirmish, in which several lives were lost, became known with subsequent exaggeration as the Battle of Limestone Ridge. Johnson, impatient with such quixotic gestures, issued a proclamation ordering the Fenians to disband, but the problem persisted until it was finally settled in 1871.

45

To finance the late war, Congress had authorized the issuing of the now too familiar greenbacks, and in so doing had taken the country from a gold to a paper standard. After the war, Secretary of the Treasury Hugh McCulloch—Lincoln's former comptroller of currency, an advocate of hard currency, and a close friend of financier Jay Cooke's—determined to cut back spending, reduce taxes, and return to the gold standard as quickly as possible. In 1866 McCulloch persuaded Congress to pass an act authorizing him to retire the greenbacks gradually by issuing bonds. That same year London had experienced a financial panic. A year later the war-inflated bubble burst in America. Debtors, as usual, demanded relief through more pa-

per money. Farmers, receiving for their produce greenbacks worth only half the face value, watched angrily while bondholders—many of them British—were paid off in gold. Over McCulloch's protest Congress repealed the greenback act. Johnson, as he stated in his annual message of December, 1868, favored some sort of scaling down of specie payments to bondholders. Yet, though urged by greenbackers and inflationists, he refused to remove his hard-money Secretary of the Treasury. Congress itself would go no further than repealing the greenback act, and refused to alter the terms of payment to bondholders.

In February, 1869, the Republicans in Congress passed the Radical-initiated Fifteenth Amendment and

The Irish-Americans were so politically potent that even after the Fenians had made diplomatic trouble for the United States and insulted President Johnson as a "dirty tool of the English government," New York leaders honored five Fenian heroes, just out of English jails, with a parade in 1871.

sent it on to the state legislatures for ratification. The brief amendment, a defining postscript to the Fourteenth Amendment and considered by Sumner unnecessary, established that "the right of citizens of the United States to vote shall not be denied or abridged by the United States or by any State on account of race, color, or previous condition of servitude." A halfhearted effort was made to include "sex" with "race" and "color," but in spite of Radical promises to women's rights leaders, like Susan B. Anthony and Lucretia Mott, Congress was not yet radical enough to give the vote to women.

While Johnson continued in the White House during the waning months of his term, many of his old enemies were disappearing from the political scene. Ben Wade had failed of re-election. Stanton, broken in health, would die before the new year was out. Old Thad, the agnostic, had died in August, stipulating in his will that he be buried in a Negro cemetery that "I might illustrate in death the principles which I advocated through a long life: equality of man before his Creator." The President himself, angered by the Northern Methodist Church's demand for his impeachment, had taken to attending mass at St. Patrick's Cathedral in Washington. Catholicism appealed to him both for its stately ritual and for the democracy of its congregations, with no reserved seats or rented pews. On his sixtieth birthday, December 29, 1868, he gave a large and lively children's party in the White House, the first ever held there.

Grant refused to allow his children to attend the White House birthday party, and as his inauguration approached, remained patently hostile to Johnson and his Cabinet. The general of the armies informed the Committee on Inauguration Ceremonies that he would neither speak to, nor ride in the same carriage with, the outgoing President. Dismayed, the committee pondered a plan for two separate presidential carriages. Johnson solved the dilemma by deciding not to appear at the Capitol at all on Inauguration Day. "After the silly, arrogant and insolent declarations of Grant that he would not speak to his official superior and predecessor, nor ride nor associate with him," wrote Secretary of the Navy Gideon Welles in his diary, "the President could not compose a part in the pageant to glorify Grant without a feeling of abasement."

On the morning of Inauguration Day, March 4, Johnson sat with his Cabinet in his White House office

This 1881 lithograph, Heroes of the Colored Race, *brackets abolitionist Frederick Douglass with Blanche K. Bruce and Hiram R. Revels, former senators from Mississippi. Bruce was also a planter; Revels, president of Alcorn University.*

examining and signing the miscellaneous bills that were the tag ends of his official life. A few minutes after twelve—and about an hour before Grant started down Pennsylvania Avenue to be sworn in—Johnson stood up and announced that it was time to go, shook hands feelingly with those present, and left the White House to his successor. "I fancy I can already smell the fresh mountain air of Tennessee," he told Welles. He had prepared one final gesture, a farewell address, which he now released to the newspapers. In it, and for the last time, he defended his policies and excoriated his foes. On returning to Greeneville, he found a throng of fifteen thousand townsmen and mountaineer visitors crowding the streets to see and greet their Andy. "I feel proud," he told them, "in coming back among old friends to help them bear their burdens, if I can do nothing to relieve them. . . . An old man, weary with the cares of state, has come to lay his bones among you."

During the eight years Grant was to spend in the White House, Reconstruction would persist as the bitterest, most consuming and divisive American issue. In 1888 Lord James Bryce, in *The American Com-*

47

monwealth, said of the Southern state governments under Radical Reconstruction:

Such a Saturnalia of robbery and jobbery has seldom been seen in any civilized country. . . . The position of these [Radical] adventurers was like that of a Roman provincial governor in the latter days of the Republic. . . . [All] voting power lay with those who were wholly unfit for citizenship, and had no interest as taxpayers, in good government. . . . [Since] the legislatures were reckless and corrupt, the judges for the most part subservient, the Federal military officers bound to support what purported to be the constitutional authorities of the State, Congress distant and little inclined to listen to the complaints of those whom it distrusted as rebels, greed was unchecked and roguery unabashed.

Bryce's view until quite recently was accepted without qualifications North and South. And indeed much that went on in the South during the Reconstruction era was bizarrely corrupt. In South Carolina, as the most extreme example, the Statehouse — with the majority of the legislators freedmen manipulated adroitly by carpetbaggers — had become a grotesque carnival managed by Governor Robert K. Scott, an Ohio adventurer, gold-rush prospector, and former Union officer, who had first drifted south as an agent of the Freedmen's Bureau. Within Scott's ring, "Honest John" Patterson of Penn-

sylvania, remembered as a wartime paymaster who had misappropriated the funds of an Ohio regiment, was being groomed to take his place in the line of South Carolina senators that had included John Calhoun. In 1873 Senator Patterson would observe that "there are five years more of good stealing in South Carolina."

The semiliterate or even illiterate freedmen occupying desks in the South Carolina House of Representatives found that they could legislate their dreams into fact. Reacting with predictably naïve venality, they voted themselves free bars and restaurants, they charged food and wine and furniture and women's dresses and millinery to the state, they filled their pockets with the change of petty graft. In one instance a deceased member was even allowed a free coffin. When Lincoln's former minister to The Hague, James S. Pike, asked a legislator how he got his money, he received the blunt reply: "I stole it." Pike saw the South Carolina legislature as a parody — black rustics at play in the sacred halls of one of the Original Thirteen. Between 1868 and 1876 the state's printing costs were greater than they had been from the Revolution to the end of the Civil War. When the scalawag speaker of the South Carolina House, Franklin Moses, Jr., lost a thousand dollars on a horse race, the solicitous leg-

48

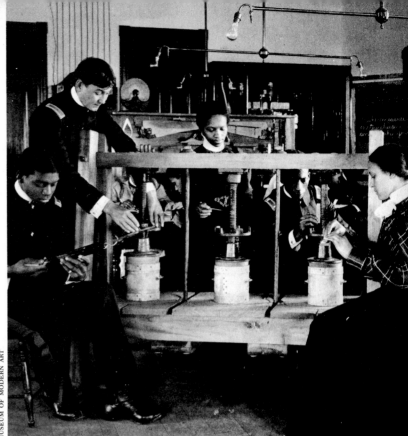

All across the South after the war, schools sprang up to educate the freedmen and their children. At left, one of the schoolhouses; center, primary students with a teacher; and above, a physics class at Hampton Institute in Virginia.

islators voted to compensate him for his loss "for the dignity and ability with which he has presided." Speaker Moses, who as a young Southern hothead had raised the Confederate flag over Fort Sumter, celebrated his postwar conversion to Radicalism by indiscriminately accepting bribes, dealing in bogus pay certificates, diverting militia funds to his own use, selling pardons, and wining and wenching with his freedmen legislators.

South Carolina and Mississippi, the two states with Negro majorities, were, with Alabama, the most blatantly corrupt, but it was merely a matter of degree. In Louisiana the twenty-six-year-old carpetbag governor from Illinois, Henry Clay Warmoth, would demonstrate how to turn an annual salary of eight thousand dollars into a million dollars in four years. The Louisiana chief justice was instrumental in selling a railroad in which the state had invested two million dollars for fifty thousand dollars. Instances accumulated like autumn leaves. A single Alabama lawmaker pocketed thirty-five thousand dollars for managing a railroad bond issue. An Arkansas Negro was paid nine thousand dollars for the repair of a bridge that had originally cost only five hundred dollars. In the cause of railroad expansion even the most aloof Southern Democrats of the old

school could be found teamed with scalawags and carpetbaggers. General Lee, when he came to Washington in 1869 and made a formal call at the White House, told Grant that he was in town on railroad business.

Throughout the postwar South taxes rose and property values declined as state debts soared. Poor bookkeeping and destruction of records make figures hard to come by, but one set of estimates shows that the Florida debt rose from $524,000 in 1868 to $5,621,000 in 1874, South Carolina's debt jumped from $7,000,000 to $29,000,000, Alabama's from $7,000,000 to $32,000,000, Louisiana's from $14,000,000 to $48,000,000. Yet, whatever the graft, much of the money, far from being squandered, went into essential and formerly neglected services. Before the war Southern states, under their Bourbon leaders, had been notably parsimonious in public expenditures. Now, under the Radical-dominated governments, roads and bridges were constructed, schools were built where there had never been schools,

49

and hospitals, insane asylums, and poorhouses were erected in impressive numbers.

Contrary to the later popular belief, Negroes did not play a dominant role in most Reconstruction governments. Only in South Carolina did they outnumber the whites in the legislature. No state had a Negro governor, although South Carolina, Mississippi, and Louisiana had Negro lieutenant governors. Fourteen Negroes were elected to the House of Representatives, along with two United States senators, Hiram R. Revels and Blanche K. Bruce, both from Mississippi. Revels, a Methodist minister, was elected by the Radical-dominated state legislature to the Senate seat formerly held by Jefferson Davis. He retired in 1871 to become president of the new Alcorn College for Negroes. He finally became so disgusted with carpetbag-scalawag-Negro rule in his state that he joined the Democrats. Equally honest and equally able was Mississippi's second Negro senator, Blanche Bruce, a Virginia-born freedman who had been educated at Oberlin College and who had come to Mississippi as a planter after the war. He remained in office until the white Democrats regained control of the state.

At the beginning of the imposed Reconstruction the military commanders in the South had divided their territories into registration districts and appointed three-man registration boards. Most registrars were federal soldiers or Freedmen's Bureau agents. No persons were permitted to register who had been "disfranchised for participation in any rebellion or civil war against the United States," and under this provision at least one hundred and fifty thousand leading whites could not vote. Registration went on through the summer of 1867. In South Carolina, Florida, Mississippi, Alabama, and Louisiana registered Negroes outnumbered registered whites. At a time when compromise on the race issue might still have been possible, Confederate leaders as distinguished as Alexander Stephens, the former vice president of the Confederacy, and Wade Hampton, the three-times-wounded cavalry general and the richest planter in the prewar South, were willing to grant voting rights to literate and property-holding Negroes. Not all scalawags were rogues like Moses.

At first a number of Southern conservatives were ready to make the best of the situation by joining and using their influence to control the Radicals. James L. Alcorn of Mississippi, a wealthy prewar planter and a Confederate brigadier general, was willing to become scalawag governor of his state with the support of the military governor, General Adelbert Ames. An honest man, Alcorn believed that only a Negro-white alliance could bring enough pressure on Northern Republicans to abolish the almost confiscatory tax on cotton and to restore political rights to proscribed ex-Confederates. But Alcorn's plans for political action did not work out, and Ames, a West Point graduate and a Civil War general, was subsequently elected governor with overwhelming freedman support. A carpetbagger, and indeed Ben Butler's son-in-law, he was nevertheless an honest man, inept as a politician but sincerely devoted to the rights of Negroes. Though the Negro bias of the state government was assailed by the whites, no major political scandal occurred in Mississippi during the Reconstruction period.

Corruption in the Reconstruction South was more blatant where semiliterate Negroes occupied legislative seats, but it was simply part of the corruption of the Gilded Age. No state government can be said to have been completely Negro dominated, and many of the emerging Negro leaders—a number of them clergymen—were men of integrity and capability like Mississippi's senators. For all the fraudulent bond issues, bribery, graft in land sales and in letting of contracts, less public money was stolen in all the South than by the Tweed Ring in New York City; no scandals were as far-reaching as those national scandals that would besmirch the Grant administration. Whatever may be said, state conventions, dominated by Negro-carpetbag-scalawag majorities, had produced revolutionary constitutions, in which for the first time in the South the right to universal manhood suffrage and free education had been made explicit.

Public education had been looked on with little favor in the prewar South. Many Johnny Rebs in the Confederate army could neither read nor write. In 1850 one white Southern adult in five was illiterate, as opposed to one in thirty-five in the Middle Atlantic States and one in two hundred in New England. Holding no great brief for education, unreconstructed Southerners found it particularly galling to watch the rapid progress of Negroes in regions where only a few years before it had been a criminal offense to instruct a slave. The schools, sponsored at first by the Freedmen's Bureau, spread rapidly. By 1869 there were nearly ten thousand teachers in Negro schools, half of them Northern and Southern Negroes, the other half whites.

Even more galling—and very closely related to the Freedmen's Bureau—were the activities of the Loyal Leagues, offshoots of the parent Union League, founded in the North in 1862. Though the leagues had only white members at first, their great potential value among Negroes was soon realized, and with a mumbo-jumbo secret ritual and a catchword of four L's—Lincoln, Liberty, Loyal, League—chapters were established throughout the South as instruments to give the freedmen a sense of political unity through ties with the Republican party. League organizers spread across the rural acres promising that Ben Butler and Thad Stevens would soon seize the land of white Confederates and give it to Negro farmers.

Southern white opposition found its embodiment in the Ku-Klux Klan and such imitative organizations as the Knights of the White Camellia, the Pale Faces, the Society of the White Rose, and the White League. The Klan had its casual origin in Pulaski, Tennessee, in December of 1865, when six young Confederate veterans with time on their hands decided to organize

themselves into a secret social society. One of the group, with a smattering of classical education, suggested that they call themselves Kuklos, from the Greek word for "circle." Another proposed adding "Klan." So the alliterative Ku-Klux Klan came into being. As a prank the Klansmen took to riding through town evenings draped in sheets and wearing masks, to the astonishment of the natives and—as they soon discovered—the terror of the more superstitious Negroes, who sometimes imagined them the ghosts of dead Confederate soldiers. What began as a prank soon turned into an instrument of intimidation. From its original den the Klan spread informally to other dens, to klaverns, and finally—after a convention of all the dens in Nashville in 1867—to an Invisible Empire of the South headed by a Grand Wizard and subordinate officials with such awesome titles as Grand Dragon, Fury, Hydra, Titan, and Nighthawk. "Troublesome" Negroes began to receive late-evening visits from squadrons of silent, white-clad riders. Carpetbaggers, scalawags, and Negroes received their warnings:

The freedman often found he was not welcome anywhere, as this cartoon of the 1870's indicates. When blacks left the South in droves in the so-called Exodus of 1879, they encountered great hostility in many new homes they had chosen.

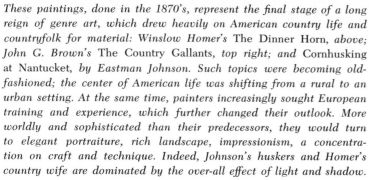

These paintings, done in the 1870's, represent the final stage of a long reign of genre art, which drew heavily on American country life and countryfolk for material: Winslow Homer's The Dinner Horn, *above; John G. Brown's* The Country Gallants, *top right; and* Cornhusking at Nantucket, *by Eastman Johnson. Such topics were becoming old-fashioned; the center of American life was shifting from a rural to an urban setting. At the same time, painters increasingly sought European training and experience, which further changed their outlook. More worldly and sophisticated than their predecessors, they would turn to elegant portraiture, rich landscape, impressionism, a concentration on craft and technique. Indeed, Johnson's huskers and Homer's country wife are dominated by the over-all effect of light and shadow.*

of which there were about two and a half billion dollars' worth outstanding, and to make a start at redeeming the third of a billion in greenbacks. A speedy retirement of the national debt seemed a happy possibility; and though financiers might be concerned about the restriction of currency, Boutwell's course struck the popular fancy.

However unorthodox Grant may have appeared in his approach to politicians, by midsummer his administration seemed to meet with general approval even among Northern Democrats. Just before leaving with his family for the Stetson House at Long Branch, New Jersey, a fashionable, if parvenu, watering place, Grant wrote to General Adam Badeau, now installed as his official biographer: "Public affairs look to me to be progressing very favorably. The revenues of the country are being collected as they have not been before, and expenditures are looked after more carefully. The first thing it seems to me is to establish the credit of the country. This is policy enough for the present."

During the dog days, while Grant sat on the veranda of the Stetson House looking out at the sea, the first great scandal of his administration was brewing. All that summer Rawlins, his guide and adviser, lay dying. No one was closer to Grant than Rawlins, no one knew his weaknesses better, no one could advise the President more reliably on men and events. Without him the President, all unknowing, would stand unprotected from the wolves.

As Boutwell continued to sell gold, the price fell. And as it fell, shipments of grain from the West eased, a process viewed with dismay by the ferret-eyed New York speculator Jay Gould, who with James Fisk, Jr., owned the overcapitalized Erie Railroad, which carried much of the grain traffic from the West to the East. Anxious to show an increase in the Erie earnings in order to water its watered stock still further, Gould assumed the patriotic stance that raising the price of gold would aid American farmers in selling their grain overseas. When gold had fallen to a price of 130 (that is, it took $1.30 in greenback paper currency to buy a gold dollar), Gould entered the gold market and bid the price up to 142. From this point on he took to buying gold when it fell below 140 and selling it when it moved above 145. Thus, he alleged, he kept the crops moving east; the profits found their way into his pocket.

Gould and Fisk as partners had one solid quality that bound them together—a calculating unscrupulousness. Otherwise they shared no resemblance, for Fisk was a gaudy rogue and Gould as prim as a deacon. Puritan in manner, upright in his family life, Gould was an indiscriminate briber of politicians and judges, a defrauder of creditors, a brilliant, indefatigable schemer. "Jubilee Jim" Fisk flaunted his mistresses in open carriages in New York, and when at sea on one of the ships of his Fall River Line, he strutted in a gold-braided uniform of self-created admiral's rank. Jubilee Jim had started out in life selling tinware from the back of a gaily painted wagon, and had ended up as a Wall Street gambler whose speculations were the hushed talk of the financial world. Gross, sensuous, flamboyant, he was the perfect foil for the mincing Gould.

As impervious to the implications of his associates as to the accepting of gifts, Grant, accompanied by his brother-in-law Abel R. Corbin, had in June sailed with Gould on the steamer *Providence* as a guest of Admiral

The Tweed Ring, which robbed New York of millions of dollars between 1869 and 1871, was so strong it wrecked itself by outraging the public and nearly breaking the city. Above is a Nast cartoon based on a bitter quote from The Nation.

Fisk to attend the Boston Peace Jubilee. Both speculators used the occasion of an elaborate supper to explain to their taciturn presidential guest the necessity of keeping up the price of gold to move the crops. Grant may even then have suspected something, although on his return to New York he and his family sat cozily in a proscenium box at the Fifth Avenue Theater with Fisk, Gould, and the Corbins.

Gould and Fisk between them had enough resources to manipulate the market on gold, but as they were well aware, its actual price depended on Boutwell. If he could be induced to suspend the Treasury's gold selling, the price would inevitably rise. But could the Secretary of the Treasury be so induced? Fisk had his doubts; Gould did not. In Corbin, the elderly real-estate speculator and lobbyist who had recently married Grant's sister Jenny, Gould found a voracious ally. The protective Rawlins died on September 6. On his way to his friend's funeral Grant stayed overnight with Corbin in New York. There he again met Gould, who spent several hours trying to persuade Grant to restrain his Secretary of the Treasury. To all Gould's persuasions the President still remained noncommittal. Nevertheless Corbin later assured Gould that he had influence with his brother-in-law and that the sales would stop. Anxious to involve a near relative of the President's, Gould had been buying gold for Corbin on credit, and to spin the web still tighter, during the summer he had purchased a half million in gold for the President's secretary, Horace Porter, and the same amount for General Daniel Butterfield, the assistant treasurer of the United States in New York City. Porter was shrewd enough and honest enough to refuse the gilded offer, but Butterfield—who had distinguished himself in the Civil War by composing the bugle call "Taps"—was neither.

Grant, behind his mask of imperturbability, had at last become genuinely suspicious and wrote Boutwell privately not to change his policy. Misinterpreting his brother-in-law's silence, the eager Corbin again reassured Gould, who now approached Fisk. The portly Jim was wary, warning his emaciated partner that if they attempted to corner gold, the government would release its stocks. "Oh, this matter is all fixed up," Gould told him. "Butterfield is all right . . . Corbin has got Grant all right." Fisk, still dubious, hurried to Corbin, who informed him in whispers that Julia Grant was in on the scheme and that he himself had two

million in the market, a quarter of which belonged to the President's wife.

About eighteen million dollars in gold and gold certificates usually circulated in New York's financial world, an amount sufficient to carry on business so long as it did circulate. Trading in gold was carried on in the Gold Exchange, which was housed in the Gold Room of the New York Stock Exchange. Nobody held the metal for more than a few days. Gould and Fisk, knowing that if the government held back its gold they could push the price where they pleased, set out to corner the market.

Beneath his confidence, Gould remained wary. Waiting until Grant had left Washington for a remote resort in the mountains of Pennsylvania thirty miles from any railroad or telegraph, he sent his agents to the Gold Exchange with orders to buy. Jubilee Jim appeared in person on the floor of the Gold Room, exuding confidence like eau de cologne. Gould had persuaded Corbin to write his brother-in-law urging him not to interfere in the battle of the speculators. A trusted agent of Fisk's carried the letter to Grant in his rustic seclusion. The President, interrupted in a game of croquet, read the letter and announced curtly that there was no reply. At the nearest station the agent telegraphed to Fisk, "Letter delivered all right." Somehow the message came through, "Letter delivered. All right," an assurance to the conspirators that Grant had been taken care of. But when Gould called on Corbin, he found that agitated old man waving a letter from Julia Grant, in which she had written that her husband was very annoyed and that Corbin must close his speculations at once. Gould calmed him down by promising to buy out his interest in the gold pool for a hundred thousand dollars and to keep the matter quiet.

On September 22 Grant arrived back in Washington. The next day Gould, tipped off by Julia Grant's letter that the President was not to be relied on, locked himself in his office and began secretly to release his gold holdings, openly buying "merely enough to make believe I was still a bull." Fisk, unwarned and unaware of the contretemps, bought heavily all day. The next day, September 24, was to be long remembered on Wall Street as Black Friday. Fisk continued to buy gold. In the center of the pandemonium that was the Gold Room he stood near the bronze cupid-and-dolphin fountain bidding up the price of gold in his bellowing voice as a shouting mass of clerks and speculators crowded round him. By noon, he said later, he had bought more than sixty million dollars' worth. Investors, businessmen, importers, forced to pay exorbitant prices for the gold necessary in their transactions, observed their own ruin as the pointer on the gold dial moved relentlessly upward by quarters—from 141 and 142 to 145, to 155, 160, 162. Jubilee Jim announced that the price would reach 200.

An alarmed Boutwell called at the White House to urge that the Treasury sell its store in order to stay the panic and protect the country's business interests. He suggested that selling three million dollars in gold and buying bonds would be enough to break the Gould-Fisk combination. Grant told him to sell five million dollars if necessary. Boutwell telegraphed Butterfield in New York to sell four million at once. Within fifteen minutes the price of gold had fallen twenty-nine points. To avoid further panic the directors closed the Gold Room. Black Friday had come to an end.

That day left jagged scars on the financial world in the shape of bankruptcies, ruined businesses, and broker-age house failures. Gould, forewarned, escaped with only minor losses. Fisk, at least on paper, went bank-rupt, although this in no way seemed to disturb his future amiable relations with his uncommunicative partner. Butterfield and Corbin were too obviously implicated to attempt to conceal or deny the fact, and Butterfield was forced to resign. Although Democrats tried to implicate Grant, he was apparently guilty of nothing more than being indiscreet in his associations. Yet the indulgence with which Grant was absolved is a measure of the low moral tone of the era, and Henry Adams, meditating a generation later in his *Education,* observed: "That Grant should have fallen within six months into such a morass—or should have let Boutwell drop into it—rendered the outlook . . . mysterious or frankly opaque to a young man who had hitched his wagon . . . to the star of reform." Adams concluded that "the worst scandals of the eighteenth century were rel-atively harmless by the side of this, which smirched executive, judiciary, banks, corporate system, profes-sions, and people . . . in one dirty cesspool of vulgar corruption."

In itself Black Friday was a symbol of the times, of the postwar reaction, of the get-rich-quick era with its ripe odor of corruption. Washington swarmed with lobbyists and favor seekers—even female lobbyists were appearing on the scene. Sam Ward, the debonair

"King of the Lobby," with a rose in his lapel and a huge sapphire ring on his right hand, became a tourist attrac-tion to equal the unfinished Washington Monument. Sam's expansive talents were for hire. The urbane brother of Julia Ward Howe, Sam, a subtle judge of men and wine, with his white imperial, domed bald head and rapacious nose, moving intimately with the mighty, was the crowned influence-peddler of the Capital. Though he had no need to descend to outright bribery, others less regal did not hesitate.

The Capital, experiencing a building boom after the shabbiness of the war years, was beginning to emerge at last as a smart city. Hotels overflowed with visitors. John Chamberlain turned the former British Legation on Connecticut Avenue into Washington's most luxuri-ous gambling establishment. Even more noted was John Welcker's elegant restaurant, the headquarters of every politician and lobbyist, where Grant's nomination was plotted and where perhaps the majority of congres-sional measures took shape. A new and fluid society had sprung up. Mark Twain observed that Washington was divided into the Antiques, the Parvenus, and the Middle Aristocracy. He looked sympathetically on the Middle Aristocracy, but it was the Parvenus who were taking over.

Aroused by opposition to his Reconstruction pro-gram, disturbed by such disparate events as Black Fri-day and the refusal of the Senate to repeal the Tenure of Office Act, Grant was shifting from his stance of pas-sive instrument of the people's will to that of active politician. As he did so, he drew closer to the party professionals, the practical spoilsmen, the Stalwarts, as they came to be called. New York's towering Senator Roscoe Conkling, of the grandiloquent speech and "turkey gobbler strut," became the orator of the ad-ministration while the deft Senator Zachariah Chandler took care of back-room manipulations. They were joined by the eloquent Oliver Morton of Indiana, like the others a master of the politics of spoils although per-sonally incorruptible. Lincoln had removed Pennsyl-vania's Simon Cameron as Secretary of War because of corruption, but Grant, to the dismay of the purists, found him a congenial trout-fishing companion. Even Ben Butler was adroitly maneuvering into the inner circle of the leader who had removed him from com-mand in the war. For high-flown idealists like Sumner and reformers like Carl Schurz, the German-born senator from Missouri, Grant had little use and little liking.

That Thomas Nast took himself something less than seriously is evident in this self-portrait. He was an illustrator, cartoonist, painter, and staff artist on Harper's Weekly *from 1862 to 1886, and his work abides as the period's autograph.*

The President's prestige suffered its first blow in his ill-advised attempt to revive Seward's expansionist dream of annexing the Dominican Republic. Knowing little or nothing of the island's turbulent corruption, Grant was intrigued when an American adventurer, Colonel Joseph W. Fabens, arrived in the spring of 1869 as representative of the President of the Dominican Republic, Buenaventura Báez, to offer that country to the United States. The mulatto Báez—a political jockey, Sumner later labeled him—whose embezzlements during previous terms in office had aroused armed opposition, previously had sought help from France and England. Now with Haiti, which occupied the western half of the island, threatening invasion and with another revolt on his hands, he turned in desperation to the United States. His emissary, Fabens,

had lived a speculative existence on the island for at least ten years, and his interest was in securing American support for his own exploitation of the country's land and resources. Deftly persuasive, he painted for Grant so fabulous a picture of the Dominican Republic's fertility and wealth that the President sent his private secretary, Orville E. Babcock, to investigate. Babcock, taken in tow by Fabens, toured the republic and returned not only with glowing accounts but with a treaty of annexation for which Báez demanded a million and a half dollars. As Grant explained to his silent Cabinet: "Babcock has returned, as you see, and has brought a treaty of annexation. I suppose it is not formal, as he had no diplomatic powers; but we can easily cure that."

The President again dispatched Babcock to the Dominican Republic, this time with official instructions from Secretary of State Fish, who, though less enthusiastic, felt the acquisition would be advantageous on the whole and was willing to go along with it. Meanwhile information was trickling into the American press about Báez' very precarious position and Fabens' self-interested maneuverings. Even as Grant and Fish were sending the Dominican treaty to the Senate, the public was surprised to learn that United States warships in the Dominican Republic's Samaná Bay were not only bolstering up the shaky Báez by their formidable presence but were also furnishing his armies with American supplies and munitions.

Early in 1870 the treaty hung fire in the Senate. Grant, urging immediate ratification, found himself opposed by Sumner, who as chairman of the Committee on Foreign Relations predicted portentously that the expenses of taking over such a bankrupt land would prove enormous and that annexation would not stop until it had included Haiti and then all the West Indies. Spring was giving way to summer as the debate continued. Grant attempted to cajole reluctant senators into line. If the Dominican treaty should be rejected, "with what grace can we prevent a foreign power from attempting to secure the prize?" he asked in an unwonted burst of angry eloquence. Unimpressed, the Senate divided, twenty-eight senators voting for ratification and twenty-eight against.

Grant never forgave Sumner for leading the attack against his pet project. For the first time the general who saw himself as President of all the people found himself confronted with a solid, implacable opposi-

In the 1870's a few men were already aware of a need to defend some of America's wilderness against exploitation. Thanks in part to a dramatic canvas by Thomas Moran, Yellowstone Park was created in 1872; above is a print of one of Moran's later Yellowstone scenes. Below and right are Albert Bierstadt paintings of Yosemite Valley and redwoods, natural wonders California had by then begun to protect.

tion. His military mind outraged by such insubordination, he laid plans to destroy the senator from Massachusetts even as he moved closer to Sumner's enemy the rabble-rousing Ben Butler. Grant found more opposition facing him in Missouri, where Senator Carl Schurz, who had opposed the treaty, had joined with a splinter group of Liberal Republicans to oppose the state's disfranchisement clauses, which had been enacted by the Radical constitutional convention of 1865 to punish former Rebels.

Butler was particularly anxious to have Grant get rid of Sumner's friend Attorney General E. Rockwood Hoar, whose brother had for long been an unrelenting Butler opponent in Massachusetts. The urbane and cultured Hoar had in any case aroused much opposition among practical politicians for his refusal to acquiesce in what they considered the just claims of patronage. In June, 1870, Grant finally asked for his resignation, appointing in his place Amos T. Akerman, a political nobody from Georgia. Reform-minded Republicans were still further disturbed by the President's removal of the upright Moses Grinnell from the New York Custom House. As collector of customs, Grinnell controlled the richest single area of patronage in the country, but to the disgust of Ben Butler and New York's Senator Conkling, he had based his appointments on merit, had abolished sinecure positions and turned out useless employees in the custom house over the protests of their congressmen, and had even appointed qualified men from outside New York. Urged by Conkling and Butler, Grant finally replaced Grinnell with Thomas Murphy, a Republican politician closely connected with Boss Tweed. Reform Republicans were even further shocked when in October Secretary of the Interior Jacob D. Cox abruptly resigned. Congressman James Garfield wrote consolingly to Cox: "It is a clear case of surrender on the part of the President to the political vermin which infest the government and keep it in a state of perpetual lousiness."

By the time of the mid-term elections in November, 1870, Grant's image had suffered considerable erosion. The Democrats gained six seats in the Senate, while in the House the Republicans lost, and lost for good, their two-thirds majority. And already the South's Radical façade was showing cracks. A sharp break appeared in Virginia, which had been under relatively mild military control until 1869 and which was the only Southern state to have avoided an imposed Radical government.

In 1869 a Virginia convention ratified a new constitution, and in June of that year an election was held. Two rival Republicans had declared themselves candidates for governor: the appointed civil governor, the Radical H. H. Wells; and the Virginia-born conservative Unionist General Gilbert C. Walker. There was a minimum of intimidation during the campaign, and Walker was elected, carrying with him a conservative Democratic legislature. Radicals, fearful of the spread of the revolt against Radical Republicanism, urged that Virginia be kept under military control. But Walker promised Grant that the legislature would ratify the Fifteenth Amendment, and the President in spite of some misgivings took no action.

Democratic revival in Virginia was followed soon, and more violently, by a similar resurgence in Ten-

To look at Horace Greeley, remarked a contemporary, "you would take him for a small farmer of the Quaker persuasion, who had lost all the neatness of the sect, but had appropriated in his disposition a double portion of its meekness."

nessee, where the Ku-Klux Klan and Governor "Parson" Brownlow's militia had been conducting their own private war. When Parson Brownlow gave up the governorship to move on to the United States Senate, the Republicans split, as they had in Virginia, and the Democrats, headed by ex-President Johnson, joined with the conservative Republicans to elect their candidate governor. Shortly afterward the Democratic legislature called a new state constitutional convention to repeal all suffrage disabilities. Georgia's attempt in August of 1868 to restore all-white rule had been thwarted by federal action, but only temporarily, for it elected a Democratic-dominated legislature in 1870. In North Carolina the Democrats, by August of 1870, had won two-thirds of both houses of the legislature and elected six of the state's nine congressmen. The Democratic revival in all three states, unlike in Virginia, was aided by savage Ku-Klux Klan intimidation.

In Texas and Mississippi the Republican party also split into radical and conservative factions. But Grant, fearful of the damage that would be done to his party by a repetition of its Virginia defeat, threw the weight of federal power and patronage behind the Radicals, assuring them of victory and continued control of the two states.

Moderate Republicans were by this time growing weary of the proscriptive policies of Butler and Boutwell, of the constant Southern agitation and the equally constant appeals by carpetbag governments for federal aid and protection. Even an old Radical like Horace Greeley was now ready to assert in his New York *Tribune* that it was time for Southern Republicans to stand on their own feet. Increasingly Reconstruction was to find its defenders in the Stalwarts around Grant, who saw the survival of the Radical Southern regimes as a practical necessity for preserving the Republican party's national control, particularly after the defection of New York and Missouri in the 1870 elections.

Although General Forrest had formally disbanded the Klan, informally and on a state and local level it continued its murderously effective course. In 1871 Butler's son-in-law Adelbert Ames testified in the Senate that there had been sixty-three murders by night riders in Mississippi alone during the preceding three months. Butler, after a congressional investigating committee had reported on night-rider outrages, prepared his Force Bill, known as Butler's KKK Bill, which he pushed through a reluctant Congress. Among its drastic provisions was one specifying that any person who deprived another of his constitutional rights and privileges could be sued for damages. The bill also authorized the President to suspend the writ of habeas corpus and employ the Army to enforce the Fourteenth Amendment, although Grant would use this provision only in the case of South Carolina. During the debate on his KKK Bill in the House of Representatives, Butler at one point brandished a blood-stained shirt worn by a carpetbag official who had been horsewhipped by a band of night riders in Mississippi. Butler's flamboyant gesture gave rise to the expression "waving the bloody shirt" to describe the inflammatory denunciations of the South, which would remain the stock in trade of Republican orators for almost a generation.

The President, in his first message to Congress after the mid-term elections, still urged the annexation of the Dominican Republic and portrayed the calamities that would follow nonannexation. Senator Charles Sumner replied with bitter eloquence, allying himself with the Democrats to expose Babcock and the frauds behind the annexation scheme. So bitter did the chairman of the Committee on Foreign Relations grow that he would not even condescend to speak to the Secretary of State. Fish's negotiations with Britain over the long-dormant claims for damages done by the English-built Confederate commerce raider *Alabama* and over relations with Canada were condemned by Sumner, who was further outraged by the removal of his friend John L. Motley as minister to England. Grant now took direct action, using the full force of his administration to oust the isolated senator from his long-held committee chairmanship. Such bitter feeling remained between the two men that once Grant, on walking past Sumner's house, was seen to stop and shake his fist. Sumner, following his departing guests to the door, would at times denounce the President in such a stentorian voice that they feared it might carry to the White House.

As the 1872 presidential election approached, the ground swell of country-wide good will for the great general was recognized by politicians as making Grant the only possible candidate that the Republicans could elect with certainty. Disaffected Republicans there were in plenty: moralists, like Horace Greeley, who had tried in vain to come to terms with Grant; Westerners, like Garfield, and reformers, like Schurz, anxious to get rid of the high protective tariff that had served well in the war for producing sorely needed revenue but now was of benefit chiefly to favored Eastern manufacturers; the outraged Sumner, who was proposing a constitutional amendment limiting Presidents to a single term. Grant's Stalwarts pointed to administration achievements: a reduced national debt; gold selling near 114; the Treaty of Washington with England; Ku-Klux Klan legislation; a peace policy with the Indians; increased receipts from the Post Office; proposed—if only proposed—civil service reforms; in fine, an idyllic picture marred only by night-rider activities in the South, polygamy in Utah, and the great Chicago fire.

Democrats under the old Copperhead Clement Vallandigham were calling for a "New Departure" that would relegate the past and concentrate on present issues. The New Departure demanded universal amnesty in the South, a swift return to specie payments, debt reduction with moderate taxation, tariff for revenue only, civil service reform, no grants of public land to private corporations. In addition the administration was attacked for its Dominican policy, for the Ku-Klux Klan acts, and for creeping corruption. The Democrats—not yet strong enough to stand alone—looked for a Liberal Republican candidate to lead them in opposing Grant.

Organized in Carl Schurz's Missouri two years before, the Liberal Republicans, determined to defeat Grant the "despot," called their own presidential convention in Cincinnati in May, 1872. Cranks, idealists, suffragettes, intellectuals, reformers, and politicians from the South were drawn to Cincinnati like iron filings to a magnet. The platform, the work of Carl Schurz, accused the Grant administration of corruption, incapacity, and despotism. Charles Francis Adams, son and grandson of Presidents, a man of a chilly rectitude not unworthy of his ancestors, seemed the favored candidate. But after the first ballot the Liberal Republican governor of Missouri, B. Gratz Brown, threw the decisive weight of his influence to Horace Greeley, and to the astonishment of all and the dismay of the more astute the New York *Tribune* editor was nominated on the sixth ballot.

Even from a century's distance, the idea of Horace Greeley as President of the United States, his baby-pink moon face framed by an alfalfa crop of white whiskers, is comically disconcerting. One observer wrote that "no two men could look each other in the face and say 'Greeley' without laughing!" With his white overcoat, shapeless trousers, and wide-brimmed hat he was a cartoonist's delight, and Thomas Nast's sharp pen

made the most of the opportunity during the campaign. Yet for all his hayseed appearance, Greeley, the country boy who had started from nothing, had made his *Tribune* one of the best of American newspapers and himself a power in the land. Abolitionist, Radical, he could still call for an end to sectional differences after the war, and to show that he was in earnest, sign the bond for Jefferson Davis' release in 1867—a quixotic but decent gesture that cost him half his *Tribune* readers. He had supported Grant for the Presidency and his disillusionment was the greater because he had done so in good faith, the faith he felt that Grant had not kept. On being nominated, Greeley said that both North and South were eager to "clasp hands across the bloody chasm." With no very hearty clasp, the Democrats nominated him in Baltimore in July, as did a Louisiana Convention of Liberal Colored Republicans in September. "If the Baltimore Convention puts Greeley in our hymn book," remarked North Carolina's governor, "we will sing him through if it kills us." The regular Republican convention, meeting in Philadelphia, nominated Grant as a matter of routine, replacing Vice President Schuyler Colfax, however, by a former Massachusetts cobbler, Senator Henry Wilson. Grant remained silent during the campaign. "I am no speaker and don't want to be beaten," he wrote. By contrast, Greeley wore himself out speaking across the country, trying to reconcile all the divergences of his supporters: his high-tariff past with the low-tariff Democrats, his abolitionism and the bloody chasm to be bridged.

With almost solid Negro support in the South, with the backing of the Boys in Blue and all the wavers of the "bloody shirt," with the entire Eastern financial world behind him, Grant could not fail to be re-elected. Greeley was so savagely denounced as crank, fool, and traitor that he sometimes wondered, he said, whether he was running for the Presidency or the penitentiary. On Election Day Grant overwhelmed him, carrying thirty-one of the thirty-seven states, including every Northern state. In the popular voting Grant received 3,597,000 votes to his rival's 2,834,000. Exhausted in mind and body, his wife dying a few days before the election, the broken-spirited Greeley saw himself "the worst beaten man who ever ran for high office." Returning to the New York *Tribune*, he attempted to resume his editorship, but he was so distraught that within a few days he retired to his country home. Three weeks after the election Horace Greeley died a madman.

Rebels and
Reconstructors

President Lincoln in 1865 urged a gentle approach toward the defeated Rebels. So did his successor, Andrew Johnson. But the Radical Republicans promoted a sterner policy, which the South helped provoke, for under the lenient terms of Johnson's Reconstruction the Southern states began to issue discriminatory Black Codes and to elect Rebel leaders to public office. Revengeful, seeking to make permanent the federal superiority decided by the war, determined to eradicate the old secessionist aristocracy, anxious to protect the freedmen, and loath to give up political dominance, the Radicals overturned presidential Reconstruction. In Congress they fastened military rule on the Southern states and passed pro-Negro legislation that in effect applied only below the Mason-Dixon Line. They encouraged the development and sustenance, by tactics frequently corrupt, of Republican state governments in the South. It was a self-destructive policy, whatever else may be said for it; from it grew political chaos and a violent reaction. By the close of Grant's first term, sectional antagonism and national race bias had set an irreversible course, and during the next four years Reconstruction fell apart under the weight of the accumulated ill will. The following documents, beginning with a cry of rage published in a South Carolina newspaper on November 20, 1872, trace that disintegration.

[It is] a hell-born policy which has trampled the fairest and noblest of states of our great sisterhood beneath the unholy hoofs of African savages and shoulder-strapped brigands—the policy which has given up millions of our free-born, high-souled brothers and sisters, countrymen and countrywomen of Washington, Rutledge, Marion and Lee, to the rule of gibbering, louse-eaten, devil-worshipping barbarians, from the jungles of Dahomey, and peripatetic buccaneers from Cape Cod, Memphremagog, Hell and Boston.

Fairfield (S. C.) *Herald*, November 20, 1872

Observant Northerners, too, were troubled by what they found in the South. Charles Nordhoff, Washington correspondent for the New York Herald, described the state of political affairs in Louisiana in 1875. Louisiana had one of the more pungent of the Radical state governments.

You can not travel far in Louisiana without discovering that the politicians who, in the name of the Republican party, rule it, and have done so for the last seven years, in all the departments of its government, State and local, are vehemently and unanimously detested by the white people. I have been amazed to see how all white men, and many blacks to my own knowledge—whether rich or poor; whether merchants, mechanics, or professional men; whether Americans, French, Germans, Irish, or Italian by birth: absolutely all except the office-holders and their relatives—unite in this feeling of detestation of their rulers. It expresses itself so vividly at the polls that . . . only five thousand whites out of over ninety thousand supported the Republican ticket at the last election; and it is a fact that most of these five thousand are office-holders, the greater part are strangers in the State, and very many of them may justly be called adventurers. It is so universal a sentiment that I have found scarcely a colored man out of office, who did not

An 1869 Harper's Weekly *satire,* "Democratic Platform Made Easy," *was made up of anti-Southern cartoons, including the one above.*

A magazine of 1880 idealized the progress of the Negro (from top): from slavery to West Point cadet to candidate for Vice President.

complain to me that the Republican whites are as faithless to their duty as they believe the other side would be.

Now, this small band of white men have for more than six years monopolized all political power and preferment in the State. They have laid, collected, and spent (and largely misspent) all the taxes, local taxes as well as State; they have not only made all the laws, but they have arbitrarily changed them, and have miserably failed to enforce any which were for the people's good; they have openly and scandalously corrupted the colored men whom they have brought into political life; they have used unjust laws to perpetuate and extend their own power; and they have practiced all the basest arts of ballot-stuffing, false registration, and repeating, at election after election.

In the last election, it was proved before a committee of Congress that the Republican leaders had, in the city of New Orleans alone, made no less than five thousand two hundred false registrations. A few days ago I went down the river to attend court, in order to see the working of a negro jury. The court had to adjourn for lack of a jury; and no panel had been drawn, because, the names being taken from the registration lists of the parish, thirty-six out of forty-eight were found to be fictitious—and this in a country parish. The Republican returning board was condemned as a transparent fraud by two Congressional committees, and has, so far as I know, no defender in Louisiana or in the country.

I know of one case in the last election where, the Conservative ticket being elected, the records of the election were carried by the supervisor from the parish to New Orleans, and concealed in a house of prostitution, one of whose inmates was sent to drive a bargain with the Conservatives for their return.

Charles Nordhoff
The Cotton States in the Spring and Summer of 1875, 1876

By no means was Louisiana a special case. And although corruption was evident to a greater or lesser degree all over the Reconstruction South, the South was not a special case in that sense either. One would have been hard pressed to find high moral tone in government anywhere in the United States—in Washington, D.C., particularly. Men in government adulated free enterprise and frontier hardfistedness and the power of impersonal machinery; they concerned themselves with getting office and wealth. They scorned refinement, contemplation, culture. At the top of the national pyramid—its elected epitome—stood the bearded, stolid figure of Ulysses S. Grant. Henry Adams, back in his native country after a number of years in England, was appalled at Grant, and later recalled his reactions in his autobiography.

Thus far in life he had met with but one man of the same intellectual or unintellectual type,—Garibaldi. Of the two, Garibaldi seemed to him a trifle the more intellectual, but, in both, the intellect counted for nothing;—only the energy counted. The type was pre-intellectual, archaic, and would have seemed so even to the cave-dwellers. Adam, according to legend, was such a man.

In time one came to recognise the type in other men, with differences and variations, as normal;—men whose energies were the greater, the less they wasted on thought; men who sprang from the soil to power; apt to be distrustful of themselves and of others; shy; jealous; sometimes vindictive; more or less dull in outward appearance; always needing stimulants, but for whom action was the highest stimulant,—the instinct of fight. Such men were forces of nature, energies of the prime, like the *Pteraspis*, but they made short work of scholars. They had commanded thousands of such and saw no more in them than in others. The fact was certain; it crushed argument and intellect at once.

Adams did not feel Grant as a hostile force; like Badeau he saw only an uncertain one. When in action he was superb and safe to follow; only when torpid he was dangerous. To deal with him one must stand near, like Rawlins, and practice more or less sympathetic habits. Simple-minded beyond the experience of Wall Street or State Street, he resorted, like most men of the same intellectual calibre, to commonplaces when at a loss for expression:—"Let us have peace!" or "The best way to treat a bad law is to execute it;" or a score of such reversible sentences generally to be gauged by their sententiousness; but sometimes he made one doubt his good faith; as when he seriously remarked to a particularly bright young woman that Venice would be a fine city if it were drained. In Mark Twain, this suggestion would have taken rank among his best witticisms; in Grant it was a measure of simplicity not singular. Robert E. Lee betrayed the same intellectual common-place, in a Virginian form, not to the same degree but quite distinctly enough for one who knew the American. What worried Adams was not the common-place; it was, as usual, his own education. Grant fretted and irritated him, like the *Terebratula*, as a defiance of first principles. He had no right to exist. He should have been extinct for ages. The idea that, as society grew older, it grew one-sided, upset evolution, and made of education a fraud. That, two thousand years after Alexander the Great and Julius Cæsar, a man like Grant should be called—and should actually and truly be—the highest product of the most advanced evolution, made evolution ludicrous. One must be as commonplace as Grant's own common-places to maintain such an absurdity. The progress of evolution from President Washington to President Grant, was alone evidence enough to upset Darwin.

Henry Adams
The Education of Henry Adams, 1907

Henry Adams criticized America's crudity, but admired his country's strength. This portrait sketch was made in 1868.

*D*uring the Grant years, Mark Twain and Charles Dudley Warner collaborated *on a satire about the national character, whose title,* The Gilded Age, *gave a name to those years. Among their targets was the sorry condition of patriotism, evidenced by, among other things, the condition of the Washington Monument. Construction of the obelisk had begun in 1848, was left off ten years later, and was not begun again until 1878.*

. . . close to [the water's] edge, the Monument to the Father of his Country towers out of the mud—sacred soil is the customary term. It has the aspect of a factory chimney with the top broken off. The skeleton of a decaying scaffolding lingers about its summit, and tradition says that the spirit of Washington often comes down and sits on those rafters to enjoy this tribute of respect which the nation has reared as the symbol of its unappeasable gratitude. The Monument is to be finished, some day, and at that time our Washington will have risen still higher in the nation's veneration, and will be known as the Great-Great-Grandfather of his Country. The memorial Chimney stands in a quiet pastoral locality that is full of reposeful expression. With a glass you can see the cow-sheds about its base, and the contented sheep nibbling pebbles in the desert solitudes that surround it, and the tired pigs dozing in the holy calm of its protecting shadow. . . .

The legislative process in Washington also symbolized the times, providing an example followed with splendid faithfulness in state capitals and county seats. Twain and Warner drew this caricature:

" . . . A Congressional appropriation costs money. Just reflect, for instance. A majority of the House Committee, say $10,000 apiece—$40,000; a majority of the Senate Committee, the same each—say $40,000; a little extra to one or two chairmen of one or two such committees, say $10,000 each—$20,000; and there's $100,000 . . . gone, to begin with. Then, seven male lobbyists, at $3,000 each—$21,000; one female lobbyist, $10,000; a high moral Congressman or Senator here and there—the high moral ones cost more, because they give tone to a measure—say ten of these at $3,000 each, is $30,000; then a lot of small-fry country members who won't vote for anything whatever without pay—say twenty at $500 apiece, is $10,000; a lot of dinners to members—say $10,000 altogether; lot of jimcracks for Congressmen's wives and children—those go a long way—you can't spend too much money in that line—well, those things cost in a lump, say $10,000—along there somewhere;—and then comes your printed documents—your maps, your tinted engravings, your pamphlets, your illuminated show cards, your advertisements in a hundred and fifty papers at ever so much a line—because you've *got* to keep the papers all right or you are gone up, you know. . . . "

Mark Twain and Charles Dudley Warner
The Gilded Age, 1873

This view shows the Washington Monument not long before work stopped for twenty years, as Mark Twain relates at the left.

*O*ne of the most remarkable aspects of life in the postwar South was the sudden sizable participation in government of the newly freed Negroes. They needed the kind of self-defense political power provided, but perhaps the turnabout was too rapid. Certainly a good many of these new voters and officials were relatively unqualified and were at the beck and call of sharp politicos, a situation that has existed wherever new Americans of limited educations appeared in numbers. The black involvement in public affairs reached its peak in South Carolina, seedbed of the secession, where for a while Negroes were in the majority in the House of Representatives. Race prejudice was by no means confined to the South, and in 1874 Northerner James Pike, in the excerpt below, blamed the condition of South Carolina's lower house on negritude alone. But one must bear in mind the universal bad odor of legislatures. Mark Twain won laughs with his lecture line: "Suppose you were an idiot. And suppose you were a member of Congress. But I repeat myself." And General Robert E. Lee, writing to his son in 1864 after a visit

69

to the Confederate Congress, remarked acidly: " . . . they do not seem to be able to do anything except eat peanuts and chew tobacco, while my army is starving."

The Speaker is black, the Clerk is black, the door-keepers are black, the little pages are black, the chairman of the Ways and Means is black, and the chaplain is coal-black. At some of the desks sit colored men whose types it would be hard to find outside of Congo; whose costume, visages, attitudes, and expression, only befit the forecastle of a buccaneer. . . .

One of the things that first strike a casual observer in this . . . assembly is the fluency of debate, if the endless chatter that goes on there can be dignified with this term. The leading topics of discussion are all well understood by the members, as they are of a practical character, and appeal directly to the personal interests of every legislator, as well as to those of his constituents. When an appropriation bill is up to raise money to catch and punish the Ku-klux, they know exactly what it means. They feel it in their bones. So, too, with educational measures. The free school comes right home to them; then the business of arming and drilling the black militia. They are eager on this point. Sambo can talk on these topics and those of a kindred character, and their endless ramifications, day in and day out. There is no end to his gush and babble. The intellectual level is that of a bevy of fresh converts at a negro camp-meeting. . . .

At times, nothing goes on but alternating questions of order and of privilege. The inefficient colored friend who sits in the Speaker's chair cannot suppress this extraordinary element of the debate. Some of the blackest members exhibit a pertinacity of intrusion in raising these points of order and questions of privilege that few white men can equal. Their struggles to get the floor, their bellowings and physical contortions, baffle description. The Speaker's hammer plays a perpetual tattoo all to no purpose. The talking and the interruptions from all quarters go on with the utmost license. Every one esteems himself as good as his neighbor, and puts in his oar, apparently as often for love of riot and confusion as for any thing else. It is easy to imagine what are his ideas of propriety and dignity among a crowd of his own color, and these are illustrated without reserve. The Speaker orders a member whom he has discovered to be particularly unruly to take his seat. The member obeys, and with the same motion that he sits down, throws his feet on to his desk, hiding himself from the Speaker by the soles of his boots. In an instant he appears again on the floor. After a few experiences of this sort, the Speaker threatens, in a laugh, to call "the gemman" to order. This is considered a capital joke, and a guffaw follows. The laugh goes round, and then the peanuts are cracked and munched faster than ever; one hand being employed in fortifying the inner man with this nutriment of universal use, while the other enforces the views of the orator. . . .

But underneath all this shocking burlesque upon legislative proceedings, we must not forget that there is something very real to this uncouth and untutored multitude. It is not all sham, nor all burlesque. They have a genuine interest and a genuine earnestness in the business of the assembly which we are bound to recognize and respect, unless we would be accounted shallow critics. They have an earnest purpose, born of a conviction that their position and condition are not fully assured, which lends a sort of dignity to their proceedings. The barbarous, animated jargon in which they so often indulge is on occasion seen

Though meant to show evils of Negro rule, this picture makes 1868 colored South Carolina legislators look much like most politicians.

to be so transparently sincere and weighty in their own minds that sympathy supplants disgust. The whole thing is a wonderful novelty to them as well as to observers. Seven years ago these men were raising corn and cotton under the whip of the overseer. To-day they are raising points of order and questions of privilege. They find they can raise one as well as the other. They prefer the latter. It is easier, and better paid. Then, it is the evidence of an accomplished result. It means escape and defense from old oppressors. It means liberty. It means the destruction of prison-walls only too real to them. It is the sunshine of their lives. It is their day of jubilee. It is their long-promised vision of the Lord God Almighty.

James S. Pike
The Prostrate State, 1874

Besides the extreme cultural shock to the White South of this elevation of former chattel, and the Republican vindictiveness and grabbery, there were other sources of a sense of oppression. In 1875 Edward King discussed the cash-crop agricultural economy of the former slave states.

There must, and will be, a radical change in the conduct of the rising generation of planters. The younger men are, I think, convinced that it is a mistake to depend on Western and Northern markets for the articles of daily consumption, and for nearly everything which goes to make life tolerable. But the elders, grounded by a lifetime of habit in the methods which served them well under a slave *régime*, but which are ruinous now-a-days, will never change their course. They will continue to bewail the unfortunate fate to which they think themselves condemned—or will rest in the assurance that they can do very well in the present chaotic condition of things, provided Providence does not allow their crops to fail. They cannot be brought to see that their only safety lies in making cotton their surplus crop; that they must absolutely dig their sustenance, as well as their riches, out of the ground. . . .

Imagine a farming country which depends absolutely for its food on the West and North-west; where every barrel of flour which the farmer buys, the bacon which he seems to prefer to the beef and mutton which he might raise on his own lands, the clothes on his back, the shoes on his feet, the very vegetables which the poorest laborer in the Northern agricultural regions grows in his door-yard—everything, in fact,—has been brought hundreds of miles by steamer or by rail, and has passed through the hands of the shipper, the carrier, the wharfmen, the reshipper (if the planter live in a remote section), and the local merchant!

Imagine a people possessed of superior facilities, who might live, as the vulgar saying has it, on the fat of the land, who are yet so dependent that a worm crawling over a few cotton leaves, or the rise of one or two streams, may reduce them to misery and indebtedness from which it will take years to recover! Men who consider themselves poorly paid and badly treated in Northern farming and manufacturing regions live better and have more than do the overseers of huge plantations in this cotton country. If you enter into conversation with people who fare thus poorly, they will tell you that, if they raise vegetables, the "niggers" will steal them; that if times were not so hard, and seasons were not so disastrous, the supply system would work very well; that they cannot organize their labor so as to secure a basis on which to calculate safely; and will finally end by declaring that the South is ruined forever.

Edward King
The Great South, 1875

The loss of slavery did indeed force the South to change its economic structure — to become more like the North. Some, though not all, Southerners resented it, but Northerners like Charles Nordhoff saw it as a useful conformity.

Almost everywhere, except in Louisiana, Mississippi, and perhaps Arkansas, I noticed an increase of the towns. I saw many new buildings, and others going up; and observant Southern men remarked upon this to me also. Wherever the people have been even moderately prosperous, these improvements begin to make a show. The reason for this growth of towns was pointed out to me by Mr. Goodloe, a North Carolinian, and an Abolitionist before the war, whose essay [in the Report of the Bureau of Agriculture for 1865] touching this question seemed to me both curious and valuable. Under the slave-system, whenever a man had saved a thousand dollars he bought a slave; and the accumulated wealth of the South was almost entirely invested in this species of property. Hence there was no money to build dwellings in the towns, to carry on retail shops, to make all those improvements which mark our Northern civilization. "But," as Mr. Goodloe remarks, "the money paid for slaves was substantially wasted, because the negro will work in freedom." A horse, a cow, or a sheep must be owned, in order to be of service to man. Not so a man, a negro man. It was not necessary to enslave him in order to make him industrious and useful to the community of which he forms a part. Experience since the war shows that he will work without being owned. It is true, therefore, that the money invested in slaves was wasted, so far as the general community was concerned; it was a misapplication of capital. With the extinction of slavery, this waste of the savings of the Southern people stopped. As wealth once more begins to accumulate, some other and sound forms of investment are, and will be, sought for it. It will be turned into houses, town improvements, and, above all, I believe, into factories of various kinds. Of course the accumulations of the community will no longer be in so few hands as before; but this also is already found to be a great advantage in the South, where employments are becoming more varied, and there is more work for mechanics of different kinds. . . . It is among the factory workers and the small farmers of Georgia that one finds the chief prosperity of the State. Here there is little or no debt; money circulates rapidly; improvements are seen; and there are patient, hopeful labor, thrift, and enterprise, which affect, as it seems to me, the whole population. I heard here and there of instances of poor young mechanics working steadily and earnestly, in a New England way, at their trades, making labor respectable, accumulating property, and taking honorable places in their communities; and some such men talked to me of their past and their future, of the hopeful change which the extinction of slavery had produced in the prospects of their

In spite of emancipation, said a Northern observer (at left), Negroes would toil as hard as ever. Above, a Georgia rice plantation.

class, in language which showed me that there is a new-born hope of better things in the poor white people of the State.

Charles Nordhoff
The Cotton States in the Spring and Summer of 1875, 1876

For many the changes were too great, too sudden. They fled to new homes in the West and the Southwest, or if they stayed, fought a guerrilla warfare against the new order. Intimidating the blacks with violence, restricting them with legislation, they prevented the fledgling citizens from gaining a secure economic and political foothold in the culture. The Radicals, meanwhile, committed to their own program of coercion and corruption, rapidly lost Northern support for and interest in the idea of rebuilding the Southern social system. The Old South reasserted itself with increasing effect in the mid-1870's. Below is the testimony of three black sharecroppers.

We worked, or made a contract to work, and make a crop on shares on Mr. McMoring's place, and worked for one-third (⅓) of the crop, and he (McMoring) was to find us all of our provisions; and in July, 1875, we was working along in the field, and Mr. McMoring and McBorinton came to us and says, "Well, boys, you all got to get away from here; and that they had gone as far as they could go, and you all must live agreeable, or you shall take what follows;" and the two white men went and got sticks and guns, and told us that we must leave the place; and we told them that we would not leave it, because we don't want to give up our crop for nothing; and they told us that we had better leave, or we would not get anything; and we wanted to justice, but he would not let us have justice; and we told them that we would get judges to judge the crop, to say what it is worth; and the white men told us that no judge should come on his place; and we did not want to leave the place, but they beat Isiah Fuller, and whipped him, and then we got afraid, and we left the place; and we got about thirty acres in cotton, and the best cotton crop in that part of the parish; and we have about twenty-nine acres of corn, and about the best corn in the parish, and it is ripe, and the fodder ready to pull, and our cotton laid by; and runned us off from the place, and told us not to come back any more; and we were due McMoring the sum of one hundred and eighty dollars, ($180;) and they told us that if they ever heard of it any more that they would fix us; and all the time that we were living and working on the place they would not half feed us; and we had to pay for all, or half of our rashings, or what we had to eat, and that is all that was due them for; and we worked for them as though we were slaves, and then treated like dogs all the time.

GEORGE UNDERWOOD, his x mark.
BEN. HARRIS, his x mark.
ISIAH FULLER, his x mark.

Sworn before me this the 3d day of August, A.D. 1875, Caddo Parish, Louisiana.

H. ADAMS.

House Executive Document No. 30
44th Congress, 2nd Session, 1877

In 1875 Harper's Weekly still insisted, with cartoons like this, that Union troops should remain in the South to protect Negroes.

Charles Caldwell was a former slave who helped write the Mississippi constitution of 1868. For being uppity he was shot at one day in Jackson. He returned the fire, killing his assailant, who happened to be the son of a white judge; he was acquitted of murder by an all-white jury — a landmark in Mississippi jurisprudence. He subsequently served in the state Senate and commanded a troop of militiamen in Clinton. The militia units were predominantly Negro and were hated by whites. In the late summer of 1875 Caldwell tried unsuccessfully to prevent a race riot in the village of Moss Hill; the riot led to four days of murder by a Vicksburg version of the Ku-Klux Klan known as the Modocs. He survived that purge, but on Christmas Day, 1875, he was killed. His wife, Margaret Ann Caldwell, told Senate investigators what she knew about his murder.

Mr. Nelson said that Buck Cabell carried him [Charles Caldwell] into the cellar; persuaded him to go out and drink; insisted upon his taking a drink with him, and him and Buck Cabell never knowed anything against each other in his life; never had no hard words. My husband told him no, he didn't want any Christmas. He said, "You must take a drink with me," and entreated him, and said, "You must take a drink." He then took him by the arm and told him to drink for a Christmas treat; that he must drink, and carried him into Chilton's cellar, and they jingled the glasses, and at the tap of the glasses, and while each one held the glass . . . somebody shot right through the back from the outside of the gate window, and he fell to the ground. . . .

When he was first shot, he called for Judge Cabinis, and called for Mr. Chilton; I don't know who else. They were all around, and nobody went to his relief; all them men standing around with their guns. Nobody went to the cellar, and he called for Preacher Nelson, called for him, and Preacher Nelson said that when he went to the cellar door he was afraid to go in, and called to him two or three times, "Don't shoot me," and Charles said, "Come in," he wouldn't hurt him, and "take me out of the cellar;" that he wanted to die in the open air, and did not want to die like a dog closed up.

When they taken him out, he was in a manner dead, just from that one shot; and they brings him out then, and he only asked one question, so Parson Nelson told me — to take him home and let him see his wife before he died; that he could not live long.

It was only a few steps to my house, and they would not do it, and some said this. . . .

Whether he stood right there in the street while they riddled him with thirty or forty of their loads, of course, I do not know, but they shot him all that many times when he was in a manner dead. All those balls went in him.

I understood that a young gentleman told that they shot him as he lay on the ground until they turned him over. He said so. I did not hear him.

Mr. Nelson said when he asked them to let him see me they told him no, and he then said, taking both sides of his coat and bringing them up this way so, he said, "Remember when you kill me you kill a gentleman and a brave man. Never say you killed a coward. I want you to remember it when I am gone."

Testimony of Mrs. Margaret Ann Caldwell
Senate Report No. 527
44th Congress, 1st Session, 1876

The bloody Memphis riots of 1868 were among the first of many acts of violent repression by Southerners against their former slaves.

The tenuous quality of Negro rights under Radical Reconstruction was well expressed by contrasts: Negroes might serve in Congress but be denied lodgings or a first-class seat in a railroad car. Black Congressmen James Rapier of Alabama and John Lynch of Mississippi angrily called this to the attention of their colleagues in the House.

. . . there is not an inn between Washington and Montgomery, a distance of more than a thousand miles, that will accommodate me to a bed or meal. Now, then, is there a man upon this floor who is so heartless, whose breast is so void of the better feelings, as to say that this brutal custom needs no regulation? I hold that it does and that Congress is the body to regulate it.

James T. Rapier
Congressional record, June 9, 1874

Think of it for a moment; here am I, a member of your honorable body, representing one of the largest and wealthiest districts in the State of Mississippi, and possibly in the South; a district composed of persons of different races, religions, and nationalities; and yet, when I leave my home to come to the capital of the nation, to take part in the deliberations of the House and to participate with you in making laws for the government of this great Republic . . . I am treated, not as an American citizen, but as a brute. Forced to occupy a filthy smoking-car both night and day, with drunkards, gamblers, and criminals; and for what? Not that I am unable or unwilling to pay my way; not that I am obnoxious in my personal appearance or disrespectful in my conduct; but simply because I happen to be of a darker complexion. If this treatment was confined to persons of our own sex we could possibly afford to endure it. But such is not the case. Our wives and our daughters, our sisters and our mothers are subjected to the same insults and to the same uncivilized treatment.

John R. Lynch
Congressional record, February 3, 1875

As Southern whites found political elbow room they became boldly outspoken in their denial of constitutional rights to blacks. Witness the so-called Pike County Platform, in which the good Democrats of an Alabama beat, or precinct, named Troy, responded to a civil rights bill in 1874.

"Whereas the republican party of Alabama, for years past, has distinctly made and tendered to the people of this State an open, square issue of race; and

"Whereas the tendencies of the doctrines, teachings, and practices of said party, as more recently illustrated and evidenced by the passage by the United States Senate of what is known as the civil-rights bill, are to the effect that the negro, by reason of his emancipation, is elevated to, and ought of right to enjoy, social as well as political equality; and

"Whereas the white people of the South have sedulously endeavored to prevent this issue of race, and in various ways sought to escape and avoid the said issue, well knowing the direful consequences that would follow it; and

"Whereas the white people of the South have hitherto forborne, and hoped to escape the consequences thus hurled defiantly into their faces by the poor negroes, at the instance of the thieving crew known as carpet-baggers, and the more contemptible and infamous gang known as scalawags, who, in full view of this issue, have, for the sake of plunder, power, and spoils, sided with the aforesaid deluded negroes, regardless of the hateful and direful consequences to ensue from the passage of said odious civil-rights bill, which is the culmination of all radical diabolism:

"Therefore, we respectfully suggest to our county convention for consideration the following resolutions:

"*Resolved*, That we, the people of Troy beat, for the protection of our dearest and most sacred interests, our homes, our honor, the purity and integrity of our race, and to conserve the peace and tranquillity of the country, accept the issue of race thus defiantly tendered and forced upon us, notwithstanding our determination and repeated efforts to avoid it; and further

"*Resolved*, That nothing is left to the white man's party but social ostracism of all those who act, sympathize, or side with the negro party, or who support or advocate the odious, unjust, and unreasonable measure known as the civil-rights bill; and that from henceforth we will hold all such persons as the enemies of our race, and will not in the future have intercourse with them in any of the social relations of life."

These are the sentiments of the democrats and conservatives of Pike County, with their fifteen hundred white majority.

House Report No. 262
43rd Congress, 2nd Session, 1875

This flag, with snakes as stripes and heads of Negroes instead of stars to represent Southern states, appeared in an Alabama weekly.

By 1876 the old order was resettling itself in the Southern saddle, and from the blacks who had dared to fight for their political rights came anguished cries for help. George Boutwell, recipient of the following appeal, was then senator from Massachusetts. But the Senate, in which he had been a powerful Radical leader, had been prodigal with its strength, and no testimony or investigating committee would now be able to halt the destructive trend that the Radicals had done so much to set in motion.

HORN LAKES MISSISSIPPI
June 29, 1876

HON. GEORGE W. BOUTWELL
DEAR SIR:
Fore God Sake.? do not forget the county of De Soto: I canvass this county for the Republicans last-fall. The Black and dirty work the Democrats done in this county is to honorable for an Honest man to believe. Mr. Senator I ask to be summon before your committee. It is a hard matter to get Republican from this county to com befor that committee and tell the truth. for fir of being kell on their return: the Democrats brought two boxes of Guns. I saw the Guns when they came to Hernando: I ask the White People what they was going to do wit the Guns: they told me: We will kill you Dam Black Radicles if we voted the Re-

76

publicans ticket they also brought a boat load men and Guns from Memphis the night before the election and landed them at Star Landing this county. I can not write you half of the Black Acts I know on them: I know the name of the boat and some of the men that came on her: they shot in colored men houses also in some of the churches: in publick Houses where colored men ware wont to visit. The Democrats told the colored voters if they went to the Polls on election day thay would be kill they inteneded to carry this election with Powder and Shot. and that—thay would kill every Republican Speaker in the county if it did not go Democratic. I was a Slave in this county before the war. I was Deputy Sheriff and tax collector last year.

Let this county have justice before the Committee: and we will tell enough to make the Democratic North Sick if they have any Shame: The Chairman of our county committee write to you in a few day. he was shot in the last canvass.

Sir, Hoping to hear from you soon

Yours Truly,

E. M. ALBRETTON

HORN LAKE DESOTO COUNTY MISSISSIPPI

Smith-Brady Papers, unpublished mss.

The contested election of 1876, though it finally produced a Republican President, Rutherford Hayes, effectively closed the books on Reconstruction. By nature gentle and middle-of-the-road anyway, Hayes was forced by the unusual electoral situation and the moribundity of Southern Republicanism to compromise with the determined White South. The selections below, spanning three and a half years, are from Hayes's diary.

[8th November, 1876.—] . . . we heard that in some 200 districts of N.Y. City Tilden had about 20,000 majority which indicated 50,000 in the City. The returns received from the rural districts did not warrant the belief that they would overcome such a large City majority. From that time I never supposed there was a chance for Republican success. I went to bed at 12 to 1 o'clock. Talked with Lucy consoling her with such topics as readily occurred of a nature to make us feel satisfied on merely personal grounds with the result. We soon fell into a refreshing sleep and the affair seemed over. Both of us felt more anxiety about the South—about the colored people especially than about anything else sinister in the result. My hope of a sound currency will somehow be realized. Civil Service reform will be delayed, but the great injury is in the South. There the amendments will be nullified, disorder will continue, prosperity to both whites and colored people, will be pushed off for years. . . .

17th February, [1877].—Last evening Louisiana was decided by the Commission in our favor. There is still some doubt, but apparently very little, of the result. The inaugural and cabinet making are now in order. I would like to get support from good men of the South—late rebels. How to do it is the question. I have the best disposition towards the Southern people—rebels and all. I could appoint a Southern Democrat in the Cabinet. . . .

The above cartoon, from the same paper as the flag, was entitled "A Sample Grant Voter" and purported to portray a former slave.

77

11th April, 1880. — . . . I know, of course, very little of what was expected. The truth is I had no confidants in regard to it. My judgment was that the time had come to put an end to bayonet rule. I saw things done in the South which could only be accounted for on the theory that the War was not yet ended. Many Southern people evidently felt that they were justified in acts which could only be justified in time of war towards the common enemy. The Republicans, the North, the colored people if active in politics, were regarded and treated as the public enemy. My task was to wipe out the color line, to abolish sectionalism, to end the war and bring peace. To do this I was ready to resort to unusual measures, and to risk my own standing and reputation with my party and the country. For the first time in our history a gentleman who had opposed the election of the President was by that President invited into his cabinet. Judge Key a confederate soldier and a Democrat who had supported Mr. Tilden against me was made Post Master General and one of my Constitutional advisers. A number of other appointments were made of Southern Democrats. My object was to end the War — to restore confidence in the South in the justice and good will of a Republican Administration. The army was withdrawn because I believed it a constitutional duty and a wise thing to do. . . . It is not true that tried Republicans at the South were totally abandoned. The possible support which could lawfully be extended to them was their appointment to office. Altogether the loudest complaints I have heard is that so many of "the tried Republicans" referred to have been appointed to office. I am not aware of a single instance in which a conspicuous Republican of the South can be said to have been abandoned. . . . The practical destruction of the Republican organization in the South was accomplished before my Southern Policy was announced. . . .

Rutherford B. Hayes

Hayes, The Diary of a President 1875–1881, T. Harry Williams, Editor

*P*erhaps the best commentary on the central question of the Reconstruction period was provided by the quiet voice of George W. Cable. Cable is not so well-known now as he once was, when he used to share lecture platforms with Mark Twain. He was born and raised in Louisiana, fought on the side of the Confederacy, and believed that the white race was superior. But such a belief, he felt, imposed on whites the duty of being just and honest with the race they considered inferior. He saw no reason, for example, why whites and Negroes should not attend the same schools and be treated the same under the law. In a magazine article written in 1885 and called "The Freedman's Case in Equity," he talked about how the slaveholding White South — and by implication the whole of White America — had come to treat the blacks unfairly and had then perpetuated the treatment after the war had ended slavery.

Their acts were not always right; whose are? But for their peace of mind they had to believe them so. They therefore spoke much of the negro's contentment with that servile condition for which nature had designed him. Yet there was no escaping the knowledge that we dared not trust the slave caste with any power that could be withheld from them. So the perpetual alien was made also a perpetual

Hayes and Grant leave the White House for the former's inauguration. With the election of Hayes, Reconstruction came to an end.

menial, and the belief became fixed that this, too, was nature's decree, not ours. . . .

This perpetuation of the alien, menial relation tended to perpetuate the vices that naturally cling to servility, dense ignorance and a hopeless separation from true liberty; and as we could not find it in our minds to blame slavery with this perpetuation, we could only assume as a further axiom that there was, by nature, a disqualifying moral taint in every drop of negro blood. The testimony of an Irish, German, Italian, French, or Spanish beggar in a court of justice was taken on its merits; but the colored man's was excluded by law wherever it weighed against a white man. The colored man was a prejudged culprit. The discipline of the plantation required that the difference between master and slave be never lost sight of by either. It made our master caste a solid mass, and fixed a common masterhood and subserviency between the ruling and the serving race. Every one of us grew up in the idea that he had, by birth and race, certain broad powers of police over any and every person of color.

. . . the old alien relation [might readily] have given way if we could only, while letting that pass, have held fast by the other old ideas. But they were all bound together. See our embarrassment. For more than a hundred years we had made these sentiments the absolute essentials to our self-respect. And yet if we clung to them, how could we meet the freedman on equal terms in the political field? Even to lead would not compensate us; for the fundamental profession of American politics is that the leader is servant to his followers. It was too much. The ex-master and ex-slave—the quarter-deck and the forecastle, as it were—could not come together. But neither could the American mind tolerate a continuance of martial law. The agonies of reconstruction followed.

The vote, after all, was a secondary point, and the robbery and bribery on one side, and whipping and killing on the other, were but huge accidents of the situation. The two main questions were really these: on the freedman's side, how to establish republican State government under the same recognition of his rights that the rest of Christendom accorded him; and on the former master's side, how to get back to the old semblance of republican State government, and—allowing that the freedman was *de facto* a voter—still to maintain a purely arbitrary superiority of all whites over all blacks, and a purely arbitrary equality of all blacks among themselves as an alien, menial, and dangerous class. . . .

Are the freedman's liberties suffering any real abridgment? The answer is easy. The letter of the laws, with but few exceptions, recognizes him as entitled to every right of an American citizen; and to some it may seem unimportant that there is scarcely one public relation of life in the South where he is not arbitrarily and unlawfully compelled to hold toward the white man the attitude of an alien, a menial, and a probable reprobate, by reason of his race and color. One of the marvels of future history will be that it was counted a small matter, by a majority of our nation, for six millions of people within it, made by its own decree a component part of it, to be subjected to a system of oppression so rank that nothing could make it seem small except the fact that they had already been ground under it for a century and a half.

George W. Cable
"The Freedman's Case in Equity"
The Century Magazine, January, 1885

PICTURE CREDITS. PAGE 65: *Harper's Weekly*, AUGUST 15, 1868; PAGE 66: *Harper's Weekly*, NOVEMBER 6, 1869; PAGE 67 (ALL): *The Daily Graphic*, MAY 28, 1880, NEW-YORK HISTORICAL SOCIETY; PAGE 68: WORTHINGTON C. FORD, ED., *Letters of Henry Adams*, VOL. I, 1930; PAGES 68–69: CULVER PICTURES; PAGES 70–71: EDWARD S. ELLIS, *The History of Our Country*, VOL. 5, 1900; PAGES 72–73 (TOP): *Harper's Weekly*, JANUARY 5, 1867, NEW-YORK HISTORICAL SOCIETY; PAGES 72–73 (BOTTOM): *Harper's Weekly*, JANUARY 9, 1875; PAGES 74–75: *Harper's Weekly*, SEPTEMBER 1, 1866; PAGES 76 AND 77 (BOTH): ALABAMA DEPARTMENT OF ARCHIVES AND HISTORY; PAGES 78–79: *The Daily Graphic*, MARCH 9, 1877

The Politics
of Boodle

*W*hen Julia Grant became the First Lady, the frigid neoclassicism of her new surroundings overawed her. She would have preferred to keep to her own house, using the White House only for official business and public receptions. Transplanted from the simplicities of Galena, awkward and timid, she dreaded receptions and levees. At first she relied for support and advice on that urbane and assured hostess Mrs. Hamilton Fish, the wife of the Secretary of State. Once when Fish was considering resigning, Grant protested that his wife could not manage without Mrs. Fish. In time Julia developed her own assurance, which became in the end a kind of arrogance. Mrs. Fish, the mentor, was discarded. For the first time since Buchanan's day, the White House became the social magnet of Washington. Julia, elegant in black velvet and diamonds, grew so enamored of her role that she came to welcome suggestions of a third term.

By the beginning of Grant's second term in 1873, his oldest son, Fred, who had graduated close to the bottom of his class at West Point, was a lieutenant in the Fourth Cavalry. Ulysses, Jr., known as Buck, had left Harvard to go into banking, while the youngest, Jesse, the jester of the family, was being tutored at the White House. Nellie, the pretty and petulant only daughter, assumed at sixteen the leadership of the "younger set." She delighted to head a cotillion and to dance all night. Before she was nineteen she would marry an Englishman, Algernon Sartoris, whom she met on shipboard coming back from Europe.

Grant himself remained unaffected by the White House atmosphere. Awkward and reticent at receptions, he kept to his small circle of friends. Beyond cigars and horses he seemed to have few personal interests. Impervious to art, music, and literature, surprisingly he liked flowers. Unconcerned with organized religion, he attended the Methodist church irregularly. There were, he remarked once, three parties in the country: Republicans, Democrats, and Methodists.

It was Grant's second term, sterile and scandal-ridden, that would break his reputation and leave him with the permanent label of least of American Presidents of his

The simple patriotism expressed in this print of F. A. Chapman's In-
dependence Day painting was honored much less in the observ-
ance than in the breach by most politicians of the Gilded Age.

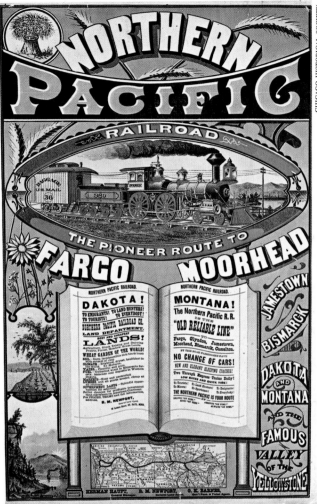

"The generation between 1865 and 1895," wrote Henry Adams, "was . . . mortgaged to the railways. . . ." The 35,000 miles of American road operating in 1865 more than quintupled in those thirty years. Above, a poster touting rail travel.

century. The first scandal, that of the oddly named Crédit Mobilier, occurred before his second inauguration, and although it could not be attributed to him or his associates, it nevertheless hovered like a somber cloud over the inaugural festivities.

The Crédit Mobilier was a construction company formed in 1864 by a group of leaders of the Union Pacific Railroad in order to obtain for themselves excessive profits from building the road. These men, in their dual capacity as stockholders of both the Union Pacific and the Crédit Mobilier, awarded themselves the contract to build the road, paying the costs and them-

selves from the mortgage bonds and common stock of the Union Pacific. In 1868, during the rush to complete the railroad, the company paid five separate dividends, amounting in all to $341.85 on each $100 share. To head off any awkward congressional queries on dividends and costs, the chief director of the Crédit Mobilier, the Massachusetts congressman and wealthy shovel manufacturer Oakes Ames, in that same year distributed 160 shares of Crédit Mobilier stock among his fellow congressmen, where it would "produce most good to us." The congressmen paid only the par value of $100 for shares worth at least double that. In many cases they paid nothing, for Ames was willing to carry them on his books until the interest paid the principal. Some of his colleagues refused the shining offer, others accepted and then had doubts, and still others accepted without qualifications. Among those involved were the two men who would serve as Vice Presidents under Grant: Speaker of the House Schuyler "Smiler" Colfax and Senator Henry Wilson.

Ames never doubted his own peculiar rectitude, although even he admitted that the Crédit Mobilier was "a diamond mine." In his enthusiasm for extending the road westward he had undertaken a daring enterprise from which "the capital of the world shrank" and he had invested a large amount of his own money in the project. His incidental favors to congressmen were revealed four years later when he had a falling out with one of his Crédit Mobilier associates and the transactions came to the notice of the New York *Sun*. A report about this "King of Frauds" in the *Sun*'s columns brought a double congressional investigation. Some of those accused, among them Smiler Colfax and James A. Garfield, denied they had ever received any stock. The investigators were in any case not willing to push matters too far. A white-faced Ames, facing Congress and reading from his memorandum book, indicated that Colfax was a liar, while Garfield's story of having merely received a loan from Ames left a permanent, though probably unjustified, stain on his political reputation. In the end a House committee voted that Ames and the Democratic minority leader, James Brooks—a director of the Union Pacific—be ejected for bribery. A Senate committee dealt in a like manner with New Hampshire Senator J. W. Patterson. The House modified to a vote of censure its committee's recommendation, and in the Senate Patterson was allowed to serve out the few remaining days of his term. Ames and

Brooks retired in disgrace, both to die a few months later. The Crédit Mobilier affair was aptly summed up by *The Nation:* "Total loss, one Senator; badly damaged and not serviceable for future political use, two Vice-Presidents and eight Congressmen."

The scandal seemed to confirm the worst beliefs of the informed public about the railroads and their influence. Nor could the Grant administration escape the popular disapproval directed against the Republican Congress. This disapproval became sharply focused by the "salary grab" at the session's end, a bill introduced by Ben Butler to raise the salaries of the President and the Cabinet members, the Supreme Court justices, and all congressmen and senators. Not only were the in-creases themselves felt by most people to be unjustified, but Butler had made them retroactive for the previous two years. The "back-pay steal" became so unpopular across the country that a number of congressmen, a few from personal scruples but most from fear of the wrath of their constituents, refused to accept the increase.

Grant's second Inauguration Day was bitter cold, with brief snow squalls and a high wind gusting from the still-ice-covered Potomac. As he read his address, frost crystals formed in his closely cropped beard. Surprisingly, in his conclusion the President laid bare his personal feelings:

... from my candidacy for my present office in 1868 to the close of the last Presidential campaign I have been the subject of abuse and slander scarcely ever equaled in political history, which today I feel that I can afford to disregard in view of your verdict, which I gratefully accept as my vindication.

The vindication would prove more nearly a disaster, and the ominous weather of his second inauguration

In 1874 Grant visited that stronghold of Methodists and tourists Oak Bluffs, on Martha's Vineyard Island, Massachusetts. With him were his wife, here standing at his side, and his troublous friend and private secretary, Orville Babcock, left.

After the 1874 elections only four states—Mississippi, South Carolina, Florida, and Louisiana—remained under Radical control. The following year Mississippi Democrats, organizing themselves into local irregular militia companies, put into effect the so-called Shotgun Plan for the state election. White militiamen provoked riots, in which scores of Negroes were killed, broke up Republican meetings at rifle point, and posted armed pickets to keep freedmen from voting. On Election Day thousands of Negroes stayed in their cabins or hid in the swamps, too terrified to vote. Governor Adelbert Ames's attempts to muster a Negro militia were of no avail, and he could get no backing from Grant, who was advised against stirring up Northern hostility. The new and overwhelmingly Democratic legislature prepared to impeach Ames, and the carpetbag governor, aware of the uselessness of further struggle, agreed to resign if the proceedings against him were dropped.

South Carolina, Florida, and Louisiana remained under the thumb of the Radicals. In South Carolina and Florida control remained secure until the end of Reconstruction in 1877, although in Florida whites outnumbered Negroes. Louisiana, rivaling South Carolina as the most blatantly corrupt state under Reconstruction, by 1870 displayed the familiar factional split among the Radicals. There Governor Henry Clay Warmoth had a falling out with Grant's brother-in-law James F. Casey, whom Grant had appointed to the politically potent post of collector of customs. Casey and United States Marshal Stephen B. Packard, who controlled federal troops, became the leaders of the Custom House Ring, which was determined to remove Warmoth from power. In his need Warmoth turned to the Democrats and in 1872 endorsed the Liberal Republican-Democratic candidate for governor, the native-born John McEnery. Casey and Packard threw the weight of their Custom House Ring behind a carpetbagger, William P. Kellogg. In a campaign that featured fraud and violence on both sides, McEnery won by some 10,000 votes. Casey and Packard, however, using spurious affidavits and juggled figures, maintained that Kellogg was the winner by 18,000 votes. Grant recognized Kellogg as the legitimate governor, and federal bayonets sustained the Kellogg legislature and excluded members elected on the McEnery ticket. McEnery refused to give way. For the next three years Louisiana would continue with a *de facto* and a *de jure* government.

Resistance to Louisiana's Radical government culminated in April, 1873, in a bloody clash between whites and Negroes in the little town of Colfax in Grant Parish. After Governor Kellogg had replaced the judge and the sheriff of Grant Parish appointed by "Governor" McEnery, a band of several hundred Negroes gathered in Colfax to defend the new appointees. They were attacked by some 125 white vigilantes, who had advanced on Colfax with military precision. The Negroes proved no match for the superior discipline and fire power of the whites. The black defenders retreated into the courthouse, but were driven out when the building was set on fire. The end was a sodden butchery in which between 60 and 300 Negroes lost their lives to the unrelenting whites, who did not bother to count the dead. Further outrages continued all over the state, most of them originating with the Knights of the White Camellia, the Louisiana counterpart of the Klan.

Within a year of the Colfax riot, vigilantes were organizing the White League along the lines of the Mississippi Shotgun Plan. In New Orleans, White Leaguers, in an encounter known as the Second Battle of New Orleans, drove Kellogg's supporters from the streets. Forced to flee the state capitol, Governor Kellogg took refuge with Casey in the custom house, where he remained until rescued by federal troops. The 1874 state elections repeated the pattern of 1872. Although the White Leaguers elected a large Democratic majority in the legislature, Radical returning boards manipulated this into a slight Republican majority. As disorders rose, Grant dispatched General Philip Sheridan, who of all his generals most hated Southerners, to command the federal troops in Louisiana. Under this bayonet threat, McEnery announced that he would submit to national authority, but in the two turbulent and indecisive years that followed, white Democrats continued to defy both Kellogg and Sheridan.

After the 1874 elections Grant's leadership of the Republican party was shattered. His military mind failed to sense the civilian mood of the depression, the popular disgust with machine politicians, the demand for civil service reform, the North's disillusionment with Reconstruction, the shadows that Black Friday and Cooke's failure had cast on the administration, the discontent that focused more and more on the person of the President. Scandals associated with Grant's administration proliferated. Yet whatever the scandal, Grant remained stubbornly loyal to the subordinate involved. When a congressional committee reported that his

Jules Tavernier made this water color of Parsons, Kansas, in 1873. Kansas was expanding; every Kansan, said General Sherman in 1879, swore that it was the "very best state in the union. . . . There is not a discontented soul in Kansas."

brother-in-law Collector of Customs Casey was guilty of gross misconduct in New Orleans, Grant's answer was to reappoint him to another term. In 1871 Congress had created a Territorial government for the District of Columbia, and Grant had appointed Jay Cooke's brother Henry as governor, with Alexander R. Shepherd to head the Board of Public Works. "Boss" Shepherd had started out in life as a plumber and later became a large-scale contractor. A man of ruthlessness and energy, in a few

years he transformed the external aspects of the District, grading and paving streets, improving parks and squares, reclaiming swamps. The sums he spent were vast and many of the contracts he negotiated hasty and some dishonest. Though the Board of Public Works was credited with "pulling Washington out of the mire," dismayed taxpayers protested widely and vehemently, and Shepherd's unpopularity grew. Rightly or wrongly, Boss Shepherd was generally considered corrupt, and the public was aghast when Grant, with his customary insensitivity, appointed him governor of the District following Cooke's resignation.

If Shepherd's case was ambiguous, there was no ambiguity at all about contracts involving Ben Butler's Massachusetts henchman John D. Sanborn. Butler, his

Victorian private life was, for most well-off Americans, restrained. At left, The Music
Lesson *by John G. Brown; below,* Mrs. John Hudson Hall of New York and children,
a portrait in oil by Michele Gordigiani; above, J. W. Champney's Wedding Presents.

fingers in every legislative pie, had got a clause inserted in the Revenue Act of 1872 that allowed the Treasury to contract with up to three outsiders to collect delinquent taxes. Such contractors would receive a percentage of any back taxes that they were able to collect. Assistant Secretary of the Treasury Richardson assigned one such contract to Sanborn. In itself the contract was not illegal, although it allowed Sanborn to retain half of anything he collected—an exorbitant percentage. Sanborn entered the Boston office of the collector of internal revenue, demanded a list of delinquents, and ordered that any and all back taxes be sent to him. On receiving them, he deducted his half. From a railroad guide he copied the names of six hundred railroads and sent them notice that they were tax evaders—as indeed it turned out most of them were. Although his minimal efforts did not bring a cent more to the Treasury than would have come in the normal process of collection, in a year he received $213,500 for his alleged services. When the news of his easy pickings was made public, Congress appointed an investigating committee,

which reported that Richardson—now Secretary of the Treasury—by assigning a contract to Sanborn, deserved a severe condemnation for "marauding upon the public Treasury." Before a vote of censure could be passed on him, Richardson resigned, only to be appointed by Grant as a judge on the Court of Claims.

Grant, Vice President Wilson told Garfield, was "the millstone around the neck of our party that would sink it." Even the President, insulated by his associates from public opinion, now grew vaguely aware of his diminished popularity and took belated steps to clean his Washington stables. In the Justice Department he attempted to relieve widespread inefficiency and corruption by replacing the unpopular Attorney General George H. Williams, the "Secretary of State for Southern affairs," with the virtuous Edwards Pierrepont. Marshall Jewell, minister to Russia, became Postmaster General and expressed the honest determination to run that department under civil service rules. The upright and energetic Benjamin H. Bristow succeeded the devious and morally slack William Richardson to

Opened in 1874—the year in which the above lithograph was published—the Eads Bridge crossed the Mississippi at St. Louis. It was named after its designer and builder, James Eads, and was the first bridge to use steel on a large scale.

become the new head of the Treasury Department.

Ironically, Bristow's appointment gave rise to the exposure of the Whiskey Ring, the most corroding scandal of Grant's two administrations. Ever since Andrew Johnson's day, distillers and their accomplices had been defrauding the government of millions of dollars in liquor taxes by falsifying reports on the amounts of spirits manufactured, by forging revenue stamps, and by bribing the poorly paid government gaugers who checked liquor production at distilleries. The corruption in many cases went up to and beyond the collectors of internal revenue, to the Treasury Department and even to the portals of the White House. By checking freight records, Bristow discovered that far more whiskey was being shipped out of warehouses than was being reported to the government. Unable to trust the subordinates in his own department, he secretly gathered a small force of reliable agents and on May 10, 1875, staged sudden raids on thirty-two distilleries in Milwaukee, St. Louis, and Chicago. In Milwaukee he learned that Wisconsin's Republican patronage boss had been tapping the Whiskey Ring funds, and in Illinois every prominent Republican politician seemed to have his hand out under the table to the distillers. But the real Whiskey Ring, obscuring all others in its brazen activity, functioned in St. Louis under the benign direction of Grant's supervisor of internal revenue, John McDonald. Since his appointment McDonald had grown very intimate with Grant. On frequent visits to Washington he was often a White House dinner guest, and drove through the streets of the Capital with the President. When Grant visited the 1874 St. Louis fair, he toured the city behind McDonald's matched team, which he later purchased from his host.

The Whiskey Ring was unexampled both in its thievery and its political influence. Distillers caught in minor infractions of the liquor laws were blackmailed into cooperation with the ring. Honest officials were forced to give up their jobs or their honesty. McDonald's ring business became so encompassing that he had to bring in an experienced manager to take care of collections and pay-offs. Until Bristow's intrusion, he had shaken down the distillers for more than two and a half million dollars. Among those paid off were the chief clerk of the Treasury, William Avery, and Grant's ubiquitous and ingratiating secretary, Orville Babcock. "He fished for gold in every stinking cesspool," Grant's political biographer wrote of the secretary, "and served more

than any other man to blacken the record of Grant's administration." Babcock's loot from the Whiskey Ring was extensive and varied — cigar boxes containing thousand-dollar bills, letters with an odd five-hundred-dollar bill tucked in them, diamonds of large size, receipted hotel bills, choice liquors, even the charms of an accommodating "sylph." The secretary received more than twenty-five thousand dollars in cash alone.

When Bristow first began his investigations, McDonald hurried to the White House to complain that the Attorney General was stirring up baseless scandal and ruining the Republican party. The President was sympathetic, but McDonald, after an interview with the less sympathetic Bristow, prudently resigned. From Washington Babcock kept telegraphing warnings to the errant McDonald of the arrival of government inspectors. Early in June McDonald found himself indicted by a federal grand jury, which in subsequent weeks returned indictments against more than three hundred and fifty distillers and government officials.

After preparing evidence against Babcock and the ring, Bristow and Attorney General Pierrepont called on Grant and set forth their case. "Let no guilty man escape," Grant ordered them, and later declared to Pierrepont that "if Babcock is guilty, there is no man who wants him so proven guilty as I do, for it is the greatest piece of traitorism to me that a man could possibly practice." Yet, after this forthright declaration, Grant soon wavered, persuaded by Babcock that the whiskey raids were merely a means by which Bristow hoped to advance his presidential ambitions.

During McDonald's trial, evidence revealed Babcock as an active partner in the ring. Still maintaining his innocence, Babcock demanded that he be given a trial, then on more prudent second thought requested a military-court investigation. Whatever Grant's opinion, the grand jury in St. Louis was not convinced of Babcock's innocence and indicted him. Rumors swept the country that the jury would also indict the President's brother Orville, his brother-in-law Fred Dent, and even Grant himself as receivers of stolen goods. Nevertheless, the wily secretary still managed to keep the President's confidence. In February, 1876, Babcock at last went on trial. Grant sent a deposition, sworn to before the Chief Justice, that his secretary had been a faithful and efficient officer since Vicksburg and that he had great confidence in his integrity. With this deposition plus the skill of his lawyers Babcock was acquitted.

But though legally free, he was condemned by public opinion for having been implicated in Black Friday, in the Whiskey Ring, in Shepherd's District Ring, and in other malversations, among them a burglary. Even to Grant it was clear that the secretary had become too much of a liability to the imperiled Republicans to remain a presidential confidant. After Babcock returned from St. Louis, he was closeted for an hour with the President, and though he avoided official disgrace and even secured a sinecure appointment, never again was he an intimate of the White House. On the other hand Grant, angered by the muddy waters Bristow had stirred up, was ready to dismiss his zealous Secretary of the Treasury. Only the quick reaction of the press to the mere rumor made the President postpone any such step until after the approaching national convention.

Grant, as well as his wife, had long nursed ambitions for a third term, and the Stalwarts had seen him as their best hope of controlling the Negro vote. But in the spring elections in Connecticut in 1875 the Republicans fared very badly, and many politicians blamed the results on Grant's challenge to the third-term taboo. With second thoughts about running again, Grant wrote late in May to the presiding officer of a Pennsylvania convention to protest that he had no desire for a third term: "I do not want it any more than I did the first. . . . I would not accept a nomination even if it were tendered unless it should come under such circumstances as to make it an imperative duty, circumstances not likely to arise." Knowing his wife's ambitions, Grant released this letter to the press without letting her know, and the chagrined Julia first learned of her husband's renunciation only when she read about it in the paper.

With Grant out of the presidential race, the principal Republican contenders were Secretary of the Treasury Benjamin Bristow, former Speaker of the House of Representatives James G. Blaine, the Stalwart Senators Roscoe Conkling and Oliver P. Morton, and Ohio's Governor Rutherford B. Hayes. Bristow, the reform candidate, was the choice of the Liberal Republicans. Morton's strength came from the party's carpetbaggers and scalawags, Conkling's from the administration and boss-incrusted New York. But no other candidate had the popular appeal of the dynamic and persuasive Blaine of Maine. A hawk-nosed, handsome man of forty-five with close-cropped gray beard and hair, and eyes that seemed to flash sparks, Blaine was a commanding figure, a born leader, exuding a magnetism that drew men to

ILLUSTRATED CHRISTIAN WEEKLY, AUGUST 5, 1876

Rutherford Hayes thought that winning the Presidency might be a mixed blessing: ". . . to be deceived by the rogues, to find many a trusted reformer no better than he should be, —here would be humiliations and troubles without end."

him and commanded their allegiance through thick and thin. His voice could hypnotize the galleries. He had one flaw that would in the end defeat his highest ambition: his love of money blunted his ethical sense.

Born of a Whig family in Pennsylvania, Blaine had married at twenty and settled in Augusta, Maine, near his wife's relatives. In 1854 he became the editor of the Kennebec *Journal* and that same year he joined the Republican party. Journalism propelled him into politics. He was a delegate to the first Republican National Convention in 1856, and two years later was elected to the state legislature. The following year he became chairman of the Republican State Committee. Preferring politics to soldiering, he ran successfully for the House of Representatives in 1862 as the Maine regiments went marching away. In 1869 he was elected Speaker and held that position until the Democratic comeback of 1874. As Speaker, Blaine controlled, and enforced order in, that often turbulent assembly more adroitly than any other Speaker since Henry Clay.

Although an Easterner by choice, Blaine was more Western in temperament, being drawn to leaders like James A. Garfield rather than to Thad Stevens and Charles Sumner. He had not been in favor of Johnson's impeachment. Stevens he detested and regarded his death as "an emancipation for the Republican party." He opposed Grant's coercive measures in the South, and he used his congressional leadership to defeat a force bill. In spite of Conkling's unbridled dislike for him, he would undoubtedly have been the Republican choice and the elected President in 1876 if it had not been for the revelation that there were strong suspicions of corruption in his connection with an Arkansas railroad.

While serving as Speaker of the House, Blaine had saved from revocation a land grant for the Little Rock and Fort Smith Railroad. In return the directors had privately granted him a generous commission to sell the railroad's bonds. Many of Blaine's friends in Maine bought the bonds, stimulated by the offer of equal amounts of preferred and of common stock, which ostensibly tripled the bonds' value. Blaine kept some $125,000 worth of land grant bonds, which should have accompanied the railroad bonds, as his commission, plus $32,500 of the railroad bonds as a brokerage fee. When hard times engulfed the Little Rock and Fort Smith, the value of all the bonds plummeted, and Blaine's friends blamed him for their losses. To placate them and keep the transactions hidden, Blaine bought their bonds back with money acquired from the sale of his land grant bonds to three other railroads. Since even these bonds had become almost worthless, rumor had it that the railroad directors, in purchasing them at book value, were purchasing the Speaker's good will and influence.

So widespread were the rumors of Blaine's misfeasance that the newly Democratic House of Representatives appointed an investigating committee to look into his conduct. At first the committee could find no evidence against its former Speaker; then a Boston witness, James Mulligan, informed the committee that he had letters from Blaine to a director of the Union Pacific Railroad. Visibly shaken, Blaine went that evening to Mulligan's hotel and with tears in his eyes begged to borrow his letters. Reluctant at first, Mulligan finally allowed him to take them. Once the letters were in his possession, Blaine refused either to return them to Mulligan or to turn them over to the committee. As news

reached the press the Mulligan letters became the scandal sensation of the day.

With the Republican National Convention less than two weeks off, Blaine appeared to have destroyed his chances for nomination. But a few days later he appeared before a full House and packed galleries. With his mesmerizing voice he explained that he had the right to refuse to give up his private correspondence. Having asserted his right, he was now willing to produce the letters. "I am not ashamed to show them," he said, raising a string-tied packet above his head. "There is the very original package." Then, untying the packet, he invited "the confidence of forty-four million of my countrymen." He read from the letters at random, interpolating and omitting where he pleased, carrying the House, almost spellbound, with him until he climaxed his defense by stalking down the aisle and accusing the committee chairman of withholding a telegram that would have completely exonerated him. To the crowded chamber he seemed the embodiment of outraged innocence. Congressmen echoed the applause and shouting of the galleries. The young Congressman Joseph G. Cannon recalled in his old age how he had "cheered Blaine that day until my voice frazzled to a squeak and weakness made me inarticulate."

Outshone by the overpowering, though tarnished, brilliance of Blaine, Ohio's Governor Rutherford B. Hayes could not take his own candidacy wholly seriously. In April, 1875, he had written in his diary: "Several suggest that if elected governor now, I will stand well for the Presidency next year. How wild! What a queer lot we are becoming!" Hayes was a quiet man, honest, honorable, on the reflective side. Educated at Kenyon College, he had later studied at Harvard Law School in a time when most law students read law in some lawyer's office. When in 1850 he began to practice in Cincinnati, he was so poor that he slept in his office. He soon prospered. He then gave up law for soldiering during the Civil War, was wounded, and almost at the war's end was brevetted major general of volunteers. In 1864, while still in uniform, he was elected to Congress, but did not take his seat until after the war, in late 1865. During his brief congressional career he generally followed the Radical Republican line. In 1867 he resigned from Congress to campaign successfully for governor of Ohio. During two terms as governor he proved an able administrator and reformer, recognizing merit above party in his appointments, taking a firm stand against extravagance in government and railroad abuses. Although he sympathized with the Liberal Republicans, he was still enough of a regular to support Grant for a second term. Because of the party split he refused to run for a third term in 1873 and the Democrats took control of the state for two years. But in 1875 he was again elected governor, and his triumph over the Democrats in that year made him a national figure. To Senators John Sherman and James Garfield their fellow Ohioan seemed an ideal presidential candidate—a liberal, a reformer, popular, with a fine war record and demonstrated party loyalty.

The hundredth birthday of the United States came inopportunely in the midst of the depression. Grant, attempting to mend the tattered fortunes of his party in a presidential election year, used the occasion of the Centennial to promulgate his program for the new century. In his seventh annual message he proposed a constitutional amendment requiring each state to "establish and forever maintain free public schools" for all children regardless of "sex, color, birthplace or religion." The amendment, which would also have forbidden the teaching of religious tenets in the public schools, was not as liberal as it seemed, for it also forbade the use of public funds to support parochial schools. It was thus aimed primarily at the Catholics and was designed to appeal to the country's latent Know-Nothing sentiments. Grant also proposed to tax church property, estimated to be worth a billion dollars, saying that "so vast a sum . . . will not be looked upon acquiescently by those who have to pay the taxes." He also asked for a literacy test for voters after 1890, an end to "polygamy and the importation of women for illegitimate purposes," and laws to "insure a speedy return to a sound currency."

Grant was well aware that his program, contrived to appeal for votes, had not the ghost of a chance in the new Congress. Whatever outside propaganda effect it might have had was soon blotted out by the furor over the Whiskey Ring. And this was followed by the resignation and disgrace of Secretary of War William W. Belknap, a nonentity from Iowa whom Grant had appointed after Rawlins' death. There had been earlier hints of corruption in Belknap's War Department following his sale of government arms to France. But his exposure came through his wife, an extravagant woman who connived with one C. P. Marsh to have Marsh appointed post trader at Fort Sill in Indian Territory. So lucrative was the position that the incumbent trader

agreed to pay Marsh twelve thousand dollars a year for not taking up his appointment, with half this sum going to Mrs. Belknap to help sustain her position in Washington society. After her death, Marsh continued to pay the money to Belknap, who probably needed it to underwrite the social ambitions of his second wife, his first wife's sister.

Treasury Secretary Benjamin Bristow, the Republican incorruptible, was the first to suggest to Grant that he should look into the growing evidence of wrongdoing against his Secretary of War. Belknap, somehow tipped off that he was being investigated, appeared at the White House greatly agitated and asked to resign immediately. Grant, from a brief talk with his War Secretary, received the impression that Belknap's wife was in difficulties and that he wanted to resign to protect her. At once the President had his secretary bring a form letter accepting the resignation. Only later did Grant discover that the resignation was an attempt to forestall impeachment. Despite Belknap's hasty withdrawal, the scandal became an open one and he was impeached by the House and tried before the Senate. Although almost all the senators were convinced of his guilt, enough doubted the Senate's jurisdiction over a resigned official to withhold the two-thirds majority necessary for conviction.

Harried by the Whiskey Ring and the Belknap scandals, the Mulligan letters, and the increasing disrepute of the Grant administration, the Republican delegates gathered in Cincinnati on June 14 for their quadrennial national convention—Bristow reformers, Grant third termers, fervid Blaine partisans, independents, carpetbaggers and scalawags, Southern Negroes. After a platform had been adopted calling for sound money, protection of labor and Negroes, nonsectarian public schools, civil service reform, and endorsement of Grant, the nominations followed in lackluster sequence. Only Senators Oliver P. Morton and James G. Blaine called up enthusiasm. At the mention of Morton's name the Southern delegates set up a wild demonstration. Blaine's name was presented by Robert G. Ingersoll, still comparatively unknown, an orator with a superb presence, a golden voice, and words that he could pour out as from a cornucopia. It was late in the afternoon when Ingersoll made his nominating speech. "Like an armed warrior, like a plumed knight," he told his transfixed listeners, "James G. Blaine marched down the halls of the American Congress and threw his shining lance full and fair against the brazen forehead of every traitor to his country." From that incandescent moment Blaine became the "Plumed Knight" to his followers. The hall resounded with shouts of "Blaine! Blaine! Blaine!" If in that waning afternoon a ballot had been taken, Blaine would have swept the convention. But Blaine's opponents—Bristow's followers have been blamed—cut the main pipe supplying the gaslights, and as evening fell and the hall grew dark, it was necessary to adjourn until the next day.

During the night anti-Blaine leaders worked diligently at stopping the steam roller. In the morning Blaine led on the first ballot with 285 votes to 124 for Morton, 113 for Bristow, 99 for Conkling, and 61 for Hayes. For the next four ballots there was little change. Blaine gained a few votes, Morton lost more. Most remarkable was Hayes's steady rise. On the sixth ballot the quiet Ohioan had 113 votes to Blaine's 308. Then on the next ballot Blaine's enemies gave up their individual candidates and combined to nominate Hayes with six votes to spare. ". . . a third-rate nonentity, whose only recommendation is that he is obnoxious to no one," Henry Adams observed acidly. In his letter of acceptance Hayes announced that he would serve for only one term, and he parted from Grantism by promising civil

The horse is still master of lower Broadway in this 1875 lithograph, but he would not be for long. Already New York had steam-powered elevateds; electric trolleys would be introduced in 1889 and horseless carriages soon afterward.

DRAFTING THE DECLARATION OF INDEPENDENCE—THE COMMITTEE

READING THE DECLARATION OF INDEPENDENCE

BATTLE OF LAKE ERIE

GREAT WORLD FAIR

GROUND FLOOR 872,320 SQR.FT. 20.02 ACRES
UPPER FLOORS 63,688   "   "   1.45   "

MAIN EXHIBITION BUILDING, FAIRMOUNT PARK.   PH

FORT SUMTER

INDEPENDENCE HALL OR STATE HOUSE, PHIL'A.

SURRENDER OF LEE.

1776, CENTENNIAL INTERNATIO

Tributes to Washington at the Centennial were many and varied. They included the above and an Italian sculpture that had him "perched," one observer wrote, "on an eagle much too small for him."

service reform and by pledging himself to allow the Southern states to govern themselves.

Meeting in St. Louis two weeks later, the Democrats picked the wealthy corporation lawyer and reform governor of New York, Samuel J. Tilden, as their presidential candidate. In his sixty-two years Tilden had been many things—a protégé of the wily Martin Van Buren's, a Free-Soiler, a Copperhead. Then he made his name as a reformer when, as chairman of the New York State Democratic Committee, he ousted New York City's apparently invulnerable Tweed Ring. As a reward for his civic zeal he was elected governor of New York in 1874. While governor, he remained a reformer, and he fittingly led the Democrats with their reform platform. As a vote-enticing contrast to Tilden, a hard-money Easterner, the Democrats chose the soft-money Thomas A. Hendricks of Indiana for their vice-presidential candidate. The Greenback party, advocating paper money, nominated the New York philanthropist Peter Cooper.

With reform blazoned on their banners and a promise of better times as their stock in trade the Democrats made political history by hiring professional publicity men to manage their campaign. Republicans, to distract attention from the reform issue, fell back on bloodyshirt waving as they denounced Democratic disloyalty in the late war and portrayed themselves as the saviors of the Union. For the first time since 1860 the outcome was in doubt, but as Election Day neared, the odds seemed to favor Tilden. By midnight of election night, with the major returns in, Democrats and Republicans alike were convinced that Tilden had won. Hayes went to bed certain he had been defeated. While he slept, four Republican journalists sitting in the office of *The New York Times* watching the returns saw that the electoral vote was so close that the result hinged on what happened in the South. With this realization John C. Reid, the managing editor of the *Times*, rushed to the hotel where Zach Chandler, Grant's Secretary of the Interior and chairman of the Republican National Committee, was sleeping. Waking that weary statesman from his somewhat alcohol-befuddled slumber, Reid explained that all was not lost for the Republicans. If they could only hold Louisiana, South Carolina, and Florida, Hayes would have a single-vote majority in the Electoral College. At once telegrams were sent to the Republican leaders in the three Radical-held states, telling them that Hayes was elected if they could bring in Republican majorities when the votes were counted.

The next day the sobered Chandler confidently announced that "Hayes has 185 electoral votes and is elected."

In those three critical Southern states the Radicals had waged a savage rear-guard action to sustain themselves. Even more savagely the resurgent Democrats had struggled to "redeem" their states. Both sides resorted to fraud and intimidation, the weight of fraud resting with the Radicals and the weight of intimidation with the Democrats. The White Leagues of Louisiana, the Red Shirts of South Carolina, and allied white-supremacy groups in Florida set out to conjure up a Democratic majority. Louisiana Democrats, with that kind of help, and with former Confederate General Francis Tillou Nicholls as their candidate for governor, carried the state for Tilden by at least 6,000 votes.

Nationwide Tilden mustered 4,300,000 votes to 4,036,000 for Hayes. And Tilden and the Democrats carried South Carolina and Florida as well as Louisiana. But in all three states the Radical-controlled returning boards proceeded to overturn the results. Outright bribery in some cases, as well as promises of patronage, insured that the boards ruled in favor of Hayes. In a free election without trickery, violence, and racial intimidation, the preponderance of Negroes in South Carolina and Louisiana would probably have given the electoral

Thomas A. Hendricks of Indiana, Tilden's running mate, was a perennial candidate for President who twice was awarded the second spot on the Democratic ticket. Elected Vice President with Cleveland in 1884, he died the following autumn.

votes of both states to Hayes. But Florida, with its white majority and its undisputed Democratic government, might well have gone for Tilden, giving the New York governor the Presidency by 7 electoral votes.

In all three states the Democrats challenged the findings of the returning boards. So bitter was the reaction to Radical vote juggling that men spoke of armed resistance and there were rumors of a possible clash between the small Regular Army and the state National Guards, controlled largely by Democratic governors. Meanwhile conservative Republican leaders met secretly with conservative Southern Democrats to try to work out concessions that both sides might accept. Privately the Northerners assured the Southerners that Hayes as President would prove a friend of the South, supporting internal improvements—above all railroad subsidies—and home rule for Louisiana and South Carolina. When the electoral certificates were returned in December, two sets arrived from each of the disputed states. It seemed possible that the issue might not be settled and that there would be no new President to replace Grant on March 4. Since the House remained Democratic and the Senate Republican, the party leaders finally found an alternative in the Electoral Count Bill, which turned the disputed returns over to a special Electoral Commission, composed of five representatives, five senators, and five justices of the Supreme Court. The congressional members were divided equally between Republicans and Democrats, while two Democratic and two Republican justices selected their fifth colleague, the politically independent Justice David Davis. Davis, thought to favor Tilden, announced his resignation from the Court five days before the commission met in order to become senator from Illinois. His place on the commission was taken by a Republican, Justice Joseph P. Bradley.

Through February until the second of March the commission met daily to evaluate the disputed votes. Bradley sided with his fellow Republicans to recognize the Hayes electors, and by the irreducible margin of 8 to 7 the commission voted down every Democratic claim. Moderate Democrats were hopeful that the commission would throw out Louisiana's electoral returns after a Treasury agent had testified that Louisiana's former carpetbag Governor J. Madison Wells had offered to sell the electoral vote of his state to Tilden for two hundred thousand dollars for himself, a like sum for the other white man on the state returning board, plus "a smaller amount for the niggers." But even here, at the core of corruption, "The Eight" held firm, giving all the disputed votes to Hayes. As the discussions became public, there were more mutterings of armed revolt. Henry Watterson, a Kentucky editor and a Liberal Republican-turned-Democrat, called for a march of a hundred thousand Tilden supporters on Washington. "Tilden or blood!" became a slogan. A bullet was fired into Hayes's house in Columbus as he sat at dinner. The Radical Stephen Packard, who claimed to have won the Louisiana governorship, was shot and wounded. In state after state Democratic ex-soldiers were forming into militia companies to meet any Radical challenge.

In this electric atmosphere a conference was held between Republican and Democratic leaders at Washington's Wormley Hotel. With Senators John Sherman and James A. Garfield—a member of the Electoral Commission—and Editor Watterson among those present in the Wormley, the conferees agreed to abandon the Radical governments of Louisiana and South Carolina in return for a Democratic promise to deal fairly with the Negroes and the castaway Republicans. Grant himself privately promised that there would be no more intervention by federal troops. Southerners promised not to join any filibuster to oppose Hayes's inauguration. The Great Swap, the conference came to be labeled. Actually, there were very few points of agreement reached at the Wormley Conference that had not previously been worked out in private meetings between Northerners and Southerners. In brief, the agreement turned the South back to the white Southerners and finally wrote off the policy of Reconstruction as a failure.

Tilden's supporters in Congress conducted wild demonstrations of protest. Tilden himself, ailing and hypochondriacal, declined to contest the decision. Tilden's manager declared that he preferred "four years of Hayes's administration to four years of civil war." At four in the morning of March 2, the Electoral Commission declared Hayes duly elected President. Hayes always maintained that he had not been party to the Great Swap or any other deal, but he could not have remained innocently ignorant. Rutherfraud, the Tilden Democrats called him in their anger.

Hayes arrived in Washington the day of the commission's decision. Since March 4 fell on a Sunday, the Monday Inauguration Day would leave the country for twenty-four hours without a President. To obviate this, Hayes took his oath of office privately on Saturday evening in the Red Room of the White House, disregarding the resolution that Democrats had forced through the House that Sam Tilden had been "duly elected president of the United States. . . ." The public inauguration took place on Monday, with the parades and festivities somehow lackluster. Men referred to the new President as His Fraudulency or the Boss Thief, while urchins bawled out "Old Eight to Seven!" Hayes rode with his predecessor from the White House to the Capitol in Grant's four-horse carriage. But all eyes, and most affections, were on the outgoing rather than the incoming President.

In Rutherford Hayes the country had the paradox of a reform President elected to office by a minority of the voters through corrupt bargains. Though he personally made none of the bargains, the bargains were made—and kept—in his name. The month after his inauguration he withdrew the federal troops from South Carolina and Louisiana. With their bayonet props removed, the last two Radical governments collapsed. In South Carolina, Daniel Henry Chamberlain, the best of the carpetbag governors, was defeated by the former Confederate General Wade Hampton. Louisiana saw the last of the Custom House Ring when Governor Packard was ousted by the one-armed, one-footed former Confederate General Francis Tillou Nicholls. For the Stalwarts the news was wormwood. Conkling observed that Packard's dismissal removed the legal ground for Hayes's election. Grant, still treasuring loyalty above virtue, told his son Jesse: "If I had been in Mr. Hayes's place, I would have insisted upon the Republican Governor being seated, or I would have refused to accept the electoral vote of Louisiana." Blaine in later years thought that "no act of President Hayes did so much to create discontent within the ranks of the Republican Party."

With the disappearance of the blue federal uniforms in the South the decade of Reconstruction came to an end, leaving behind it corrosive bitterness, a legend, and two inoperative constitutional amendments. Ironically the Fourteenth Amendment, providing that no state could "deprive any person of life, liberty or property without due process of law," would find its most immediate application in the exemption of corporations from state control. For once the corporation had been defined in the legal sense as a "person," the amendment became "the Magna Charta of accumulated wealth and organized capital."

In the wake of Hayes's inauguration the carpetbaggers flocked north like migrating birds, many of them to find places there for their talents. All the members of the Louisiana Returning Board were taken care of, most of them with comfortable nests in the Treasury Department. Taking over the Southern state governments were the Bourbons—the name first applied by the New York *Herald* to Southerners of substance, members of the old planter aristocracy who remained Whigs beneath their Democratic skin and saw themselves as the receivers for the "redeemed" though bankrupt South. The announced goal of the Bourbons was a repudiation of Radical extravagance and a return to honesty in government. "Spend nothing unless absolutely necessary," was the order of the millionaire Whig-Democratic governor of Florida, George F. Drew. Bourbon governors reduced salaries, abolished offices, and cut all government services, including the Radical-conceived program of education. An even more drastic step, the "redeemed" state governments repudiated most of the debts incurred in the Reconstruction period, claiming that these had been imposed at bayonet point.

Economy proved easier to reintroduce in the South than honesty. In Louisiana, as the most flagrant example, Major E. A. Burke, who had been one of the principals at the Wormley Conference and had become one of his state's most powerful political figures, in his ten years as state treasurer stole $1,777,000 in state bonds. Six other Southern Democratic state treasurers absconded with public funds in the post-Reconstruction period.

Though the Bourbons preferred to look backward, they had no objections to Negro voting as such. General Pierre G. T. Beauregard, the South's most dashingly romantic military leader, even organized the Unification Movement in 1873 in Louisiana, which would have given the Negro complete political equality in a party that united honest white and black men to fight political corruption. Few Bourbons were as extreme as Beauregard, but most of them felt that with a limited Negro franchise, they could manipulate the freedman vote. In 1878 the old Boston abolitionist Colonel Thomas Wentworth Higginson, after an extended Southern journey, wrote about Negroes and the ballot: "The Southern whites accept them precisely as Northern men in cities accept the ignorant Irish vote—not cheerfully, but with acquiescence in the inevitable. . . ."

Those who did not acquiesce in the inevitable were the Rednecks—the sunburned men behind the plow,

POLITICAL SUICIDE OF PRESIDENT HAYES.

Californians were furious, but Hayes felt that the Chinese exclusion bill violated a treaty with China and that he must veto it. "We should deal with China," he wrote, ". . . precisely as we expect and wish other nations to deal with us."

the crackers, the hillbillies. The Rednecks remained the real black-haters, fearing the Negro as an economic rival, jealous and resentful of the complacent Bourbon. In turn the Bourbons, with their zeal for retrenchment and limited government, their intimate links with the railroad oligarchy, failed to perceive the needs and demands of the farmers and the poor whites. Once more, under the new names Bourbons and Rednecks, the old quarrel was renewed between the aristocratic Whigs and the Jacksonian Democrats. When the Negro was seen as potentially holding the balance of power between the two groups, he was eliminated from political life, and the internecine struggle within the Democratic party was fought behind the barriers of white supremacy. To the North the fate of the Negro became increasingly a matter of indifference. As Republican strength expanded in Ohio, Indiana, and Illinois—the old Demo-

cratic Northwest—the more astute Republican politicians wrote off the South.

Segregation was a more gradual process in the South, particularly in the cities, than has been commonly realized. For a quarter of a century after Reconstruction Negroes were admitted without hindrance to theaters and parks and other public places in many parts of the South. There was no restriction for any passenger on many Southern railroads. Segregation existed chiefly in schools, churches, and social life. Not until the savage and prolonged political contest between the Bourbons and their Redneck opponents did the public barriers go up between the races. Not until the nineties did the rigid pattern of separation down to the drinking-fountain level emerge, along with the wholesale rigging of state constitutions to deny the Negro the ballot while keeping within the letter of federal law. Various Supreme Court rulings, particularly that of separate but equal facilities being admissible under the Constitution, aided the inexorable process.

A few months after his inauguration, Hayes made a conciliatory tour of the South to find himself welcomed with enthusiasm in the cities of Virginia, Tennessee, Kentucky, and Georgia. As an old Northern Whig he hoped to win over former Southern Whigs to support a renewed conservative Republican party of the North and the South, a business party of high tariffs and a sound dollar. Yet in spite of the warmth of Hayes's Southern reception, his goal would prove unattainable because of bitter memories of Republican Radicalism.

On April 22, 1877, Hayes had written in his diary, "Now for Civil Service Reform." The new President saw himself as the chief civil servant of the United States, an administrator rather than a leader. Like Carl Schurz he believed that the country's political evils could be overcome by appointing honest men to public office. In line with this belief he appointed to high position independents and reformers without considerations of patronage. His Cabinet, the most able and upright since that of Lincoln's second term, contained Senator John Sherman of Ohio as Secretary of the Treasury and—to the outrage of the Stalwarts—the incorruptible Carl Schurz, now an editor, as Secretary of the Interior. Unglamourous, lacking aggressiveness, Hayes felt—as weak Presidents have generally felt—that the initiative for legislative action should come from Congress. By the time his term was half over, he was recording in his voluminous diary that he was "heartily

101

tired of this life of bondage, responsibility and toil." The social life of the White House became as pallid in its virtuous domesticity as the President's official life. His wife, whom he called "the Golden Rule incarnate," established White House teetotalism upstairs and down. At state dinners even wine was banished; Mrs. Hayes received the sobriquet Lemonade Lucy.

In May, Hayes issued his first policy statements on civil service reform, declaring in a letter to Secretary Sherman that "the collection of revenues should be free from partisan control, and organized on a strictly business basis . . . the party leaders should have no more influence on appointments than other equally respectable citizens." Schurz inaugurated a strict merit system in the Interior Department, while Sherman took the unheard-of step of dismissing redundant clerks from the Treasury. Prompted by his Secretary of State, the New York corporation lawyer William Evarts, Hayes, through Sherman, appointed a committee to investigate the United States custom houses, the source of the most constant corruption in the country.

The most corrupt of these was the huge New York Custom House, the bailiwick of Senator Roscoe Conkling, regal dispenser of hundreds of postmasterships, marshalships, and other federal appointments, Grant's Stalwart favorite, and powerful Republican boss of the Empire State. Six feet three inches tall, with auburn curls falling over his square forehead and a golden-blond beard, the senator bore himself with an air of truculent elegance, which extended to his clothes — cream-colored pantaloons, silk scarves, yellow satin waistcoats. Rumor, and more than rumor, linked him with the dazzling Kate Chase Sprague, daughter of Chief Justice Chase and wife of the Rhode Island former senator and millionaire alcoholic William Sprague. Conkling regarded federal patronage in New York as his to dispense by divine Republican right. "A government," he pronounced, "is a machine . . . a political party is a machine." And he felt it superfluous to add that such machines ran on the fuel of patronage.

Such federal patronage became even more vital to his political fief after the New York state government had been lost to Tilden's reform Democrats in the 1876 elections. Hayes's gestures toward reform were a challenge to the New York senator's very position. Soon Conkling could not speak of the President or of "snivel service" without a sneering curl of the lip. Hayes's investigating committee found all the long-existing ac-

cusations of bribery and political shakedowns in the custom house service to be true. In June the President issued an order for stringent reform, indicating at the same time that the resignation of Conkling's chief lieutenants, Collector of the Port of New York Chester A. Arthur and Alonzo Cornell, who bore the odd title Naval Officer, would be acceptable.

"A scandalous system of robbery," Schurz had called the whole custom house establishment centered in New York under Arthur's facile direction. A sleek party man with blond sideburns, Chester Arthur lent unction to the political boss's trade. Ingratiating where Conkling was arrogant, he was as much of a dandy, rumor holding that he owned a hundred pairs of trousers. More sedate than his chief, he usually wore a Prince Albert with a colored silk handkerchief in the corner pocket and a flower pinned on the lapel. He had started humbly enough, working his way through Union College in Schenectady. He was a competent student, and after college became a schoolmaster. He studied law for five years in his free time and was finally admitted to the bar. His main chance came during the Civil War when he became state quartermaster general and brought professional order out of amateur confusion in feeding and equipping the thousands of soldiers arriving in New York from all over the Northeast on their way to the war. He returned to the law in 1863, and soon prospered through his handling of war-claims cases and through his increasing prominence as a lawyer. Politically he attached himself to the coattails of the rising Senator Conkling, until by 1868 he had become chairman of New York's Republican Executive Committee. When scandals in the New York Custom House under Collector Thomas Murphy became too blatant and gross even for Grant, Murphy resigned in 1871 — with a letter of commendation from Grant — and Arthur replaced him.

As collector of customs, Arthur received half of any fines or forfeits, a lucrative arrangement that often netted him more than forty thousand dollars a year. Under his adroit direction the thousand or more employees of the custom house toiled principally for the Republican party. Several hundred customs workers did nothing but partisan political chores. Regarded as honest in private, Arthur ran his office at Conkling's bidding. The senator looked on the custom house as his preserve, a perquisite of his office. That his henchmen, Arthur and Cornell, should step down at the President's bidding

The gentle Lucy Hayes, first First Lady to have graduated from college, bore her husband eight children, five of whom lived to adulthood. The photograph at right was taken in Fremont, Ohio, long after the Hayeses had left the White House.

was an unthinkable surrender of his sovereign powers. His reply was to use the September, 1877, Republican State Convention at Rochester as a platform for declaring war against the reformers—the Half-Breeds, as they were becoming scornfully known by the Stalwarts. Through the New York senator the convention was turned into a spectacular demonstration against the President. Hayes was denounced in searing terms by Roscoe Conkling's most trusted lieutenant, Congressman Thomas Platt of Owego, while the mention of Grant's name brought forth almost hysterical cheers. Conkling, strutting his full-blown presence on the rostrum, proclaimed that "when Dr. Johnson defined patriotism as the last refuge of a scoundrel," he had had no idea of the uses of the word "reform."

Hayes's counter to this carefully measured effort was to send to the Senate the names of two men of unblemished reputation to replace Cornell and Arthur: L. Bradford Prince, a New York lawyer and politician, and

Theodore Roosevelt, the father of the future President. Conkling appealed to his fellow senators to preserve "the dignity of the Senate," and they, with traditional solidarity in defense of their privileges, voted down the President's appointees by 35 to 21. "In the language of the press, 'Senator Conkling has won a great victory,'" Hayes noted in his diary, ". . . but the end is not yet. I am right, and shall not give up the contest."

Biding his time until Congress had adjourned, Hayes then suspended Arthur and Cornell by executive order, replacing Arthur with Edwin A. Merritt, a minor Republican faithful, since Roosevelt had just died. At the opening of the new Congress, Secretary Sherman took charge of the struggle for confirmation. He underscored the derelictions of Arthur and Cornell while using the full weight of his office and the force of patronage to bring reluctant senators into line, pursuing them to their offices and even to their lodgings. Although a narrow majority of Senate Republicans stood by the

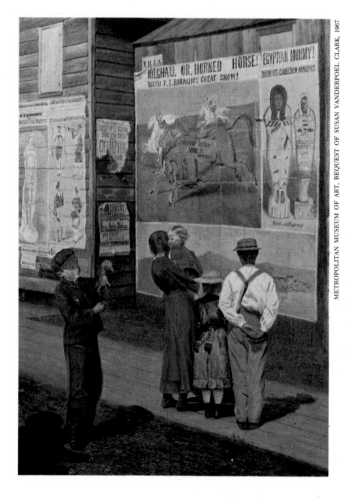

These were boom years for the circus in America. The ballyhoo, as in Charles C. Ward's 1871 painting at left, may have regularly overstated the attractions to come, but the ani-

highhanded Conkling, enough Half-Breeds voted with the Democrats to confirm the new appointees. Conkling never forgave Hayes for this setback, even going so far as to maintain that Tilden had been rightfully elected President, and to egg on the Democrats—who were, after the mid-term elections, in control of both houses of Congress—to challenge the 1876 decision.

With the Republicans riven between the Stalwarts and the Half-Breeds, Hayes found himself a President without a party. Nor did the country-wide depression show any sign of lessening. Between 1873 and 1877 wages fell between one-third and two-thirds. The unemployed numbered three million, and in the West farmers were burning their unsold corn. In the anthracite mining region of Pennsylvania, "Molly Maguire" terrorist groups sprang up among the Irish-born miners, the most poorly paid and exploited of white American workmen. In 1877 came the great railroad strike, more widespread and disruptive than any labor disturbance

that had yet occurred on the American scene.

The strike began during the depths of the depression with a walkout of the Trainmen's Union—engineers, conductors, brakemen, and firemen—on the Baltimore and Ohio Railroad after their wages had been cut 25 per cent in four years. It spread with increasing violence until soon the whole network of American railroads was shut down. Strikers seized railroad yards and junctions and blocked all movement of freight. Business came to a standstill. At least a hundred thousand union men went on strike. In Pittsburgh they destroyed hundreds of freight cars, and the night sky was red from the glow of burning yards, warehouses, and factories. When state governors called out the militia, in many cases the mob drove back the amateur soldiers. With the militia unable to cope with the disorder in the larger cities, Hayes finally issued a proclamation calling on the strikers to disperse, and at the same time he sent Regular Army troops to the trouble spots in West Virginia, Maryland,

mals, the acts of precision and daring, and spectacles like the equestrian round dance of a center-ring finale, above, did indeed make a good circus "The Greatest Show on Earth."

An Era of Expansion

To Americans of the late nineteenth century, as indeed to people in most times, politics was the froth on the stream, brightly visible, in constant motion, even odoriferous, but still on the surface. Below its evanescent bubbles ran the deeper currents of men's lives, carrying along their own private, contrasting, and mostly anonymous destinies. There were industrialists as well as the scurfy children tending the textile spindles, mineowners in their furbelowed wooden mansions and Paddies grubbing underground, Indians fighting for survival in the West, railroad magnates as well as the coolies laying the tracks across the Sierras, freedmen in the South, Americans of farm and mill, city and country, sea and prairie, on the whole expanse of continent that Whitman was cataloguing so lovingly and at such length.

The vibrant activity seemed normal to ordinary Americans. The humming and expanding continent, for all its corruption and crudities, its setbacks and depressions, embodied progress, the one permanence beyond all change. To those who had absorbed the idea while knowing nothing of its origins, progress seemed part of the very scheme of things. What had begun in France as a purely philosophical concept was accepted by Americans as a practical principle for daily life. As Whitman at seventy saw his United States:

> Here first the duties of to-day, the lessons of the concrete,
> Wealth, order, travel, shelter, products, plenty;
> As of the building of some varied, vast, perpetual edifice,
> Whence to arise inevitable in time, the towering roofs, the lamps,
> The solid-planted spires tall shooting to the stars.

From the beginning most of those who had migrated to America had done so in the hope of improving their lot in life. They had made their settlements at the edge of the wilderness, had seen the settlements grow to towns and the towns become cities. Their sons had watched the newly formed United States expand in giant steps across a continent. They had seen power mills spring up at the waterfalls, mines in the valleys,

Life on the Great Plains was full of sunlight and drudgery—a feeling reflected in Harvey Dunn's The Homesteader's Wife. *Dunn was born on a South Dakota homestead in 1884 and grew up there.*

industries in the frontier towns and old seaports. They had followed the expanding network of roads and canals and then railroads. They had seen the population grow from five million to fifty million in the nineteenth century's first eighty years. In the aftermath of the Civil War the smokestacks of industry proliferated, bringing an abundance of new goods, new manufactures. More would follow, a higher standard of living, a better way of life, a still-vaster population, in an endless progression.

Progress, however crassly defined, was the sustaining faith of the pioneers in their westward sweep, giving them the fortitude to endure change. Only partially interrupted by the Civil War, the migrant waves continued across the Mississippi for the next three decades, settlers often with the skimpiest of means and equipment— miners, prospectors, adventurers, sharpers, cattlemen, traders. Most ardent in their hopes for quick wealth were the prospectors, who even during the war continued to push into the mountainous regions of the West. Not long after California's forty-niner gold rush, new strikes were made in Colorado, Nevada, and British Columbia. Rumor, fanned by cupidity, brought a horde of prospectors to Colorado's mountain country. Wagons daubed with "Pike's Peak or Bust" became a familiar trail sight, and before long many of the same wagons, retreating, proclaimed, "Busted, by God!" Only after capital had been supplied by the East and machinery had been hauled in,

could most of the underground treasure be tapped. For the shoestring prospector, opportunity in the Rockies seemed to have dried up.

Then, in 1859 in the Sierras in Nevada, two prospectors, digging to increase the flow of water to their gold-mining site at the head of Six Mile Canyon on the side of Davidson Mountain, found silver and gold. The vein of ore, named the Comstock Lode for a shiftless prospector who had talked his way into a share of the claim, would develop into one of the richest finds in the history of mining. To the locality—called the Washoe District because Indians of that tribe lived in the region—the foot-loose prospectors swarmed like flies to carrion, staking their claims and making their camps on and about Davidson Mountain. The largest collection of tents and ramshackle saloons became known as Virginia City after a drunken miner nicknamed Old Virginny had stumbled on his way to his tent one night, breaking a bottle of whiskey. Rather than waste the liquid, he bellowed that he was baptizing the camp Virginia Town.

Virginia City grew like a mushroom of a rather gaudy and somewhat toxic variety. A few years after its baptism the young Samuel Clemens, who would first call himself Mark Twain a year later, became a reporter on the infant Virginia City *Territorial Enterprise*. He described his new stopping place, the archetype of all such ephemeral mining towns:

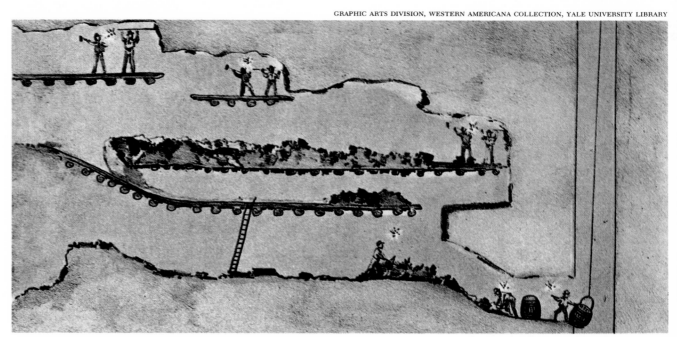

Following the vein of gold-bearing rock, men in the Gregory mine in Colorado stand on scaffolding to drill, with hand drills and sledges, holes that will hold explosive charges. Other men below are removing the ore already blasted loose.

The great "Comstock lode" stretched its opulent length straight through the town from north to south, and every mine on it was in diligent process of development. . . . Laboring men's wages were four and six dollars a day, and they worked in three "shifts" or gangs, and the blasting and picking and shoveling went on without ceasing, night and day.

The "city" of Virginia roosted royally midway up the steep side of Mount Davidson, seven thousand two hundred feet above the level of the sea, and in the clear Nevada atmosphere was visible from a distance of fifty miles! It claimed a population of fifteen thousand to eighteen thousand, and all day long half of this little army swarmed the streets like bees and the other half swarmed among the drifts and tunnels of the "Comstock," hundreds of feet down in the earth directly under those same streets. Often we felt our chairs jar, and heard the faint boom of a blast down in the bowels of the earth under the office.

The mountain side was so steep that the entire town had a slant to it like a roof. Each street was a terrace, and from each to the next street below the descent was forty or fifty feet. The fronts of the houses were level with the street they faced, but their rear first floors were propped on lofty stilts; a man could stand at a rear first-floor window of a C street house and look down the chimneys of the row of houses below him facing D street. . . . The thin atmosphere seemed to carry healing to gunshot wounds, and, therefore, to simply shoot your adversary through both lungs was a thing not likely to afford you any permanent satisfaction, for he would be nearly certain to be around looking for you within the month, and not with an opera glass, either.

Other strikes were followed by other rushes: into Idaho's Snake River valley; the great Montana gold rush of 1863; into Last Chance Gulch in the upper Missouri River country; into the Salmon River region in Idaho Territory; and finally, against Indian resistance, into the domed Black Hills of Dakota, where the gaudy wild West made its last stand in such roaring towns as Rapid City and Deadwood and Lead. Near Lead two brothers struck what would be the Homestake Mine, which has produced more than one-third of a billion dollars' worth of gold and is still operating today. However, the impatient brothers sold their claim to a San Francisco syndicate headed by George Hearst for a mere $150,000. The frontier West, perpetuated in myth and film, the West of prospectors seeking El Dorado and cowboys in town on a spree, of bad men and vigilantes, of boom towns with their saloons and jangling music halls and painted ladies, of gold nuggets and gunplay at high noon, of fabled names, like Wild Bill Hickok and Calamity Jane, flickered out in the Black Hills, which the Indians called Paha Sapa and considered holy.

Almost from the first settlements land speculation had been an American fever. Even the Father of His Country had acquired enormous holdings in the Ohio region. As the new country expanded, empty lands to the West were regarded by the government primarily as a source of revenue. Before the Constitution was adopted, the Land Ordinance of 1785 allowed the public lands to be auctioned off in square-mile sections (640 acres) at a minimum price of a dollar an acre, payable in gold or soldiers' land bounty certificates (many of which had been bought up on the cheap by speculators). Such sizable tracts in any case favored the land company and the speculator over the pioneer. From the settler and the frontiersman came the reiterated demand for free land for free men. In response, the Land Act of 1800 cut the plot size to half a section, which a buyer could pay for over a four-year period. Four years later the size was cut to a quarter section, or 160 acres. Land speculation soared in Jackson's administration, only to sink in the 1837 Panic. In 1841 the Distribution–Pre-emption Act allowed squatters to legalize their possession of up to 160 acres of land and to buy it later at $1.25 an acre.

Eastern magnates and Southern planters united in their opposition to a freer land policy, Easterners fearing the loss of their laborers, Southerners seeing hordes of new settlers as a challenge to their cotton economy and their "peculiar institution"—slavery. But the Western surge continued and the Western pressure for free land grew. "Go West, young man," the phrase Horace Greeley had used in a *Tribune* editorial, became a slogan. Frontiersmen insisted profanely that land swindles would vanish if the government gave each settler a quarter section of homestead land, enough for him to sustain himself and his family. The first of such homestead bills was introduced in Congress in 1846 but received scant support. Subsequent bills, also unsuccessful, were sponsored by Andrew Johnson. With the flood of cheap labor arriving in the wake of the Irish famine, Northern industrialists lost their fear of losing workmen and began to see the new settlers of the West as potential customers. Only in the South did resistance to a homestead policy persist. A homestead measure, advocated in the Republican platform of 1860, had passed both houses of Congress earlier that same year, only to be vetoed by Buchanan. Finally, as the settlement of the Great Plains got under way, the Homestead Act of 1862 was passed, granting 160 acres of public domain to every adult American on payment of a ten-dollar fee, title to the land to go

Steam power was well established in logging by 1908, when Darius Kinsey took this photograph. The donkey engine at far left and the locomotive nearby were used—in place of oxen and horses—to move the cut timber out of the woods. Kinsey made a career recording lumbermen in the Northwest.

to the settler after he had "resided upon or cultivated the same for a term of five years." At the end of six months a settler could "commute" his homestead to a pre-emption claim by paying $1.25 an acre.

The homesteads, demanded so vociferously for a generation by Eastern workers and Western pioneers, turned out in many cases to be disappointments. Eastern laborers earning two hundred and fifty or three hundred dollars a year lacked the means to equip themselves to take Greeley's advice. Besides, what in the Mississippi Valley or the Ohio country would have seemed a generous grant, turned out in the arid Great Plains to be inadequate. Such land was not suited for intensive cultivation, as the drought years would soon demonstrate. A rancher needed several thousand acres at a minimum to exist, and a farmer there could not make do with less

than a whole section of land under cultivation.

As with most poorly planned laws, ways were soon found to circumvent the Homestead Act. In making its huge grants to the railroads to subsidize their westward expansion, Congress had attempted to thwart speculation by assigning the land in a checkerboard pattern: a square mile to the railroads, with the adjacent square mile reserved for the public domain. The attempt for the most part failed. Fly-by-night settlers took to moving in on quarter sections to make their pre-emption claim after six months and then move on to the next claim. Some of the shacks they built were no bigger than dolls' houses; some were even conveniently set on wheels, ready to be moved to the next vacant section. Railroads and speculative companies took over from the fly-by-nighters, scooping up the acreage, trying to lure the new arrival in the West by advertising their track-centered lands as "Better Than A Homestead." In 1862 the Morrill Land-Grant Act gave large tracts of Western land to the states to raise funds for agricultural colleges, and most of this bonus land found its way cheaply and readily into the hands of large-scale speculators.

Pressed by homesteaders, Congress in 1871, in an at-

tempt to patch up matters, refused to grant any more land to the railroads. Two years later, after a more realistic appraisal of Western conditions, it passed the Timber Culture Act, by which any homesteader could obtain an additional 160 acres if within four years he planted a quarter of his new land with trees. In the fifteen years that this law remained in effect, 65,292 homesteaders acquired ten million additional acres for their forestation efforts.

The Timber Culture Act was followed by the Desert Land Act of 1877, a measure ostensibly designed to aid farmers but actually to serve the large-scale cattlemen. By that act a man could claim a section of 640 acres in the Great Plains or the Southwest by paying an initial twenty-five cents an acre. After three years, if he could prove that he had irrigated part of his land, the tract became his on payment of an additional one dollar an acre. Cattlemen had their cowhands and workmen file claims. Irrigation often consisted of pouring a bucket of water on the land before witnesses. With the consolidation of such dummy claims—95 per cent of which are estimated to have been fraudulent—cattlemen in the West and the Southwest were able to expand their holdings by thousands of acres at the end of the open-range period.

Spurred by the cattlemen's bonanza, the lumber magnates of the West, with all the means of persuasion at their disposal, lobbied through Congress the Timber and Stone Act of 1878. By this act any citizen or alien with first papers could obtain a quarter section of some of the nation's richest forest lands in California, Nevada, Oregon, or Washington. Such land, described as "unfit for cultivation" and "valuable chiefly for timber" or stone, could be bought for two and a half dollars an acre—the price of a good log. Company agents rounded up foreign seamen in the sleazy water-front boardinghouses of West coast ports, herding them to the nearest courthouse for their first papers, then to a land office to claim a quarter section, and finally to a notary public to deed over their claim to the lumber company. At first such floaters were paid fifty dollars a claim, then the price dropped to five or ten dollars, and finally as low as a glass of beer. By 1900 the Timber and Stone Act put more than three and a half million acres of rich forest land into the hands of speculators and big timber interests.

The Homestead Act for the most part failed in its intent to realize the Jeffersonian ideal of transforming the

123

landless worker into the sturdy yeoman, the backbone of the republic, cultivating his acres. For all the government's bounty with the public domain, not more than one acre in eight of Western land went to the small settler-farmer. The lion's share found its way to the speculator, the jobber, the land company, the railroads. Often the hopeful pioneer discovered that the only homestead acres available were isolated or on poor soil, or both. To obtain good land he had to buy it from speculators who had arrived before him or from the railroads, which had amassed their vast acreage through construction grants. Nevertheless, whatever its deficiencies, the Homestead Act did stimulate the imaginations of ordinary men on both sides of the Atlantic. Millions of farmers and immigrants, enticed by the Western dream, filled Kansas and Nebraska and spread across the grasslands of the Dakotas into the rolling hill country of Wyoming and Montana. Between 1870 and 1900 more new acres were occupied—four hundred and thirty million in all—than had been settled from the seventeenth century to 1870.

In the South, entry into the un-pre-empted public lands of Alabama, Arkansas, Florida, Louisiana, and Mississippi had been halted during Reconstruction, waiting in vain for Congress to pass a Southern homestead act. Then in 1876 all restrictions were lifted, and in the next decade more than five and a half million acres were sold, most to timber and mining concerns and large-scale speculators. The states disposed of their own lands for next to nothing, granting huge free tracts to railroad companies. Texas, as the most prodigal example, turned over to twelve railroad companies an area larger than the whole state of Indiana.

At the beginning of the Civil War the frontier had been dotted from Canada to Mexico with Army forts whose names are today forgotten, and others, like Fort Leavenworth, Fort Snelling, Fort Scott, Fort Riley, that have won places in history. Beyond them lay the Great American Desert, where the Indians had gathered in their forced retreat westward. These federal garrisons, with their own carpenters, blacksmiths, masons, machinists, pharmacists, farmers, cobblers, tailors, bakers, and even printers and teachers, were almost self-sufficient in their isolation. To protect the settlers and emigrants and to keep the Indian nations in their own Western country, the Army stationed mounted troops on the Plains, units called dragoons until the Civil War, but actually the lighter, faster cavalry. And cavalry was indeed necessary, for on the treeless Great Plains the

hostile Indians had developed into superb horsemen skilled in the use of firearms. Faced with predatory hordes of trappers, miners, traders, and squatters united in the long-held American conviction that "the only good Indian is a dead Indian," the Western tribes grew increasingly restive.

In 1860 probably a quarter of a million Indians still inhabited the prairies and the Great Plains. No longer a threat were the Five Civilized Tribes—Creeks, Cherokees, Choctaws, Chickasaws, and Seminoles—who had been forced across the Mississippi in President Jackson's time and who looked to the whites for protection against the indigenous Indians of the Great Plains. These Plains Indians—Comanches, Kiowas, Arapahoes, Sioux, Cheyennes, Blackfeet, and Crows—were nomadic tribesmen, and as fearless and unyielding as the Iroquois of a century earlier. The horse, descended from the mounts brought long ago from Spain, they had adopted as their own until they seemed a race of centaurs. Guns, with which they were well provided, had come to them through traders even before the Revolution. For food and clothing they relied on the great buffalo herds. Now the surge of scouts and settlers along the main trails—the Sante Fe, the Smoky River, and the Oregon—threatened the herds and their very existence.

To some tribes, the Civil War seemed an opportunity to remove this threat as federal troops were withdrawn from frontier forts to Eastern battlefields. The Santee Sioux, long peaceful but mercilessly defrauded by traders, rose in August of 1862, and under Chief Little Crow, ranged up and down the Minnesota River valley, killing an estimated seven hundred settlers and soldiers. Most of the victims were taken by surprise in the first days of the uprising; the Sioux sweep of the valley was halted by epic defenses of strategic, refugee-swollen Fort Ridgely and of the town of New Ulm, which was 90 per cent burned before the Indians drew back. In the end, growing white strength was decisive. Ex-Governor Henry Sibley—commissioned a colonel—raised a force that eventually amounted to sixteen hundred and defeated Little Crow's forces at the Battle of Wood Lake. Most of the Indians responsible for the uprising fled into Dakota Territory, but Sibley rounded up some two thousand Sioux, among whom he found four hundred who appeared culpable enough to be tried. Of these, three hundred and six were sentenced to death, but President Lincoln pardoned all but thirty-eight, who were hanged simultaneously on a single gallows.

In Colorado the buffalo ranges of the Cheyennes and the Arapahoes had been ruined by the heavy traffic to and from the gold fields, and the two tribes had been given a sterile reservation. During the uneasy summer of 1864 a series of raids for food by hungry Indians and indiscriminate retaliation by local militias led to open war. A dreadful climax came when a regiment of Colorado volunteers, led by Colonel John M. Chivington, rode against the camp of Black Kettle, a Cheyenne chief who had declared his peaceful intentions and placed himself under the protection of the commanding officer of Fort Lyon. Chivington, a former minister, attacked the sleeping camp of Black Kettle on Sand Creek in the dawning light of November 29, 1864, almost before his men were seen. The chief raised an American flag and a white flag but they were ignored. The militia charged with a blaze of rifle and cannon fire, killing women and infants as indiscriminately as men, and committing unspeakable atrocities. Probably two hundred Indians were killed, and the white warriors returned laden with scalps to Denver, to be acclaimed heroes.

However, the applause was not general; revulsion spread across the rest of the nation when the facts became known. As for the Indians, they reacted with fury, attacking all whites, although their war had been petering out at the time of the Sand Creek Massacre.

An important road of the West, the Bozeman Trail, branched off the Oregon Trail not far west of Fort Laramie in Wyoming (then part of Dakota Territory) and angled northwestward to Virginia City in the rich gold diggings in Montana Territory. It ran, however, through the choicest hunting lands of the Sioux and the Northern Cheyennes, and traveling the road from end to end was hazardous. In June of 1866, when the Army sent a bat-

Like the cowboy's quarter horse, the horse an Indian rode to hunt buffalo had to be quick and intuitive, particularly when—as in the painting above by muralist and illustrator Walter Shirlaw—the kill was made in close, with a lance.

talion under Colonel Henry B. Carrington to build and garrison forts along the trail, most of the Sioux and their Cheyenne allies, under Chief Red Cloud, accepted the move as a declaration of war and prepared to defend their hunting grounds against these intruders.

Colonel Carrington, an able officer, strengthened Fort Reno, a post already established near the southern end of the Bozeman Trail, built his main stronghold, Fort Philip Kearny, sixty-five miles to the northwest, and sent two companies of infantry another ninety miles up the trail to build a third post, Fort C. F. Smith. Red Cloud and his warriors followed, lurking in the cover of the hills, striking at every sign of white carelessness. In December the Indian leader decoyed a detachment of eighty troops under a hell-for-leather cavalryman, Captain William J. Fetterman, into ambush. Fetterman, ironically, had earlier boasted that he could conquer the entire Sioux nation with only eighty men; he was wrong, for hundreds of Sioux rose up from hiding and destroyed his detachment to the last man.

In spite of the reinforcements arriving at Fort Philip Kearny, Red Cloud remained a menace, on the alert to strike at working parties from the fort. One such encounter occurred the following summer, on August 2, 1867, when a woodcutting crew guarded by a detail under Captain James Powell—thirty-two men in all—was attacked by fifteen hundred warriors led by Red Cloud. But Powell, a defter and more prudent man than Fetterman, took shelter in a corral of dismounted wagon bodies and held off the attack with sustained fire from new breech-loading rifles, whose rapid firing caught the Indians by surprise. No one knows how many Indians were killed in this Wagon Box Fight before the dispirited warriors withdrew; Captain Powell estimated sixty, with twice as many badly wounded. Only the day before, Indians had attacked a haymaking detail at Fort C. F. Smith and had been driven off.

Finally, in 1868, the government agreed to close the trail and to abandon Forts Philip Kearny, Reno, and C. F. Smith. As the troops moved out for the last time, the Sioux moved in. Troops glancing backward saw the smoke columns rise from their old barracks. Along with the closing of the Bozeman Trail came a change in the government's Indian policy, a determination to reduce the mobility of the Indians by restricting them to reservations. Yet, as in previous settlement attempts, the questions remained: Were these new reservations permanent or temporary? How would encroachments by

The beginning of the end for the Plains Indians is depicted in these scenes—six from a panorama by John Stevens—of the bloody 1862 uprising by the Santee Sioux in Minnesota.

predatory whites be prevented? Commissioners from the Bureau of Indian Affairs, political hacks for the most part, had often signed absurd treaties with the chiefs, who had been deviously willing to accept government rations while preparing later attacks. To the cynical cavalrymen it was a policy of "feed 'em in the winter and fight 'em in the summer."

In 1868 General Philip Sheridan, then in command in the Nebraska area, opened a campaign to drive the Indians of the southern Plains onto their reservations. Sheridan acted with characteristic harshness. Where it had been customary to end campaigning with the coming of cold weather, he sent out, along with less-remembered officers, George Armstrong Custer, the "Boy General" of the Civil War, to pursue Indians to their winter quarters. So unrelenting was Sheridan's campaign that within a few years only three real centers of Indian resistance remained. In the North many Sioux, under their chiefs Sitting Bull and Crazy Horse, as well as a number of Cheyennes, were on their unceded hunting grounds in the Powder River country of Wyoming and Montana—where they had a right to be under the 1868 treaty between Red Cloud and the government. When they failed to obey an order to return to their Dakota reservation by January 31, 1876—a near impossibility in the depths of winter—they were declared to be at war with the Army. In the Southwest the Apaches, most relentless of all tribes, had been intermittently at war with the settlers of Arizona and New Mexico since during the Civil War. Swindled by agents and traders, their women and children often cut down by white vigilantes, the Apaches from 1861 to 1890 kept up their resistance to white intruders. A third combination of Kiowas, Comanches, and Southern Cheyennes became particularly troublesome on the southern Plains.

Custer and Sheridan in 1869 forced the Cheyennes and Arapahoes onto a reservation in Indian Territory (Oklahoma today), the Comanches and Kiowas onto an adjoining one. But the nomadic nature of the tribes did not change, and they continued to hunt buffalo, riding north into Kansas and west into Texas. Nor, except for the Arapahoes, had defeat broken their fighting spirit; the Comanches and Kiowas, especially, remained truculent and frequently raided wagon trains and settlements. Indian resentment of the white man increased with the wholesale slaughter of the buffalo by professional hide hunters. By the fall of 1873 the millions of bison in Kansas and Colorado had been all but annihilated, and a

Some whites were spared as being "good men," but hundreds were not. Ultimately the beaten Sioux gave up their prisoners, and a mass execution put a bitter period to the tragedy.

large herd in the Texas Panhandle was the only one left on all the southern Plains. White hunters were forbidden to enter the region, but it was believed that once the buffalo were destroyed, the nomadic tribes would settle down to farming, and so the Army winked when a party of hide hunters headed south from Kansas in the spring of 1874 and began killing and skinning buffalo in northern Texas. The Indians reacted predictably to this invasion of their last hunting ground. A war party of Comanches, with some Cheyennes and Kiowas, struck the hide men's camp at dawn on the morning of June 27. The two-dozen-odd whites eventually drove off the warriors, but with four dead they abandoned the camp and returned to Kansas. They had stirred up a hornets' nest, and the embittered Indians now began ranging far afield, into Colorado, Kansas, Texas, and New Mexico, slaying settlers who had had nothing to do with killing buffalo. Very shortly still another Indian war, the Red River War of 1874–75, was under way. In the summer of 1874 five Army columns, under the over-all command of Colonel Nelson A. Miles, converged from all directions on the Texas Panhandle, attacking and harrying all

Indian bands that were off their reservations. The tribesmen were given no chance to hunt or rest, their camps were burned, and one by one the destitute bands returned to the reservations in a starving condition. There was little fight left in them, and soon the buffalo hunters returned and wiped out the last possibility of the tribes' returning to the old life on the Plains.

No other episode of that protracted conflict in the West would become so legendary, so part of the folk memory, as the annihilation of George Armstrong Custer and five companies of his soldiers at the hands of Crazy Horse and Gall in the Battle of the Little Bighorn on June 26, 1876. A late winter expedition against the Sioux, led by Brigadier General George Crook, from Fort Fetterman, Wyoming, had been thrown back by the Cheyenne chief Two Moon. After this reverse Sheridan planned a three-pronged attack against the Sioux stronghold in the Powder River country of Wyoming and Montana. One detachment, under Colonel John Gibbon, was to march east from Fort Ellis in Montana; another, under Brigadier General Alfred H. Terry, who was also the over-all commander, was to move west from Fort

Custer, commemorated often in Last Stand paintings, as above, sought "fresh laurels" heedlessly, according to a cavalry private. Honor, said the trooper, "weighed lightly in the scale against the 'glorious?' name of 'Geo. A. Custer.''

Abraham Lincoln in Dakota Territory; while a third, under General Crook, would again march north from Fort Fetterman.

The neatly dovetailed paper plan bore little relation to the actual situation that developed. Crook was again attacked by some fifteen hundred Sioux and Cheyenne warriors under Crazy Horse, on upper Rosebud Creek, and though the Indians were driven from the field, Crook's men suffered such heavy losses that he felt compelled to withdraw to his supply depot. Meanwhile Terry and Gibbon met on the Yellowstone River at the mouth of Rosebud Creek. With Terry rode the flamboyant Custer and his Seventh Cavalry.

George Armstrong Custer was only thirty-six years old when he fell in battle. He had graduated from West Point in 1861 at the bottom of his class. A lieutenant he remained until his gallant conduct at the Battle of Aldie in June, 1863, translated him into brigadier general overnight. Soon he became one of the Union's most dashing cavalry leaders, conspicuous in wide-brimmed cavalry hat, velveteen uniform spangled with gold braid, a scarlet kerchief round his neck, and long golden hair. Before he was twenty-five, he became a major general of volunteers, commanding the Third Cavalry Division. His division led in the pursuit of Lee after the fall of Richmond in 1865, and it was to Custer that the Confederate flag of truce was tendered. With the war's end the disbanding of the volunteer army stripped him of his temporary rank, leaving him a mere cavalry captain. But when the Seventh Cavalry was organized, he was assigned to it as second-in-command and raised to the rank of lieutenant colonel. However, as the regiment's colonel was always away, Custer was in actual command. There were those who failed to be impressed by his dashing nonregulation figure and impulsive ways, among them the commanding general, Winfield Hancock. In 1867 Custer was court-martialed and suspended from duty for a year for deliberately deserting his command. Sheridan, on replacing Hancock, restored his friend Custer to favor, and the long-haired commander went on to make a name for himself as an Indian-fighter. In 1876 he was again in trouble after he had gone to Washington to testify against Secretary of War Belknap, accused of corruption in sharing the profits of a post trader. Custer included the President's brother and even the President in some of his wilder accusations, and Grant removed Custer from command of the eastern prong of the campaign against the Sioux. General Terry, though in over-

all command, would also personally lead the eastern column. Custer, Grant ordered, should not even accompany the expedition he was to have led. Only Terry's plea made Grant relent enough to restore Custer to the command of his regiment, which, however, made up the greater part of the eastern column's strength.

After joining up with Gibbon at Rosebud Creek, Terry sent Lieutenant Colonel Custer and his Seventh Cavalry with written instructions to ride up the valley of Rosebud Creek, swing across to the headwaters of the Little Bighorn River, and ride down that stream while Gibbon was marching up it to meet him. Thus the Indian camp would be caught between the two forces. Under no circumstances was Custer to attack before Gibbon's column was in position. After three days of riding, Custer located the Indian encampment of between twenty-five hundred and four thousand warriors in the valley of the Little Bighorn. Warned by his scouts that the Indians were aware of his presence and that there were far too many of them for his regiment to handle, he paid as little heed to this information as he did to his written instructions. Dividing his force—about six hundred and fifty men—into three battalions, he sent the first, three companies, under Captain Frederick Benteen on a scouting mission into hills to the south. The second, of three companies, under Major Marcus Reno, he ordered to proceed to the Little Bighorn River and attack the Indian village on sight, while he, Custer, whose battalion included five companies, would support him as soon as the attack was under way. The remaining company of the regiment was detailed to guard the pack train.

Reno reached and crossed the river and for the first time saw the Indian village, a huge one, two miles ahead of him. He immediately charged it with his force of one hundred and twelve men and some two dozen Indian scouts. Almost at once he found himself overwhelmed on all sides, but managed finally to pull back to a wooded area beside the river and then make a panicky withdrawal across the stream. Meanwhile Benteen, wearying of scouting empty land, returned to the river just in time to join forces with Reno's beleaguered troops and form a defense against the Sioux.

Custer had no chance to support Reno. He was struck from one direction by Chief Gall, whose warriors had just thrown Reno back, and from another by Crazy Horse and a force of Cheyennes under Chief Two Moon. The fierce and swirling Last Stand was soon over, and at its end the colonel and all his men were dead, the only

OVERLEAF: *At Big Hole Basin in Montana Territory the Nez Percés were surprised in a dawn attack by federal troops, but escaped. The painting of the battle is by Olaf Seltzer.*
GILCREASE INSTITUTE OF AMERICAN HISTORY AND ART

education he had, he received from his mother. An early attack of scarlet fever affected his hearing, and as he matured he grew progressively deafer. Even as a boy he was preoccupied with chemistry and physics, selling newspapers and candy on trains to get money for his home experiments. From 1863 to 1868 he worked as an itinerant telegrapher, ending up employed by Western Union in Boston, where in off moments he read the complete works of Michael Faraday and developed his first patented invention, an electric voting machine. The machine proved much too efficient for its own good. "Young man, that is just what we do *not* want," a congressman told him when he demonstrated his apparatus in Washington. "Your invention would destroy the only hope that the minority would have of influencing legislation. . . ."

By this time Edison had left Western Union to take his chances in the world as a free-lance inventor. The chances at first seemed murky. Arriving in New York City almost penniless, he managed, through an engineer friend, to find a place to sleep nights in the offices of the Laws Gold Indicator Company on Broad Street while subsisting days on coffee and five-cent apple dumplings. One day while he was waiting for a job interview at the indicator company, the master stock ticker broke down. At once several hundred office boys swarmed in from the neighboring brokerage houses demanding quotations, and Samuel Laws was in a panic. Edison stepped for-

ward like an Alger hero to make the repairs—a matter of a broken contact spring—and Laws hired him on the spot. When, however, the company was absorbed by Western Union, Edison quit. Once more a free-lance inventor, he developed a number of improvements for stock tickers, which he took to Western Union, hoping to market them for five thousand dollars but willing to take less. To his amazement the company's president offered him forty thousand dollars. With this unexpected bounty he opened his own shop at Newark, New Jersey, to design and make stock tickers for Western Union.

In five years at Newark he managed to take out a new patent almost every month. He invented an electric pen for cutting stencils, the mimeograph, and dozens of

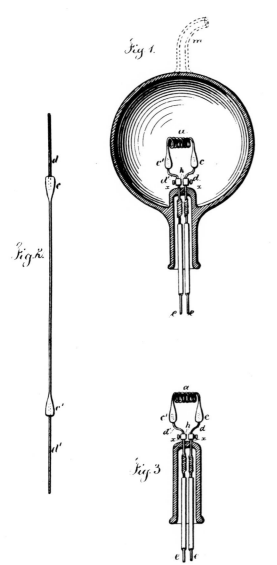

At left, a wondering group listens to a phonograph. Above is a patent-application drawing of Edison's incandescent lamp: "a" is the carbon filament, the suitable material that he sought so long; tube "m" drew the air from the globe.

other devices. So engrossed did he become in his inventions that he slept only a few hours a day. Kindly, friendly, but somewhat short-tempered, he was comically absent-minded and impractical outside his laboratory. Much of the money he made from his Western Union patents he lost to mismanagement and to swindlers. Once, when he went to Newark City Hall to pay his taxes, he found he could not remember his own name. One Christmas Day he married a buxom young woman from his laboratory, Mary Stilwell, then after the wedding went back to his workbench and stayed there far into the night, quite forgetting that he had a bride at home. In 1876, at the age of twenty-nine, he established a "village of science" in Menlo Park, New Jersey, and in a barnlike structure there over the next twelve years the "Wizard of Menlo Park" invented, along with a host of lesser devices, the carbon telephone transmitter and the phonograph and made the first practical electric light. Because of his increasing deafness, his conversations with his assistants developed into shouting contests, but he refused to get a hearing aid, since outside noises distracted him and besides "my wife would want to talk to me all the time."

The idea of the phonograph came to him in 1877 when he noticed a telegraph repeater in his laboratory giving out curiously speechlike sounds as its disks revolved. The thought struck him that sounds might be recorded on a moving surface and played back. He experimented first with waxed paper drawn under a needle attached to a diaphragm. After several months of experiments, he evolved a machine like a small lathe on which a tin-foil-wrapped cylinder revolved. As the handle was turned, a needle attached to a diaphragm cut a groove around the cylinder. When it was ready for its first trial, Edison turned the handle and shouted into the diaphragm. Then, using another needle and placing it back in the starting position, he turned the crank again. Squeakily but still recognizably his voice and words echoed back from the cylinder:

Mary had a little lamb,
Its fleece was white as snow.

Although his machine that talked gave Edison much publicity, he postponed any further work on it for almost a decade in order to devote himself to the problem of the electric light. The principle of the arc light had been discovered in England early in the century by Sir Humphrey Davy. With the arrival of the steam-driven generator, capable of supplying electricity in isolated areas, its brilliant illumination could by mid-century be used in lighthouses, and later it was adapted to even more practical ends by the American Charles F. Brush, who developed a system of arc lighting for streets.

Arc lights were far too glaring for indoor lighting; nor was it possible to dim them. A crude type of incandescent lamp was contrived in France as early as 1820, and its possibilities were explored elsewhere. Most early experimenters used thick carbon rods for the light-producing element. Edison, when he put his mind to the problem, conceived of a filament as the source of light. For this incandescent filament he tried many kinds of metals, from nickel and chromium to boron, molybdenum, and osmium. For a time he thought he had found the answer in platinum, but this metal proved to have too low a melting point. A thin thread of carbon, he concluded, was the solution, and he tried all sorts of carbonized substances: cedar shavings, fishline, flax, punk, tissue paper, twine, even hairs plucked from a friend's beard. Finally by chance he shredded a Japanese fan and discovered his best substance in its bamboo fiber. Carbonized bamboo remained the standard filament in electric lamps for nine years, until superseded first by a cellulose substance and finally by tungsten. In September, 1882, the first New York buildings were glowing with electric light, and from that bright moment, illuminating gas, which had seemed such a wonder two generations earlier, was doomed.

Edison is remembered most spectacularly in connection with the electric light. Yet even more essential than the light itself was his designing and developing of a generating and distributing system for electricity that would make the incandescent light practical.

Second only to Edison's as a household name in the roll of American inventors of the post-Civil War period is that of the Scottish immigrant Alexander Graham Bell. Born in Edinburgh in the same year as Edison, the son and grandson of speech teachers, he had gone to London as a young man to become himself a teacher of elocution. A meeting with Sir Charles Wheatstone, one of the European developers of the telegraph, first roused his interest in science. He also came in professional contact with Alexander Ellis, the president of the London Philological Society, and through him learned of recent German investigations into the nature of sound. London's dampness and fogs, however, brought him down with tuberculosis — his two brothers had died of it — and to re-

The circle-shaped pamphlet sampled here celebrates both the Pan-American Exposition of 1901 and an instrument that was billed as the "Acme of Perfection for Family Sewing" that (with a million sold each year) "Conquers all Competition."

cover his health he left for Canada. For a time he worked near Montreal transcribing the language of the Mohawk Indians into a phonetic alphabet called Visible Speech, invented by his father. Learning of his work, the Boston Board of Education asked him to come to Boston and introduce his system to a new school for deaf-mutes.

Unlike the rough-diamond Edison, Bell was a courtly man, gracious in speech and manner, tall, thin, rather shabby, with a drooping mustache. While he taught his deaf-mutes — and fell in love with a deaf girl, whom he later married — he experimented in his spare time in the basement of the house where he boarded. Two ambitions obsessed him: to build a musical telegraph over which as many messages could be sent as there were notes on a piano and to construct a "telephone" that would transmit vocal sounds over a wire.

Bell had given up all other work except for tutoring two pupils: George Sanders, the deaf-mute grandson of his landlord; and his future wife, Mabel Hubbard. Both the Hubbards and the Sanderses believed in him enough

VIEW OF COURT.—PAN-AM. EXP9

NIAGARA – AMERICAN SIDE.

to help him out financially and to pay nine dollars a week to his brilliant young assistant, Thomas A. Watson. The two experimenters rented a workshop in the attic of the shop of a manufacturer of telegraph instruments in Boston. Their most baffling problem in developing the telephone was to devise a transmitter, and Bell had even obtained the ear of a corpse from a friendly surgeon to aid his experiments. As so often happens, an accident put the men on the right path; on June 2, 1875, a wrong adjustment of their apparatus showed them the principle that was to lead to the telephone.

For nine more months the two men worked. Then one day—March 10, 1876—Watson over his receiver in one room heard Bell, who had just spilled acid on his trousers, say in the next room: "Mr. Watson, come here, I want you." Watson bounded through the door, shouting, "I can hear the *words!*"

Sometimes an invention simple to the point of triviality carries consequences so momentous that they alter the face of a country. Such was the invention of barbed wire in 1874 by an Illinois farmer, Joseph F. Glidden. "The advent of barbed wire," Walter Prescott Webb wrote in his study of the Great Plains, "brought about the disappearance of the open, free range and converted the range country into the big-pasture country." The larger ranchers, long troubled by chaotic conditions of land ownership and by problems of water rights, cattle rustling, and overcrowding of the ranges, banded together in self-protective cattlemen's associations. These associations, as well as many independent ranchers, now began to use barbed wire to fence off sections of the public domain that they considered theirs by right. In a few years thousands of miles of fence wire crisscrossed the Plains, restricting access to water and to roads, sometimes even surrounding whole townships. "Fence-cutter wars" ensued, with cattlemen against sheepmen, herders against farmers, and sometimes ranchers against other ranchers. When the associations tried to police their fences and post trespass signs, violence often ensued. "The Son of a Bitch who opens this fence had better look out for his scalp," a typical sign warned succinctly. The new fences blocked the free movement of cattle, and in the winters thousands of beasts died as they piled up against the wire barbs. Whether the cattlemen realized it or not, fencing marked the range's end.

Other agricultural inventions had preceded the Civil War: John Lane's and John Deere's steel plows, which would make the cultivation of the Great Plains possible; Cyrus McCormick's reaper; machines for planting, threshing, and haying. The war, with its Moloch-like consumption of young men, made a rapid introduction of laborsaving farm machinery essential. At the war's end old inventions were improved while new ones proliferated. A Scottish immigrant, James Oliver, spent a dozen years in developing a "chilled plow" with a body, or moldboard, of tough iron with a hardened surface and with a cutting edge of tempered steel that could be easily removed for sharpening. So superior were his chilled-iron-moldboard plows that it is estimated farmers could have saved themselves forty-five million dollars a year if all had switched to them from the ordinary iron or steel plows.

Cyrus McCormick continued to improve his reaping machine as well as to absorb the patented improvements of others whenever he could. The Gordon brothers of Rochester, New York, who had invented a wire grain-binder, sold their rights to McCormick. When it was found that bits of wire were getting into the feed and being swallowed by the cattle, John F. Appleby finally evolved a binder that used twine. Other inventions, bringing equally profound change to the processes and the condition of agriculture, followed: the corn cutter and shocker, corn binders, clover hullers, bean and pea threshers, manure spreaders, and the great harvester-thresher combines that made farming big business.

Equally revolutionary were some of the changes in the processing of foods. Charles A. Pillsbury in Minneapolis had developed a new process for milling spring wheat, and by 1883 had built the world's largest mill. In Chicago, Massachusetts-born Gustavus Swift conceived of shipping dressed meat under refrigeration and to do so built refrigerator cars at his own expense.

Many prewar inventions only came into general use later. The postwar country-wide acceptance of Isaac Singer's sewing machine owed as much to his extraordinary business ability as to the excellence of the machine. With "A machine in every home" as their slogan, his agents went into the small towns and rural areas. To bring his machine within reach of the poor, Singer depended to a large extent on installment selling. Alfred E. Beach's typewriter of 1847, further developed by a Wisconsin newspaperman, Christopher L. Sholes, and two printer friends, was taken over and built up into a commercial success by the firearms manufacturer Philo Remington. Postwar inventions included the Burroughs adding machine, the safety razor, the fountain pen, and the cash register. In the newspaper world Richard Hoe's prewar rotary press was followed by the web press and folding machinery, which made it possible to print twenty-four thousand twelve-page papers in an hour. This would scarcely have been possible, however, without Ottmar Mergenthaler's invention of the linotype machine, first used by Whitelaw Reid's New York *Tribune* in 1886.

Swift's refrigerator cars, for all their importance to food transport, were only a minor matter to the expanding and consolidating railroads. Like George M. Pullman's sleeping cars, they were ingeniously useful rather than essential. Pullman, as a young contractor jolting his way on night journeys across New York State in primitive bunk cars, had conceived of a car in which one could sleep as comfortably as in a hotel. In 1858 he experimented with ordinary cars divided into ten sleeping sections, each with an upper berth that folded out of the way in the daytime—his own invention—and two washrooms; but not until 1864 did he build his first real Pullman car, the *Pioneer*, at the then astronomical cost of twenty thousand dollars. Acceptance was rapid, for in 1865 the government hired the *Pioneer* to carry Lincoln's body from Chicago to Springfield and the success of the Pullman Palace Car Company was assured. By 1867 Pullman had built and was operating forty-seven

cars staffed by the Negro porters and crews that would become the Pullman trademark.

All-steel cars, replacing the wooden ones, had made the railroads much safer in case of accident. But accidents themselves often could not be averted because of the inadequacy of the hand-braking system. Young George Westinghouse, just out of the Union navy, and with a mechanical bent, had witnessed two locomotives in a head-on collision and ever since had been obsessed by the thought of how all the brakes on a train might be applied simultaneously. His idea of a brake operated by air came to him as he was reading about a compressed-air rock drill used for tunneling in the Alps. With only this to go by, he devised the air brake named after him, which he patented when he was only twenty-three years old. The first unscheduled demonstration on a train of the Panhandle Railroad west of Pittsburgh was impres-

A hotel car was equipped with folding overhead berths, tables that were put away when not in use, and a kitchen. The food on trains was often excellent: an 1872 menu of the line advertised here included buffalo, antelope, elk, and grouse.

sively convincing. A heavy wagon had stuck on a crossing before the oncoming test train. Attempting to whip up his horses, the driver was thrown onto the track. The engineer pulled the new brake valve, and the train ground to a stop with a jolt that sent Westinghouse and the railroad officials sprawling from their seats. On tumbling out of their carriage, they found that the engine had stopped within four feet of the driver and his wagon. Before Westinghouse's invention it took a train traveling twenty miles an hour 794 feet to stop. With the new air brakes it took a mere 166 feet.

From their short-line beginnings in the East before the Civil War, the small railroads were absorbed by bits and pieces into the trunk lines—the New York Central, the Pennsylvania, the Erie, the Baltimore and Ohio. After the war the railroads East and West became America's most important industry, the backbone of commercial expansion. They were vital to the growth of the iron and steel industries; they made possible the rapid settlement of the wheat and cattle countries; they opened the West to farmers and immigrants; financing their construction absorbed domestic savings and (thanks to high interest on their bonds) brought in a steady flow of foreign capital. Nurtured on public lands, new railroad empires sprang up in the West, as ruthless as they were essential. By 1890 all American cities were linked by rail.

The oldest and in many ways the most flamboyant of the railroad empire builders was the self-appointed "Commodore" Cornelius Vanderbilt. Born late in the previous century, son of a poor Dutch farmer, he grew up on the water, first as a Staten Island ferry boy, then in his young manhood as a master of river and coastal vessels. From a master he became a shipowner, a piratical competitor, grasping early the still-unfamiliar profit principle of a greater volume of traffic at a lower rate. His big chance and fortune came to him with the California Gold Rush when, competing against the Collins Line, he sent his passengers by ship to Nicaragua and then by stagecoach across that country, working his men and himself fourteen to sixteen hours a day in spite of plague, heat, and sporadic revolutions. By the end of the 1850's he had more than a hundred ships earning him well over a million dollars annually. With the passing years he became a bald-headed, lecherous, miserly, profane old man who wore a fur coat and a high silk hat winter and summer. Never was he able to speak or spell correctly, although he was long remembered for his one aphorism: "What do I care about the law? Hain't I got the power?" He had it and used it ruthlessly.

The Commodore was four years short of seventy when in 1860 he became interested in acquiring railroads. First he bought up the New York and Harlem Railroad, running from Forty-second Street to Brewster, New York, paying nine dollars a share for stock that soon climbed to fifty dollars. When "Uncle" Daniel Drew, the great short seller, connived with members of the legislature to drive the price of the Harlem down, Vanderbilt manipulated it to $179 a share and forced Drew and his legislators to the wall. The Commodore then acquired the Hudson River Railroad, and this time Drew, in his thirst for revenge, almost succeeded in ruining Vanderbilt. But the Commodore, in what was admittedly "the darkest hour" of his life, held firm and at last, in his own words, "busted the whole legislature." He now expanded his empire rapidly, picking up broken-down companies "for a song," absorbing the New York Central, which he had earlier helped put together from nine short lines. In 1869 he secured passage of a bill allowing him to consolidate his holdings into the New York Central system. Recapitalizing the new corporation at almost twice its previous value, he demonstrated that though the stock might be watered, his touch was golden. With the new capital he double-tracked his lines, substituted steel rails for iron, built modern bridges, and finally built New York City's Grand Central Depot.

The Commodore met his match, however, in the combination of Drew, Jay Gould, and Jim Fisk when he attempted to take over the Erie Railroad. That line of misfortune, started in 1832, ran 460 miles from the Hudson to Lake Erie. In 1859, when it went bankrupt, Uncle Daniel took over. As soon as Vanderbilt attempted to buy up Erie stock, Drew, with Gould and Fisk, issued ten million dollars' worth of new stock, and when threatened by court action, fled with bundles of greenbacks across the Hudson to Jersey City. Waiting until the legislature was in session, Gould arrived at Albany with a trunkful of currency, and after discreetly passing out half a million dollars' worth of greenbacks and promising another half million, succeeded in having a bill passed authorizing the stock issue and forbidding interlocking directorates among Vanderbilt's railroads and the Erie. The Erie war finally ended in a negotiated peace that left Gould and Fisk as managers of the railroad with Uncle Daniel in the background. Once in control, Gould and Fisk started up the printing presses again, expanded the Erie stock by sixty-five million dollars, sold it short, and finally manipulated financial panics, in which hundreds of businessmen were ruined but in which the manipulators were able to buy up Erie and other stock at enormous profits. The Erie never recovered. Although it was able to advertise "1,400 miles under one management" and provided an unbroken connection between New York and St. Louis, Gould left it in 1872 with worn-out equipment and weighed down with debts. Three years later it went bankrupt (as it would once more in 1893) and the sanctimonious Gould made another killing by selling the stock short.

In 1828 Charles Carroll of Carrollton, last surviving signer of the Declaration of Independence, had turned the first shovelful of earth for the Baltimore and Ohio Railroad, saying that he considered it the second most important act of his life. From its horse-drawn beginnings, the line had extended slowly westward, finally reaching St. Louis in 1857. "Look at the great enterprises," Mayor Thomas Swann of Baltimore then proclaimed with windy pride, "the New York and Erie, the Central Pennsylvania, and the Baltimore and Ohio Railroads. What country on the face of the earth can boast of such enterprises?" The fourth trunk line from east to west, the Pennsylvania, had originated as a response to the twin threats to Philadelphia of the Baltimore and Ohio Railroad and the Erie Canal. Begun in 1846, its lines reached Pittsburgh from Philadelphia in 1858. Unlike the other railroads, headed by looters like Drew and manipulators like Vanderbilt, the Pennsylvania had at its head J. Edgar Thomson, a man of advanced managerial notions whose interest and pride lay primarily in developing the Pennsylvania and extending it into the growing West. By 1869 his railroad had a thousand miles of track in Pennsylvania and controlled lines to Lake Erie. The next year Thomson acquired the Pittsburgh, Fort Wayne and Chicago line, giving the Pennsylvania a continuous system from Philadelphia to Lake Michigan. While Vanderbilt was reaching out through Ohio, Indiana, and Illinois, while Gould pushed the Erie westward, Thomson absorbed the Cleveland and Pittsburgh plus various small lines in Ohio and finally the large "Panhandle line" extending from Pittsburgh to St. Louis. Besides its direct line to St. Louis, the Pennsylvania maintained two other lines as well—to Chicago and Cincinnati.

There were in 1850 not quite nine thousand miles of railroad track in the United States. Just before the Civil War the figure had tripled. By 1870 there were 52,922

miles, extending over the country like metal filaments. The most spectacular advance, of course, was the spanning of the continent, the extension of the rails across the Central and Western deserts, mountains, and rivers.

As early as 1849 Missouri's Senator Thomas Hart Benton had introduced a bill in the Senate calling for the construction of a rail line from St. Louis to San Francisco. Talk of a transcontinental railroad achieved official recognition in 1853 when government engineers made surveys for suitable routes. Then in 1862 Congress passed the Pacific Railway Act, by which the Union Pacific Railroad was chartered to build a line from Omaha in Nebraska Territory to the eastern boundary of California. At the same time California's Central Pacific Railroad was authorized to build from Sacramento eastward until it linked up with the advancing tracks of the Union Pacific. Since so massive an undertaking was beyond the power and resources of the two companies, outside assistance was essential. The government agreed to give the railroads free rights of way plus whatever wood, earth, and stone they needed from the public lands. For every mile of track laid down, the railroads would receive ten alternate sections (each a mile square) on each side of the right of way, and the government would also lend them sixteen thousand dollars for every mile completed in the plains, double that for each mile completed in the foothills, and forty-eight thousand dollars for each mountain mile.

At Sacramento on a rainy morning of January, 1863, the aggressive Governor Leland Stanford, to the accompaniment of brass bands and gunfire, thrust a spade into the damp earth to break ground for the Central Pacific Railroad. Besides being governor of California, Stanford was one of the four Pacific Associates who controlled the railroad, the others being Charles Crocker, a minor politician vast in bulk and, like Stanford, a San Francisco dry-goods merchant, and two Sacramento hardware dealers, Collis P. Huntington and Mark Hopkins. All four were adventurous, willing to chance such a hazardous enterprise as an eight-hundred-mile railroad (longer than any yet attempted) across impossible terrain, and willing to use any means to achieve their end—bribery of politicians, intimidation, trickery, financial hocuspocus, and human exploitation. Their less-publicized equivalent of Oakes Ames's Crédit Mobilier was the Credit and Finance Corporation. Ames and his brother Oliver with Thomas C. Durant formed the triumvirate controlling the Union Pacific, and ground for their rail-

The transcontinental rails had recently been joined when this photograph was taken at Devil's Gate Bridge east of Promontory Summit. Aboard was Senator James Patterson, later to become a casualty of the Crédit Mobilier scandal.

road was broken in December, 1863, at Omaha.

The difficulties both groups found in raising money slowed construction. By mid-1866 only three hundred miles of Union Pacific track had been spiked down and all of the hazardous mountain track-laying still lay ahead. But by the next year the tempo was increasing, and as it increased, it drew the attention of the country as if to some gigantic and extended horse race. Crocker had formed his own construction company within the

Central Pacific and pressed on. When his Irish laborers quit to go to the Nevada mining fields, he brought in Chinese at half the white rate of pay. Scouring California, recruiting overseas, he eventually had more than ten thousand pig-tailed coolies working for him, to the dismay of nativists, who would remain voluble against "the yellow peril." Outnumbering the whites 3 or 4 to 1, the coolies took on the heaviest and most grinding jobs of hauling and grading. A New York *Tribune* reporter on a Central Pacific excursion saw swarms of them working in the Sierra Nevadas "shovelling, wheeling, carting, drilling and blasting rocks and earth, while their dull moony eyes stared out from under immense bucket hats, like umbrellas."

Once each railroad had completed its allotted section,

143

it was allowed to continue laying tracks beyond that point toward its rival and to claim the additional bounty. Competition for the triple-subsidy mountain construction grew sharp. Five hundred miles of the Central Pacific route had an elevation of over 5,000 feet, while two hundred miles were over 6,500 feet. Tunnels had to be blasted out. Through the winter of 1867 the coolie crews toiled, cutting through drifts sometimes sixty feet deep in the Sierra Nevadas. Accidents were inevitable. At least four times entire camps of buildings and men were hurled into canyons by avalanches and buried until spring. The company was forced to build thirty-seven miles of snow sheds. But the huge project grew systematized, and the work became a routine, a rhythm. After the roadbed had been scraped and leveled, one gang distributed the ties, another the rails. A team of eight men laid each rail in place. Gangs of drivers and bolters followed. Ten spikes held each rail, three sledge-hammer strokes drove each spike, four hundred rails were laid to the mile.

As the gap narrowed, both forces stepped up their rate to two miles a day, five miles, seven miles, and finally in one stupendous effort the Central Pacific won a ten-thousand-dollar wager by laying ten miles and two hundred feet of track between sunrise and sunset with an hour's halt for lunch. The Union Pacific crews were made up mostly of Irish immigrants and war veterans, and to their other hazards was added that of marauding Indians, who accounted for several hundred railroad workers before the two lines finally met at barren Promontory Summit, about forty miles northwest of Ogden, Utah. From that point, 1,085 miles of Union Pacific main-line track stretched east to Omaha, while 690 miles of Central Pacific track reached back west to Sacramento. May 8, 1869, was set for the official rail-linking of the continent, but the event was postponed until May 10 because heavy rains damaged some bridges.

In preparation for the day the companies had brought their respective tracks to within one rail-length of each other, and the materials for this last section were stacked in readiness. The Western Union Company had prepared a nationwide telegraph hookup to announce from Promontory Summit that the last spike had been driven in. Leland Stanford, Thomas Durant, and a crowd of notables and officials were present in top-hatted formality. At noon a coolie gang on one side and Irishmen on the other put the last two rails in place. All work was completed except for spiking the rail to the last tie, of polished laurel with six predrilled holes, and the Central Pacific's wood-burning locomotive *Jupiter* and the Union Pacific's coal-burning *No. 119* puffed to within yards of each other. A succession of dignitaries hammered home five ceremonial spikes from several Western states. Then the last golden spike was placed in the laurel tie. Stanford swung at it with a silver sledge hammer and missed. Then Durant swung and also missed. Finally someone—history is unclear on the point—drove down the spike, and the rails were linked at last as the two engines touched noses.

Other lines followed in the pattern of expansion. James J. Hill, the stocky, one-eyed storekeeper of St. Paul, Minnesota, built up his Great Northern Railway empire in the Northwest with extraordinary care and caution. By 1883 four different transcontinental routes were in operation and a fifth was under construction, and branch lines proliferated.

In addition to their massive support from the federal government, the railroads borrowed from state and city governments. Increasing numbers of foreigners turned to American railroad bonds for investment. By 1890 about one-third of all American railroad stocks and bonds was held abroad. In the scramble of railroad construction, overexpansion was inevitable and did much to contribute to the depression of the seventies. The building up of the great railroad empires was a haphazard, brutal, and often corrupt process. Empire builders of the stripe of Huntington and Cooke and Vanderbilt did not hesitate to break their rivals or to bribe public officials to obtain charters or grants. Promoters, speculators, and politicians were on hand to take their slice of the railroad melon. In the struggles for freight traffic, large shippers received rate cuts and rebates, to the angry and impotent dismay of farmers and small proprietors.

To subsequent generations many of the postwar entrepreneurs have appeared grasping and repellent figures, labeled with some glibness and a certain justice the robber barons. Indeed, a Platonic philosopher-ruler would have constructed the American railroad network more tidily, more honestly, and more cheaply, though probably more slowly. Yet the United States after the Civil War bore scant resemblance to Plato's ideal republic. No federal government under any conceivable circumstances would have undertaken the necessary railroad construction or other industrial expansion on its own. The robber barons were not always attractive, but they served a purpose.

American Agriculturist

MAY 1885
VOL. XLIV.

ESTABLISHED
1842
For Farm
Garden
and
Household

751 BROADWAY New York
$1.50 A YEAR · SINGLE NUMBER 15 CENTS ·
GERMAN EDITION SAME AS ENGLISH.

KNOWLEDGE

In Rural America

The industrial revolution of the nineteenth century could just as well be called the agricultural revolution. In the fifty years after the Civil War the power of steam and then of gasoline opened vast new territories to the production of crops and sharply reduced the man-hours it took to raise a bushel of corn or wheat, for example, and get it to market. In rural communities there was more leisure time; the railroads and, latterly, the Model T, made communication and travel easier; people could buy by mail instead of making the goods themselves or trading at the local store. Yet farming remained tied to the soil and the seasons; and farm communities retained much of their old individualism, isolation, order, and quiet. As a matter of fact, in those respects rural life was becoming something of an anachronism as the cities grew in importance. Still, urbanites often felt they were missing something—the oneness with their earth, the reassurance in nature's cycles. And like many in his generation and in the one to follow, journalist Ray Stannard Baker cemented his ancestral tie to the land by writing about it. Baker went even further: he farmed some.

It was the personal relationship between man and soil, as in the advertisement above, that drew and held many Americans to the farm.

It is astonishing how many people there are in cities and towns who have a secret longing to get back into quiet country places, to own a bit of the soil of the earth, and to cultivate it. To some it appears as a troublesome malady only in spring, and will be relieved by a whirl or two in country roads, by a glimpse of the hills, or a day by the sea; but to others the homesickness is deeper seated and will be quieted by no hasty visits. These must actually go home. . . .

If one has drained his land, and plowed it, and fertilized it, and planted it and harvested it—even though it be only a few acres—how he comes to know and to love every rod of it. He knows the wet spots, and the stony spots, and the warmest and most fertile spots, until his acres have all the qualities of a personality, whose every characteristic he knows. . . .

One who thus takes part in the whole process of the year comes soon to have an indescribable affection for his land, his garden, his animals. There are thoughts of his in every tree, memories in every fence corner. Just now, the fourth of June, I walked down past my blackberry patch, now come gorgeously into full white bloom, and heavy with fragrance. I set out these plants with my own hands. I have fed them, cultivated them, mulched them, pruned them, staked them, and helped every year to pick the berries. How could they be otherwise than full of associations. They bear a fruit more beautiful than can be found in any catalogue, and stranger and wilder than in any learned botany book.

Ray Stannard Baker (pseud. David Grayson)
"This Wonderful, Beautiful and Incalculably Interesting Earth!"
The American Magazine, November, 1917

Country life seemed poetic. But what made it so? In the two selections that follow, Mary Dean first tackles the question and then seems to provide an unstated answer: there was time and space enough to enjoy very basic things.

The boy cannot conceive what poetry there is about oxen. From the moment a calf hides in the hay with its mother's help, and makes believe there is no calf born yet, until it becomes an ox, it cannot for an instant be considered poetic by a boy. The calf is a creature that insists, whenever it drinks, on thrusting its head to the bottom of the pail with a splash that deluges the boy with milk: it drinks until it is out of breath, and then withdraws its head with another splash and an explosion of milk-steam from its nostrils—performances which cause the boy's friends to remark wherever he goes, "You smell of sour milk." The boy likes well enough to feed the oxen their full measures of meal; he likes to see them get down on their knees to lick up morsels that roll into corners of the stable-floor; he stretches his hand in before them for little balls of meal they cannot reach with their long tongues, at which they draw back with a thwack against the stanchion, breathing hard and gazing at him with their large black eyes; and when the off ox [in yoke, the right-hand ox] tries to capture the nigh ox's portion, the boy raps him back to his place. Quite a pastoral friendship exists between the boy and the nigh ox, which, being continually bullied by the off ox, needs the boy's protection, and is therefore placed next him at work. But, for all that, he does not see the romance of such matters.

The yoking of oxen is decidedly not matter for a flying smile to a boy. He lays one end of the yoke's beam on the ground, lifts the other end with his hand, and, waving one of the ox-bows in his left, cries to the nigh ox, "Come under!" The "nigh" slowly obeys, bending its head low to accommodate the boy's stature, and permitting itself to be fastened by the ox-bow to the yoke. The boy now lifts the free end of the yoke's beam as high as he can and calls the off ox to come under. It also obeys, treading deliberately with its heavy feet, and waiting patiently for the boy's small fingers to fasten the weighty bow with a clumsy bow-key. Then the boy lifts the ponderous cart-neap and attaches it to the ring in the yoke—a labor that causes his heart to "beat like a tabor;" and thus the beasts are wedded to their daily toil. Occasionally, however, the ox will not come under at all, but will require the boy to follow it about the barnyard, dragging the jingling yoke and waving the bow with infinite fatigue; and occasionally the boy makes the mistake (no greater could be made) of yoking the off ox first. The off ox, finding a yoke sans yokefellow dangling at its neck, is much amazed, not being "broke" to that, and takes to whirling round and round and galloping up and down the barnyard in a manner suggestive of nightmare. This is a circumstance that makes a boy hopeful of going somewhere else.

Mary Dean
"The Boy on a Hill-Farm"
Lippincott's Magazine, September, 1878

Whether in New York or, as here, on the Kansas prairie, oxen were used in much of the heavy hauling.

Two o'clock by the kitchen-clock. At four it will be dark. The dim red sunset of fine days can hardly shine through the December windows, and now a storm is blowing and it is intensely cold. The tavern stands knee-deep in snow. Snow is piled high on window-ledges and sashes, and the rooms are muffled in a peculiar hush caused by the woolly frost on the panes, which thickened to bold *alto rilievos* when the kettles were boiling for dinner; you have to scratch a hole half an inch deep in order to see out. Nevertheless, "flowers of all heavens" grow in the landlady's windows. A large, dark, able woman, she sews beside her flowers, half remembering the brief dream of summer . . . half hoping for the first heavenly day of spring when the wind, blowing hundreds of miles from sea to the New York hills, will begin to melt the snow under its icy crust. The remark common to women, "I can't have anything as I want it," is not one of hers. She has made a sitting-room of her ample old kitchen, has fitted it up with a rag-carpet, a cherry bureau inlaid with birch, and a stand having gorgeous brass handles and a pair of green-glass candlesticks, and has moved her kitchen, according to a fashion dear to country wives, back to a little pantry-surrounded room in the rear. From her chair she can hear Ann Smallhoof in the kitchen singing with the voice of a wild bird,—screech-owl, for instance,—

> I wants none of your rings nor money,
>   Fal de rang,
>   De rang edang eday;
> I'm for the man that calls me honey,
>   Fal de rang,
>   De rang edang eday.

And she can look across the yellow-painted dining-room to a door of the bar-room, which opens occasionally with the announcement, "Two travellers for dinner!" Whenever this happens, the little pot standing full of peeled potatoes in cold water in the kitchen is clapped on the fire, and twenty minutes later those potatoes, mashed, enter the dining-room in the company of ham and eggs and hot coffee. There are long, level roads about Wet Fells and the Malleable Iron-Works where the railroads have killed the taverns, but among the hills a great deal of riding and driving still goes on, and this tavern, on a plateau of the valley, with woody sweeps rising far above it, and below it a cedar-scented stream running in woody beds, lacks no company. Many a traveller breasts the storm miles and miles for the sake of the landlady's cookery.

Mary Dean
"A Country Tavern in Winter"
Lippincott's Magazine, February, 1881

A *path is dug and bread crumbs are scattered to the birds in the 1871 engraving by Winslow Homer* A Winter-Morning,—Shovelling Out.

*A*nne Sneller spent her girlhood in the 1880's and '90's in upstate New York. *Of the schoolhouse paraphernalia she mentions in the following excerpt, a form of the slate is still in use, enlarged from tablet to blackboard size. But the slate pencil is gone, and unlamented. It was made of soft slate or soapstone.*

Every child had a slate, large or small. [The slates] had inch-wide wood frames that made a loud noise when they were slammed down on top of one another in the rush of an arithmetic match. When the wood frames began to be bound with strips of red wool they looked less drab and made less noise. But slates had to be companioned by slate pencils, and of all the sounds to rasp a teacher's nerves, a squeaking slate pencil was the most trying. Any slate pencil could be made to squeak if you held it just right and it was one of your bad days. The law requiring a flag flying over every school building did not exist in our earlier schooldays. The nearest thing to it was the paper picture of the Stars and Stripes pasted around the top of our slate pencils.

A pencil was not enough for a slate. It demanded the constant use of a slate rag.

On almost every child's desk stood an old bottle filled with water and with a folded paper wedged in its neck in place of a cork. Water could be poured on the slate rag and all the mistakes and sorrows of misspelled words and wrong answers to arithmetic examples could be wiped out. Slate rags were repulsive to sight, smell, and touch. The alternative—only employed by a child who had not been taught better—was to spit plentifully on the slate and rub it off on a sleeve already dirty. Pencil and paper were thought too expensive except for some special purpose. A penny would buy a pencil that had a tiny rubber eraser in the end, and five cents bought a tablet of ruled white paper. To make the tablet last longer, we used any scraps of wrapping paper we could find at home. But the slate remained the backbone of our school equipment. On it we worked our arithmetic examples, drew our maps for the geography class, and constructed diagrams for sentences in the grammar lesson. Some of the pleasures of the slate were not for the teacher's inspection. Such were the houses that covered both sides with an upstairs and a down or a floor plan for playing tic-tac-toe. . . .

Anne Gertrude Sneller
A Vanished World, 1964

The plain and virtuous life of the Tennessee parson and his family implicitly promised the city man that if the pace of urban America became too fast, there would always be this to return to.

On our way up the mountain we had passed "the church." It was a rude structure of boards and logs, which we should have mistaken for some deserted shanty, had not our friend of the "moonshine" whiskey pointed it out.

The parson's cabin stood in an enclosure, guarded by a rough fence, and, as we approached, a stalwart young fellow opened the little gate, and some hounds followed him out, making the woods ring with their yelping. A tall matron and two of "the girls"—young women, at least five and a-half feet high, dressed in straight, homespun gowns—peered out at us, and we were presently invited to remain at the cabin all night, as "the parson never refuses nobody."

The pigs and the geese had just come home together from their day's ramble in the woods, and were quarreling over the trough which ran along the fence. The cows wandered about the clearing, watched by the hounds; and the "boys" busied themselves in hewing logs of wood into sticks for the fire. Behind the cabin rose a rib of the mountain, on which was a corn-field, and near this ran a brook.

The whole cabin did not seem large enough to house a family of four; yet Parson Caton's stalwart brood of ten children lived there happily with himself and wife, and found the shelter ample. There were but two rooms on the lower floor, each lighted by the doors only; above was a loft, in which were laid truckle-beds. Supper was speedily cooking on the coals in the fire-place; the scent of bacon was omnipresent. In the smaller of the two rooms there were four large beds, covered with gay quilts, and shoved closely together. Around the room hung collections of herbs and several rifles; for furniture there were a few rude chairs, and a small table, on which were some antiquated books.

One school recess game was snap-the-whip, here drawn by Homer; boys on the whip end, left, tried to keep from being snapped loose.

149

As we returned from a wash at the brook the parson came home, and was greeted with a cheery welcome from the hounds. Every inch of his face was filled with rugged lines, which told of strong character. He stood leaning on his staff and looking us over intently for some moments before he said, "Good evening, men." Then he greeted us heartily, and our invalid wagon was forthwith dispatched to the rustic forge near the cabin for repairs. . . .

This old man, in his mountain home, was as simple and courteous in his demeanor as any citizen. After the frugal supper was over, he asked us many questions of the outer world, which he had never visited; New York and Louisville seemed to him like dreams. By and by the family came crowding in to evening prayers. It was quite dark, and the forest around us was still.

The parson took down a well-worn Bible, and opening it at the Psalms, read, in a loud voice, and with occasional quaint expoundings, one or two selections; after which, taking up a hymn-book, he read a hymn, and the family sang line by line as he gave them out. They sung in quavering, high-pitched voices, to the same tunes which were heard in the Tennessee mountains when Nolichucky was an infant settlement, and the banks of the French Broad were crimsoned with the blood of white settlers, shed by the Indians.

The echoes of the hymn died away into the depths of the forest, and were succeeded by a prayer of earnestness and fervor, marked here and there by strong phrases of dialect, but one which made our little company bow their heads, for the parson prayed for us and for our journey, and brought the prayer home to us. Another hymn was lined, during which the hounds now and then joined in with their musical howls, and at last the family withdrew, leaving us in the spare-room. Presently, however, the parson reappeared, and announced that he and his wife would share the room with us, which they did; and we were wakened to the six o'clock breakfast by the good woman, who joined with her husband in reproving us for continuing our journey on the Sabbath day.

Edward King
The Great South, 1875

Unsophisticated, possibly, in an urban sense, the capable farmer or farm worker nonetheless had a highly refined canon of behavior and sense of his own worth. Robert Frost wrote about it in "The Code," part of which appears here.

"The hand that knows his business won't be told
To do work better or faster—those two things. . . .
Tell you a story of what happened once:
I was up here in Salem at a man's
Named Sanders with a gang of four or five
Doing the haying. No one liked the boss.
He was one of the kind sports call a spider,
All wiry arms and legs that spread out wavy
From a humped body nigh as big's a biscuit.
But work! that man could work, especially
If by so doing he could get more work

150

Out of his hired help. I'm not denying
He was hard on himself. I couldn't find
That he kept any hours — not for himself.
Daylight and lantern-light were one to him:
I've heard him pounding in the barn all night.
But what he liked was someone to encourage.
Them that he couldn't lead he'd get behind
And drive, the way you can, you know, in mowing —
Keep at their heels and threaten to mow their legs off.
I'd seen about enough of his bulling tricks
(We call that bulling). I'd been watching him.
So when he paired off with me in the hayfield
To load the load, thinks I, Look out for trouble.
I built the load and topped it off; old Sanders
Combed it down with a rake and says, 'O.K.'
Everything went well till we reached the barn
With a big catch to empty in a bay.
You understand that meant the easy job
For the man up on top of throwing *down*
The hay and rolling it off wholesale,
Where on a mow it would have been slow lifting.
You wouldn't think a fellow'd need much urging
Under these circumstances, would you now?
But the old fool seizes his fork in both hands,
And looking up bewhiskered out of the pit,
Shouts like an army captain, 'Let her come!'
Thinks I, D'ye mean it? 'What was that you said?'
I asked out loud, so's there'd be no mistake,
'Did you say, Let her come?' 'Yes, let her come.'
He said it over, but he said it softer.
Never you say a thing like that to a man,
Not if he values what he is. God, I'd as soon
Murdered him as left out his middle name.
I'd built the load and knew right where to find it.
Two or three forkfuls I picked lightly round for
Like meditating, and then I just dug in
And dumped the rackful on him in ten lots.
I looked over the side once in the dust
And caught sight of him treading-water-like,
Keeping his head above. 'Damn ye,' I says,
'That gets ye!' He squeaked like a squeezed rat.
That was the last I saw or heard of him.
I cleaned the rack and drove out to cool off.
As I sat mopping hayseed from my neck,
And sort of waiting to be asked about it,
One of the boys sings out, 'Where's the old man?'
'I left him in the barn under the hay.
If ye want him, ye can go and dig him out.'

An 1874 wash drawing of Montana farmers carting home the hay was done by illustrator William Cary.

They realized from the way I swobbed my neck
More than was needed something must be up.
They headed for the barn; I stayed where I was.
They told me afterward. First they forked hay,
A lot of it, out into the barn floor.
Nothing! They listened for him. Not a rustle.
I guess they thought I'd spiked him in the temple
Before I buried him, or I couldn't have managed.
They excavated more. 'Go keep his wife
Out of the barn.' Someone looked in a window,
And curse me if he wasn't in the kitchen
Slumped way down in a chair, with both his feet
Stuck in the oven, the hottest day that summer.
He looked so clean disgusted from behind
There was no one that dared to stir him up,
Or let him know that he was being looked at.
Apparently I hadn't buried him
(I may have knocked him down); but my just trying
To bury him had hurt his dignity.
He had gone to the house so's not to meet me.
He kept away from us all afternoon.
We tended to his hay. We saw him out
After a while picking peas in his garden:
He couldn't keep away from doing something."

Robert Frost
"The Code"
North of Boston, 1914

Because of the fabled Indian ability to cure ills with wild plants, a red man's image was often used in patent medicine advertisements.

*I*nformation about scientific advances was often slow to reach beyond the cities. Some thirty years after Queen Victoria first used an anesthetic in childbirth, such a practice was literally unknown in Onondaga County, New York, where Anne Sneller was born in 1883.

Doctor Blynn, who attended mother, was both a general practitioner and a surgeon who had made a fine record in the Civil War. He had used chloroform when he could get it in performing the countless amputations on wounded soldiers, and he regarded it as suitable and desirable for lessening pain. He suggested to mother that she permit him to try chloroform if things got bad. The proposal was startling. No such thing as a woman's escaping the pangs of childbirth had ever been heard of in the village. Chloroform was dangerous. Who knew what it might do? But mother was no fonder of pain than most women and she was, besides, courageous and open to new ideas. She agreed at once, and I suppose father must have agreed too. The objections came from Aunt Sophy. She was to stay with mother, and the thought that her dear sister might be lost under the influence of a medicine no doctor had ever prescribed before for such a purpose frightened her into protests and prophecies.

"Sarah," she wept, "if you let the doctor do this you will die, or if you don't die, the baby will be an idiot!"

In spite of Aunt Sophy's implorings, mother decided to take the risk. Dr. Blynn's method was simple. He called for a clean white cloth, which Aunt Sophy tearfully produced. By mother's account, he sprinkled chloroform on the cloth and laid it over her face, and the idiot baby was on its way. The only thing that turned out wrong was that father had set his heart on having a boy.

Anne Gertrude Sneller
A Vanished World, 1964

*S*ocial life and entertainment were furnished by such community enterprises *as harvests, barn-raisings, and Grange functions. And "Uncle Tom" companies, minstrel shows, circuses, and vaudeville troupes visited the towns.*

All the Uncle Tom shows and some of the vaudeville shows had parades, and often they enlisted local talent to make the parades look good. I recall the savage envy with which I saw a young acquaintance of mine named Lyle Burnham riding a horse in an Uncle Tom parade, down past the J. K. Linton store and as far as the school house and the Pool Bridge. Lyle looked as though he might fall off the horse at any moment, and I earnestly hoped he would, but he was wearing a bright red coat with gilt epaulettes and a soldier hat; and for this he was about to get a free ticket to the show.

I don't know how many Uncle Tom shows we saw in the course of our life in Williamstown. It could not have been more than three or four. But my father always said we certainly wouldn't want to see an Uncle Tom show again, because we had already seen it, and had read the book, and knew all about it, and he wouldn't have any boy of his carrying water to an elephant or a horse or even to Little Eva herself. Then, when we had given up hope, he would fish in his pocket and come up with whatever it cost to go. He did the same thing with firecrackers on the Fourth of July. . . .

A few traveling vaudeville shows came through, too. . . . Before I left Williamstown these shows usually carried a few reels of film and a motion picture projector. We thought this was wonderful and in many ways better than the magic lanterns we had at home.

What I chiefly recall of the vaudeville shows are the girls or women who kicked up their heels and danced and sang. There was one who had red ruffles under her dress, practically all the way down to her knees but no further, and I wondered if I ought to look at them.

The rest of the family, including my parents, my brother, and, I have no doubt, my sister, thought it foolish of me to waste ten hard-bitten cents on such an exhibition. My mother was willing enough to take me to an instrumental concert, or to a lecture which might be entitled "Hitch Your Wagon to a Star"; she wanted me to grow up to be a thoughtful and cultivated man; but she apparently didn't see how a girl kicking up her heels on the stage of the Town Hall could be of the least use to me.

But neither my mother nor my father told me not to go. This I gratefully re-

Vaudeville ladies like this singing soubrette could make small boys uneasy; R. L. Duffus talks about it in the excerpt at right.

153

member. It was my ten cents, not theirs. If I spent it the way I wanted to, I couldn't spend it for candy or a baseball or a bat.

Afterward, and it was very late, almost ten, perhaps, I ran all the way home, pelting over the Pool Bridge with the suspicion that something might be lying in wait for me there to punish me for my small sin; but it wasn't.

R. L. Duffus
Williamstown Branch, 1958

*P*olitical campaigns also served to bring rural people together. One E. V. S. — probably correspondent Eugene Virgil Smalley — reported in the New York Daily Tribune *on a huge political gathering in Cambridge City, Indiana, in 1876.*

A hasty dinner is eaten and we set out for the place of meeting, which of course is out-of-doors. The marshals dashing about on fine horses, with much display of gay-colored sashes, rosettes and saddle-cloths, get the procession in shape. As we leave the mile-long street at the top of a hill and turn into the fields we get a view of the line — a river of bright lines moving through the darker margin of lookers-on that line the way. What a striking spectacle it is! And what masses of people — men, women, and children! Where could they all have come from, for the village could not have contributed a hundredth part of them? They have come by rail from the towns, big and little, for twenty miles around, and in wagons, on horseback and on foot from all the neighboring country. Even more striking is the scene when the tide of humanity has spread itself over the great green field around the little beech grove where the seats and the platform are. The escort clubs in their many-colored uniforms move to and fro, or break ranks with volleys of cheers; the ponderous wagons unload their joyous freight; family parties in holiday attire picnic upon the grass; new delegations are constantly arriving with music and banners; there are troops of romping children, knots of rosy-cheeked girls walking with interlocked arms, young couples making love and eating luncheon at the same time; booths where rustics feast on lemonade and gingerbread. The earnestness of politics is tempered with much merry-making, and the air is vocal with laughter, cheers, and songs. What a scene for a painter! How characteristically American and how rich in elements of the picturesque!

A *husking bee, such as the one in the barn above, was often held in conjunction with a barn dance (below). Both institutions played important parts in rural courting.*

Only a small part of the throng can get within range of the orator's voice, but the rest seem none the less happy, for it is the holiday diversion, the crowds, the bravery of the procession, the music, and the fun of the occasion they came chiefly to enjoy. As many people as can possibly hear pack in upon the seats rising amphitheater-like against a sloping hill, or make a thick fringe around their margin. It is an attentive audience, quick to applaud a good point, and relishing keenly a funny story or witty remark. Nearly half the listeners are ladies. . . .

In the evening the citizens, such as are not Democrats, light up their houses and hang out Chinese lanterns, and the uniformed clubs parade the streets with torches. There is more speaking, this time from a rude platform at a street corner, and wherever one goes about the place there is a blaze of light and an uproar of drums and fifes and brass bands, of men vociferating campaign songs or hurrahing for Hayes and Wheeler, for Harrison, and for "Tom" Browne (the candidate

for Congress) as if they were wound up and could not stop. It is nearly midnight before the last club gets away on the cars and the last string of vehicles departs for the country.

E. V. S.
"Indiana Mass Meetings"
New York *Daily Tribune*, September 23, 1876

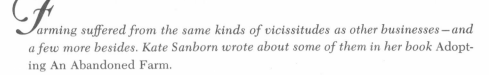

Farming suffered from the same kinds of vicissitudes as other businesses—and a few more besides. Kate Sanborn wrote about some of them in her book Adopting An Abandoned Farm.

At a recent auction I obtained twenty-one volumes of State Agricultural Reports for seventeen cents; and what I read in them of the Advantages of Rural Pursuits, The Dignity of Labor, The Relation of Agriculture to Longevity and to Nations, and, above all, of the Golden Egg, seem decidedly florid, unpractical, misleading, and very little permanent popularity can be gained by such self-interested buncombe from these eloquent orators.

The idealized farmer, as he is depicted by these white-handed rhetoricians who, like John Paul, "would never lay hand to a plow, unless said plow should actually pursue him to a second story, and then lay hands on it only to throw it out of the window," and the phlegmatic, over-worked, horny-handed tillers of the soil are no more alike than Fenimore Cooper's handsome, romantic, noble, and impressive red man of the forest and the actual Sioux or Apache, as regarded by the cowboy of the West.

It's all work, with no play and no proper pay, for Western competition now prevents all chance of decent profits. Little can be laid up for old age, except by the most painful economy and daily scrimping; and how can the children consent to stay on, starving body and soul? *That* explains the 3,318 abandoned farms in Maine at present. And the farmers' wives! what monotonous, treadmill lives! Constant toil with no wages, no allowance, no pocket money, no vacations, no pleasure trips to the city nearest them, little of the pleasures of correspondence; no time to write, unless a near relative is dead or dying. Some one says that their only chance for social life is in going to some insane asylum! There have been four cases of suicide in farmers' families near me within eighteen months. . . .

Think of the New England climate in summer. Rufus Choate describes it eloquently: "Take the climate of New England in summer, hot to-day, cold to-morrow, mercury at eighty degrees in the shade in the morning, with a sultry wind southwest. In three hours more a sea turn, wind at east, a thick fog from the bottom of the ocean, and a fall of forty degrees. Now so dry as to kill all the beans in New Hampshire, then floods carrying off all the dams and bridges on the Penobscot and Androscoggin. Snow in Portsmouth in July, and the next day a man and a yoke of oxen killed by lightning in Rhode Island. You would think the world was coming to an end. But we go along. Seed time and harvest never fail. We have the early and the latter rains; the sixty days of hot corn weather are pretty sure to be measured out to us; the Indian summer, with its bland south winds and mitigated sunshine, brings all up, and about the 25th of November,

155

being Thursday, a grateful people gather about the Thanksgiving board, with hearts full of gratitude for the blessings that have been vouchsafed to them."

Kate Sanborn
Adopting An Abandoned Farm, 1891

Yankee farmers had long been leaving their rocky hillsides for more fertile acres, and abandoned farms had become a common sight in New England.

Few roads can be followed far without coming upon some broken-windowed ruin of a house, now for years unoccupied, and wholly given over to decay. The children left, drawn by dreams of the gains the city or the sea or the far West offered; and the parents are gone, too, now. The shingles and clapboards loosen and the roof sags, and within, damp, mossy decay has fastened itself to walls, floor, and ceiling of every room. Gaps have broken in the stone walls along the roadway, and the brambles are thick springing on either side. In the front yard is a gnarled, untrimmed apple-tree with a great broken limb sagging to the ground, and about a ragged growth of bushes. As time goes on, the house falls piece by piece, and at last only the shattered chimney stands, a . . . memorial of the dead past.

Clifton Johnson
The New England Country, 1898

As had thousands before them, many Easterners went west, now to farm the rolling prairie lands and the great flat plains. Howard Ruede wrote home from Kansas to his family in Pennsylvania in 1877 and described the raising of a house in a land where wood and stone were scarce.

Perhaps you will be interested in the way a sod house is built. Sod is the most available material, in fact, the only material the homesteader has at hand, unless he happens to be one of the fortunates who secured a creek claim with timber suitable for house logs.

Occasionally a new comer has a "bee," and the neighbors for miles around gather at his claim and put up his house in a day. . . . The women come too, and while the men lay up the sod walls, they prepare dinner for the crowd, and have a very sociable hour at noon. A house put up in this way is very likely to settle and get out of shape, but it is seldom deserted for that reason. . . .

When the prairie is thoroughly soaked by rain or snow is the best time for breaking sod for building. The regulation thickness is 2½ inches, buffalo sod preferred on account of its superior toughness. The furrow slices are laid flat and as straight as a steady-walking team can be driven. These furrow slices, 12 inches wide, are cut with a sharp spade into 18-inch lengths, and carefully handled as they are laid in the wall, one length reaching across the wall, which rises rapidly even when the builders are green hands. Care must be taken to break joints and bind the corners of the house. "Seven feet to the square" [top of the wall] is the

To chink the cracks in a sod house and keep it warm despite the bitter winds of a plains winter, the farmer banked his walls with snow.

156

A dilapidated mill was one concomitant of the abandoned farms Clifton Johnson describes (left).

rule, as the wall is likely to settle a good deal, especially if the sod is very wet when laid. The door and window frames are set in place first and the wall built around them. Building such a house is hard work.

When the square is reached, the crotches (forks of a tree) are set at the ends and in the middle of the house and the ridge pole—usually a single tree trunk the length of the building, but sometimes spliced—is raised to its place by sheer strength of arm, it being impossible to use any other power. Then rails are laid from the ridge log to the walls and covered with any available material—straight sorghum stalks, willow switches and straw, or anything that will prevent the sod on the roof from falling between the rafters. From the comb of the roof to the earthen floor is usually about nine feet.

The gables are finished before the roof is put on, as in roofing the layer of sod is started at the outer edge of the wall. If the builder is able, he has sawed cottonwood rafters and a pine or cottonwood board roof covered with sod. Occasionally a sod house with a shingle roof is seen, but of course this costs more money.

At first these sod houses are unplastered, and this is thought perfectly all right, but such a house is somewhat cold in the winter, as the crevices between the sods admit some cold air; so some of the houses are plastered with a kind of "native lime," made of sand and a very sticky native clay. This plaster is very good unless it happens to get wet. In a few of the houses this plaster is whitewashed, and this helps the looks very much. Some sod houses are mighty comfortable places to go into in cold weather, and it don't take much fire to keep them warm. I will have to be contented with a very modest affair for a while, but perhaps I can improve it later.

Howard Ruede
Sod-House Days, 1937

Once again, in the Plains states and the great Northwest, Americans were pioneers—deprived of comforts, breaking virgin soil, and, as the second selection below demonstrates, finding that their rich new land was not exempt from agricultural disasters.

Many of the pioneer teachers taught in small log or frame houses so open that the sun could enter through the crevices . . . . the sod school houses were far more comfortable than the frame or log buildings. The boarding places of the teachers, were of a necessity, often a mile or more away from the school house and accommodations much like camping out. A former teacher explained that the school house she taught in was made of logs and was so open where the "chinks" had been left out between the logs that a fairly good view of the outdoor landscape was possible. Then with a limited supply of green cottonwood fuel, that the teacher must use to warm the school house in time for morning classes, after walking a mile from her boarding place, did not provide an atmosphere conducive to study. She boarded with a family whose small house was so open that everything freezable suffered from frost during the night. There was but one bed in the house and she slept with the wife in the bed while the husband slept with the children on the floor. Bread making under such environments required originality to make it a success. In such an atmosphere only dry yeast could be used. It would be started at noon and at night worked down hard and kept till morning when it would be set by the stove till it had risen enough to make into loaves and then it was baked. To keep it warm and from freezing at night the wife wrapped it up well and placed it in the bed at the teacher's feet.

Cass G. Barns, M.D.
The Sod House, 1930

By July, 1873 . . . we had a field of corn of which we were very proud indeed. It was tall and strong and early, and bid fair to produce a crop so large that we would make a little, even at the low price we were almost certain to get. I went to town the day I have in mind, and noticed as I started home that the sunlight was growing hazy. I thought little of it, however, and having forded the river, drove along fairly pleased with our prospects. What my mind was on I do not know, but I saw nothing coming, when suddenly the grasshoppers were about me in such infinite numbers as to seem impossible. They flew into the horses' faces until the poor beasts backed and tried to turn around. They actually hurt me as they flew against my face and hands. The wagon I was driving was literally filled with them. The road was seething; the grass along the way was hidden. The horses' hoofs crushed scores of them at every step. The wagon wheels sounded as if they were running over popcorn.

I struggled with the horses every step of the way home, and when I got there I saw Father standing almost in despair. So thick were the grasshoppers in the cornfield of which both of us had been so proud, that not a spot of green could be seen. And within two hours of the time that they had come not a leaf was left in all that field. The stalks that still were left were merely ragged stumps, and where many a stalk had stood, a hole in the ground was all that remained — a hole where the grasshoppers had eaten the stalk off an inch or more below the ground.

Our wheat, too, was ruined, for though it was too ripe for them to eat, they cut almost every head from the stalks. We salvaged some of that, it is true, but the corn was utterly, completed gone.

I was drawing a pension for my wound at Shiloh — a pension of eight dollars a month, paid twice a year. How fortunate that was! Without that forty-eight dollars coming twice a year I do not know what would have happened to us. There were many in the country 'round about who had no such anchor to windward, and settlers heading back toward where relatives lived in the states farther east were common enough. They took it good-naturedly, it is true, and painted humorous signs on their wagons, but it was more than serious enough.

"Going home to Mother," read one sign on a wagon. "Going east to my wife's folks," read another. These were common sights in the seventies in Nebraska.

James H. Kyner
End of Track, 1937

New contrivances that made rural life easier were legion; one such was the water pump shown here.

$\mathcal{E}$ugene Smalley was a farming authority. This excerpt from an article he published in 1894 serves to remind us that no matter how acute a man's judgments may be about the past and present, the future is likely to surprise him.

The late President Garfield once told me that, having a small field of wheat on his Mentor farm, he thought he would hire a man to cut the grain with a cradle, because there was not enough of it to warrant the use of a harvesting-machine. He had great difficulty in finding a man who knew how to swing a cradle and was willing to undertake the hard physical labor. The young men on the neighboring farms knew nothing of the use of the old implement, and the older men did not wish to undertake the job. A single lifetime has spanned the entire period from the sickle to the self-binder and the header and the gigantic California machine, which, propelled by twenty-six horses, moves across the wheat-fields, cutting and threshing as it goes. . . .

An interesting question might be raised as to the influence of labor-saving machinery on the intellectual development of the farmer of the present day. Most men of the generation that is passing away who have given thought to this question will, I imagine, say that it has not been beneficial and will argue that the farmer of their boyhood, who had to do a multitude of things that are now done by factories or by farm machinery, was a brighter, more original, and more manly fellow than his successor of this day. He made his own axe-helves, plough-handles, and flails, split fence-rails and built fences, did a little carpentry, cobbling, and blacksmithing, and sharpened his wits by many makeshifts and contrivances; and his wife carried on a little factory in the house, where wool was spun, dyed, and woven, clothing was made, and fruits were dried and preserved. Now everything is bought at the stores and all the little farm arts and handicrafts have departed from the rural districts. I admit that some loss of intellectual fibre must have resulted from this great change, but I hold that it has been more than made up by the universal habit of reading that has come with more leisure and with the multiplication of cheap books and newspapers. Instead of spending the evenings shelling corn by the light of a tallow candle, the farmer now reads the newspapers in the glow of a kerosene lamp, and his wife, released from the drudgery of spinning and knitting, will be found reading a novel or a magazine. Farm machinery now gives the farmer an amount of leisure unknown in the old times of hand labor. All the really hard work is done by machines. We cannot suppose this to be detrimental to the intellect and character of the farm population. Leisure is the golden dream of the working classes all over the world, and if the modern farmer has secured release in part from the grinding toil that made of his father an old man at fifty, wrinkled and rheumatic, who shall say that he has been injured thereby in brain force or moral stamina?

I believe that we are now in a transition period in agriculture. The influence of machinery has been fully exerted. It is doubtful whether the next century will see any important new inventions that will further eliminate the man from the land and do his work with cog-wheels, levers, and knives. There are no more fertile lands on the globe to be conquered by civilization and to increase the food-supply. With growth of population will come better prices for farm products. Farm life will become more attractive. The tendency to large farms will be checked. A hundred acres, even with exclusive grain farming, will afford a good living to a family. Better times for American agriculture are not far off.

E. V. Smalley
"Has Farm Machinery Destroyed Farm Life?"
The Forum, April, 1894

PICTURE CREDITS. PAGE 146: LIBRARY OF CONGRESS; PAGES 146–47: *Harper's Weekly,* MAY 9, 1868; PAGES 148–49 (TOP): *Every Saturday,* JANUARY 14, 1871, NEW YORK PUBLIC LIBRARY; PAGES 148–49 (BOTTOM): BUTLER INSTITUTE OF AMERICAN ART; PAGES 150–51: GILCREASE INSTITUTE OF AMERICAN HISTORY AND ART; PAGE 152: WARSHAW COLLECTION OF BUSINESS AMERICANA; PAGE 153: LIBRARY OF CONGRESS; PAGES 154–55 (BOTH): *Scribner's Magazine,* MAY–OCTOBER, 1874; PAGES 156–57 (TOP): METROPOLITAN MUSEUM OF ART, GIFT OF MRS. ANDREW FISHER BUNNER, 1899; PAGES 156–57 (BOTTOM): *Harper's Weekly,* JANUARY 17, 1885; PAGES 158–59: LANDAUER COLLECTION, NEW-YORK HISTORICAL SOCIETY

Rise of the Tycoons

The post-Civil War era has been called many things, but it can aptly be called the age of steel, for that refinement of iron was becoming the foundation of all industries, even as petroleum would become their lubricant. Henry Bessemer's process of making steel from pig iron by blowing cold air into it had been first used in America in 1865; the previous year steel had been made by a similar process patented in 1857 by a Kentuckian, William Kelly. With the introduction of the Kelly-Bessemer process began the "American plan" of producing steel on an enormous scale. Steel rails—eight to fifteen times as durable as iron—replaced the older type, making the sudden network of railroads and street railways practical.

In 1868 the first open-hearth furnace for manufacturing steel was erected in Trenton, New Jersey. Developed originally in France and England, it burned preheated gas and air in the furnace, and though a slower process, it produced a higher grade of steel than the Bessemer converter while at the same time using cheaper raw materials and equipment. An American engineer, Samuel T. Wellman, through his ingenious adaptations of the process, became known as the "father of the open hearth in America."

In the first part of the century most of the iron ore in the United States had come from New York and Pennsylvania, with smaller amounts from Virginia, Tennessee, and Alabama. Then in 1844 iron was discovered along Lake Superior in upper Michigan, near the present city of Marquette, though so remote and undeveloped was the region that it was a dozen years before the new iron range was sending ore in quantity to steel mills in the East. A second iron range, the Menominee, a short distance to the south, was discovered and was in large-scale production by 1872, and not long after, the Gogebic Range, straddling the Michigan-Wisconsin border, was opened. But the richest find was still to come. Lewis H. Merritt, a timber prospector in northeastern Minnesota, had become convinced that the iron deposits in the Lake Superior area extended also into his state. As he and his sons—he raised eight, and several followed him into the lumber business—ranged the forests, they also looked for iron, and when the father retired, the sons continued the search. In 1890 they found their first ore in quantity,

The moving force in America after the Civil War was industrial energy—an energy captured here in Charles Graham's 1886 drawing for Harper's Weekly *of steelmaking by the Bessemer process.*

not as a hard mineral in veins in rocks, from which it had to be removed by underground shaft mines, but as huge deposits lying close to the surface and so soft the ore could be scooped up with steam shovels.

Thus was opened the almost unbelievably rich Mesabi Range. To exploit their discovery the Merritts constructed a railroad to Lake Superior and docking facilities on the water front. For aid in financing such a large development they went to John D. Rockefeller. But they had hardly gotten their operations well under way before the Panic of 1893 came and strained their already overextended resources. They were builders and men of action but they knew little about finance, and very soon everything—mines, railroad, and docks—was in the possession of the astute John D. Rockefeller, who later sold out to the Carnegie interests.

In each developing industrial field the names of the great entrepreneurs stood out, the relentlessly ambitious men who made their own names almost synonymous with that of their industry—Vanderbilt and Hill and Huntington with the railroads, McCormick with farm implements, Swift with meat packing, Rockefeller with oil. In steel the important name would be that of Andrew Carnegie.

Born in Dunfermline, Scotland, the son of a poor weaver, Carnegie emigrated with his family to America in 1848 at the age of thirteen, settling across the river from Pittsburgh. His first job was as a bobbin boy in a cotton mill at $1.20 a week. Sharp-witted, competitive, with a fierce desire to succeed, he acquired skills as he went along. From a tender of bobbins he became a telegraph messenger boy, and by the time he was fifteen, a telegraph operator. At eighteen he was earning $40 a month as confidential clerk of the Pennsylvania Railroad's western division superintendent, and in 1859 he became the manager of the division. He began to invest

America's pride in its brawn and its romanticizing of the workingman's life are both evident in this Ivory Soap advertisement dated about 1890. The ad seems to derive from Thomas Anshutz' famous painting Steelworkers' Noontime.

early, and his persistent speculations—usually with borrowed money—were as shrewd as they were fortunate. So notable was his reputation in 1861 that he was placed in charge of the operation of military railroads and telegraphs for the Army. After serving for a year he returned to the Pennsylvania Railroad.

Because the future of railroads was linked to iron, young Carnegie gravitated to that industry. He first bought a small wrought-iron plant, then acquired control of a rail works, a locomotive works, and what Carnegie believed was the first iron-bridge company in the world. He cannily expanded into steel through prosperity and depression, developing new uses for his products and taking full advantage of tariffs and rebates; as his empire grew, he established relations with the international financiers: the Morgans, the Rothschilds, the house of Baring. In the early 1870's he decided to rid himself of all his other enterprises in order, in his own words, to "concentrate on the manufacture of iron and steel and be master in that." By 1873 he had organized the first large Bessemer steel rail company. Even in the long depression, demand for steel remained insatiable and the business of the Carnegie companies soared. In 1881 Carnegie Brothers and Company, Limited, was formed, and within four years was producing ten thousand tons of steel a month and making a profit of $1,192,-000 a year. From 1880 to 1900 Carnegie dominated the steel industry, absorbing, consolidating, expanding production. In 1883 he bought controlling interest in the H. C. Frick Coke Company and the labor-plagued Homestead Mills—acquisitions that would in time cast a dark shadow over the reputation of which he was so proud. Henry Clay Frick later became general manager of the new combination, Carnegie Associates; he, Carnegie, and a few others formed a loyal compact group against which no outsiders could hope to compete.

What Carnegie was in the structured world of steel, John D. Rockefeller would become in the disorderly world of oil production. Like Carnegie and most of the great entrepreneurs of the period, he actualized the rags-to-riches myth, recorded with stilted repetition by the clergyman turned hack writer Horatio Alger. Like the other entrepreneurs, Rockefeller arrived at the opportune moment.

For a hundred years before Rockefeller's birth, travelers through the Appalachian Mountain region in and near western Pennsylvania had observed hollows where a viscid, blue-green, foul-smelling substance, which they called petroleum, oozed from the earth. To farmers seeking fresh water and to borers for salt wells, petroleum was a continuing nuisance, but promoters bottled the substance and—under such names as Snake Oil, American Oil, or Seneca Oil—hawked it as a remedy for rheumatism, bronchitis, cholera, consumption, and a variety of other ailments. At the same time that Americans were gulping this nauseous cure-all, the lamp was evolving from the flickering rushlight holder into the unwavering flame induced by the glass chimney. By the 1840's lamps had become far more general as the costly sperm oil from whales was superseded by the cheaper, if volatile, hazardous camphene made from turpentine. In the 1850's a still less expensive and far safer oil, distilled from coal and patented as "kerosene" by a young Canadian geologist, was coming into use as an illuminant beyond the gaslit cities. Coal oil was soon being distilled at the rate of several million gallons a year.

In 1851 Francis Beattie Brewer, a New England doctor who had turned lumberman and settled in the frontier village of Titusville in Venango County, Pennsylvania, became interested in the commercial possibilities of a petroleum spring in his neighborhood. With several promoters he formed the Pennsylvania Rock Oil Company. One of his partners sent some of their oil to Yale's professor of chemistry Benjamin Silliman, Jr., with the request for a detailed report as to its value. The modern history of petroleum begins in 1855 with Silliman's "Report on the Rock Oil, or Petroleum, from Venango Co., Pennsylvania." The professor's startling conclusion was that 50 per cent of the rock oil could be distilled as an illuminant and 40 per cent more recovered as naphtha and paraffin, leaving only a 10 per cent residue.

Great interest in the commercial possibilities of petroleum was stirred up by the report. The Rock Oil Company was reorganized several times, and after the setback of the 1857 Panic, Silliman became for a time its president. Then a New Haven banker, James M. Townsend, took over the faltering company and hit on the idea of drilling for oil. "Oh, Townsend," one of his New Haven friends exclaimed, "oil coming out of the ground, pumping oil out of the earth as you pump water? Nonsense! You're crazy." Determined nevertheless to try out his revolutionary idea, Townsend hired as a driller Edwin L. Drake, a former railroad express agent and odd-jobs man whose principal qualifications were that he was available and that he could obtain a railroad pass to Titusville. Assuming the equivocal title of "colonel,"

Drake arrived at the village of three hundred inhabitants and was shown the petroleum spring by Brewer. "Within ten minutes after my arrival upon the ground with Dr. Brewer," Drake wrote in reminiscence, "I had made up my mind that it [petroleum] could be obtained in large quantities by Boreing as for Salt Water. I also determined that I should be the one to do it."

Drake was indeed the one to do it, but it took him fifteen months of frustrating struggle, during which the general opinion grew that "Drake was fooling away his time and money." Then at the end of August, 1859, when the drill had reached down almost seventy feet, it at last struck oil. Before long oil was being pumped out at the unprecedented rate of eight to ten gallons a day.

For all his lack of experience, Drake had demonstrated beyond dispute that petroleum lying underground could be tapped by drilling. From his "folly" the petroleum industry took its start. The area around Titusville soon assumed the aspect of a boom town, an "Oildorado." Hundreds of prospectors—oil forty-niners—rushed to the region. Diviners and hunch players made their appearance, and there were even those who set themselves up as "oil smellers." By January, 1861, Venango County was producing seven hundred and fifty barrels of oil a day, a figure that would double by spring. Prospectors followed the Appalachian oil-field trail beyond Pennsylvania to western Virginia, Ohio, New York, Kentucky, and Tennessee. By the end of the year it was becoming apparent that petroleum would soon challenge coal oil's position in the illuminating-oil market.

That same year the first gusher was struck in the Pennsylvania Oil Creek field, but the oil caught fire and burned the promoter, one Henry Rouse, and eighteen others to death. A less disastrous gusher, the Fountain well, amazed oilmen with its 300-barrel-a-day flow, only to be eclipsed shortly by the Empire with 2,500 barrels, and finally the Phillips No. 2 well on Oil Creek with 3,000 barrels. Production rose from between 200,000 and 500,000 barrels in 1860—early statistics are vague—to three million barrels two years later.

After an initial depression caused by overproduction, the new industry by 1864 had created a wildly flourishing nationwide market in oil stocks. The speculative boom grew for two years, until its inevitable collapse. In that time stock salesmen, promoters, and fly-by-nighters swarmed over the Pennsylvania oil fields like locusts as oil wells spouted and the price per barrel soared from $3.00 to $13.75. On Pithole Creek in Venango County,

scene of enormous strikes, Pithole, called aptly "the sewer city," sprang up overnight, only to disappear in 1867–68 with the drying up of many wells and the falling of oil prices to as low as ten cents a barrel.

Among those brought to the oil fields by the news of Oildorado was a thin, tight-lipped young wholesale produce merchant from Cleveland, Ohio, John D. Rockefeller. To his calculating eyes the chaotic conditions made the oil trade appear too risky for prudent investment, and he so advised his fellow Ohio merchants who had sent him in 1860 to investigate the oil fields. But two years later he had shifted his views enough to back a Clevelander, Samuel Andrews, who worked in a small coal-oil refinery. The pair, with three brothers named Clark, started their own refinery, where Andrews developed new methods of extracting kerosene from petroleum and of utilizing the by-products. While Andrews took care of the manufacturing, Rockefeller took enough

time from his other affairs to keep the books and organize the business with his characteristic economy and efficiency. In 1865 he gave up his produce business and invested all his capital and his uncanny commercial skills in the oil-refining trade.

Rockefeller, when he made this momentous step, was only twenty-six years old and already rich, a goal he had set for himself as a country boy in upper New York State when he informed a playmate that he intended to make one hundred thousand dollars. His early poverty has been exaggerated—he liked in later life to exaggerate it himself—but though he was not poor as Carnegie had been poor, his education was scant and while still a child he worked in the fields. His father, a quack doctor, patent medicine vendor, and cancer curer, was an itinerant sport, a tavern tippler, at home only on occasion and only occasionally supporting his family. It was from his Baptist mother that the boy inherited a pietistic zeal, a fru-

Despite the rudimentary look of oil mining in 1865, when this photograph was taken of Pioneer Run in the Oil Creek district of Pennsylvania, the United States that year exported some 30,000,000 gallons of crude oil and oil products.

gal, evangelical approach to life, which was apparent in everything he did. Indeed, he scarcely seemed to have been a child at all, but a miniature adult of solemn, unwavering propriety and enterprise. When he was seven years old, he started raising turkeys with his mother's help. With time for only a few years' schooling, he worked for local farmers, hoeing potatoes for thirty-seven cents a day and hoarding his earnings in a blue bowl that he kept on a chest in his room. Before he reached his teens he had saved fifty dollars. When he lent this nest egg to a farmer at 7 per cent, he discovered that he could get as much interest in a year "as I could

165

earn by digging potatoes for ten days." Then and there he resolved that it was better "to let the money be my slave than to be the slave of money."

The family moved to Cleveland, Ohio, in 1854, where John attended Central High School for a year, following this with a three-month course at Folsom's Commercial College, where he learned double-entry bookkeeping and the rudiments of banking and commercial law. Figures delighted and fascinated him. Later it was said of him that "he had the soul of a bookkeeper." He would describe himself as "a man of figures." At sixteen this reticent, methodical, determined young man went as assistant bookkeeper to a Cleveland firm of produce shippers and commission merchants, at a starting salary of one hundred and eighty-two dollars a year. He spent no more than enough to keep himself fed and neatly dressed, eschewing all sports and amusements, neither drinking nor playing cards nor going with girls, finding few friends, but as his mother's son, attending the Baptist Church regularly and later teaching in the Sunday school. To the church he gave ten cents weekly, which he later raised to twenty-five cents, and as his earnings grew, he practiced tithing. Within three years he had saved eight hundred dollars and had thoroughly absorbed the ins and outs of the commission business. In 1859 with his saved-up capital he opened his own produce business with a young Englishman, Maurice Clark. As an embryo entrepreneur he picked up the technique of obtaining credit, and soon he was borrowing against warehouse receipts. In a few months he had moved from small purchases to buying grain and produce by the carload. As he prospered he began to dress the part of the successful merchant, acquiring fluffy sideburns, a frock coat, striped trousers, and a silk hat. But beneath this conventional, almost austere, exterior there lurked a rapacious, alert, intense intelligence. "Mad about money, though sane in everything else," his high school friend Mark Hanna later described him. Days he made his fortune, nights he read the Bible in his room and lay in bed talking to himself in admonishing intimate lectures, which, he wrote later, "had a great influence on my life." Relentless in details, a hard bargainer, he said little, rarely smiled and almost never laughed. Only a well-planned business deal broke through the crust of his reserve, sometimes moving him to cavort or even throw his hat in the air. Once and only once, in his early merchant days, he was so carried away by a successful coup that he shouted triumphantly: "I'm bound to be rich! *Bound to be rich!*"

The Civil War evoked none of the martial response in the breast of the young merchant that it did in that of his friend Mark Hanna. Rockefeller was far too concerned with business to waste his time in soldiering. His sister Mary Ann recalled that while everyone else was talking war, her brother and his associates "were talking oil all the time. It was all foreign to me and I got sick of it. . . ."

Not long after entering the oil business Rockefeller bought out the Clark brothers, who had become increasingly alarmed as the firm's borrowings reached the one-hundred-thousand-dollar mark. In February, 1865, the new firm of Rockefeller and Andrews was born under Rockefeller's guiding hand. William Rockefeller, a shrewd and successful younger brother, came into the new company. Henry M. Flagler, who would develop into Rockefeller's closest, most trusted, and ablest associate, joined in 1867, and the company became Rockefeller, Andrews and Flagler, which in three years evolved into the Standard Oil Company of Ohio.

Into the chaotic boom-and-bust competition of the nascent oil industry, epitomized by such free-living cities as the ephemeral Pithole, Rockefeller brought order and economy. It has been said of him that what had to be done, he did. What he did, in the cold elimination of competitors and the development of big business, made him for some time one of the most hated men in the country and brought the name Standard Oil into odious repute. Yet, from a perspective long in developing, he is seen to have created an industry that is vital to America and that probably could not have been built up in any other way.

From the beginning Rockefeller aimed to make his refineries self-contained, to "pay a profit to no one" if he could help it. Bypassing the jobbers, he bought oil directly from the producers. He built his own wagons and did his own hauling; to cut down the cost of barrels he set up his own cooperage. Besides producing kerosene and gasoline—then the least useful petroleum by-product—Rockefeller, Andrews and Flagler developed great efficiency in refining paraffin, petrolatum—used in ointments—and lubricating oils. The firm, with ships and storage tanks and the recently introduced pipelines, soon became the largest in Cleveland.

The growth of a Cleveland oil refining firm to the corporation colossus of the industry, the nation's first trust, came about primarily through the advantages accruing from secret rebates from the railroads patronized by Rockefeller. His first rebate came from the Lake Shore and Michigan Southern Railroad as early as 1867. Rockefeller considered, and would always consider, such rebates justified as discounts for large-scale use of the railroads' facilities. It was at best a partial truth.

The granting of rebates was at that time a general railroad practice, the published rate being considered both by shippers and the road management as only a starting point for haggling. Often a railroad would grant a special rate to meet the competition of a rival. Nothing in the law as yet compelled any road to give equal rates as a common carrier to all users. Railroad heads facing competition tended to prefer secret rebates to a general reduction of their announced rates. Smaller producers and refiners who were not in a position to extract rebates were, of course, forced to the wall.

From its organization in 1870 with a capitalization of one million dollars the Standard Oil Company of Ohio moved forward with giant steps, soon gaining almost complete control of all oil refining facilities. With such power behind it, Standard Oil was able to demand and receive rate favors from the lines it used.

By 1871 overproduction had brought about a general depression in the refining industry, and although Standard Oil itself still managed to make money, it seemed to Rockefeller that the time had come to get together with other large refiners and stabilize the oil industry and its rail traffic, to eliminate the smaller operators and their price cutting, and to reduce refining to consumption levels. The means to his ends he found in the South Improvement Company, a name that would later have sinister connotations to the public at large. The company had been given a charter in 1870 by the corrupt Pennsylvania legislature for unspecified ends, which Rockefeller, after obtaining the charter, would make specific. His plan was brutally simple. Railroads such as the New York Central, the Erie, the Atlantic and Great Western, and the Pennsylvania would be told to double their rates for carrying both crude and refined oil. But the refiners subscribing to the South Improvement Company plan would get rebates that almost covered the cost of the rate raises. And, as if this were not enough, additional payments would be made to the company from the gross rates paid by refiners and producers outside the association. Under this scheme railroads by agreement with South Improvement would at last eliminate unproductive competition among themselves, while refiners would, on their part, be able to control the amount of oil refined and at the same time get rid of their fringe competitors. Individual large refiners benefited, but the greatest benefit accrued to the Rockefeller interests.

The power of the railroads and the large refiners had come to seem unassailable. Yet the South Improvement plan was too blatant. Oil producers, fearful of the threat to their independence, staged demonstrations in Titusville and Oil City and formed the Petroleum Producers' Union, which pledged itself to sell no oil to members of the South Improvement Company. The Oil Men's League sprang up, meeting in secret, with the trappings and ritual of the defunct Ku-Klux Klan. Rockefeller, pried out of his self-sought obscurity, found himself attacked in the Oil City *Derrick* as the "Mephistopheles

In this angry painting by Thomas Nast, The Devil and the Businessman, *pocket-picking Scratch will have his due even as the businessman enters church. Presumably the collection plate will be that much lighter and the man's soul, heavier.*

OVERLEAF: *The sketches, most of them lighthearted, of scenes at* The New Oil Field *by Theodore R. Davis were printed in* Harper's Weekly *in August, 1882. By then both the oil industry and John D. Rockefeller had become American institutions.*

Garfield Pa.

DANGER No SMOKING.

"Hay! Yer Got er Match."

Hotel de Gunny Sack.

Pump Station near Garfield.

A 1000 Barrel Well.

Burnt Well.

of Cleveland." So great was the uproar over South Improvement that the railroads finally agreed to drop the plan, the harassed Pennsylvania legislature revoked the company's charter, and Rockefeller himself felt it wise to make it known that Standard Oil had canceled all its prior contracts with the railroads. Only then, with the written promise of the railroads to establish public and equal rates with no rebates and with Rockefeller's announcement that Standard Oil's agreements with the railroads and the South Improvement Company had been canceled, was the oil producers' boycott finally lifted on April 10, 1872.

It was a promise that scarcely survived the drying of the ink on the pact. For the rails in their cut-throat competition felt forced to continue their rebates and favors to their largest shipper, and counted on Standard Oil to divide the traffic equitably among them. Before long it was apparent that the failure of the South Improvement plan had turned out to be less than a defeat for Rocke-

feller, for he had used the plan deftly and silently to undercut his rivals. Before the plan was dropped, he had managed to take over twenty-one of the twenty-six Cleveland refineries with a quarter of the refining capacity of the whole country. Where he could not eliminate his opponents he absorbed them, making their officials part of his own organization. "You can't compete with Standard," he told Mark Hanna's uncle, head of an independent refining firm. "We have all the large refineries now. If you refuse to sell, it will end in your being crushed." And Rockefeller did not hesitate to crush. He drove hard bargains and would drive even harder ones, although when he thought good executives and good will worth it, he paid amply in stock or cash. By 1876 he was able to say that "the coal-oil industry belongs to us." Standard Oil had achieved a monopoly of 95 per cent of the country's oil refining capacity.

The impression of Rockefeller created by Ida Tarbell and other reformers at the turn of the century was as a

THE VERDICT, JANUARY 22, 1900

"The Trust Giant's Point of View" was The Verdict's *caption on this cartoon by Horace Taylor. "'What a Funny Little Government?'" murmurs Rockefeller, whose interests are satirized as enormous smokestacked versions of federal buildings.*

business buccaneer who scuttled the ships of his opponents until he was left master of the oily seas. Rockefeller forced the railroads, including the most powerful in the land — the Pennsylvania — to knuckle under to him, as he would later even more ruthlessly bend the individualistic oil producer to his will. But Miss Tarbell's simplistic explanation of the rise of Standard Oil glossed over significant factors. Rockefeller indeed brought a harsh discipline to the refining business. But during those years of his consolidation, technical improvements were making it increasingly difficult for small refiners to survive. Bankruptcies among refiners were common, and in the depression years after 1873 many would in any case have gone out of business. Standard Oil succeeded as much by its phenomenal efficiency and by the brains and foresight of its management as by restraint and intimidation.

Secure in the monopoly of refining, Rockefeller moved to make his Standard Oil equally strong in the fields of transportation and production. The Pennsylvania Railroad had dared to challenge him by backing the rival Empire Transportation Company, which, despite its name, was competing with Rockefeller in oil refining. But even the Pennsylvania was no match for Standard Oil. Weakened by the rail strike of 1877, it could not prevent Rockefeller from buying the Empire Transportation Company. However, it was Rockefeller's struggle with the producers that would make his name anathema in the oil regions and that would at last bring him an indictment for criminal conspiracy. To Rockefeller the producers were an undisciplined lot and the oil region itself a "mining camp." They in turn found in him what they dreaded most, a single monopoly buyer, and in a desperate defensive move formed the Petroleum Producers' Union. But for all its threats of boycott the union could not in the long, or even middle-distance, run stand up against Standard Oil and its control of the railroads. After 1875, a Standard Oil subsidiary, United Pipelines, engaged in constructing pipelines in a thousand directions as new oil fields were discovered. In the end the producers were forced to come to terms with Standard Oil, receiving some concessions, but yielding in all essentials to the economic and political power of the Rockefeller interests.

Faced with the problem of the interstate operations of Standard's accumulating state-chartered companies, the Rockefeller lawyers evolved the trust as a way of maintaining centralized control of this multifaceted empire

whose products included, to name a very few: macadam binder; asphalt; raw material for fertilizers; scores of types of greases and oils; and benzines and naphthas for highly specialized uses, such as removing grease from wool. The first tentative trust arrangement in 1879 was superseded three years later by a more flexible formula in which all the stock of the Standard Oil interests was conveyed to nine trustees, headed by Rockefeller, to "exercise general supervision over the affairs of the said Standard Oil companies, and as far as practicable over the other Companies or Partnerships any portion of whose stock is held in said trust." The new trust included fourteen companies, the largest of which was Standard Oil of Ohio, and controlled twenty-six more. It was capitalized at seventy million dollars, and a quarter of its shares was owned by Rockefeller, who also headed the controlling Executive Committee. Of this first American trust Miss Tarbell wrote:

Thirty-nine corporations [actually forty], each of them having legal existence, obliged by the laws of the state creating it to limit its operations to certain lines and to make certain reports, had turned over their affairs to an organization having no legal existence, independent of all authority, able to do anything it wanted anywhere; and . . . working in absolute darkness. . . . You could argue its existence from its effects but you could never prove it. You could no more grasp it than you could an eel.

With the Standard Oil trust as its model, big business acquired the legal fiction needful to surmount state and local barriers to its growth. The trend to consolidation and centralization was no phenomenon unique to the oil industry but the prevailing pattern of the economic revolution of the latter half of the nineteenth century in which larger units and standardized products were becoming the norm. Similar trust combinations followed in such disparate fields as liquor, sugar, tobacco, cattle, nails, linseed and cottonseed oil, salt, lead, leather, and even bicycles. "The day of combination is here to stay. Individualism has gone, never to return," was Rockefeller's verdict. The binding together of the nation by railroads had doomed many local industries. Pillsbury's grain rollers stopped the wheels of small flour mills, the Bessemer process damped the fires of local steel furnaces, neighborhood slaughterers were forced to give way to Swift's refrigerator cars.

And as the industrial cities grew, the villages faded away. The often repeated story of small failures and little men pushed aside seemed an affront to the indigenous

American tradition of independence. In this general process of expansion and absorption through which the trusts emerged, what would happen to Jefferson's pioneer farmer sustaining himself on his modest holdings? How would the artisan and mechanic fare who had rallied to Andrew Johnson? The answer, troubling as it was to those who felt themselves crowded or threatened by the new behemoths, was in the time-spirit. Jefferson and Jackson had spoken for a bygone day when the republic was dominated by farmers and merchants. The new domination of business found its philosophical justification—whenever it felt it needed one—in Charles Darwin's 1859 book, *On the Origin of Species*. However dismaying the notion of man descended from the lower animals may have been to theologians, the struggle for existence, through which all living species adapted themselves to a changing environment, seemed to the industrial capitalists the very key to their world. Only through the cold eyes of that detached New England pessimist Henry Adams did the world seem otherwise: "The progress of evolution from President Washington to President Grant," he wrote, "was alone evidence enough to upset Darwin."

Social Darwinism found its most eloquent and convincing spokesman in the English philosopher and sociologist Herbert Spencer, who applied the evolutionary hypothesis to the whole domain of human knowledge. As the foremost proponent of laissez faire, the survival of the fittest in the business and industrial world, he achieved a vogue in the United States between 1870 and 1900 beyond any other thinker of his day. Businessmen who had never read a book of philosophy or even of science read Spencer and found a justification of their vaguely formed beliefs.

Spencer saw society as an organism and history as a progression from more to less government. He contrasted the efficiency and vigor of private business with the inefficiency and bureaucratic sloth of state enterprises, and held that all government action except preventing internal and external aggression was destructive both of the freedom of the individual and of progress. State aid of any kind was harmful, nor did the state have the right to tax individuals to mitigate distress. Spencer opposed sanitary laws, poor laws, post offices, state-supported education, a government currency, and regulation of labor conditions and tariffs as violations of the principles of evolutionary justice.

The entrepreneurs were not prepared to go all the way down the laissez-faire road. They were certainly not prepared to give up a national banking system, a high protective tariff, federal land grants to the railroads, and the importation of contract labor; nor could they quite conceive of doing away with public education or the post office. But Spencer's coldly serene view of tooth-and-claw competition, of a society in which selection was unrestrained by government intervention, rang in their willing ears like a secular gospel. Carnegie, later to become Spencer's friend, wrote in his autobiography of the revelation he had experienced in his first reading of Spencer:

. . . I remember that light came as in a flood and all was clear. Not only had I got rid of theology and the supernatural, but I had found the truth of evolution. "All is well since all grows better" became my motto, my true source of comfort. Man was not created with an instinct for his own degradation, but from the lower he had risen to the higher forms. Nor is there any conceivable end to his march to perfection.

Nevertheless in his article "The Gospel of Wealth," published in 1889, Carnegie parted from his mentor. Although still defending in Spencerian phrases the "concentration of business industrial and commercial, in the hands of a few," he now asserted—and he was to follow his assertion with his own practice—that it was the duty of the rich man to get rid of his "surplus revenues" in such a way as to benefit the community. And Carnegie libraries across the country still bear witness that he did as he urged others to do.

As for Rockefeller, he resorted to a horticultural metaphor to explain the meaning of Spencer's teachings: "The American Beauty rose can be produced in its splendor and fragrance only by sacrificing the early buds which grow up around it. This is not an evil tendency in business. It is merely the working-out of a law of nature and a law of God."

For the young, the gospel of success was propounded in the volumes of Horatio Alger, whose titles—*Ragged Dick, Luck and Pluck, Tattered Tom*, and more than a hundred others—seemed to hint at mean beginnings and a successful outcome. The adventures of Alger's heroes shaped the thoughts and dreams of success of American boys for two generations. Intelligence, initiative, and hard work marked the Alger road from rags to riches, and to these familiar ingredients the author added an unSpencerian final ingredient—luck. Only with luck, the propitious accident, the rescue from drowning, the train

The life of Andrew Carnegie, who rose from immigrant messenger boy to millionaire philanthropist, was the kind of American experience that spawned and made popular the Horatio Alger books, frontispieces of which are shown above.

or runaway carriage brought to a halt, did the young Alger hero attain the first rung of the ladder of success. Destiny, even in these hack works, was still inscrutable.

There was another side to Alger glimmering fitfully through his prose, for behind the mask of success in progressive, expanding America he saw the sullen face of urban poverty. Living in New York, doing much of his writing in his office at the Newsboys' Lodging House, he was a familiar of the waifs who came for refuge there, and who served as his models. He knew the degradation

of the Five Points, the Bowery, Mulberry Bend, all places where the derelicts congregated. He saw the abandoned children of the streets sleeping in boxes or under stairways. In one of his books he exposed the brutality of the *padrone* system, by which little Italian children were brought to New York in a state of slavery. For him, at least, whatever his contribution to the American success myth, the harshness of natural selection was mitigated by compassion.

To the orthodox Spencerian, trade unions with their wage demands and strike threats were obstacles in the path of progress. Wages and hours could only be determined by the inflexible laws of supply and demand. By interfering with these laws, unions were destructive of the rights of individual laborers.

In the depressive first year of the Civil War, trade-union membership had sunk almost as low as during the Panic of 1857. But with the full employment of the war's later years, trade assemblies—general organizations of unions in cities to bring pressure, including boycotts, against unfair employers—revived. By 1870 more than thirty national unions had been founded. Unionism gathered its strength primarily from those workers whose skills were threatened by industrial progress or cheap immigrant labor: bricklayers, masons, carpenters, iron molders, machinists, hatters, printers, railroad engineers, cigar makers. Until 1890 only a fraction of the labor force belonged to any union at all.

The period from 1865 to 1897 was one of steadily declining prices, and thirty years after the war labor's standard of living in terms of actual buying power was higher than it had ever been. Even the unskilled operatives earning a dollar a day were able to get along on their wages—as long as they were employed. Nevertheless, living in their slum warrens, working the daylight hours and beyond in dark, unsafe, and unsanitary factories, they could not have been too aware of their good fortune. Entrepreneurs gave little thought to improving working conditions or increasing labor efficiency. The ten-hour day, object of agitation since Jackson's time, had become a reality for most workers by 1890, although many women toiled for sixty-five hours a week in sweatshops for a few dollars, as did the children tending the looms in factories. As late as 1910 the average wage for a fifty-six-hour week in a Massachusetts textile mill was $8.76 for adults and less than $5.00 for the many child workers. The docile newcomers from overseas, who constantly filled the country's unskilled labor pool, were unresponsive at first to unionization attempts.

In 1865 an unsuccessful effort had been made to combine the various craft unions in an International Industrial Assembly of North America. This was followed the next year by the National Labor Union, whose demands included an eight-hour day, consumers' cooperatives, public land only for settlers and not speculators, restriction of immigration, a Department of Labor, and legal-tender greenbacks. Collective bargaining was not one of their aims, and workers were advised not to strike. Most of the delegates to the National Labor Union conventions were not workingmen but reformers, utopians, and politicians without a party; and the loose association foundered at last in 1872. In 1873 the craft unions tried to set up a less visionary Industrial Brotherhood, and might have succeeded but for the panic of that year. The ensuing depression, the worst that the United States was to endure until that of the 1930's, devastated union membership and reduced the number of national unions from thirty to eight or nine.

The one union that achieved an embracing national status in those years was the Noble Order of the Knights of Labor, founded as a secret society by a small group of garment cutters in 1869. Although intended as a craft union, it was soon taking in skilled workers from many crafts, including ship carpenters, machinists, miners, blacksmiths, stonecutters, masons, ironworkers, and others. Only lawyers, physicians, bankers, saloonkeepers, gamblers, and stockbrokers were denied membership. Its secret ritual, derived from Freemasonry, made it at first suspect to the Catholic Church, and it might have expired early had it not been for its Grand Master Workman, Terence V. Powderly, who took over the Knights in 1879. The Catholic Powderly, a talkative, flamboyant Celt, was one of twelve children of a Pennsylvania teamster. After scant schooling he had worked on a railroad, then in 1866, at the age of seventeen, was apprenticed to a machinist, a trade he remained in until he was twenty-eight. He joined a machinist's union, holding various offices in it and in the Knights of Labor, which he joined in 1874. Class- and political-minded, in 1878 he was elected mayor of Scranton as the candidate of the Greenback-Labor party. As head of the Knights of Labor, he persuaded the organization to drop some of its veil of secrecy, making it acceptable to the Catholic Church—and thus to Catholic workers.

Powderly did not believe in class war but in a collaboration of owners and workmen for the goal of a coopera-

tive commonwealth that would completely abolish the wage system. Under his mastership the Knights demanded an eight-hour day, arbitration of labor disputes, a graduated income tax, equal wages for women, and greenbacks, while opposing child and convict labor and the importation of contract laborers. In 1878 the Knights of Labor had nine thousand members. The organization grew rapidly in the great wave of strikes that swept the country in 1884 following wage reductions during a depression year. That year the Knights won strikes against the Union Pacific, forcing that railroad to rescind several wage cuts. The following year successful strikes against Jay Gould's Erie Railroad left the Knights undisputed leaders of the labor movement. Membership, which had risen sharply to one hundred thousand by 1885, soared in a year to more than seven hundred thousand. Workers, still harboring the bitter memories of the great railroad strike of 1877 and filled with resentment over wage cuts and the use by employers of black lists and yellow-dog contracts—an employee's agreement not to join a union if hired—and even, as in the coal fields of Ohio, of the armed force of militia and Pinkerton detectives, flocked to the Knights' increasingly militant banners.

In a time of rapid economic and social transformation, with the rise of the great corporations, relations between the classes grew in every way more impersonal. An artisan like Paul Revere in the eighteenth century had lived in his simple wooden house in Boston's North End near Governor Thomas Hutchinson's elegant brick mansion—and neither governor nor artisan had thought twice about it. A hundred years later, faced with the wave of Irish immigrants fleeing the famine, the Yankee upper classes abandoned first physical and then political control of the city, retreating to their Beacon Hill-Back Bay redoubt. Workingmen might live in the same city with the middle and upper classes, but the three no longer shared the same streets and rarely knew each other. "I once knew a wealthy manufacturer who personally visited and looked after the comforts of his invalid operatives," a Boston clergyman wrote. "I know of no such case now." Charles Francis Adams, grandson of the yeoman President, observed with blunt hauteur: "I don't associate with the laborers on my place, nor would the association be agreeable to either of us. Their customs, language, habits and conventionalities differ from mine; as do those of their children."

Fluid from its beginnings, having severed its eighteenth-century links with an aristocratic tradition, Amer-

In 1868 the first national eight-hour-day law affected persons employed by or for the federal government. This symbol-filled poster published by the Mechanics' State Council of California features the Mare Island Navy Yard at Vallejo.

ica was weak in social continuity. At best an attenuated family tradition still held sway in cities like Philadelphia and Boston. There could be little social permanence in a country of unlimited land that lacked the stabilizing Old World props of primogeniture and entail. Captain Frederick Marryat, an English visitor, commenting on the American scene at its industrial beginnings, noted: "The stream flows inland, and those who are here today are gone tomorrow, and their places in society filled up by others who ten years back had no prospect of ever being admitted. All is transition, the waves follow one another to the far west, the froth and scum boiling in the advance."

What the American social structure faced in the decades after the Civil War was the emergence of a new upper class in all its crudities, a periodic phenomenon well known to the United States. Only the abundance of new wealth was extraordinary. The emergent American industrial millionaires had been far more concerned with the making of money than with the thought of what they might do with it. Jim Fisk and Diamond Jim Brady wallowed in the gaudy sensual moment, but the goal of most of the *arrivistes*—and particularly of their wives— was social acceptance and assimilation.

As the commercial and financial center of the United States, its largest, most opulent and indulgent city, New York rather than Washington became the social center of the country, the magnet to which the new rich were

OVERLEAF: *The marble mansion in Childe Hassam's painting was built in 1869 for dry-goods king A. T. Stewart and cost $2,000,000. Then known as one of America's finest homes, it stood at Thirty-fourth Street and Fifth Avenue in New York.*
SANTA BARBARA MUSEUM OF ART, PRESTON MORTON COLLECTION

drawn. Leader of that social world was Mrs. William Astor, half-estranged wife of the roué great-grandson of a German butcher. The butcher's son, John Jacob Astor, had arrived in New York in 1783 with seven German flutes as his stock in trade. Even after he had risen through the fur trade and real estate to become one of the country's richest men, he could still barely read and write, and according to former Secretary of the Treasury Albert Gallatin, still "ate his ice cream and peas with a knife." Two generations later his granddaughter-in-law was New York's "Queen of the Four Hundred." It was the self-styled "Autocrat of Drawing Rooms," Ward McAllister, cousin of lobby king Sam Ward, who had established Mrs. Astor above the older Knickerbocker families and who coined the phrase "the Four Hundred" to designate the members of fashionable New York society—reputedly the number that would fit into Mrs. Astor's ballroom. The Southern-born McAllister, insignificant in appearance, short, balding, with a drooping Van Dyke beard and the beginnings of a potbelly, found his mission in life in molding a plutocracy into an American aristocracy. In 1860 he traveled abroad to observe the manners, habits, and ways of life of the actual nobility. Returning, he saw he could organize Society by reviving the eighteenth-century assemblies. Shortly after the Civil War he arranged several cotillion suppers at Delmonico's as a preliminary to the setting up of a series of select balls, called the Patriarch Balls. As organizer and with the sponsorship of Mrs. Astor, McAllister made himself New York's social arbiter. To Mrs. Astor, scarcely removed from the memory of her husband's grasping old German grandfather, who had died in 1848, the Vanderbilts were not acceptable.

In Commodore Vanderbilt's dozen years of railroad manipulations after the Civil War, he had run up his fortune from ten million to one hundred million dollars. Whether he would be accepted by Society, with or without the capital S, never concerned him. But it was his grandson William who would set the social pattern of the next age, to be imitated by oil magnates, financiers, tin-plate kings, industrial barons, nobles of meat packing, and other newcomers to riches. Until William Kissam Vanderbilt and his wife, the former Alva Smith of Mobile, Alabama, surfaced in the New York social world, the living pattern of the rich was still bounded by the rows of brownstone-front mansions that had ousted the graceful Federalist style. The Vanderbilts shattered this pattern with a grandiose landmark in limestone when

they commissioned the Vermont-born architect Richard Morris Hunt to build them a house on the corner of Fifty-second Street and Fifth Avenue, a stupendous turreted contrivance in imitation of the Château de Blois.

Hunt was the first American student to be trained at the Ecole des Beaux Arts in Paris, where he enrolled in 1846 at the age of nineteen. For nine years he remained in France, assuming a Parisian manner in speech and dress and behavior, so successful in his studies that he even assisted the Paris architect Hector Lefuel in completing the Louvre. He was twenty-seven years old when he returned to the United States, started his practice in New York, and set up a small school of architecture there embodying the Beaux Arts methods. At the time of the Civil War he went back to Europe, staying this time until 1868. On his second return to the booming postwar city he prospered, but not until the late seventies did there come to him through the Vanderbilts the opportunity to amaze blasé New Yorkers and make his reputation across the land. Though a present-day critic has labeled Hunt's Fifth Avenue château "formalized barbarism," it seemed to passers-by in its spectacular newness a thing of "glittering beauty." Charles F. McKim, of the architectural firm of McKim, Mead and White, used to walk up Fifth Avenue late in the evening because he found he slept better after feasting his eyes on so much loveliness. If the château's outside was de Blois, the white, pink, and green marble interior was eclectic, with grand staircases, a three-story entrance hall, Moorish and Byzantine rooms, Italianate allegorical ceilings, classical friezes and gold-leafed nymphs, tapestries, armor, and medieval and Renaissance furniture. The total cost was more than three million dollars.

As a housewarming, Alva Vanderbilt prepared the most ornate and costly ($250,000) fancy-dress ball ever to be given in the United States. It was held in March, 1883, and twelve hundred guests were invited, not including Mrs. Astor until she—in her anxiety to have her daughter shine at the festivities—paid a capitulating call on the Vanderbilts. Alva appeared at her ball as a Venetian princess, surrounded by live white doves, while her brother-in-law, named after the old Commodore, assumed the guise of Louis XVI. An actual French nobleman, the Duc de Morny, was among the guests, as was ex-President Grant. From that high moment of pageantry, the Vanderbilts became a power in the social as well as the financial world. The mansion convinced

Though chronically ill for much of his adult life, and fat, Henry Hobson Richardson (above in a portrait he admired) was still full of energy. He designed a remarkable variety of buildings—from churches to railroad stations. Below is a drawing of his proposed cathedral for Albany, New York.

even Ward McAllister that the Vanderbilts had earned their ticket to the Patriarch Ball.

For Hunt, the éclat of the Vanderbilt château made him the country's most sought-after architect, the founding father of what architects of the time fondly referred to as the American Renaissance. Soon he was building town castles for the Astors and other wealthy patrons on Fifth Avenue, and transforming Newport from a staid New England resort into the turreted fashion center of McAllister's dreams. The new rich, truly seeing their homes as their castles, flocked to him. Gothic palaces soon lined Fifth Avenue, to be emulated in Chicago, San Francisco, and even Boston. Few patrons were like Collis Huntington, who had his dream castle built at Fifth Avenue and Fifty-seventh Street, then, tormented by the thought that men build houses only to die in them, never lived in it. Near Asheville, North Carolina, Hunt designed Biltmore, another Château de Blois for another Vanderbilt, the most palatial country house

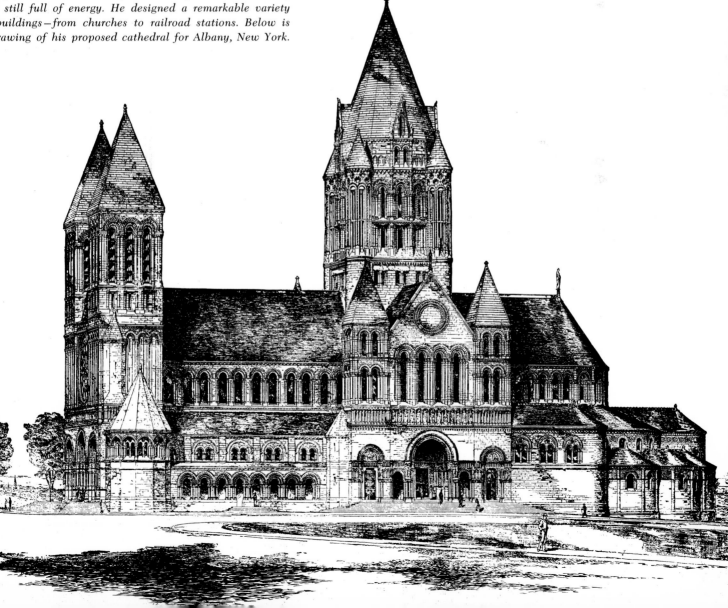

ever seen in America. But it was in the grandiose classical-inspired Administration Building in the Great White City of Chicago's 1893 Columbian Exposition that his career reached its peak.

The advent of the American Renaissance brought with it the battle of the styles. From the mid-1860's past 1880, Victorian Gothic had reigned triumphant, particularly in church architecture and in such brick monsters — once scorned, but now regarded with some interest — as Harvard's Memorial Hall. By 1885 Gothic was succumbing to the reconstituted French Romanesque, introduced to America by the Boston architect Henry H. Richardson. Richardson had studied in Paris at the Beaux Arts and was a more fundamental architect than Hunt, using the ponderous Romanesque as a viable medium for commercial and public buildings across America, stripping it of superfluous ornamentation, adapting it to private houses, railroad stations, libraries, stores and offices, and Harvard's fortresslike Sever Hall. His masterpiece, Trinity Church on Boston's Copley Square, is still regarded as one of the great churches of the North American continent.

In the wave of applause and imitation that followed Hunt's Vanderbilt mansion-château there were a few dissenters. The most important was the Boston-born architect Louis Henri Sullivan, who wondered at the time why passers-by did not laugh to see a cut-down Château de Blois on a New York street. Sullivan, the son of an improvident dancing teacher, had followed the arid architectural course then prescribed by the Massachusetts Institute of Technology, but soon found himself at variance with cut and dried imitations of the past. For his purposes he needed neither the framework of the Romanesque nor the Renaissance. Called the father of modernism, he believed that the solution to every architectural problem was contained in itself. However, his Transportation Building for the Columbian Exposition of 1893, while spectacular in appearance, was planned with little relation between form and the function it was to serve. His famous dictum "form follows function" became the slogan of a whole school of architects, among them Frank Lloyd Wright, who joined Sullivan in 1887 at the age of eighteen when the latter was designing Chicago's Auditorium Building, his last essay in traditional architecture. Sullivan, much influenced by *Leaves of Grass*, aimed to translate Walt Whitman's democratic vistas into stone. "With me," he wrote, "architecture is not an art but a religion, and that religion but a part of the greater religion of democracy." Already in 1885 a band of architects who, like Sullivan, had sensed the opportunities in Chicago after the great fire of 1871 were building the first metal-framed tall building there for the Home Insurance Company. Commercial buildings began to sprout up from five to twenty-five stories high. Though Sullivan did not invent the skyscraper, he can be said to be its foster father in the sense that he was the leader in developing not just height but an American functional style to go with it. A tall building, he wrote, "must be every inch a proud and soaring thing, rising in sheer exultation . . . from bottom to top . . . a unit without a single dissenting line." His first steel and stone demonstration of this maxim was the Wainwright Building in St. Louis, which may be said to have opened the age of the skyscraper.

The two most celebrated and enduring architectural monuments of the period are a statue and a bridge: the Frenchman Frédéric Auguste Bartholdi's Statue of Liberty, dominating New York's harbor, and the German-American engineer John Roebling's suspension bridge over the East River to Brooklyn. In their day bridge and statue were rivals for the claim of eighth wonder of the world. The 151-foot-tall goddess was 50 feet taller than the Colossus of Rhodes, and her pedestal raised her 100 feet, to bring her torch 251 feet above the water. The span of the Brooklyn Bridge was half again as long as any bridge that had yet been built.

In the eight decades since its unveiling, the Statue of Liberty — the gift of the French to the American people to honor (a decade late) the centennial of the Declaration of Independence — has become almost as revered as the Stars and Stripes and, like the flag, so familiar that it is no longer possible to judge it solely by aesthetic standards. Marking the gateway to the New World, inscribed with Emma Lazarus' idealistic lines, it has become as integral a landmark of New York as the Eiffel Tower is of Paris. Oddly enough, Gustave Eiffel, who gave his name to the tower, designed the interior framework that supports the statue.

The Brooklyn Bridge was begun in 1869. Roebling designed it as a suspension bridge with two stone towers and four woven steel cables capable of sustaining a weight of eighteen thousand tons. He viewed his creation "as a great work of art, and as a successful specimen of advanced bridge engineering," a structure that would "forever testify to the energy, enterprise and wealth of that community which shall secure its erection." Four-

The Statue of Liberty (left arm under construction, above) was truly a people-to-people gift. No government aid was involved: thousands of Frenchmen contributed to underwriting the statue, and American citizens paid for the pedestal.

teen years of struggle, disasters, disappointments, followed. Roebling himself had a foot crushed and died of lockjaw in 1869. His son Washington Roebling carried on with his father's dream. More than twenty men died in the course of construction. Sand hogs working on the piers in caissons seventy-eight feet under water suffered from deafness, pneumonia, and the bends. Explosion, fire, and flood were constant dangers. The younger Roebling was a victim of the bends. He became partially paralyzed and was slowly growing deaf and blind so that finally he was reduced to following the progress of construction with binoculars from his Brooklyn window. At last, on May 24, 1883, to the pealing of the bells of Trinity Church and cannonades from Castle William, President Chester Arthur and Governor Grover Cleveland opened the soaring, unforgettably graceful span.

The Columbian Exposition of 1893 gave the world a chance to see something of American artistic attainments, and if those attainments fell short of genius, they were surprisingly high for a crass and ostentatious era that had enthroned money as the highest good. The Chicago architects John W. Root and Daniel Burnham saw an exposition that would be an exuberant mixture of many styles — Romanesque, Grecian, Spanish, Moorish mosques, Chinese pagodas — and that would be laced by canals and reflecting pools on which gondolas moved. However, Eastern architects prevailed with their concept of a city of Greek, Roman, and Renaissance elegance. As a result, there was little that was original in concept even though the noted architects of the day had been commissioned to design the individual buildings.

A myriad of statues was required to embellish this pseudoclassic city by Lake Michigan, and the best of the American sculptors, under the guidance of Augustus Saint-Gaudens, joined in creating art works of plaster of Paris. Saint-Gaudens, in his enthusiasm, exclaimed, "Do you realize that this is the greatest meeting of artists since the fifteenth century?" But although many of the

181

works that resulted were imposing, few were memorable. The most noteworthy was Daniel C. French's sixty-five-foot-tall *The Republic*. Of all the sculptors who took part, only Saint-Gaudens and French would prove to have durable reputations. Saint-Gaudens' 1881 statue of Admiral David Farragut had made him famous, though his enduring fame came from his memorial to Henry Adams' wife in Washington's Rock Creek Cemetery, the enigmatic female figure that may be either pity or grief or both. His *Sherman* in New York City is considered the greatest equestrian statue of modern times. The largely self-taught Daniel French had won his first fame with his *The Minuteman*, unveiled at Concord in 1875. He also did the figure of the seated John Harvard at Cambridge and the great brooding Abraham Lincoln in the white-columned Lincoln Memorial in Washington.

Though the majority of those who visited the Columbian Exposition's Great White City were undoubtedly impressed by French's huge plaster and gilt female statue *The Republic*, in their hearts they still felt most at ease with the homespun sentimental realism of the mass-produced statuary groups of John Rogers, just as they preferred above all other pictures at the exhibition Thomas Hovenden's meticulously painted tear-jerker *Breaking Home Ties*, of the farm boy leaving his family for the city. Most of the paintings exhibited were of the every-picture-tells-a-story variety or else the pallid classical allegories preferred by rich New Yorkers; but there were countertrends that, though passed over, would in the end come to be regarded as the flesh and bone of American art. The illustrators Frederic Remington and Arthur Frost were represented, and there were nine portraits by John Singer Sargent. Thomas Eakins' *Agnew Clinic* stood out in a realism that seemed alive against the thin imitations of Titian and Raphael. But Winslow Homer, with his group of paintings, which included *Fog Warning*—and that did at least win a medal—would later come to be acknowledged as the great artist of the exhibition, remembered long after the popular artists of the moment who showed their paintings at the White City had been forgotten.

Born in Boston in 1836, two years after James McNeill Whistler had been born in nearby Lowell, Homer remained rooted all his life in the granite-strewn New England landscape. At nineteen his impoverished father apprenticed him to a lithographer. Reaching his majority, he became a free-lance artist, doing much of his work for *Harper's Weekly*. Then, at the outbreak of the Civil War, he followed the troops as an artist-reporter, sending back sketches to *Harper's* and other periodicals. His view of the war was far from heroic, and the increasingly somber nature of the conflict turned him from wood-block engraving to painting in oil. His first canvases were homely scenes of army life in the field, themes—such as soldiers listening to the regimental band play "Home, Sweet Home"—that might easily have turned maudlin yet with him remained austerely, if wistfully, realistic. After the war he sketched and painted his native rural New England—the farmers and fields and summer resorts—in the naturalistic tradition of William Sydney Mount and George Caleb Bingham but with his own sense of composition and his intense feeling for the immediacy of the sun-drenched moment. From his sunny landscapes Homer would move on to his great final theme of men against the sea, which he would develop for the rest of his long life in self-imposed isolation on Prouts Neck on the Maine coast.

Only a degree less in their achievement were his fellow artists Albert Pinkham Ryder and Thomas Eakins. With Homer, they made a trio worthy to stand against any of the impressionists or any foreign school. Ryder, an American William Blake, had passed his formative days in the greatest squalor in New York, and drew from an elemental world of dreams in which the sea became the great symbol, mist-shrouded and enigmatic, over which men sailed on the mysterious voyage of life. Thomas Eakins on the other hand was a hardheaded realist who painted things just as he saw them: clinics, operating rooms, prize fights, oarsmen, and hard-faced businessmen. Like Homer, he refused to compromise, and was so unbending in his delineations that friends who sat for him were known to refuse their portraits when he offered them as gifts. Neither Homer, Ryder, nor Eakins graced the walls of an Astor or a Vanderbilt.

The stream of American literature ran low during the second half of the nineteenth century. Mark Twain was, without doubt, the commanding figure among the prose writers of the period, and of his works the greatest, *Adventures of Huckleberry Finn*, was published in 1885. Viewed at the time as essentially a juvenile book and a sequel to *The Adventures of Tom Sawyer*, that account of the summer voyage of the boy Huck Finn and the Negro Jim down the Mississippi on a raft has since come to be considered almost as an allegorical recounting of the American experience.

The same year that saw *Huckleberry Finn* also noted the publication of William Dean Howells' *The Rise of Silas Lapham*, marking the emergence of a realism of sorts in New England. For all that the great reading public preferred the exotic, religion-tinged romanticism of Lew Wallace's *Ben Hur*, the general trend of literature after the war was toward realism. Today most of the authors' names are embalmed in histories of literature, their works scarcely read, but in their day they opened new windows. Bret Harte, writing in prose and verse of the mining camps, became for a time the most celebrated author in the country. Lincoln's biographer, John Hay, used the dialect of ordinary people in his *Pike County Ballads and Other Pieces*. George Washington Cable enlarged the local color of New Orleans until those qualities took on something of the universal, as did the Maine of Sarah Orne Jewett's "country of the pointed firs" and the Massachusetts of the darker vision of Mary Wilkins Freeman. After Whitman's *Leaves of Grass*, subsequent poetry seemed a thin path to nowhere, lined with poetasters like Bayard Taylor, Richard Henry Stoddard, and Thomas Bailey Aldrich. Henry W. Longfellow and John Greenleaf Whittier still wrote, but they had long since written their best, and in the face of the new age James Russell Lowell retreated into an Anglophile Toryism.

The rise of national large-circulation magazines gave authors unrivaled opportunities for finding their way into print. First appearing in 1883, the *Ladies Home Journal*, which had started out as the "Woman and the Home" section of Cyrus Curtis' *Tribune and Farmer*, would publish such noted American writers as Mark Twain, Bret Harte, Hamlin Garland, Joel Chandler Harris, and Sarah Orne Jewett. A rash of new magazines was made possible when Congress, in a postal act in 1875, provided low-cost mailing rates. Such high-priced magazines as the literary-minded *Harper's New Monthly Magazine*, the New England-oriented *Atlantic Monthly*, and the political-minded, reformist *The Nation*, which was founded by E. L. Godkin in 1865—all of which appealed to an intellectual elite—would be followed by cut-rate magazines of popular appeal: *Munsey's Magazine*, *McClure's Magazine*, *The Cosmopolitan*, and the revivified *The Saturday Evening Post*—the latter cost Curtis a thousand dollars in 1897.

From 1865 to 1885 the number of American magazines increased from seven hundred to thirty-three hundred. At the beginning of the nineties there were a number of specialized magazines, such as the *Scientific American*, *Popular Science Monthly*, *The National Geographic Magazine*, *Ladies' World*, *Home and Art*, as well as general news-summarizing journals, like the weekly *Literary Digest* and the monthly *Review of Reviews*. The rotary press, Ottmar Mergenthaler's linotype machine, conveyor systems, and production schedules were doing their part to make large-scale circulation possible. Advertising was the final ingredient. For advertising, which had once been a nuisance, now in the dawning age of the consumer with mass production, standardization of products, and the introduction of brand names, became a necessity. A recent biographer

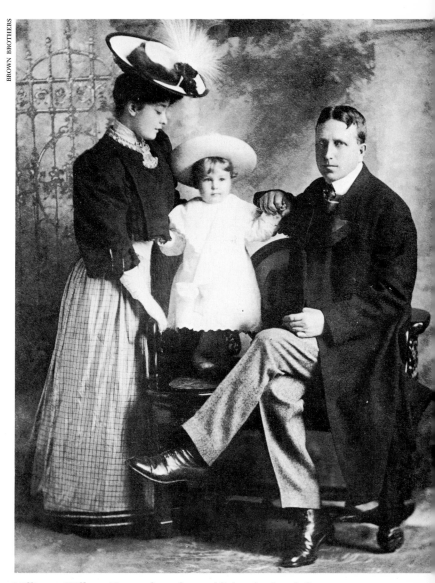

BROWN BROTHERS

Millicent Willson Hearst bore her publisher husband five sons—the eldest, George, is pictured with them—before he left her for actress Marion Davies. Millicent refused divorce, but remained friendly to him until he died in 1951.

Advertising
TAE SUN
Gives best results

COLLIER'S

March Twenty-third ♪ ♪ Price Ten Cents

Drawn by
Edward Penfield

WOMENS

EDITION
(BUFFALO)
COURIER

HARPER'S

MARCH

of Harding's wrote of that productive period, America of the mid-eighties:

America's postwar industrial expansion was shifting from capital to consumer goods. Local merchants were beginning to enlarge their stock with unheard-of novelties. Hardware men offered all sorts of new labor-saving gadgets. Dry goods merchants and clothiers, used to ordering their consignments twice a year, now took smaller and more varied monthly selections. Advertising, storekeepers were beginning to realize, could clear their loaded shelves. No longer were advertisements merely a nuisance bribe to avert the malice of an impoverished local paper, but, properly inserted, they could be the magic key to a quick turnover. The newspaper business was changing its character from that of a beggar and blackmailer to become one of the major industries of every little town.

It was Frank A. Munsey, a hand-to-mouth publisher with two failing magazines — *Munsey's* and *The Argosy* — who grasped the economic fact that a magazine could sell for less than its cost of production if it could obtain a high volume of advertising through large-scale distribution. His rate was five hundred dollars a page for a claimed circulation of seven hundred thousand, and with increased advertising he cut the price of his magazine from twenty-five to ten cents. His formula made his fortune and was soon imitated by Samuel S. McClure, Curtis, and others.

For newspapers, advertising was increasingly the staff of life, though many of the older, more established ones were slow to sense it. Newspaper readers were for the most part upper- and middle-class. Even James Gordon Bennett, using sex and crime like fireworks to build up his *Herald*, had appealed to native Americans. It was the immigrant Joseph Pulitzer who set out to create a paper for the urban working class, for immigrant groups, for those just verging on literacy. Pulitzer was a curious mixture of reformer and sensationalist, a professional friend of the people, a man who discovered that he could advance his own interests by defending those of the public. For him the world was a sensational place where sensational news had to be reported sensationally. Whenever he was faced with a dearth of sensations, he manufactured them.

Hungarian-born, a penniless ex-Union soldier, Pulitzer had wandered after the war to St. Louis, where he tended mules, worked as a stevedore, and took other odd jobs. At twenty-one he became a reporter for a German-language paper, the *Westliche Post*, his first real step upward. Ten years later, in 1878, he was able to take

over the bankrupt St. Louis *Dispatch*. He soon showed himself a brilliant editor, introducing reform and sex to the headlines, making his paper controversial, incisive, surprising, loud, and racy. In the process he made himself rich, for by the time he decided that St. Louis was too small for him, he was making forty thousand dollars a year. Moving on to New York in 1883, he dickered for the ailing *World* with Jay Gould, who had acquired it as part of a railroad deal. Although the flamboyant, red-bearded newspaperman and the phlegmatic financier were old enemies, they did eventually come to terms. Charles A. Dana's impishly clever *Sun* and the more sedate *Herald* were then the city's leading papers with circulations of about one hundred and forty thousand each. The *Tribune* and the *Times* were New York's other important journals. All four were either Republican or independent. Pulitzer envisioned a hard-hitting Democratic paper aiming for the masses with every sensational trick his fertile mind could muster. "The *World*," he announced, "is the people's newspaper." Within a year under his guidance it reached a circulation of one hundred thousand and in a little over a decade was selling more than a million copies daily. "Wonderfully peppery and noticeable," the editor of the Boston *Herald* found it shortly after Pulitzer had taken over, and noted that the New York newspaper situation was much as it had been forty years earlier when the irrepressible Bennett had arrived on the scene.

If Pulitzer fought his way up with the *World*, then his great rival William Randolph Hearst can be said to have fought his way down. For as the son of the California mineowner George Hearst, who later bought himself a seat in the United States Senate, William Randolph came into the world with more silver spoons than he could put in his mouth. As an only child, born in 1863, he was spoiled by his mother, indulged by his father. He left preparatory school in his second year at the school's request. His career at Harvard, a succession of expensive practical jokes, such as turning loose several dozen roosters in the Yard to celebrate an election victory, ended finally when he sent all his professors and instructors chamber pots with their names — or, it is said by some, their portraits — glazed on the bottom. Yet there were will and talent when he wanted to use them. His studies did not interest him, but as business manager of *The Lampoon*, Harvard's humor magazine, for the first time he made that publication pay.

The Lampoon sparked his fascination with the world

In an age of flamboyance and expansion in American journalism some of the most striking work was done by the illustrators. Clockwise here, from top left, the artists are Louis J. Rhead, Edward Penfield (twice), and Alice Glenny.

of print. To learn journalism he went to work for a year as a reporter on Pulitzer's New York *World,* captivated by that paper's mixture of scandalmongering and idealism. Some years before, George Hearst had taken over the San Francisco *Examiner* for the debts it owed him, but even under his management it had never really prospered. In his Harvard days William had begged his reluctant father for the paper, and had been refused. Now, accepting his son's term on the *World* as evidence that he was serious about journalism, the elder Hearst gave William the *Examiner.*

Shortly before his twenty-fourth birthday, William Randolph Hearst became publisher and editor of the *Examiner* and set out to apply his own radical cure to that ailing paper. His prescription: to out-Pulitzer Pulitzer. No expense was too large, no effort too great, no action too outrageous, to obtain or concoct the sensational story. *Examiner* reporters plunged off ferryboats, had themselves committed to jails, public hospitals, and institutions for the insane. Their editor was one of the first users of the sob sister, and he initiated a dozen other features. He lived his paper in all its garishness. He even had the temerity to challenge Collis Huntington's Southern Pacific Railroad, an institution regarded by most California editors and politicians as too potent to criticize. Against all expectations, including his father's, the *Examiner* began to make money.

San Francisco nevertheless remained peripheral. New York, the nerve center of national influence, was Hearst's real goal. For some time he had been prospecting for a New York paper. At last in 1895 he was able to buy the *Morning Journal,* owned by a publisher of dubious reputation, John R. McLean of Cincinnati. Founded by Pulitzer's brother Albert, the *Journal*—known as the chambermaid's delight—had been sold to McLean the year before for a million dollars and had been a heavy money loser for him. Hearst, even with a broken-down paper, at last had his foot in the door of the journalistic metropolis.

With that foot the thirty-two-year-old newcomer soon kicked the door open. A David in New York publishing, he strode in with brash pugnacity to challenge the Goliath Pulitzer's *World,* which with its three editions was the most thriving and opulent paper in the country. Hearst began by dropping the price of his *Journal* to one cent, enlarging it, and starting a ferocious circulation campaign. His recipe was "crime and underwear," his aim, to shock. If the *World* set itself up as the paper of

the underdog, the *Journal* would be the paper that *fought* for the underdog. Hearst advertised his paper on streetcars and billboards, set up *Journal* soup kitchens, cultivated the masses in ways Pulitzer had never thought of. Unabashed at a deficit of one hundred thousand dollars a month, he hired away Pulitzer's best men, heedless of the cost—to the great indignation of the nervous and now partially blind Pulitzer, who had done the same thing to other publishers ten years before. Hearst came out with evening and Sunday editions to rival Pulitzer's. The latter's Sunday edition was the most lurid of his papers. Hearst made his *Sunday Journal* more so. With cartoons and pictures he pitched his appeal to those who could scarcely read the headlines. He was a Democrat, he was for labor, and above everything else he was out to astonish and stupefy. A critic wrote of his paper at the time: "An ideal morning edition . . . would have been one in which the Prince of Wales had gone into vaudeville, Queen Victoria had married her cook, the Pope had issued an encyclical favoring free love . . . France had declared war on Germany, the President of the United States had secured a divorce in order to marry the Dowager Empress of China . . . and the Sultan of Turkey had been converted to Christianity—all of these being 'scoops' in the form of 'signed statements.'"

Within a year of Hearst's explosive take-over, the circulation of the *Journal* was second only to that of the *World* with the prospect of soon overtaking it altogether. Hearst continued to lose money—his recent inheritance—with the indifference he had always shown.

For all his flamboyance, Hearst was more astute than his critics. He had come to New York because he knew—as who did not?—that the city as well as the country was growing. Subtracting from the number of New Yorkers the combined circulation of the existing newspapers, he had become confident that there was room for still another paper—if the new readers could be reached. Hearst in his presumption was right. For America was growth, was indeed the living water that had started out as a small, relatively clean stream. Fed by tributaries from other nations, it had grown into a mighty, unifying river, gathering dirt and debris as it moved swiftly toward the twentieth century frothed with politics, mottled by privilege, too often clogged with the sediment of corruption, but impossible to hold back in its surge toward that sea of the future in which the overwhelming number of Americans believed and trusted.

A Time for Sports

In 1899 satirist George Ade wrote of two devotees of a sport relatively new to America: "They followed the Gutta Percha Balls with the intent swiftness of trained Bird Dogs, and each talked feverishly of Brassy Lies, and getting past the Bunker, and Lofting to the Green, and Slicing into the Bramble — each telling his own Game to the Ambient Air, and ignoring what the other Fellow had to say." As leisure time increased with mechanization, Americans enthusiastically sought ways to fill it. There were the gentle pastimes, such as bathing, above; and one could play, or watch others play, an increasing variety of more or less energetic games. In the half century after the Civil War, cycling and roller skating crazes swept the country, golf, lawn tennis, and ice hockey were introduced, basketball was invented, and football and baseball became sports that, as British diplomat James Bryce said, excited "an interest greater than any other public events except the Presidential election, and that comes only once in four years."

The various versions of baseball played on city streets, in 1910 (at left) as now, were enriched by fantasies of professional heroics. One player who fired young imaginations was Ty Cobb, above, star of the Detroit Tigers, a team that had just won three consecutive American League championships.

Pictured here is an early football match, a rugbylike contest between Harvard College and a Canadian team. Harvard played McGill at Cambridge and Montreal in 1874 and an all-star team at Montreal in 1875; which game this depicts is not certain.

In the days before fast films, the composite photograph was used to catch such populated action after the fact. In this case players and spectators posed individually for William Notman; then, with various embellishments, the scene was put together.

WIDE WORLD

The "Boston Strong Boy," John L. Sullivan, above, was the last of the bare-knuckle champions, ruling for ten years. The profession of boxing, considered brutal and outside the law in many communities, began to reform during the 1880's. The first championship fight in which the fists were covered by padded gloves was held in 1892: James J. Corbett—as he had promised, "without getting my hair mussed"—beat the out-of-shape Sullivan. At the right, fashionable motorists crowd the rail at a horse track.

BROWN BROTHERS

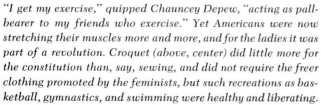

"I get my exercise," quipped Chauncey Depew, "acting as pall-bearer to my friends who exercise." Yet Americans were now stretching their muscles more and more, and for the ladies it was part of a revolution. Croquet (above, center) did little more for the constitution than, say, sewing, and did not require the freer clothing promoted by the feminists, but such recreations as basketball, gymnastics, and swimming were healthy and liberating.

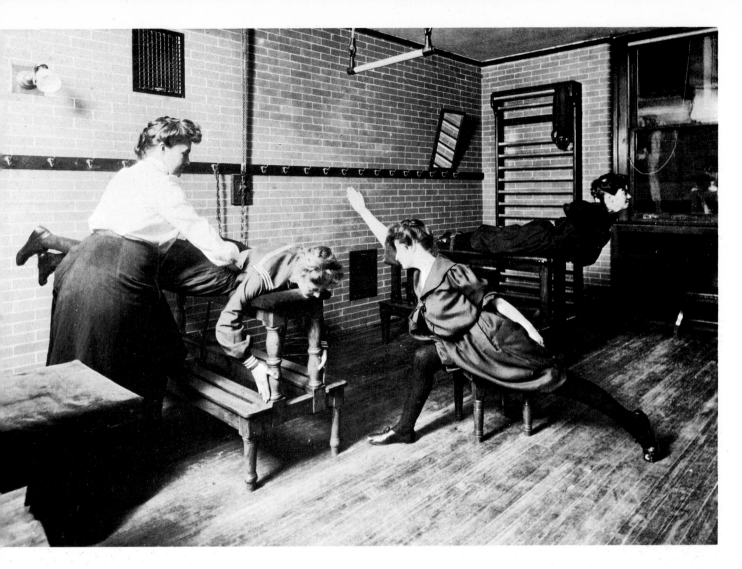

Near a lovely footbridge over the Susquehanna at Cooperstown, New York, a family poses in the wherry while Papa fishes.

The girls, their oars now carefully feathered, have nosed the boat into the bank. Mama guards the doll; the doll, the flag.

The Return of
the Democrats

*A*fter putting the White House behind him, ex-President, now once more General, Grant had embarked on a world tour, crisscrossing Europe several times before going on to the Near East, India, China, and Japan. He was entertained by the duke of Wellington and Queen Victoria, he dined with kings, he met the great men of his day—Thiers, Gladstone, Bismarck. Dutifully, phlegmatically, he saw the sights from London to Tokyo. Art, architecture, cathedrals, and ancient buildings continued to bore him. In Rome not even Marcus Aurelius' bronze horse interested him. Of Venice he remarked that it would be a pretty city if only it were drained.

Removed from the meshes of politics, the absent general again became a hero to his fellow countrymen. His tour lasted more than two years. If he had extended it a few months longer, he might have arrived back just in time to stampede the Republican convention of 1880 into nominating him. Unfortunately for his third-term ambitions he came back too soon. There were just too many receptions, there was too much fanfare, and soon the reaction set in. Anti-third-term clubs vied with Grant clubs. Grant's managers hustled him out of the country, this time on a visit to Cuba and Mexico that lasted until three months before the convention.

The 1880 convention was held in Chicago in June. The platform was carefully innocuous; it condemned polygamy and Chinese immigration, though when it cautiously expressed "sympathy" for civil service reform, an angered office-hungry carpetbagger from Texas sprang to his feet and shouted, "What are we up here for?"

For all his eroding image, Grant was still the leading Republican candidate. The Stalwarts marshaled solidly behind him, the Half-Breeds rallied around Senator James G. Blaine, while Treasury Secretary John Sherman followed a poor third. Blaine's name was placed in nomination first, followed by that of favorite son Senator William Windom of Minnesota, whose name was presented dutifully and perfunctorily. Grant was nominated by Senator John A. Logan, who took a single sentence to do so; then when the cheering had died down, Roscoe Conkling, at his magnetic best, did Grant the full honors with a spread-eagle, flag-waving seconding speech whose fervor wrung

In the scene at left, from Edgard Farasyn's end-of-the-century painting Les Emigrants, *passengers prepare to embark on the Red Star Line's S.S.* Pennland *at Antwerp for the voyage to America.*

These paintings are by Edward Lamson Henry, a leading historical artist in post-Civil War America and, as evidenced here, a fine genre artist as well. A contemporary characterized him as "the Washington Irving of a painted 'Sketch-Book'...."

thetic crowd dwindled. In a nearby police station, Inspector Bonfield had one hundred and eighty policemen standing by. In spite of the mayor's passing advice to him that no interference was needed, Bonfield, with Police Captain William Ward, marched his men out just before the meeting closed. Fielden, speaking from a wagon, was about to conclude when Ward appeared, raised his hand, and commanded those present to disperse. The indignant Fielden began to remonstrate, and while he was speaking to Ward, someone, shielded by the darkness, threw a bomb that exploded with a blinding flash among the police. Blue-uniformed bodies sprawled on the cobbles. Seven policemen died, more than fifty were injured, and the rest in a wild panic fired their revolvers at the crowd, some of whom began to return the fire. Between five and ten civilians were

killed, and some fifty were injured.

Fear and anger at the anarchist outrage swept the country. Even the labor unions joined in the outcry. The bomb thrower was never discovered, but Spies, Parsons, Fielden, and seven other anarchists were indicted as having aided and abetted the actual perpetrator. After an intense, dramatic, and certainly prejudiced trial before the biased Judge Joseph E. Gary, Spies, Parsons, Fielden, and four other anarchists were sentenced to death. Spies and Parsons and two others were hanged. Fielden and one other man had their sentences commuted to life imprisonment; they and a third man, who had been sentenced to fifteen years in prison, were freed in 1893 by the Democratic Governor J. P. Altgeld, who had become so convinced of their innocence that he ruined himself politically by pardoning them. From

The Puck cartoon, published after Cleveland's election in 1884, shows him braving the dangerous straits between Scylla and Charybdis, threatened by spoilsmen on one side and (as the nation's then most eligible bachelor) wedding bells on the other.

American art came of age in the Old World. John Singer Sargent, like many American artists, spent his life mainly in Europe and portrayed not only Americans (the Isaac N. P. Stokeses, above) but fashionable Europeans, too. James McNeill Whistler (Cremorne Gardens, top right) and impressionist Mary Cassatt (Summertime, right) did all their major work abroad and made key contributions to developments in painting.

PUCK, OCTOBER 4, 1893

HARPER'S WEEKLY, MAY 15, 1886

Anarchism's view of man and government, and its appeals for violence, deeply troubled Victorian America. So did the fact that many anarchist leaders were foreign-born. Above, an 1893 cartoon; right, a contemporary view of the Haymarket Riot.

that bomb flash in the Haymarket, anarchism—the image of a bearded madman with a smoking bomb in his hand —would remain an American bogey.

Even before the Haymarket Riot, Cleveland had been concerned with the whole problem of labor conflict. His message to Congress in April, 1886, the first ever issued by a President on the subject, recommended that the government take over the role of arbitrator in labor disputes and requested a permanent labor commission to whom disputants might appeal. House and Senate members, with an eye to the next election, diluted the President's proposals, but a bill legalizing the incorporation of national trade unions was passed and signed

into law, and toward the end of his term Cleveland put his name to an act providing for voluntary arbitration of railroad disputes.

Resentment against the railroads with their arbitrary and excessive rates had grown strong, particularly in the West, where Huntington, Stanford, and Gould prospered greatly at the expense of their often-mismanaged lines. Animosity increased when in 1886 the Supreme Court struck down all state regulation of interstate railroads. A year later a Senate committee proposed an interstate commerce commission. In the controversy attending the bill's passage Cleveland took no part, and he signed the final act "with reservations," fearing that "the cure might be worse than the disease." Actually, the commission had no real power, as the railroads soon discovered. The Pacific Railway Commission, appointed to investigate the dubious affairs of the Western railroads, recommended that the lines settle their debts to the government by paying one hundred million dol-

lars. It was a proposal that the conservative Cleveland approved of in spite of the demands by union leaders and the anticorporation press for more drastic measures. But before any such bill could be maneuvered through Congress, Cleveland's term expired.

By 1887 the redeemable public debt had been retired. Cleveland found himself confronted with the problem of a treasury surplus, the same problem that had baffled Arthur. To the ordinary politician the solution seemed both easy and palatable — spend the money, preferably in his home district. Blaine now favored turning the fund over to the states. Cleveland, like Arthur, was more concerned with shutting off the money spigot. Heavy duties were being paid on necessary imports while many luxuries escaped any payment. Money in circulation grew scarce as it accumulated in the treasury, and there was much public grumbling against "bloated bond-holders" and the "Shylocks" of Wall Street. The President felt obliged to scrutinize the tariff, the source of

this embarrassment of riches. Just after his election he had told Schurz in dismay: "I am ashamed to say it, but the truth is I know nothing about the tariff. . . . Will you tell me how to go about it to learn?" Late in 1887 he took up its study with the same relentless persistence he had once given to his law books, often working through the night in his White House study.

The President's annual message in December, 1887, was devoted wholly to the tariff. He called the existing schedule of tariffs a "vicious, inequitable and illogical source of unnecessary taxation. . . . a burden upon those with moderate means and the poor . . . a tax which with relentless grasp is fastened upon the clothing of every man, woman and child in the land." He assailed the tariff-protected industries, "which have for their object the regulation of the supply and price of commodities." He warned that if "safe, careful and deliberate reform" were rejected, there might come a time when "an abused and irritated people . . . may insist upon a radical and sweeping rectification of . . . wrongs."

What Cleveland accomplished, with an election looming, was to give the Democrats their first real issue besides reform since 1860, leading his party away from the threadbare issue of states' rights and minimal government and making it the defender of the people through a low tariff. Blaine grasped the challenge at once. After a visit to Carnegie in his feudal castle in Scotland in the autumn of 1887, he went on to Paris, and from there issued a counterblast to the President's message. In the Republican leader's interpretation, reducing the tariff would benefit British manufacturers at the expense of American industry, American labor would suffer from the competition of cheap foreign labor, and farmers would suffer equally. Blaine looked forward to "a full and fair contest on the question of protection."

Besides arousing the protectionists, Cleveland also alienated the vast majority of the Civil War veterans, who wielded great political power through the Grand Army of the Republic. Not only had Cleveland hired a substitute to do his fighting for him, not only was he the leader of the old party of rebellion, not only had he consistently vetoed private pension bills, but in February, 1887, he had rejected the Dependent Pension Bill, which would have granted twelve dollars a month to all veterans who had served at least ninety days and who were unable to support themselves. He angered the veterans much more in June when he suggested to governors that it would be a gracious act to return captured

221

Confederate battle flags to the Southern states. Ohio's Governor "Fire Alarm Joe" Foraker, who had marched with Sherman across Georgia, replied that "no rebel flags will be surrendered while I am governor!" and the national commander of the G.A.R. expressed the profane hope that God would "palsy the hand that wrote that order." So great was the resentment that the President canceled his plans to attend the G.A.R. national encampment in St. Louis in September.

The 1888 campaign, fought on the issue of the tariff, was not one to send torch-carrying partisans to the streets, but it did have the effect of cementing the Republican alliance with protectionist big business. As the war receded, the old leaders disappeared from the Republican scene, and a new type of boss was emerging, no longer with the crude, unabashed roguery of a Tweed, but more amenable to the business world, subsidized by large corporations and free of the crasser forms of graft. Such a new type, "Easy Boss" Tom Platt, only temporarily discommoded by his hotel room "nymph," had become the undisputed leader of the New York Republicans, holding forth in the Fifth Avenue Hotel, where, according to President Chauncey Depew of the New York Central Railroad, "were made governors, state senators, supreme court judges, judges of the Court of Appeals, and members of Congress." A kindred easy spirit was the sad-faced, cynical dictator of the Pennsylvania Republicans, Matthew Quay, who after crude beginnings had turned suave and held the state legislature in his itchy palm. Those two came to typify the new breed of political boss, closely allied to the rulers of finance and industry.

Despite Blaine's defeat of four years earlier, he had remained the unchallenged leader of his party, the presidential candidate who by his very presence intimidated all rivals. His Paris Letter of December, 1887, on the tariff was seen as an informal announcement of his candidacy. "You have given us our platform for next year," Lincoln's old secretary, John Hay, wrote him. Messages overwhelmed him in Europe, assuring him that this time he would be elected "without raising a finger in the campaign." Then, late in January, he wrote from Florence, Italy, to the chairman of the Republican National Committee asking that his name not be presented to the June national convention. The next month he reaffirmed his stand, telling a reporter that for him the goal was no longer worth such a struggle. Nevertheless his old followers, still convinced that they could draft their Plumed Knight, brandished their slogan:

> Blaine, Blaine, James G. Blaine,
> We've had him once and we'll have him again.

But finally, while still overseas, he wrote to Whitelaw Reid, the editor of the New York *Tribune*, a month before the Republican convention in Chicago and made it absolutely definite that he would not accept the presidential nomination.

Two weeks before the Republicans met in Chicago, the Democrats held their convention in St. Louis. Cleveland was renominated by acclamation, without even the formality of a roll call. The brief platform dealt mainly with the tariff, though it did recommend the admission of the Territories of Washington, Dakota, Montana, and New Mexico to the Union. The elderly, white-bearded Allen G. Thurman was chosen as the vice-presidential candidate, more for his venerable appearance and his durability than any other reason, for he was a spoilsman of the old school, opposed to Cleveland's hard-money views, and a waverer on the tariff. He had a whimsical habit of taking a pinch of snuff and then blowing his nose on a red bandanna, and on his nomination delegates all over the floor waved similar bandannas, causing one politician to remark that the party had nominated a pocket handkerchief. In poor health, Thurman made a sorry campaign, admitting that he would rather have stayed home with his "dear old wife," and breaking down completely when he was scheduled to speak at a Madison Square Garden rally.

With Blaine out of the running, the Republican field was open to all comers. Fourteen candidates declared themselves—the largest number in convention history. Backed by Governor Joe Foraker and Congressman William McKinley from his own state, Senator John Sherman of Ohio was the leading contender. Staid, honorable, the colorless brother of the colorful general, Sherman was a party elder who had first been elected to Congress as a Whig in 1854 and who had struggled for his party's nomination in two earlier conventions. Among the other candidates were Walter Q. Gresham and Benjamin Harrison, both of Indiana; New York's favorite son, Chauncey M. Depew; former Governor Russell A. Alger of Michigan; and Senator William B. Allison of Iowa. Gresham, Arthur's former Secretary of the Treasury and now a federal judge, was the ablest candidate, but as a reformer who believed in civil service and moderate tariff reduction, he had little chance of being nomi-

The blizzard of '88 (left) was New York City's worst, with drifts up to thirty feet deep. At its peak, old Roscoe Conkling left his office for home—on foot, as usual. He walked three miles before he collapsed; he died a few weeks later.

nated. Harrison, a frigid, intellectual man, an archprotectionist, a Civil War general and grandson of William Henry Harrison—hero of Tippecanoe and briefly America's ninth President—was a more probable dark horse in a convention of dark horses. After serving a term in the United States Senate he had failed of re-election in 1886. But he was ahead of the other dark horses in that he came equipped with a slogan, having in an address referred to himself as "a dead statesman, but . . . a living and a rejuvenated Republican." The phrase "rejuvenated Republican" stuck.

On the first ballot Sherman led with 229 votes to 111 for Gresham, 99 for Depew, 84 for Alger, and 80 for Harrison. But by the fifth ballot Sherman, with 224 votes, had failed to hold his own, while Harrison's vote had risen to 213 and Gresham's had sunk to 87. Forty-eight delegates insisted on voting for Blaine, still in Europe. What the various managers feared was an incident that would start a stampede for Blaine. Then word arrived by cable from Scotland that the Plumed Knight wanted Harrison, word that was law to Boss Tom Platt, who passed it on to his New York delegation. The next ballot showed that the Harrison tide had set in, and by the eighth ballot, when Harrison's majority was clear, the fiery Foraker sprang to his feet and moved that the nomination be made unanimous. Judge John M. Thurston of Nebraska declared that Americans were "tired of avoirdupois and cussedness" and were "ready for loyalty and statesmanship." Stirred by these inspiring sentiments, the delegates by a rising vote approved Foraker's motion. The New York banker and former minister to France Levi Morton was named the vice-presidential candidate.

With Pennsylvania's Boss Matthew Quay as chairman of the Republican National Committee—according to Platt "the ablest politician this country ever produced"—industrialists who had grown rich behind the high tariff walls opened their purses for the Harrison campaign. "Put the manufacturers of Pennsylvania under the fire and fry all the fat out of them," the Republican fund raisers were advised. Quay persuaded John Wanamaker to enlist a huge committee of businessmen under the high-tariff banner. Blaine returned to campaign for his party, and Harrison himself proved an effective speaker. Many a Republican manufacturer had the warning printed on his employees' pay envelopes that if Cleveland won, the factory would close, and workers were told with ominous repetition and in graphic detail that a Cleveland victory would mean depression, unemployment, and hunger.

By contrast the Democratic campaign was limited in funds and amateurish in operation, handicapped by Cleveland's rigid insistence that for him to campaign was beneath the dignity of his office and by the nonprofessional efforts of men like reformer George Curtis and William Graham Sumner, an educator and social scientist. Cleveland was damaged when the British minister, Sir Lionel Sackville-West, was trapped into writing a private letter stating that Cleveland was the better choice for maintaining friendly relations with Great Britain. When this indiscretion was made public, Cleveland requested Sackville-West's recall, but the damage was done and his Irish Democratic support permanently lost. There was treachery in the key state of New York, where the Tammany Governor David B. Hill worked out a deal whereby the Republican organization would surreptitiously support him in return for his own underground efforts in behalf of Harrison.

The Saturday before the election, the Republican National Committee paid one hundred and fifty thousand dollars to a New York State leader to stimulate the balloting. As reinforcements for Election Day, Boss Quay took gangs of his Pennsylvanians into Indiana, several hundred at a time, to vote for Harrison. In the brisk Republican vote market the usual price of two dollars a floating vote rose to five, and much higher in key states like Indiana, where floaters were openly collected and impounded in local G.A.R. halls. The Republican national treasurer issued a circular instructing party workers to divide the floaters into groups of five "and put a trusted man with the necessary funds in charge of these five, and make him responsible that none get away, and that all vote our ticket." The price of a vote in Indiana ran to fifteen dollars in five-dollar gold pieces or twenty dollars in paper money.

In the popular voting Cleveland won a plurality—5,540,329 votes to Harrison's 5,439,853—but the returns as they came in that evening showed Harrison with 233 electoral votes to Cleveland's 168. New York's 36 votes went this time to Harrison by 13,002 popular votes and Indiana's by 2,348. "Providence," said President-elect Harrison when he heard the news, "has given us the victory." But Matt Quay read the celestial signs differently. "Think of the man!" he said later about Harrison's pious remark. "He ought to know that Providence hadn't a damned thing to do with it!"

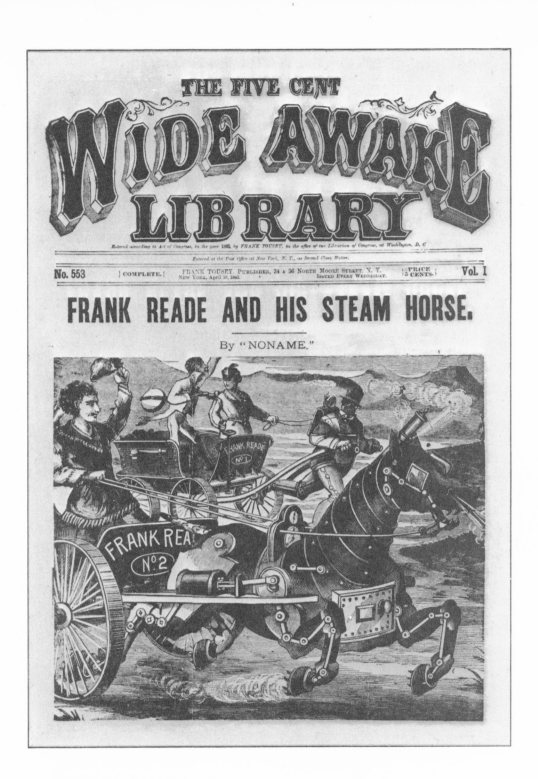

THE FIVE CENT

WIDE AWAKE

LIBRARY

Entered according to Act of Congress, in the year 1883, by FRANK TOUSEY, in the office of the Librarian of Congress, at Washington, D. C

Entered at the Post Office at New York, N. Y., as Second Class Matter.

No. 553 | COMPLETE. | FRANK TOUSEY. PUBLISHER, 34 & 36 NORTH MOORE STREET, N. Y. | PRICE | Vol. I
New York, April 18, 1883. | 5 CENTS. | Issued Every Wednesday.

FRANK READE AND HIS STEAM HORSE.

By "NONAME."

Builders and Doers

These were years of tremendous energy in America. The continent was tied by railroad lines, and its last frontiers vanished before the press of migrants from the East, of immigrants from Europe. A complicated and productive industrial organization was created, fed by seemingly limitless supplies of raw materials, men, and inventions. What patriotism managed to survive the debacle of the Civil War found, in the fields of industry and economic progress, new ground in which to flower. America was a "go-ahead country." By degrees she came to think of herself as a world leader. A key moment in the development of this national self-esteem was May 10, 1869. Below are selections from the lead story in The New York Times *the following day.*

PROMONTORY, Utah, Monday, May 10.

The long-looked-for moment has arrived. The construction of the Pacific Railroad is *un fait accompli.* The inhabitants of the Atlantic seaboard and the dwellers on the Pacific slopes are henceforth emphatically one people. Your correspondent is writing on Promontory Summit amid the deafening shouts of the multitude, with the tick, tick, of the telegraph close to his ear. . . .

WASHINGTON, Monday, May 10.

The completion of the Pacific Railroad has monopolized public attention here to-day to the exclusion of everything else. The feeling is one of hearty rejoicing at the completion of this great work. There were no public observances, but the arrangements made by the telegraph company to announce the completion of the road simultaneously with the driving of the last spike were perfect. At 2:20 this afternoon, Washington time, all the telegraph offices in the country were notified by the Omaha telegraph office to be ready to receive the signals corresponding to the blows of the hammer that drove the last spike in the last rail that united New-York and San Francisco with a band of iron. Accordingly Mr. TINKER, Manager of the Western Union Telegraph Office in this city, placed a magnetic bell-sounder in the public office of that Company . . . connected the same with the main lines, and notified the various offices that he was ready. New-Orleans instantly responded, the answer being read from the bell-taps. New-York did the same. At 2:27 o'clock offices over the country began to make all sorts of inquiries of Omaha, to which that office replied:

"*To Everybody:* Keep quiet. When the last spike is driven at Promontory Point they will say 'Done.' Don't break the circuit, but watch for the signals of the blows of the hammer."

At 2:27 P.M., Promontory Point, 2,400 miles west of Washington, said to the people congregated in the various telegraph offices:

"Almost ready. Hats off; prayer is being offered."

A silence for the prayer ensued. At 2:40 the bell tapped again, and the office at the Point said:

"We have got done praying. The spike is about to be presented."

Chicago replied:

"We understand: all are ready in the East."

Promontory Point: "All ready now; the spike will be driven. The signal will be three dots for the commencement of the blows."

For a moment the instrument was silent; then the hammer of the magnet tapped the bell, "One, two, three," the signal; another pause of a few seconds, and the lightning came flashing eastward, vibrating over 2,400 miles between the junction of the two roads and Washington, and the blows of the hammer upon the spike were measured instantly in telegraphic accents on the bell here. At 2:47 P.M., Promontory Point gave the signal, "Done," and the Continent was spanned with iron.

The New-York Times
May 11, 1869

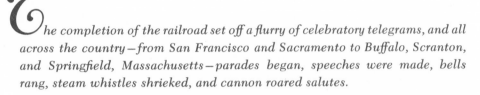

The completion of the railroad set off a flurry of celebratory telegrams, and all across the country — from San Francisco and Sacramento to Buffalo, Scranton, and Springfield, Massachusetts — parades began, speeches were made, bells rang, steam whistles shrieked, and cannon roared salutes.

The time of the event in San Francisco was 11:45, in the forenoon. A telegraph wire had been attached to a fifteen-inch gun, and as the first stroke on the last spike was telegraphed from Promontory Point, the gun was fired by electricity, and by the same agent all the fire-bells in the city were rung. . . .

On the announcement of the completion of the road in New York, the mayor ordered a salute of one hundred guns, and himself saluted the mayor of San Francisco with a dispatch conceived in the most jubilant spirit, — informing him that "our flags are now flying, our cannon are now booming, and in old Trinity a Te Deum imparts thankful harmonies to the busy hum about her church walls." The Chambers of Commerce of the two cities also exchanged congratulations, the New York chamber recognizing in the new highway an agent that would not only "develop the resources, extend the commerce, increase the power, exalt the dignity and perpetuate the unity of our republic, but in its broader relations, as the segment of a world-embracing circle, directly connecting the nations of Europe with those of Asia, would materially facilitate the enlightened and advancing civilization of our age." The services in Trinity were conducted with great solemnity, in the presence of a crowded congregation. After prayer, and the reading of a portion of the Episcopal service, the organ pealed forth in its grandest fullness and majesty, and, as the assembly dispersed, the church chimes added to the joyousness of the occasion by ringing out "Old Hundred," the "Ascension Carol," and the national airs.

The detail from Joseph Becker's painting shows, in the background, part of the system of snowsheds the Central Pacific constructed to protect its track in the Sierra Nevadas.

In Philadelphia, the authorities improvised a celebration so suddenly, that the ringing of the bells on Independence Hall, and at the various fire stations, was mistaken for a general alarm of fire, till the news was announced. The sudden flocking of the people to the state-house resembled that which followed the reception of the news of Lee's surrender to Grant. . . .

More wonderful still, a trans-continental train, which left New York early on the morning of June 1st, 1876, reached San Francisco at twenty-five minutes past nine, June 4th, in the morning; thus accomplishing the journey in eighty-three hours and twenty minutes, without stoppages and without accident.

R. M. Devens
Our First Century, 1876

With one main highway laid across the country, and others soon to come, the empty spaces in the West began to be filled in. As had already happened where American civilization rooted, the wild competitors of that fittest species, Man, were to suffer. Amazingly numerous at first, the birds and animals were hunted hard—some of them to extinction. Even men who truly loved Nature behaved as if she were endlessly bountiful, endlessly forgiving. And there were many who hunted not for food or pleasure but for plunder, in the manner of those who were at the same time leveling forests and littering streams with the offal of their factories and mines. Richard Irving Dodge wrote about both kinds.

. . . I confess that my taste for sport is rather of the vagabond order. I like to bag these large animals; but I like better to ride through a country where game is in great variety, rifle and shot-gun both ready for use, bagging now a deer or an antelope, now getting into a flock of turkeys; at one time banging into a flock of ducks, at another beating a marsh for snipe, or quartering the grass for grouse or quail in true Eastern style. One gets less large game in this kind of hunting, but he has a vast deal more enjoyment.

The most delightful hunting of this kind I have ever had was in the country south-east of Fort Dodge, on the small tributaries of the Cimarron River. I append the record of a hunt of twenty days in this section, in October 1872, in which one officer besides myself and three English gentlemen participated. Everything bagged was counted as one, and an idea of the sport can be formed from this list:—

127	buffalo.	6	cranes.
2	deer (red).	187	quail.
11	antelope.	32	grouse.
154	turkeys.	84	field-plover.
5	geese.	33	yellow legs (snipe).
223	teal.	12	jack snipe.
45	mallard.	1	pigeon.
49	shovel-bill.	9	hawks.
57	widgeon.	3	owls.
38	butter-ducks.	2	badgers.
3	shell-ducks.	7	racoons.
17	herons.	11	rattlesnakes.

143 meadow larks, doves, robins, &c.
1 blue bird, for his sweetheart's hat.
Total head bagged, 1,262.

. . . In 1868 I took a small party of gentlemen on a short excursion to the "heads of the Muddy." We remained but two days. Each morning, before 9 o'clock breakfast, we had killed an ordinary horse-bucket full of trout, and between breakfast and dinner bagged so many grouse that, although we mustered, including hunters and escort, some thirty persons, and all ate what they wanted, we yet carried into the post nearly 200 birds, of a weight of almost 1,000 pounds.

In 1872 some enemy of the buffalo race discovered that their hides were merchantable, and could be sold in the market for a goodly sum. The Union Pacific,

Kansas Pacific, and Atchison Topeka and Santa Fé Railroads soon swarmed with "hard cases" from the East, each excited with the prospect of having a buffalo hunt that would pay. By waggon, on horseback, and a-foot, the pot-hunters poured in, and soon the unfortunate buffalo was without a moment's peace or rest. Though hundreds of thousands of skins were sent to market, they scarcely indicated the slaughter that, from want of skill in shooting, and want of knowledge in preserving the hides of those slain, on the part of these green hunters, one hide sent to market represented three, four, or even five dead buffalo.

The merchants of the small towns along the railroads were not slow to take advantage of this new opening. They furnished outfits, arms, ammunition, &c., to needy parties, and established great trades, by which many now ride in their carriages. . . .

In 1872 I was stationed at Fort Dodge, on the Arkansas, and was not on many hunting excursions. Except that one or two would be shot, as occasion required, for beef, no attention whatever was paid to buffalo, though our march led through countless throngs, unless there were strangers with us. . . . From within a few miles of the post our pleasure was actually marred by their numbers, as they interfered with our pursuit of other game.

In the fall of 1873 I went with some [British] gentlemen over the same ground.

As William Dean Howells indicated in the excerpt that begins at the right, this huge Corliss engine powered all machinery at the Centennial Exhibition's Machinery Hall.

Where there were myriads of buffalo the year before, there were now myriads of carcasses. The air was foul with sickening stench, and the vast plain, which only a short twelvemonth before teemed with animal life, was a dead, solitary, putrid desert. We were obliged to travel south-east to the Cimarron, a distance of nearly ninety miles, before we found a respectable herd. Even there we found the inevitable hunter, the southern line of the State of Kansas being picketed by them. They were wary of going into Indian territory, where they might be arrested; but an unfortunate herd no sooner crossed the line going north than it was destroyed. The butchery still goes on. Comparatively few buffalo are now killed, for there are comparatively few to kill. In October 1874 I was on a short trip to the buffalo region south of Sidney Barracks. A few buffalo were encountered, but there seemed to be more hunters than buffalo.

Richard Irving Dodge
The Plains of the Great West and Their Inhabitants, 1877

One of the most notable qualities of American writing in this period was the vibrancy and awe with which machinery was described—particularly big machinery made in the United States. Below, William Dean Howells talks about his visit to the Centennial Exhibition in Philadelphia.

We went . . . to the Machinery Hall, through the far extent of which we walked, looking merely to the right and left as we passed down the great aisle. Of that first impression the majesty of the great Corliss engine, which drives the infinitely varied machinery, remains most distinct. . . . The Corliss engine does not lend itself to description; its personal acquaintance must be sought by those who would understand its vast and almost silent grandeur. It rises loftily in the

229

centre of the huge structure, an athlete of steel and iron with not a superfluous ounce of metal on it; the mighty walking-beams plunge their pistons downward, the enormous fly-wheel revolves with a hoarded power that makes all tremble, the hundred life-like details do their office with unerring intelligence. In the midst of this ineffably strong mechanism is a chair where the engineer sits reading his newspaper, as in a peaceful bower. Now and then he lays down his paper and clambers up one of the stairways that cover the framework, and touches some irritated spot on the giant's body with a drop of oil, and goes down again and takes up his newspaper; he is like some potent enchanter there, and this prodigious Afreet is his slave who could crush him past all semblance of humanity with his lightest touch. It is, alas! what the Afreet has done to humanity too often, where his strength has superseded men's industry; but of such things the Machinery Hall is no place to speak, and to be honest, one never thinks of such things there. One thinks only of the glorious triumphs of skill and invention; and wherever else the national bird is mute in one's breast, here he cannot fail to utter his pride and content. It would be a barren place without the American machinery. All that Great Britain and Germany have sent is insignificant in amount when compared with our own contributions; the superior elegance, aptness, and ingenuity of our machinery is observable at a glance. Yes, it is still in these things of iron and steel that the national genius most freely speaks; by and by the inspired marbles, the breathing canvases, the great literature; for the present America is voluble in the strong metals and their infinite uses.

W. D. Howells
"A Sennight of the Centennial"
The Atlantic Monthly, July, 1876

F. L. Hunter's pen-and-ink drawing of a Brooklyn Bridge pier, above, was made while the bridge was under construction. Munsey's Magazine, *which printed Edgar Saltus' article at right, had just moved into offices on the eighteenth story of the Flatiron Building, below.*

Similar pride was manifested in the great new structures that Americans were building. Abram S. Hewitt, steel manufacturer and Democratic member of the House of Representatives, spoke at the opening of the Brooklyn Bridge in 1883. Sixteen hundred feet long from pier to pier, the bridge had taken thirteen years to finish. One accident during construction killed its designer, John Roebling, and another crippled his son Washington, who completed the project.

"What hath God wrought!" were the words of wonder, which ushered into being the magnetic telegraph, the greatest marvel of the many marvelous inventions of the present century. It was the natural impulse of the pious maiden who chose this first message of reverence and awe, to look to the Divine Power as the author of a new gospel. For it was the invisible, and not the visible agency, which addressed itself to her perceptions. Neither the bare poles, nor the slender wire, nor the silent battery, could suggest an adequate explanation of the extinction of time and space which was manifest to her senses, and she could only say, "What hath God wrought!"

But when we turn from the unsightly telegraph to the graceful structure at whose portal we stand, and when the airy outline of its curves of beauty, pendant between massive towers suggestive of art alone, is contrasted with the over-reaching vault of heaven above and the ever-moving flood of waters beneath, the work of omnipotent power, we are irresistibly moved to exclaim, "What hath *man* wrought!"

Address of Hon. Abram S. Hewitt
Opening Ceremonies of the New York and Brooklyn Bridge, 1883

Essayist Edgar Saltus, here observing New York and its people from the top of the new Flatiron Building, wrote, thought visiting Britisher H. G. Wells, "with a very typical American accent."

They hurry because everybody hurries, because haste is in the air, in the effrontery of the impudent "step lively," in the hammers of the ceaseless skyscrapers ceaselessly going up, in the ambient neurosis, in the scudding motors, in the unending noise, the pervading scramble, the metallic roar of the city.

Beyond is the slam-bang of the Sixth Avenue Elevated careering up-town and down, both ways at once. Parallelly is the Subway, rumbling relentlessly. Farther east are two additional slam-bangers. To the west is a fourth. Beneath them are great ocher brutes of cars, herds of them, stampeding violently with grinding grunts, and, on the microbish pavements, swarms such as Dante may indeed have seen, but not in paradise.

In the morning they are there, scurrying to their toil; at high noon to their food; at evening to their homes; at night to amusements more laborious than their work. When they are not there you do not know it. Save at night, when the crowd moves elsewhere, always are there compact throngs, always are there streams of incarnated preoccupations, pouring from whence you cannot say, to where you cannot tell; human streams which the Flatiron cleaves indifferently, rearing its knifish face with the same disdain of the ephemeral that the Sphinx displays, knowing that she has all time as we all have our day.

Ages ago the Sphinx was disinterred from beneath masses of sand under which it had brooded interminably. Yet in its simian paws, its avian wings, in its body which is that of animal, in its face which is that of a seer, there, before Darwin, before history, by a race that has left no other souvenir, in traits great and grave, the descent of man was told.

There remained his ascent. Ages hence the Flatiron may tell it. For as you lean and gaze from the toppest floors on houses below, which from those floors seem huts, it may occur to you that precisely as these huts were once regarded as supreme achievements, so, one of these days, from other and higher floors, the Flatiron may seem a hut itself.

Evolution has not halted. Undiscernibly but indefatigably, always it is progressing. Its final term is not in existing buildings or in existing man. If humanity sprang from gorillas, from humanity gods shall proceed. The story of Olympus is merely a tale of what might have been. That which might have been may yet come to pass. Even now, could the old divinities, hushed forevermore, awake, they would be perplexed enough to see how mortals have exceeded them. The inextinguishable laughter which was theirs is absent from the prose of life. Commerce has alarmed their afflatus away. But the telegraph is a better messenger than they had, the motor is surer than their chariots of dream. In Fifth Avenue

231

inns they could get fairer fare than ambrosia, and behold women beside whom Venus would look provincial and Juno a frump. The spectacle of electricity tamed and domesticated would surprise them not a little, the Elevated quite as much, the Flatiron still more. At sight of the latter they would recall the Titans with whom once they warred, and slink to their sacred seas outfaced.

In the same measure that we have succeeded in exceeding them, so will posterity surpass what we have done. Evolution may be slow, but it is sure; yet, however slow, it achieved an unrecognized advance when it devised buildings such as this. It is demonstrable that small rooms breed small thoughts. It will be demonstrable that as buildings ascend so do ideas. It is mental progress that skyscrapers engender. From these parturitions gods may really proceed—beings, that is, who, could we remain long enough to see them, would regard us as we regard the apes.

Edgar Saltus
"New York from the Flatiron"
Munsey's Magazine, July, 1905

Machinery in motion, men in motion, communities in motion—that was Progress, that was exciting. Another typically American voice was that of Edward King, here talking about the steel industry in St. Louis.

Let us peer into that busy suburban ward of St. Louis which still clings so fondly to its old French name of "Carondelet." The drive thither from the city carries you past the arsenal, where Government now and then has a few troops, and past many a pretty mansion, into the dusty street of a prosaic manufacturing town, near the bank of the Mississippi.

Descending toward the water-side from the street you find every available space crowded with mammoth iron and zinc-furnaces, in whose immense structures of iron, wood, and glass, half-naked men, their bodies smeared with perspiration and coal dust, are wheeling about blazing masses of metal, or guiding the pliant iron bars through rollers and moulds, or cooling their heated faces and arms in buckets of water brought up fresh from the stream. Here, in a zinc-furnace, half-a-dozen Irishmen wrestle with the long puddling rods which they thrust into the seventy-times-seven heated furnaces; the green and yellowish flames from the metal are reflected on their pale and withered features, and give them an almost unearthly expression.

Farther on, the masons are toiling at the brick-work of a new blast-furnace, which already rears its tall towers a hundred feet above the Mississippi shore; not far thence you may see the flaming chimney of the quaint old Carondelet furnace—the first built in all that section; or may linger for hours in such immense establishments as the South St. Louis or Vulcan iron works, fancying them the growth of half a century of patient upbuilding, until you are told that nearly every establishment has been created since the war.

The Vulcan Iron Works, which now employs twelve hundred men in its blast-furnaces and rolling-mills, overspreads seventeen acres, boasts $600,000 worth of machinery, and has two furnaces smelting 25,000 tons of ore annually, while

A Bessemer converter, sparks spattering from its mouth, is tilted down to pour out the molten steel.

232

its rolling-mill can turn out 45,000 tons of rail in a year, was not in existence in 1870; indeed, there was not a brick laid on the premises. There is nothing else so wonderful as this in the South or South-west; Kansas City, in the northwestern part of the State, is the only other place in Missouri which can show similar material progress.

The little *Rivière des Pères*, where the holy Catholic fathers once had a mission among the Osage Indians, empties into the Mississippi, close beside the Vulcan iron works; its banks are piled high with coal and refuse. The fathers would know it no more. They would stare aghast at the thousand horse-power pump; at the myriads of fiery snakes crawling about on the floors of the rolling-mill; at the troops of Irish laborers, the cautious groups about the doors of the sputtering blast-furnace, and the molten streams pouring into the sand-beds to form into "pigs" of iron; and could hardly credit the statement that Carondelet furnaces alone can manufacture 140,000 tons of iron yearly.

This sudden and marked progress at Carondelet is significant. Such amazing growth is indicative of a splendid future. The elder England is fading out; her iron-fields are exhausted; and her producers growl because American iron-masters can at last undersell those of England. The heart of the republic, the great commonwealth of Missouri, is to be the England of to-morrow.

Her mineral stores are inexhaustible. There are a thousand railroads locked up in the great coffers of the Iron Mountain. A thousand iron ships lie dormant in the ore-pockets scattered along the line of the Atlantic and Pacific railway, and a million fortunes await the men who shall come and take them. Missouri is one of the future great foundries of the world; the coal-fields of Indiana and Illinois are near at hand; the earth is stored with hematites; the hills are seamed with speculars. The work has already begun in earnest. . . .

What crowding, what noise and clang of machinery, what smoke and stench of coal! The workmen, with thick leather aprons about their waists, and gloves on their hands, are bringing the bars of pig-iron from the blast-furnaces, and cording them up by hundreds. Here is a crowd of perturbed Irish laborers, shrieking and dancing around a prostrate man, whose limbs have been scarred and seared by a sudden spurt of hot iron from the furnace. His comrades are bending over him, eagerly cutting away his garments with their knives, while the iron burns its way into his flesh.

Edward King
The Great South, 1875

And there, in that almost offhand picture of a man in agony, lay the rub, if there was a rub. The society seemed to accept that some men would have to suffer—have to live in shacks and on beans, have to sicken and die from silicosis in mines, have to be injured because of employers' carelessness and never have redress. Did the wealth of the society, did Progress, require such sacrifices? Some thought not. There were demands—as, indeed, there were in Europe, too—for fairer treatment of the weaker members of the society, for government control of the managers and entrepreneurs, and for less concentration of the society's wealth. But such men as Andrew Carnegie feared the possible destruction of the

American industrial system when it was, so to speak, just hitting its stride. They based their defense on social Darwinism: leave the individual alone to do his best, said Carnegie, and all will be well.

The price which society pays for the law of competition, like the price it pays for cheap comforts and luxuries, is also great; but the advantages of this law are also greater still, for it is to this law that we owe our wonderful material development, which brings improved conditions in its train. But, whether the law be benign or not, we must say of it, as we say of the change in the conditions of men to which we have referred: It is here; we cannot evade it; no substitutes for it have been found; and while the law may be sometimes hard for the individual, it is best for the race, because it insures the survival of the fittest in every department. We accept and welcome, therefore, as conditions to which we must accommodate ourselves, great inequality of environment, the concentration of business, industrial and commercial, in the hands of a few, and the law of competition between these, as being not only beneficial, but essential for the future progress of the race. Having accepted these, it follows that there must be great scope for the exercise of special ability in the merchant and in the manufacturer who has to conduct affairs upon a great scale. That this talent for organization and management is rare among men is proved by the fact that it invariably secures for its possessor enormous rewards, no matter where or under what laws or conditions. The experienced in affairs always rate the MAN whose services can be obtained as a partner as not only the first consideration, but such as to render the question of his capital scarcely worth considering, for such men soon create capital; while, without the special talent required, capital soon takes wings. Such men become interested in firms or corporations using millions; and estimating only simple interest to be made upon the capital invested, it is inevitable that their income must exceed their expenditures, and that they must accumulate wealth. Nor is there any middle ground which such men can occupy, because the great manufacturing or commercial concern which does not earn at least interest upon its capital soon becomes bankrupt. It must either go forward or fall behind: to stand still is impossible. It is a condition essential for its successful operation that it should be thus far profitable, and even that, in addition to interest on capital, it should make profit. It is a law, as certain as any of the others named, that men possessed of this peculiar talent for affairs, under the free play of economic forces, must, of necessity, soon be in receipt of more revenue than can be judiciously expended upon themselves; and this law is as beneficial for the race as the others.

Objections to the foundations upon which society is based are not in order, because the condition of the race is better with these than it has been with any others which have been tried. . . . One who studies this subject will soon be brought face to face with the conclusion that upon the sacredness of property civilization itself depends—the right of the laborer to his hundred dollars in the savings bank, and equally the legal right of the millionaire to his millions. . . . Not evil, but good, has come to the race from the accumulation of wealth by those who have the ability and energy that produce it. But even if we admit for a moment that it might be better for the race to discard its present foundation, Individualism,—that it is a nobler ideal that man should labor, not for himself

Above, a 1911 caricature of Carnegie; below, busy Chicago in 1892.

234

alone, but in and for a brotherhood of his fellows, and share with them all in common, realizing Swedenborg's idea of Heaven, where, as he says, the angels derive their happiness, not from laboring for self, but for each other, — even admit all this, and a sufficient answer is, This is not evolution, but revolution. It necessitates the changing of human nature itself—a work of æons, even if it were good to change it, which we cannot know. It is not practicable in our day or in our age. Even if desirable theoretically, it belongs to another and long-succeeding sociological stratum. Our duty is with what is practicable now; with the next step possible in our day and generation. It is criminal to waste our energies in endeavoring to uproot, when all we can profitably or possibly accomplish is to bend the universal tree of humanity a little in the direction most favorable to the production of good fruit under existing circumstances. We might as well urge the destruction of the highest existing type of man because he failed to reach our ideal as to favor the destruction of Individualism, Private Property, the Law of Accumulation of Wealth, and the Law of Competition; for these are the highest results of human experience, the soil in which society so far has produced the best fruit. Unequally or unjustly, perhaps, as these laws sometimes operate, and imperfect as they appear to the Idealist, they are, nevertheless, like the highest type of man, the best and most valuable of all that humanity has yet accomplished.

Andrew Carnegie
"Wealth"
North American Review, June, 1889

Frank Norris exuded something of the same spirit as Carnegie in his description—in The Pit—*of that metropolis of the American heartland, Chicago.*

. . . [Laura] could not forgive its dirty streets, the unspeakable squalor of some of its poorer neighborhoods that sometimes developed, like cancerous growths, in the very heart of fine residence districts. The black murk that closed every vista of the business streets oppressed her, and the soot that stained linen and gloves each time she stirred abroad was a never-ending distress.

But the life was tremendous. All around, on every side, in every direction the vast machinery of Commonwealth clashed and thundered from dawn to dark and from dark till dawn. Even now, as the car carried her farther into the business quarter, she could hear it, see it, and feel in her every fibre the trepidation of its motion. The blackened waters of the river, seen an instant between stanchions as the car trundled across the State Street bridge, disappeared under fleets of tugs, of lake steamers, of lumber barges from Sheboygan and Mackinac, of grain boats from Duluth, of coal scows that filled the air with impalpable dust, of cumbersome schooners laden with produce, of grimy rowboats dodging the prows and paddles of the larger craft, while on all sides, blocking the horizon, red in color and designated by Brobdingnagian letters, towered the hump-shouldered grain elevators.

Just before crossing the bridge on the north side of the river she had caught a glimpse of a great railway terminus. Down below there, rectilinear, scientifically paralleled and squared, the Yard disclosed itself. A system of gray rails beyond words complicated opened out and spread immeasurably. Switches, semaphores, and signal towers stood here and there. A dozen trains, freight and passenger, puffed and steamed, waiting the word to depart. Detached engines hurried in and out of sheds and roundhouses, seeking their trains, or bunted the ponderous freight cars into switches; trundling up and down, clanking, shrieking, their bells filling the air with the clangor of tocsins. Men in vizored caps shouted hoarsely, waving their arms or red flags; drays, their big dappled horses feeding in their nose bags, stood backed up to the open doors of freight cars and received their loads. A train departed roaring. Before midnight it would be leagues away boring through the Great Northwest, carrying Trade—the life-blood of nations—into communities of which Laura had never heard. Another train, reeking with fatigue, the air-brakes screaming, arrived and halted, debouching a flood of passengers, business men, bringing Trade—a galvanizing elixir—from the very ends and corners of the continent.

Or, again, it was South Water Street—a jam of delivery wagons and market carts backed to the curbs, leaving only a tortuous path between the endless files of horses, suggestive of an actual barrack of cavalry. Provisions, market produce, "garden truck" and fruits, in an infinite welter of crates and baskets, boxes and sacks, crowded the sidewalks. The gutter was choked with an overflow of refuse cabbage leaves, soft oranges, decaying beet tops. The air was thick with the heavy smell of vegetation. Food was trodden under foot, food crammed the stores and warehouses to bursting. Food mingled with the mud of the highway. The very dray horses were gorged with an unending nourishment of snatched mouthfuls picked from backboard, from barrel-top, and from the edge of the sidewalk. The entire locality reeked with the fatness of a hundred thousand furrows. A land of plenty, the inordinate abundance of the earth itself emptied itself upon the asphalt and cobbles of the quarter. It was the Mouth of the City, and drawn from all directions, over a territory of immense area, this glut of crude subsistence was sucked in, as if into a rapacious gullet, to feed the sinews and to nourish the fibres of an immeasurable colossus.

Suddenly the meaning and significance of it all dawned upon Laura. The Great Gray City, brooking no rival, imposed its dominion upon a reach of country larger than many a kingdom of the Old World. For thousands of miles beyond its confines was its influence felt. Out, far out, far away in the snow and shadow of Northern Wisconsin forests, axes and saws bit the bark of century-old trees, stimulated by this city's energy. Just as far to the southward pick and drill leaped to the assault of veins of anthracite, moved by her central power. Her force turned the wheels of harvester and seeder a thousand miles distant in Iowa and Kansas. Her force spun the screws and propellers of innumerable squadrons of lake steamers crowding the Sault Sainte Marie. For her and because of her all the Central States, all the Great Northwest roared with traffic and industry; saw-mills screamed; factories, their smoke blackening the sky, clashed and flamed; wheels turned, pistons leaped in their cylinders; cog gripped cog; beltings clasped the drums of mammoth wheels; and converters of forges belched into the clouded air their tempest breath of molten steel.

It was Empire, the resistless subjugation of all this central world of the lakes and the prairies. Here, midmost in the land, beat the Heart of the Nation, whence

American heroes of the war with Spain are featured on this shield. Richmond P. Hobson, bottom row, center, had tried to bottle up the Spanish ships in Santiago Harbor by scuttling a ship in its entrance.

inevitably must come its immeasurable power, its infinite, infinite, inexhaustible vitality. Here, of all her cities, throbbed the true life—the true power and spirit of America; gigantic, crude with the crudity of youth, disdaining rivalry; sane and healthy and vigorous; brutal in its ambition, arrogant in the new-found knowledge of its giant strength, prodigal of its wealth, infinite in its desires. In its capacity boundless, in its courage indomitable; subduing the wilderness in a single generation, defying calamity, and through the flame and the débris of a Commonwealth in ashes, rising suddenly renewed, formidable and Titanic.

Frank Norris
The Pit
The Saturday Evening Post, September 27, 1902

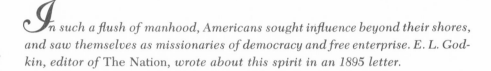

In such a flush of manhood, Americans sought influence beyond their shores, and saw themselves as missionaries of democracy and free enterprise. E. L. Godkin, editor of The Nation, *wrote about this spirit in an 1895 letter.*

The Jingoes are . . . numerous and powerful and absolutely crazy. . . . An immense democracy, mostly ignorant, and completely secluded from foreign influences, and without any knowledge of other states of society, with great contempt for history and experience, finds itself in possession of enormous power and is eager to use it in brutal fashion against any one who comes along, *without knowing how to do it,* and is therefore constantly on the brink of some frightful catastrophe. . . . The spectacle of our financial condition and legislation during the last twenty years, the general silliness and credulity begotten by the newspapers, the ferocious optimism exacted of all teachers and preachers, and the general belief that we are a peculiar or chosen people to whom the experience of other people is of no use, make a pretty dismal picture. . . .

Edwin Lawrence Godkin
Life and Letters of Edwin Lawrence Godkin, 1907, Rollo Ogden, Editor

And in 1898 the United States undertook a war with Spain. One legacy of the war was possession of the Philippine Islands; the question of whether to occupy them or to give them immediately the independence they had sought for years stirred violent controversy. Despite the opposition of prominent men like Andrew Carnegie and of the Philippine independence movement, President McKinley decided that Americans should govern the islands for a while and prepare them for self-rule. Below, columnist Finley Peter Dunne's characters Mr. Dooley and Mr. Hennessy discuss the question.

"Whin we plant what Hogan calls th' starry banner iv Freedom in th' Ph'lippeens," said Mr. Dooley, "an' give th' sacred blessin' iv liberty to the poor, downtrodden people iv thim unfortunate isles,—dam thim!—we'll larn thim a lesson."

"Sure," said Mr. Hennessy, sadly, "we have a thing or two to larn oursilves."

"But it isn't f'r thim to larn us," said Mr. Dooley. " 'Tis not f'r thim wretched an' degraded crathers, without a mind or a shirt iv their own, f'r to give lessons in politeness an' liberty to a nation that manny-facthers more dhressed beef than anny other imperyal nation in th' wurruld. We say to thim: 'Naygurs,' we say, 'poor, dissolute, uncovered wretches,' says we, 'whin th' crool hand iv Spain forged man'cles f'r ye'er limbs, as Hogan says, who was it crossed th' say an' sthruck off th' comealongs? We did,—by dad, we did. An' now, ye mis'rable, childish-minded apes, we propose f'r to larn ye th' uses iv liberty. In ivry city in this unfair land we will erect school-houses an' packin' houses an' houses iv correction; an' we'll larn ye our language, because 'tis aisier to larn ye ours than to larn oursilves yours. An' we'll give ye clothes, if ye pay f'r thim; an', if ye don't, ye can go without. An', whin ye're hungry, ye can go to th' morgue— we mane th' resth'rant—an' ate a good square meal iv ar-rmy beef. An' we'll sind th' gr-reat Gin'ral Eagan over f'r to larn ye etiquette, an' Andhrew Carnegie to larn ye pathriteism with blow-holes into it, an' Gin'ral Alger to larn ye to hould onto a job; an', whin ye've become edycated an' have all th' blessin's iv civilization that we don't want, that'll count ye one. We can't give ye anny votes, because we haven't more thin enough to go round now; but we'll threat ye th' way a father shud threat his childher if we have to break ivry bone in ye'er bodies. So come to our ar-rms,' says we. . . .

"An' there it stands, Hinnissy, with th' indulgent parent kneelin' on th' stomach iv his adopted child, while a dillygation fr'm Boston bastes him with an umbrella. There it stands, an' how will it come out I dinnaw. I'm not much iv an expansionist mesilf. F'r th' las' tin years I've been thryin' to decide whether 'twud be good policy an' thrue to me thraditions to make this here bar two or three feet longer, an manny's th' night I've laid awake tryin' to puzzle it out. But I don't know what to do with th' Ph'lippeens anny more thin I did las' summer, befure I heerd tell iv thim. We can't give thim to anny wan without makin' th' wan that gets thim feel th' way Doherty felt to Clancy whin Clancy med a frindly call an' give Doherty's childher th' measles. We can't sell thim, we can't ate thim, an' we can't throw thim into th' alley whin no wan is lookin'. An' 'twud be a disgrace f'r to lave befure we've pounded these frindless an' ongrateful people into insinsibility. So I suppose, Hinnissy, we'll have to stay an' do th' best we can, an' lave Andhrew Carnegie secede fr'm th' Union. They'se wan consolation; an' that is, if th' American people can govern thimsilves, they can govern annything that walks."

Finley Peter Dunne
Mr. Dooley In the Hearts of His Countrymen, 1899

Theodore Roosevelt was a leading jingo; as assistant secretary of the Navy he had played a key role in the taking of the Philippines. But he was also many other things—philosopher of government, conservationist, reformer. He became President in 1901, succeeding the assassinated McKinley. H. G. Wells visited him during his second term and made these observations.

Now it is a curious thing that as I talked with President Roosevelt in the garden

These caricatures of Roosevelt on his postpresidential, postsafari tour of Europe in 1910 depict him (clockwise from bottom left) in Berlin, Italy, Paris, and London.

of the White House there came back to me quite forcibly that undertone of doubt that has haunted me throughout this journey. After all, does this magnificent appearance of beginnings which is America, convey any clear and certain promise of permanence and fulfillment whatever? Much makes for construction, a great wave of reform is going on, but will it drive on to anything more than a breaking impact upon even more gigantic uncertainties and dangers. Is America a giant childhood or a gigantic futility, a mere latest phase of that long succession of experiments which has been and may be for interminable years — may be indeed altogether until the end — man's social history? I can't now recall how our discursive talk settled towards that, but it is clear to me that I struck upon a familiar vein of thought in the President's mind. He hadn't, he said, an effectual disproof of any pessimistic interpretation of the future. If one chose to say America must presently lose the impetus of her ascent, that she and all mankind must culminate and pass, he could not conclusively deny that possibility. Only he chose to live as if this were not so.

That remained in his mind. Presently he reverted to it. He made a sort of apology for his life against the doubts and scepticisms that, I fear, must be in the background of the thoughts of every modern man who is intellectually alive. He mentioned a little book of mine, an early book full of the deliberate pessimism of youth, in which I drew a picture of a future of decadence, of a time when constructive effort had fought its fight and failed, when the inevitable segregations of an individualistic system had worked themselves out and all hope and vigor of humanity had gone forever. The descendants of the workers had become etiolated, sinister, and subterranean monsters, the property-owners had degenerated into a hectic and feebly self-indulgent race, living fitfully amid the ruins of the present time. He became gesticulatory, and his straining voice a note higher in denying this as a credible interpretation of destiny. With one of those sudden movements of his, he knelt forward in a garden chair — we were standing before our parting beneath the colonnade — and addressed me very earnestly over the back, clutching it, and then thrusting out his familiar gesture, a hand first partly open and then closed.

"Suppose after all," he said, slowly, "that should prove to be right, and it all ends in your butterflies and morlocks. *That doesn't matter now.* The effort's real. It's worth going on with. It's worth it. It's worth it — even then." . . .

I can see him now and hear his unmusical voice saying "The effort — the effort's worth it," and see the gesture of his clinched hand and the — how can I describe it? the friendly peering snarl of his face, like a man with the sun in his eyes. He sticks in my mind as that, as a very symbol of the creative will in man, in its limitations, its doubtful adequacy, its valiant persistence amid perplexities and confusions. He kneels out, assertive against his setting — and his setting is the White House with a background of all America.

I could almost write, with a background of all the world — for I know of no other a tithe so representative of the creative purpose, the *good-will* in men as he. In his undisciplined hastiness, his limitations, his prejudices, his unfairness, his frequent errors, just as much as in his force, his sustained courage, his integrity, his open intelligence, he stands for his people and his kind.

H. G. Wells
The Future in America, 1906

PICTURE CREDITS. PAGES 226–27: GILCREASE INSTITUTE OF AMERICAN HISTORY AND ART; PAGES 228–29: FREE LIBRARY OF PHILADELPHIA; PAGE 230: MUSEUM OF THE CITY OF NEW YORK; PAGES 230–31: LIBRARY OF CONGRESS; PAGES 232–33: *Scientific American,* NOVEMBER 6, 1875, NEW-YORK HISTORICAL SOCIETY; PAGE 234: *The Sketch,* JUNE 7, 1911, NEW YORK PUBLIC LIBRARY; PAGES 234–35: CHICAGO HISTORICAL SOCIETY; PAGES 236–37: LIBRARY OF CONGRESS; PAGES 238 AND 239 (ALL): M. B. SCHNAPPER, *Grand Old Party,* 1955

1789
1889

Edwin H Blashfield

Unrest in the Farm Lands

*I*n his Paris letter of December, 1887, defending protection, Blaine had declared America's export market insignificant and unimportant in relation to the country's domestic trade. "It is not," he told a reporter, "our foreign trade that has caused the wonderful growth and expansion of the Republic. It is the vast domestic trade between thirty-eight States and eight Territories. . . . even now in its infancy, and destined to attain a magnitude not dreamed of twenty years ago. . . ."

To Western and Southern farmers, Blaine's rosy view lacked the color of reality. For agriculture the decade following 1877 had been a period relatively free from natural disasters, but the problem of surpluses persisted and prices fell. However fast the population might increase, farm production increased even more rapidly. Much of the surplus had been absorbed by Great Britain, for ever since the repeal of the Corn Laws in 1849 removed British import duties on grain, the United States had been the basic supplier of Britain's food needs. The tariff now hampered this trade, which was further cut into by the agricultural competition of other countries, from Russia and Australia to Canada and the Argentine. No rose-tinted tomorrow could change the fact that today American farm surpluses were not being absorbed domestically and would not be acceptable overseas as long as foreign manufacturers were barred entry to the United States.

In the early seventies the pioneer farmers of Minnesota, Dakota Territory, Iowa, Nebraska, and Kansas had found themselves faced with a concatenation of troubles. Years in which hailstorms were unusually frequent were followed by years of drought. Most destructive of all were the plagues of grasshoppers, which came in clouds, blotting out the sun and, when they descended, stripping the earth as bare as a lunar landscape. Thousands of acres of corn and potatoes and wheat were eaten away overnight. To keep the ruined farmers alive, relief committees were formed and state and federal aid hurriedly provided. The Army was ordered to distribute rations and clothing. Though men did not starve, many settlers fled the land. But with the passing of the 1870's, good times of seasonable weather and ample harvests returned. It was during

A bust of the Father of his Country is fronted by Columbia and a decorous cherub in a design by E. H. Blashfield for the Washington inauguration centennial celebration's souvenir booklet.

these good times that bonanza farming in the Red River Valley of Dakota Territory and Minnesota, which had begun in 1876, grew to a scale and a degree of mechanization approached at that time only in California. Developers were able to buy up acreage granted to the Northern Pacific Railroad, exchanging depreciated bonds for land; late-comers purchased land still owned by the government. Farms of ten thousand acres were common, and there was one of one hundred thousand acres. All were cultivated by the most up-to-date machinery. In the spring it was not unusual to see forty or fifty plows moving with military precision across the flat landscape of a single farm.

The year 1886 again ushered in a decade of searing, dry years, which cut down the lush harvests and marked an end to most farm prosperity. Frost and drought combined to make crops during all but two years from 1886 to 1895 almost total failures, particularly in the Red

River Valley. Again settlers abandoned their farms, returning from Dakota Territory, Kansas, and Nebraska with the legend painted on their covered wagons:

> In God We Trusted,
> In Kansas We Busted.

Even the crops that were harvested met with a falling market. As price levels fell, as the gold dollar bought more, farmers, mortgaged to the financial East and facing foreclosures, clamored for a silver standard, for cheap money—the constant agrarian dream. In response to such agitation Congress in 1878 had passed the Bland-Allison Bill, which allowed limited coinage of silver. Over the opposition of conservative Republicans, Congress early in 1889 raised the Department of Agriculture to Cabinet status, and Cleveland appointed Norman J. Colman to serve as the first Secretary of Agriculture.

The voice of the Western farmer spoke for rural Amer-

There is optimism and peace in this post-Civil War Kansas farming scene from a historical painting by John Steuart Curry. But by the 1880's and '90's the prevailing spirit in American agriculture was compounded of deep despair and bitterness.

ica. In New England the voice of agriculture was fading as farmers continued to abandon the thin soil of their boulder-littered upland acres. The voice was muted in the South, where the one-crop system of cotton had been expanded to the further detriment of the soil. Over most of America farmers either owned their own acres or, as tenants, were preparing to own them, but in the South the sharecropper system held farmers, both black and white, in a state of virtual peonage to the town merchant. Increasingly the Southern small farmer lapsed into tenancy, becoming a mere renter on the land he once had owned.

It was the perennial complaint of farmers even in good times that they were denied their share of the general prosperity, that they were in debt to the financial East, that they were the victims of middlemen, of hard currency, of high rates of interest, of marketing facilities rigged against them, of the overcapitalized railroads and their arbitrary and capricious rate schedules. It cost, they maintained, a bushel of corn to ship a bushel of corn to market. A North Carolina farm journal editor expressed the prevailing rural opinion when he wrote in the spring of 1887:

There is something radically wrong in our industrial system. There is a screw loose. The wheels have dropped out of balance. The railroads have never been so prosperous, and yet agriculture languishes. The banks have never done a better or more profitable business, and yet agriculture languishes. . . . Towns and cities flourish and "boom" and grow and "boom," and yet agriculture languishes. . . . Salaries and fees were never so temptingly high and desirable, and yet agriculture languishes.

As one writer noted, the farmer after the war had faced the problem of making "two spears of grass grow where one grew before. He solved that. Now he is struggling hopelessly with the question how to get as much for two spears of grass as he used to get for one."

Beyond the more obvious material causes of agricultural discontent were the psychological ones: the isolation of the settler-farmer and his family under the arching prairie skies, the brutal alternations of the seasons, the drudgery, the bleakness of a life without cultural outlets. In the first agricultural setback after the Civil War boom, farmers in their despair began to get together to form clubs in many states of the South and the Middle West. Dwarfing all other such groupings in extent and influence was the Granger Movement, which had given the farmer political strength. The movement had its almost fortuitous origin in 1866, when President Johnson's commissioner of agriculture sent an obscure government clerk, Oliver Hudson Kelley, to investigate the collapsed state of farming in the South. Kelley, despite his name a Bostonian of pre-Revolutionary stock, had left New England as a young man in the Western migration and lived for several years on a farm in Minnesota. At the time he left Washington on his Southern errand he was forty years old, a sedate, white-bearded man who concealed a burning energy behind his dignified exterior. "An engine with too much steam," his intimates called him. His finished report was pigeonholed unheeded, but what he saw of the South's crushing poverty convinced him that farmers needed above all else an organization through which they could help themselves. With six associates, he worked out elaborate plans for such an organization. It would be nonpolitical, educational and social, with an elaborate ritual derived from Freemasonry. Women would be admitted equally with men—a revolutionary proposal for its day. Possessed by his idea, Kelley resigned his job in 1867 and set out to organize Granges across the land. He found the farmers suspicious, often unwilling even to listen to him. He established his first permanent Grange at Fredonia, New York, in 1868. At the end of two years he had succeeded in founding 37 in Minnesota, where he had done most of his work, but in 1872 he started 1,105 and in 1873, the panic year, 8,400.

Not until the Panic of 1873 did the Grange come into its own as a national organization. Farmers who saw the bottom drop out of the produce market, who found interest rates soaring to 15 and 20 per cent, now swarmed into the Grange's shelter. Soon it had become a potent organization of 858,000 members. The idealistic Kelley was thrust aside. Education and social events and the monthly Feast of Pomona grew incidental to the Grange's activity as a nationwide pressure group. Developing into the Granger Movement, the National Grange became a rallying point for farmers, whether members or not, its primary practical concerns the control of railroad rates in the public interest and the establishment of cooperatives.

The first successful efforts toward railroad regulation began in Illinois with laws backed by the Grange and opposed violently by the railroads. In 1873 the Illinois legislature established a commission to prepare schedules of maximum rail rates for passengers and freight. Such regulation, the railroads continued to maintain, brought him down and buried him in debt. In his adversity he grew convinced that what the farmers needed was unity and a long-denied start in the Bourbon-dominated state government; and he stood ready to challenge the whole hierarchy of aristocratic leaders, headed by the Redeemer former governor and present United States senator, onetime Confederate General Wade Hampton.

After his own farming disaster Tillman had first attempted to form a local agricultural club in Edgefield, and when this failed, he organized a county agricultural society, of which he became president. What he first demanded was more effective agricultural education. It was at a joint meeting of the State Agricultural and Mechanical Society and the State Grange that he stepped out of his anonymity with his high, rasping voice and caustic speech. In the day of high-flown oratory he captured his audiences by falling back on a simpler manner of speech, emphasizing his points by resorting to the expressiveness of the rural vernacular. Men were aware of a new challenge as he attacked the society, the Charleston politicians, and the South Carolina College Agricultural Department. Tillman told the South Carolina farmers that they had acted like cowards and idiots in the past and that it was now up to them to decide whether or not they were going to run the state in the future. From the back roads the Rednecks swarmed to hear him with shouts of "Bring out the one-eyed plowboy!"

Tillman had earlier said that public office would have to seek him, and that time came in the spring of 1890 at a convention of the Farmers' Association, a South Carolina farmers' political action organization, called to act against "the aristocratic oligarchy." There he agreed to accept its endorsement as candidate for governor. In the campaign for delegates for the regular fall Democratic convention he was also endorsed by the Farmers' Alliance, while his alarmed opponents nominated a dignified Bourbon, whose manners they trusted would outweigh Tillman's crudities. Tillman, however, aimed his sharpest thrusts at ultra-Bourbon Wade Hampton. He swept the nominating convention and in the election overwhelmed the dissident Bourbon whom the old guard had stubbornly run against him. The largest throng ever assembled in front of the state capitol crowded there to watch his inauguration. Some Rednecks even perched in the trees or climbed public monuments to get a better view of their hero. His address was strong and progressive where he set forth requests for many long-overdue reforms. But in regard to the Negro he showed himself far more adamant than the Bourbons had ever been. "The triumph of Democracy and white supremacy over mongrelism and anarchy is most complete," he told the crowd. ". . . the whites have absolute control of the State government, and we intend at any and all hazards to retain it."

With the memory of the Reconstruction era's Black Republicanism still lurking like an ogre in the background, Bourbons and Rednecks would fight out their differences, no matter how bitter, within the protective shelter of white Democracy. Westerners, not burdened by the incubus of the race question, were more inclined to consolidate the agrarian revolt in an independent political party. The harvest of 1890 had been a good one in the West with bumper crops of grain, and yet, though Europe was again short of food, the price of wheat sank in the money scarcity following a banking crisis in England. Meanwhile the newly enacted McKinley Tariff brought sharp increases in the cost of machinery, clothing, shoes, wire, and other essentials that the farmer had to buy. Unrest in Kansas, Nebraska, Colorado, Minnesota, and the Dakotas moved beyond the Alliance to crystallize in local political third parties, bringing a revivalist fervor to the West such as Tillman had brought to the South. Supported by the Alliance, various third-party leaders of the trans-Mississippi Middle West called a convention in Topeka, Kansas, to unfurl the banner of the new People's party. A Kansas historian recalled that convention as "a religious revival, a pentecost of politics in which a tongue of flame sat upon every man, and each spake as the spirit gave him utterance." Old Greenbackers like General Weaver hailed the party as the continuation of their crusade. New leaders shot like sparks from the blaze: Minnesota's roly-poly, utopian ex-Congressman Ignatius Donnelly, benign failure in law, business, farming, and politics, popularizer of the Lost Atlantis myth, defender of Bacon as the author of Shakespeare's plays; the chin-whiskered firebrand from Kansas "Sockless" Jerry Simpson, to whom the legend clung—quite falsely—that he was too much a man of the people to wear socks. The most magnetic and spectacular orator of that 1890 campaign was, oddly, a woman— Mary Elizabeth Lease of Kansas, suffragist, prohibitionist, half socialist, and virulent denouncer of Jewish bankers and British gold. She was tall and her appearance was far from feminine, but her golden contralto voice could hypnotize. "What you farmers need to do is to raise less corn and more *Hell*!" she told her audiences. "We want money, land and transportation. We want the abolition of the National Banks, and we want the power to make loans direct from the government. We want the accursed foreclosure system wiped out. . . . We will stand by our homes and stay by our firesides by force if necessary, and we will not pay our debts to the loan-shark companies until the Government pays its debts to us. The people are at bay. . . ."

The mid-term elections of 1890 were a tidal wave, ridden in the West by the People's party—former Republicans and Democrats—to the tune of "Good-bye, My Party, Good-bye." The farmers' voting strength had been increased by the admission in 1889 of Montana, Washington, and the Dakotas to the Union. The Kansas People's party captured the governorship and the legislature, and the new party was able to take control of four other Middle Western states. As a result, the Republicans lost almost half their seats and their majority in the House of Representatives, while nine People's party congressmen and two senators were elected.

Meanwhile an austere, bearded, blue-eyed little man sat in the isolation of the White House. Once described as a typical Presbyterian deacon, President Benjamin Harrison, who had taken the offering in his church in

In the West agriculture was unsettled not only by bad years and an unfavorable economic climate but also by competition for land between the cattle ranchers (James Walker's painting above), sheep growers, and farmers raising crops.

OVERLEAF: *John Haberle's trompe l'oeil, or "deceive the eye," paintings—including* A Bachelor's Drawer, *shown here—caused considerable stir. He was accused, for instance, of pasting on, not painting, some items, such as news clippings.*

Indianapolis the Sunday before his inauguration, was characterized in ex-President Hayes's diary as "stiff, cold, distant. The elect of God—by faith, not works, to be saved." Shortly after his inauguration in 1889 Harrison had been taken across New York Harbor in a barge rowed by twelve silk-hatted oarsmen, in commemorative re-enactment of Washington's triumphant arrival for his first inauguration just a hundred years before. But the comparison verged on the ridiculous, for Harrison was less the leader than the led. "When I came into power I found that the party managers had taken it all to themselves," he once complained privately. "I could not name my own Cabinet. They had sold out every place to pay the election expenses." Harrison's Cabinet became known as the Businessmen's Cabinet. He did draw the line, however, at appointing Boss Tom Platt Secretary of the Treasury. Platt, who felt himself uniquely qualified for the post and who felt besides that he had been given a pre-election "positive pledge," resolved never again to "trust men from Ohio."

Harrison's administration, since labeled with some

The banners above are relics of the election of 1888. The message on the Cleveland-Thurman banner, which looks faintly like an ad for cigars, is affixed to netting, probably so that when strung out above a windy street, it would hang straight.

aptness The Period of No Decision, was a milepost on the bumpy transition road from an agrarian to an industrial age. The President rightly saw the future as a business future, but had little understanding of the farmer or the laborer. His Businessmen's Cabinet was made up largely of men little-known nationally and was dominated politically by Postmaster General John "One Price" Wanamaker, the great Philadelphia shopkeeper who owed his appointment to his fifty-thousand-dollar campaign donation. The most noted member of the Cabinet, independent and towering over the rest, was the Gentleman from Maine, James G. Blaine, whom Harrison, after hesitating for ten weeks, appointed to his old post of Secretary of State.

The Republican Congress accompanying Harrison to Washington, the lavish Fifty-first, became known for its spendthrift ways as the Billion Dollar Congress. But, as the newly elected Speaker of the House, Thomas B. Reed, remarked, this was "a billion dollar country." Mindful of promises to the Boys in Blue, Congress in 1890 passed an act by which any Union veteran who had served for ninety days or more and was unable to earn a living was entitled to a pension. "The old flag and an appropriation" became a Grand Army of the Republic slogan. Harrison had no objection to opening the purse strings, which Cleveland had held tight, and the surplus that had so troubled his predecessors melted away like snow in April. "God help the surplus!" Harrison's newly appointed commissioner of pensions, the "loud-mouthed Grand Army stump-speaker" James Tanner, had exclaimed with satisfaction as he doled out the money. The number of veterans receiving pensions was soon doubled, while applications increased tenfold. Nor was Congress behindhand in making appropriations for river improvements, coastal defenses, new public buildings, and other pork-barrel measures.

In his inaugural address Harrison had said that his officers would enforce the Civil Service Law "fully and without evasion," but he concluded realistically that "the ideal, or even my own ideal, I shall probably not attain." The Cabinet and the Republican elders had other ideals, expressed succinctly by Wanamaker, who advised that "full weight be given to congressional claims of patronage." Following his own advice, the Postmaster General placed Iowa Boss J. S. Clarkson in charge of post-office patronage. Working with selfless zeal, Clarkson almost immediately removed fifteen thousand fourth-class postmasters, cheered on by party

organs urging: "Go to it, Clarkson. Out with the whole 55,000 by January 1!" Clarkson's ruthlessness and the subsequent outcry finally became too much even for the irresolute Harrison, who on the advice of Congressman Henry Cabot Lodge appointed young Theodore Roosevelt to the dormant Civil Service Commission. Never a man to worry about even the most ferocious political sleeping dog, Roosevelt was soon at loud odds with the "evasive hypocrite" Wanamaker and the party's patronage dispensers. Harrison, torn between his basic, if passive, honesty and his wish to build up a strong party organization, could satisfy neither reformers nor spoilsmen. Roosevelt in his frustration complained that the President was a "cold blooded, narrow minded, prejudiced, obstinate, timid old psalm singing Indianapolis politician." Quay and Platt came to detest Harrison, and Blaine in the Cabinet kept his distance. Yet that frigid judge of men Henry Adams, though he preferred Cleveland, could say of the President that he was "a man of ability and force; perhaps the best President the Republican party had put forward since Lincoln's death."

Men of wealth and power had sought to control the government in Grant's administration by influence, but under Harrison, leaders of industry and men of sudden fortune were moving increasingly into the actual seats of power, as could be seen in the membership of the United States Senate, soon to be labeled the Millionaires' Club. Where representation had once been fiercely regional, it now was becoming economic. Kansas newspaperman William Allen White observed that a senator had come to represent "something more than a state, more even than a region. He represented principalities and powers in business." It was a process simplified by the tight boss control of the state legislatures, which elected the senators, and it went beyond party labels. Rhode Island's Nelson Aldrich, aristocratic spokesman for entrenched Eastern wealth and the high tariff, was the Senate's Republican leader. George Hearst came to the Senate from California as a mining man first, a Democrat second. The lumber senator from Wisconsin, Philetus Sawyer, semiliterate, was there; so was Chauncey Depew, the suave courtier of the Vanderbilts. Banks, railroads, silver, gold mines, oil, utilities, all claimed their proxy seats in the Senate until by the close of the century over two dozen industrial millionaires were sitting in the upper chamber.

With Harrison's election the Republicans for the first time in fourteen years controlled the Presidency and

HARPER'S WEEKLY, JUNE 15, 1889

both houses of Congress. In the House of Representatives Speaker Reed, that oddly shaped man with a round bald head and sharp pig eyes, in a series of masterly parliamentary maneuvers made himself the "Czar" of the House. After Congress' decisive success in eliminating the surplus, the chief measures of the Harrison years were the Sherman Silver Purchase Act, the Sherman Antitrust Act, and the McKinley Tariff.

One major piece of legislation, Lodge's Force Bill of 1890, failed to become law. A ghost from the Reconstruction era, the Force Bill would have provided federal control of elections to guarantee Southern Negroes the right to vote. Passed by the House, it died in the Senate. It was a landmark of sorts, for it gave a bleak demonstration that the Republican party was ready to forego the Fourteenth and Fifteenth Amendments and abandon the Negro to his segregated fate. Silver was not as easily disposed of as civil rights. Western demands for free coinage grew more vociferous as the price of

silver sank. To forestall more radical measures, Senator John Sherman, Hayes's old Secretary of the Treasury, sponsored a silver purchase bill that he himself felt to be "a thoroughly bad principle in order to avoid the enactment of that principle in a still more vicious form."

Sherman's Silver Purchase Bill, which became law on July 14, 1890, provided for issuing enough legal tender notes to purchase 4,500,000 ounces of silver each month. Then from this silver enough silver dollars were to be coined to redeem the notes. The act was a concession to Western senators in return for their support of the McKinley Tariff Bill. Sherman admitted that he had voted for his own bill with distaste. The tariff bill, introduced with all the persuasive power of Ohio's blandly open-faced Congressman William McKinley, chairman of the Ways and Means Committee, was a new concept in tariffs. No longer would the tariff be an instrument of revenue, or even an instrument of protection, but this time an instrument of exclusion, with rates raised so

high that cheap foreign goods made by cheap foreign labor would be barred from the United States for good. McKinley hated the word "cheap." "Cheap is not," he said, "a word of hope; it is not a word of inspiration! It is the badge of poverty; it is the signal of distress." His bill would take care of the surplus by eliminating its source. It was by his definition a patriotic measure, a foundation on which to anchor the "American standard" of living and of wages. The ensuing lobbying to insure the bill's passage resulted in even higher rates than McKinley himself had intended. Not only were infant industries shielded from foreign competition, but protection was extended even to industries—such as that of tin-plate manufacture—that had not yet been born. For the trusts the McKinley Tariff was manna or, more crudely, a free lunch.

One of those not stirred to fervor by the banners and battlements of the McKinley Tariff's protective wall was James G. Blaine. His handling of foreign affairs as Sec-

In 1889, the year President Cleveland left the White House for the first time, the Johnstown Flood swept through a valley in the Alleghenies in Pennsylvania. At the left is an engraving of the event; above is a photograph of the aftermath.

retary of State, particularly the success of his efforts in forming the International Bureau of American Republics—later the Pan American Union—was the most distinguished aspect of an undistinguished administration. Despite earlier protectionist views, he now had elaborate plans to expand foreign trade, which would be scuttled by the tariff. It is "a slap in the face to the South Americans," he wrote McKinley, warning him that the tariff would "benefit the farmer by adding 5 to 8 per cent to the price of his children's shoes. . . . Such movements as this for protection will protect the Republican Party only into speedy retirement." In a last effort before its passage, the Secretary of State warned the Senate's Fi-

253

nance Committee: "Pass this bill, and in 1892 there will not be a man in all the party so beggared as to accept your nomination for the Presidency."

"The Tariff," Henry O. Havemeyer, the head of the execrated Sugar Trust, remarked complacently, "is the mother of Trusts." Even without its maternal influence the trusts were thriving. Between 1880 and 1890 the number of woolen and steel mills was reduced by a third, while production soared. Such consolidation became general in all industrial and commercial fields, from railroads to sugar. As a response, or more accurately as a sop, to public opinion, and after much wrangling, both houses of Congress, just before the beginning of the 1890 campaign, passed the Sherman Antitrust Act, a law that bore the Ohio senator's name, although his role in drafting the bill was so slight that it is possible he never understood it himself. As passed, the act ostensibly gave the federal courts authority to prevent "contract, combination . . . or conspiracy, in restraint of trade or commerce" and made forming a monopoly and the "attempt to monopolize" a crime. But the act was neither seriously intended nor seriously enforced. "Trust" and "monopolize" were never adequately defined, and although the government brought eight antitrust suits during Harrison's term, it won only one and that in so limited a manner as to prove meaningless. The act became dormant, though it would later have a surprising reawakening.

Blaine with his acute political sensibilities had indeed anticipated the tidal wave of the 1890 elections. As he had surmised, farmers and workers turned out to be more influenced by a rise in the price of shoes and other basic imports than by the pejorative word "cheap." Besides the nine elected People's party congressmen and two senators, there were some fifty Democratic legislators who had been elected through the support of the Farmers' Alliance. Among other trends, the election year showed clearly that farmers were increasingly restive in the limits of the old parties. The successes of 1890 stirred up agitation to make the People's party a truly national third party, and a Western Democratic fusionist leader suggested the word "Populist" to give the movement a more convenient label. In the West it seemed a natural movement, but Southerners remained fearful of the black threat that lay outside the segregated ranks of the Democratic party.

In December, 1890, the Supreme Council of the Southern Alliance met at Ocala, Florida. There in the winter

sunshine the leading advocates of a third party debated its practicability. Midwestern leaders were determined to pledge the whole Alliance movement to the support of the third party. Southerners were hesitant when not downright opposed to giving such support. Already they had captured most branches of the Democratic party in the South, and they were hopeful of capturing the national organization. "The argument against the independent political movement in the South may be boiled down into one word—NIGGER," Georgia's farm leader Tom Watson remarked succinctly in 1892. As a delaying compromise the Western and Southern leaders agreed to assemble delegates from "all organizations of producers" in February of the 1892 election year to discuss whether a national third party was necessary. Some of the more extreme third-party advocates were not content to wait. A small group, among them two Kansas editors of the radical *Non-Conformist*, proposed an earlier convention to establish a broad movement that would go beyond the Alliance to take in farmers, laborers, veterans—black and white. This convention, the National Union Conference, was held in May, 1891, in Cincinnati, where fourteen hundred assorted delegates assembled in Music Hall under enormous banners proclaiming: "United we stand; divided we fall," "Opposition to all monopolies," and "Nine million mortgaged homes." All the city's second- and third-class hotels were overflowing, and almost any adult who showed up at Music Hall was admitted as a delegate whether he had credentials or not. There were Greenbackers; proponents of the utopianism of "Looking Backward" Bellamy, who called themselves Nationalists; single-tax followers of Henry George; Prohibitionists; suffragists; and even a group from the National Reform Press Association then meeting in the city. But the greatest single group of delegates was nevertheless from the Alliance. Ignatius Donnelly provided the compromise solution on the problem of consolidating into a third party. The delegates would elect the National Executive Committee of the People's party to attend a St. Louis convention. If no workable arrangement could be made with the other reform organizations in St. Louis, the National Committee would call a national convention to meet no later than June 1, 1892, to nominate a People's party presidential ticket.

The St. Louis convention was even more of an omnibus gathering than had been its predecessor, with more the aspect of a revival meeting than of a political gathering. Delegates from twenty-two organizations—from the Knights of Labor to the Women's Christian Temperance Union—were awarded seats. They were earnest, plain people, described by one reporter as "mostly gray-haired, sunburned and roughly clothed men. . . . The 'ward bummer,' the political 'boss,' and the 'worker at the polls' were conspicuously absent."

The platform they wrote included the usual Alliance demands for government ownership of railroads and telegraphs, free coinage of silver, abolition of national banks, restraint of alien ownership of land, restriction of gambling in stocks and futures, direct election of senators and the President, and the secret ballot. The preamble, written and delivered by Donnelly—who had drawn on the earlier Kansas Populist Manifesto—was longer and more rhetorical than the platform itself. Donnelly, with all his Celtic-inherited eloquence, denounced the ills of society while by implication offering the remedy of a third party, bringing his audience to its feet shouting and stamping approval of his passionate demands. "Hats, papers, handkerchiefs, etc., were thrown into the air; wraps, umbrellas and parasols

waved; cheer after cheer thundered and reverberated through the vast hall, reaching the outside of the building where thousands [who] had been waiting the outcome, joined in the applause till for blocks in every direction the exultation made the din indescribable. For fully ten minutes the cheering continued, reminding one of the lashing of the ocean against a rocky beach during a hurricane. . . ." After Donnelly's address the platform was adopted and the convention was adjourned. However, most of the delegates remained in their seats, becoming an assembly of "individual and independent citizens," with General James B. Weaver of Iowa as presiding officer. Weaver appointed still another committee to confer with the People's party National Committee about calling a People's party nominating convention, and it was decided to hold this in Omaha in July after the two major parties had held their nominating conventions.

During the interval until the Omaha convention met, Southern Alliance members increasingly sensed the futility of working through the Democratic party, where, in spite of the recent elections, so many of the positions

The monopoly octopus has his tentacles into everything. "The Menace of the Hour," commented The Verdict, *in which this cartoon appeared in 1899. It was drawn by George Luks, later highly respected for his painting as well as for his illustrating.*

OVERLEAF: *"Driving a coach on the road between fixed points [on schedule] . . . in imitation of old-fashioned business coaching, has a great fascination for the coaching man. . . ." So, in 1900, wrote devotee Fairman Rogers, whose coach is shown.*
PAINTING BY THOMAS EAKINS, 1879, PHILADELPHIA MUSEUM OF ART

of power were still held by the old Bourbons allied with the new industrialists. Leader in the effort to establish the Populist alternative in the South was Georgia's vociferous, red-headed Tom Watson. Watson gave tongue to the muted resentments of the tenant and the small landowner—and a considerable number of large landholders—against bankers and the new industrialism, represented in Georgia by a close-knit group that had ruled the state since before the collapse of Reconstruction. Watson liked to tell his rural audiences:

You were born in plenty and spent your childhood in plenty. I had it too. Then you lost your houses. The sheriff's red flag was planted at your front gate. You and yours took down the family pictures from the wall, picked some favorite flowers from the grave yard and took your weary march out into a strange, cold world. You walked the roads asking for work. I have done it too.

Unlike most of his followers, Watson had come from landed gentry. Born in Georgia in 1856, he, with his family, had endured dispossession and poverty in the Reconstruction era, although by the time he joined the Populist movement he had become one of the largest landowners in the state, with more tenants than his grandfather had had slaves. A farmer by birth and instinct, at twenty-three he threw in his lot with the agrarian insurgents, making stump speeches to oppose the ruling Bourbon-industrial clique. No success rewarded those early efforts, for the Georgia Bourbons, when pressed, turned to the bribable Negro vote to save themselves from the white majority—as they did in Mississippi and other states. Championing the Alliance platform, Watson was elected to Congress in 1890 as a Democrat, but soon broke with his party to organize the People's party.

As the chief Populist representative in Congress, he startled the South by becoming the first People's party leader to extend the hand of friendship to the Negro. The Republican party, he told his rural audiences, represented everything that was hateful to the whites, while the Democrats represented everything hateful to the blacks. The People's party, in his words, was called on now to explain to both blacks and whites:

You are kept apart that you may be separately fleeced of your earnings. You are made to hate each other because upon that hatred is rested the keystone of the arch of financial despotism which enslaves you both. You are deceived and blinded that you may not see how this race antagonism perpetuates a monetary system which beggars both.

Watson urged his followers to disregard skin pigmentation in favor of Populist cooperation. "The accident of color," he told his mixed audiences of black and white farmers, "can make no difference in the interests of farmers, croppers and laborers." He praised the Negro accomplishments at home and abroad, denounced lynch law (Georgia led the world in lynchings), sat on the same platform as Negroes, and nominated a Negro as a member of the new party's State Executive Committee.

The Democrats, determined to defeat Watson's reelection to Congress by any means, countered with their old shibboleth of White Supremacy. Populists were cursed, driven from churches and sometimes even from their homes. To run against Watson old-line Democrats picked a pious Baptist deacon, James Conquest Cross Black, a former Confederate private with the honorary title of major and "a Democrat because he was a Georgian." Watson, campaigning like a whirlwind through the rural areas of the state, urged his fellow farmers to "wipe out the color line, and put every man on his citizenship irrespective of color." Accused by his enemies of advocating social equality, he answered that "this is a thing each citizen decides for himself." Negroes flocked to his rallies by the thousands, standing beside Redneck farmers. Less amenable whites responded with violence. One estimate says that fifteen Negro Populists were killed during the campaign. When H. S. Doyle, an eloquent young Negro preacher who had taken the stump for Watson, was threatened, Watson took him to the shelter of his own home and sent out an appeal to his Populist farmers for armed support. Georgia was treated to the unwonted sight of whites armed with rifles riding posthaste in defense of a black.

While Watson campaigned for his nascent party in Georgia amidst increasing threats and violence, the national conventions of the two major parties began to shadow the spring of 1892. Republicans planned to hold their convention first, on June 7, in Minneapolis. Harrison, in spite of his cold manner, which had alienated so many, and in spite of the active dislike of the Eastern bosses, seemed the only possible candidate. A President sees his second term as a justification of his first, and for a party to refuse to nominate an incumbent discredits the party itself as well as the President. Harrison, after the mid-term elections debacle, had swung back toward reform policies, axing "Headsman" Clarkson and extending the civil service merit system to increase the number of federal officeholders covered by 20 per cent—

making thirty-four thousand in all. The mass of Republicans might still have hankered after the Man from Maine, but Harrison took vigorous steps through his control of patronage and of the rotten boroughs of the South to insure his own nomination on the first ballot. There was a flurry, however, three days before the convention when Blaine resigned as Secretary of State. That the President and his Secretary were at odds was common inner-circle knowledge. Suddenly it seemed that the Plumed Knight might again be a candidate. In February he had announced that he would not be, but Clarkson, Platt, Quay, and other professionals refused to take him at his word. At no time did he give his reasons for resigning as Secretary of State. In poor health, it seems doubtful that he wanted the nomination.

Blaine and Harrison were the only names presented to the convention, although Ohio's businessman-politician Mark Hanna moved behind the scenes to try to corral votes for McKinley. When Blaine's name was placed in nomination, there were the old cries of "Blaine! Blaine!" from the galleries, and the "Blaine legion" raised a white-plumed helmet to parade past the wheat sheaves and cornstalks with which the walls were decorated. But

The prohibition movement was fast gaining ground near the close of the nineteenth century, and the Chicago Figaro, *a liquor dealers' publication, opposed prohibition in Illinois, for which the journal won the encomiums of these gentlemen.*

it was a forced demonstration, nostalgic rather than ardent, and despite the shouting, stamping galleries, a requiem for a lost leader. There were even a few shouts of "sit down!" as the final Blaine orator eulogized the Plumed Knight. On the first roll call Harrison gathered $535\frac{1}{6}$ votes, nearly one hundred more than were necessary to nominate him, while Blaine trailed with $182\frac{1}{6}$, only one-sixth of a vote more than the total cast for McKinley. A motion was then carried to make the nomination unanimous, and Whitelaw Reid of the New York *Tribune* was named the candidate for Vice President.

Two weeks after the Minneapolis convention the Democrats held their convention in Chicago, with Cleveland's nomination appearing as certain as Harrison's had been for the Republicans. The former President's re-emergence had required months of assiduous preparation. In March of 1889, as the Clevelands were leaving the White House, Frances Cleveland had told an old colored servant: "Now, Jerry, I want you to take good care of all the furniture and ornaments in the house, for I want to find everything just as it is now when we come back again. We are coming back just four years from today." Cleveland, who had often felt himself a prisoner in the White House, had had no such desires. During the next four years, as a member of a sedate New York law firm, he had moved within a closed circle of friends, mellowed by his family life, which was enriched by the birth of a daughter, Ruth, in 1891. In the summers he made his home at Gray Gables on Cape Cod's Buzzard's Bay, spending some of his happiest hours fishing or sailing in a catboat named after his daughter. Buffalo and the memory of his roistering days he had come to hate, and renewed political life held little charm for him.

Nevertheless the solid, conservative Cleveland in his retirement began to seem to many Eastern capitalists and financiers the best windbreak against the Populist gales blowing from the West. In the struggle shaping up between the financial East and the agrarian West and South, between creditors and debtors, between the flexible bimetal standard and the rigid gold one, the more astute industrialists were increasingly dubious of Harrison's ability to resist the insistent demand for the free coinage of silver. On the other hand Cleveland, in February, 1891, in an open letter, had taken his stand on the currency question with "those who believe that the greatest peril would be initiated by . . . the unlimited coinage of silver." In a year when the Democrats seemed

COLLIER'S WEEKLY, MAY 30, 1903

The Gibson Girl — two samples of which species, from the pen of Charles Dana Gibson, appear here — set a standard for feminine beauty in the 1890's. In those days a lady as well put together as the one above was politely described as "a fine figure of a woman." Gibson adored his Girls, but in his caption for the drawing at the right he suggested, "These young girls who marry old millionaires should stop dreaming."

bound to win, Cleveland loomed up increasingly in sophisticated business circles as the suitable candidate, the one man who could clamp down on the rampaging free-silver heretics of his own party.

It fell to Henry Villard, German-born financier and president of the Northern Pacific Railroad, to persuade Cleveland to become a candidate again. A former abolitionist, a friend and supporter of Horace Greeley's, Villard continued on his path as a liberal capitalist by subsidizing *The Nation* and the New York *Post*. Beyond his railroad and industrial activities, he also maintained connections with powerful German banks. In his international point of view the maintenance of sound money and the gold standard was essential for a strong America attractive to foreign investors. Already apprehensive of the spreading Populist revolt with its clamor for cheap money, he had become disgusted with Harrison's approval of the McKinley Tariff and of the Sherman Silver Purchase Act as further threats to sound money. Cleveland's solid, if Democratic, bulk seemed a better insurance against the "wild radicals" of the West, even though less internationally minded manufacturers might dislike his low tariff attitude. Villard wrote in 1892 in his memoirs that "there was but one way of saving the country and the road [the Northern Pacific] from a ruinous catastrophe, viz., by the earliest possible repeal of the Sherman Act, and the election of a President in 1892 who could be relied on to exert executive influence for the repeal of the Act as well as for the establishment of the gold standard." Among the select group of conservative Easterners who followed Villard in rallying to Cleveland were two members of the first Cleveland Cabinet, Secretary of the Treasury Charles S. Fairchild and Secretary of the Navy William C. Whitney. Fairchild spoke for great banking interests; Whitney, one of the founders of the anti-Tammany County Democracy, which had helped elect Cleveland governor, was a representative of corporate finance in politics, a deft organizer of monopolies in whiskey, tobacco, and street railway lines. While Fairchild concentrated largely on securing delegates, Whitney made his chief responsibility the planning for the convention and the campaign. The chief threat to Cleveland and the sound-money Democrats lay in the rival candidacy of New York's senator and state boss, David Hill. A former governor, with black curling mustachios, which gave him the leering look of a stock company villain, Hill was an antireformist, a firm ally of Tammany's, and a bimetallist whose views on coining silver were so moderate that he alienated the free-silver people almost as much as he did the gold-standard advocates. He began by making overtures to the free-silver Westerners and to Southerners like Pitchfork Ben Tillman, who could not abide Cleveland. After touring the South on what an Atlanta newspaper called a "vote begging junket," he returned to New York to call a "snap convention" in February, which sealed his hold on the state's delegates. Yet for all his hold on New York and his incongruous Tammany–free-silver support, Hill's candidacy had flowered and faded by the time of the Democratic convention in Chicago.

In spite of the undercurrent of Tammany bitterness and the resentments of Populist-minded Democrats like Pitchfork Ben, Whitney, with his careful preparations among the Democratic leaders, felt by the time of the Chicago convention that he had enough delegates secured to insure Cleveland's nomination. From the convention hall invisible strings ran to the headquarters of the suave New Yorker in the Palmer House, a suite with Cleveland's name in electric lights over the door. For all the geysers of oratory at the convention's opening, the only challenge to Cleveland came when the ailing Tammany spokesman Bourke Cockran held the delegates spellbound with his fluid brogue-tinged voice as he denounced the former President. The effect was momentary, altering no minds or votes. Cleveland was nominated on the first ballot with $617\frac{1}{3}$ votes, $10\frac{1}{3}$ more than the necessary two-thirds majority. As a concession to the free-silver people, the Illinois bimetallist Adlai E. Stevenson was chosen for Vice President, although the platform itself did its best to mute the silver issue. Whitney wished to do the same with the McKinley Tariff, making demands for a modest reduction of rates but carefully avoiding any direct confrontation with the protectionists. Party radicals succeeded, however, in substituting a plank declaring the high tariff unconstitutional and the McKinley act "the culminating atrocity of class legislation." The increasingly conservative Cleveland warned the party's erratically liberal journalist Henry Watterson, one of those who had sponsored the radical substitution, that "if we are defeated this year, I predict a Democratic wandering in the dark wilds of discouragement for twenty-five years. I do not purpose to be at all responsible for such a result."

The third-party convention of the Populists, which opened at Omaha on July 2, aroused more enthusiasm for its platform than it did for its candidates. The dele-

A gentle view of Henry Clay Frick, who showed softness but seldom in public, is taken in this painting by Edmund C. Tarbell, portrayer of the rich and famous. Shown with the steel man in the portrait is his daughter Helen Clay Frick.

gates chose General James B. Weaver, that perennial leader of lost causes, as their presidential candidate. Then, as a balance to his Union war record, they picked a Confederate general, James G. Field of Virginia, as Weaver's running mate.

Compared to the raucous, vindictive campaigns of earlier years, that of 1892 was staid and lethargic. "The lack of interest continues," the aged Hayes wrote in his diary on Election Day. During the summer Harrison's wife had been slowly dying, and he had taken no active part in the campaign. For Cleveland, suffering from gout, his opponent's sorrow was a decent and reasonable excuse to remain at Gray Gables. The former President made only one major public appearance, at Madison Square Garden, to reply to the formal notification of his nomination. From summer through fall the usual brass and tinsel fripperies were absent. No uniformed marching clubs paraded with bands, there were no frenetic rallies, no torchlight processions. Only General Weaver,

accompanied by Mrs. Lease as he moved through the South and the West, conducted anything like a vigorous campaign. Whitney, increasingly fearful for the key state of New York, finally persuaded Cleveland to make a gesture of appeasement toward Tammany by attending a dinner at which Boss Croker and other chiefs were present. But at the meal's end, when the aggrieved Tammany leaders voiced their demands for consideration, Cleveland, according to one story, replied by pounding the table with his fist and announcing, "Gentlemen, I will not go into the White House pledged to you or to anyone else. I will make no secret promises. I'll be damned if I will!" Another, less dramatic, version has Cleveland saying simply, "No promises." Whitney and Croker pleaded for party harmony, and Croker went so far as to assure Cleveland that he was right.

One event of that summer, the strike of the ironworkers and steelworkers in Homestead, Pennsylvania, while unrelated to the campaign, had a marked effect on

the election results. The Homestead Mill on the Monongahela River was then part of the newly formed Carnegie Steel Company, of which Henry Clay Frick had become chairman with powers subordinate only to Carnegie himself. Relations between the Homestead management and the union—the powerful Amalgamated Association of Iron and Steel Workers of America—had been reasonably satisfactory until Frick's appearance. But the autocratic Frick was a ruthless businessman, uncompromising in his hostility to unionism and determined to direct labor in his plants as he saw fit. Homestead's contract with the Iron and Steel Workers expired on July 1, 1892. Before that date the union had suggested the need for a general wage increase. Frick insisted on the necessity for a reduction in wages for certain categories of workers. More important to the workers was Frick's insistence that future union contracts should expire in January, when it was difficult to find work, instead of in July, as had been the custom. When the union refused to consider this, Frick prepared for a showdown by arranging to bring three hundred Pinkerton Detective Agency guards into Homestead. In the final weeks before the contract deadline, the two sides at the bargaining table were not far apart. Union leaders were even willing to accept a slight cut, but Frick now preferred a showdown to a settlement. The question, he told the press, was "whether the Carnegie Company or the Amalgamated Association shall have absolute control of our plant and business at Homestead." Frick had the backing of Carnegie, then in Scotland, who wanted the Homestead plant to become nonunion.

At a mass meeting shortly before the July deadline, the ironworkers and steelworkers voted to strike. The strike had been in progress for three days when Frick hired the tugboat *Little Bill* to tow two barges of Pinkerton guards up the Monongahela to the Homestead landing. Five thousand people, many of them armed, waited grimly on the river banks for the arrival of the Pinkertons. On approaching the plant landing, the *Little Bill* cast off and a gangplank was pushed ashore from one barge. As the first Pinkertons attempted to land, a shot rang out. Then a volley came from the crowd and was answered by the barges. Two strikers and two guards lay dead; a number of the Pinkertons were wounded. Two hours later the guards made another attempt to land, and this too was repulsed. The *Little Bill*'s captain then took several wounded off one barge and headed toward Pittsburgh, ostensibly to get help. Strikers threw

Steel strikes, such as the one at Homestead, top left, were of considerable moment in the United States because of the rapid growth of the steel industry. At left is a panorama of steel mills in the Pittsburgh region, photographed in 1911.

dynamite sticks at the stranded barges, tried to set fire to them by igniting oil they had poured on the water, and even brought up two small cannon. Late in the afternoon the trapped Pinkertons surrendered on a promise of safe-conduct, a promise the union leaders found impossible to keep. The guards with their white flag were forced to make their way through a crowd of enraged men and women. All three hundred Pinkertons were injured to some extent before they reached safety. Sixteen of them were killed during the day, and several others died of their wounds later. The strikers were left in possession of the plant.

On receiving reports of the disturbance, the governor of Pennsylvania ordered seven thousand militiamen to Homestead to drive the strikers from the premises. Alarmed union leaders now sought a settlement on management's earlier terms, but Frick's aim was to smash the union completely, and he refused to receive them. A young anarchist, Alexander Berkman, chose this time to make his way into Frick's office, shoot Frick twice, and stab him several times with a dagger before he was overpowered. Frick's wounds were not serious; he finished out the afternoon at his office after a doctor had removed the two bullets and treated his wounds, but a great deal of sympathy that had been with the strikers shifted to Frick as a result of the senseless attack. Ironically, Berkman's attack had nothing to do with the Homestead strike; he had selected Frick as his victim simply because he epitomized the ruthless capitalist.

The Homestead Mill began limited operations again July 15, with strikebreakers and under military protection. The next day the Carnegie Company announced that it would receive work applications from strikers on an individual basis, but only until July 21; after that only new men would be hired. The American Federation of Labor—the conservative craft union that had emerged from the post-Haymarket Riot wreckage of the Knights of Labor—intervened on the side of the harassed workers, doing its best to help the steelworkers' union keep the strike going, to aid suffering strikers and their families, and to help in the legal defense of 167 unionists who had been indicted for murder and for treason. But on November 14 the beaten workers voted to end their strike. In any event, the Homestead Mill had long been back in operation by that time, and Frick was completely triumphant. As for the indicted union men, the indictments were dismissed after three men were acquitted of murder charges and the state could do no better than

win assault and battery cases against two men—one of them a cook in the mill—accused of giving poison to nonunion men.

A Carnegie house historian wrote that the strike became a national issue in the presidential election of that year and "brought defeat to the Republican hosts." Public opinion was against violence but even more against Frick's union-smashing efforts. Democratic leaders showed themselves more sympathetic to the strikers than did the Republicans. Cleveland with biting irony referred to "the tender mercy the workingman receives from those made selfish and sordid by unjust governmental favoritism." Republican leaders, unhappily faced with political realities that Carnegie could avoid, appealed in vain by cable to Carnegie at least to recognize the union. Workers were left to express their anger by voting for the Democrats or the Populists.

In spite of the Carnegie historian's judgment, Cleveland would have won handily if there had never been a strike. As it was, he won overwhelmingly, with 277 electoral votes to Harrison's 145, the greatest margin granted to any presidential candidate since Lincoln's re-election in 1864. Tammany New York went for Cleveland, but even without New York he would have succeeded. In the popular voting he polled 5,556,543 votes to Harrison's 5,175,582. The Populists, with just over 1,000,000 popular votes, received 22 electoral votes, all from Kansas and the Western silver states. In the South they had continued to court the Negro vote, with the result that the old-line Democrats took pains either to bar the Negro from the polls or to bribe and intimidate him into voting for the party of white supremacy. As a result the Populists failed to dent the Solid South, and the disfranchisement of the Negro was merely accelerated.

Cleveland's return to Washington was a triumph for his wife. Six months later Cleveland's daughter Esther was born in the White House, the first President's child to be born there. But despite this charming touch of domesticity, the national scene bore an increasingly ominous aspect to those who could view it with an economist's eye. Cleveland himself had sensed the lowering atmosphere heralding the approach of financial storms. Shortly before his inauguration, with tears in his eyes, he had told a friend, "I have a hungry party behind me and they say I am not grateful. Sometimes the pressure is most overwhelming, and the President cannot always get at the exact truth; but I want you to know that I am trying to do what is right. *I am trying to do what is right!*"

Avenue and Alley

Frank Norris described a turn-of-the-century scene outside a Chicago opera house: in a snowstorm, as richly dressed folk arrived in carriages and hurried into the lobby, there collected on the sidewalks "a crowd of miserables, shivering in rags and tattered comforters, who found . . . an unexplainable satisfaction in watching this prolonged defile of millionaires." The attitudes of rich and poor toward each other then were fascinatingly complex. The couple pictured above, who had asked their black servant to pose with them, was Virginian, but in that era—the 1890's—the maid could as well have been Irish and the couple Bostonian. Blacks and Irish may have been thought inferior as classes, but as servants, "in their place," they were often treated as indispensable old friends.

The rich gave to charity; in return, the poor frightened them with angry talk or simply with the bitter reality of being poor, as in Jacob Riis's mother-and-child photograph at right. But at heart such women as Mrs. Cornelius Vanderbilt III, above with Cornelius, Jr., were mainly concerned with Society.

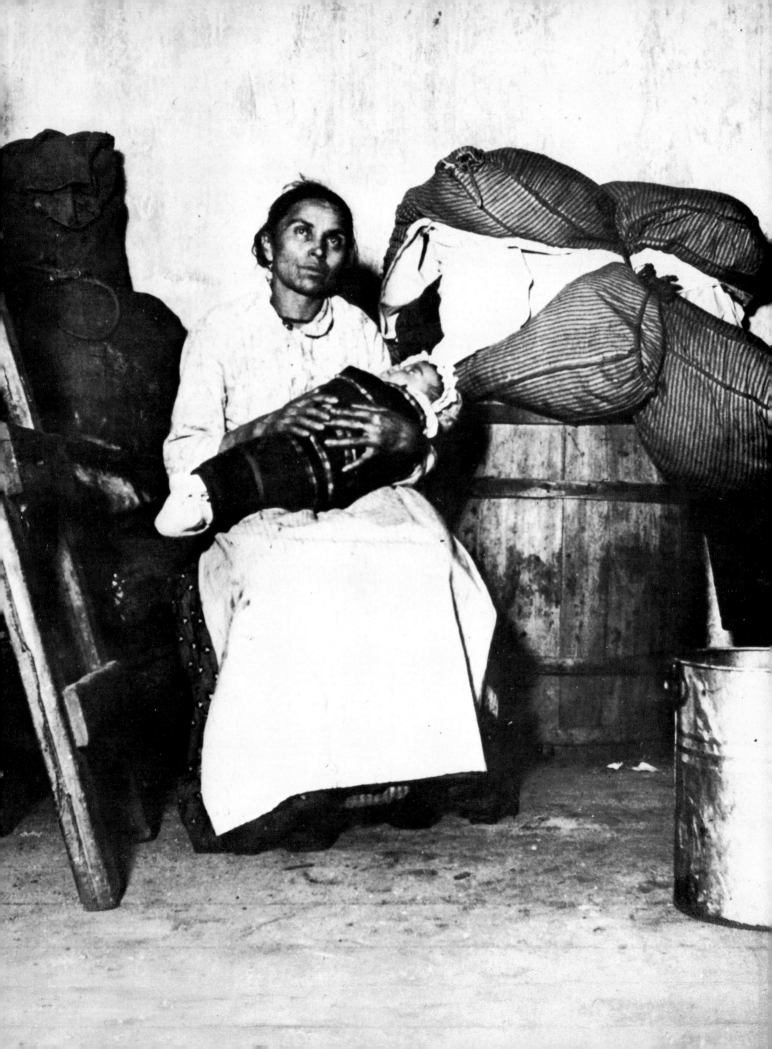

Society could make fun of itself; note the laurel-crowned diners at the left. But Mrs. William K. Vanderbilt, above in costume for a ball, took it very seriously— although she would become, as Mrs. Oliver H. P. Belmont, a prominent suffragette. "I know of no profession, art, or trade that women are working in to-day," she declared, "as taxing on mental resource as being a leader of Society."

This portrait of tenement dwellers was taken in about 1910, probably by Mrs. Jessie Tarbox Beals, a newspaper photographer.

With two rooms and the mattresses off the floor, the apartment was considerably more pleasant than many in that period.

Above, elegantly turned-out couples dance on a lawn during a meet held at Newport for devotees of horse-drawn coaches.

Below is Jacob Riis's photograph of children dancing in a rough playground in Poverty Gap on New York City's West Side.

Free Silver and Expansionism

*B*efore Cleveland's return to office, financier Henry Villard, alert to every change in the economic weather, had sensed a drop in the business barometer and had warned his German associates to keep their American investments liquid. Watching the effect of the Sherman Silver Purchase Act, he foresaw a currency crisis that would be followed by a depression. Although silver was being mined in such large quantities in the West that the price continued to fall, the government was still forced by the Sherman act to buy four and a half million ounces of the metal each month. Debtors could pay their government debts in silver dollars with an intrinsic value of only fifty-three cents. Nongovernment creditors demanded gold. The McKinley Tariff, by drastically reducing imports and so cutting off import duties, had eliminated any possible treasury surplus; the Sherman act was draining away specie. Nervous foreign investors began to withdraw gold from the United States. Cleveland at the beginning of his term found himself faced with an almost empty treasury.

Ten days before Cleveland's inauguration, the Philadelphia and Reading Railroad had gone bankrupt with debts of more than $125,000,000. The failure seemed a symbol. Prices of grain, iron, cotton, and other commodities kept falling, and the stock market churned about uneasily. The treasury's gold reserve, though bolstered by an emergency loan from New York bankers, threatened to drop below the $100,000,000 level, the magic figure popularly regarded, as Cleveland observed, "with a sort of sentimental solicitude." Villard, supported by financiers like J. P. Morgan and August Belmont, warned the President that a panic was moving in like a northeaster and begged him to call a special session of Congress to repeal the Silver Purchase Act. Confronting the widespread uneasiness that the United States would be forced onto a silver standard, Cleveland declared that the dollar would continue to be redeemed at its established gold value. Carnegie, speaking for business, said that the President's statement had "saved this country from panic and entire confusion in its industrial interests."

In spite of Carnegie's optimism, by the first week in May the great Panic of 1893 was sweeping across the land. Other railroads followed the downward path of the Phila-

The cheery, sunny charm of Maurice Prendergast's South Boston Pier *is the quality traditionally associated with the 1890's in America. But, like the moon, the "Gay Nineties" had their dark side.*

delphia and Reading. Trust after trust collapsed into bankruptcy. European banks, which had lent most of the money to finance the Western railroads, sold their American stocks and bonds, and a vast bank run followed. In the South and the West more than five hundred banks failed. Farm foreclosures soared. The harvest that year was bountiful, but farmers could not even obtain short-term loans for shipping their crops to market. Industry stagnated as the panic gave way to depression with mass unemployment. Eastern conservatives continued to blame the Silver Purchase Act for destroying confidence in the American currency. Under their persistent urging the President, though at first reluctant, in late June called a special session of Congress for August 7 to repeal "unwise laws" relating to the currency.

Richard Olney, the Boston corporation lawyer who had become Cleveland's Attorney General, wrote most of the presidential message demanding the repeal of the Sherman act. Revoking the act, he said, would make the currency "so safe . . . that those who have money will spend and invest it in business and enterprise instead of holding it." Westerners, both agrarian and mining, remained unconvinced. The silver issue divided Congress geographically rather than politically. A third of the Democratic congressmen, prodded by the Populists and urged on by Silver Dick Bland of Missouri and the tousle-haired William Jennings Bryan of Nebraska, were ready to vote against the administration, as were the "silver" senators from the West.

Cleveland remained the key figure in the fight for repeal, the one man powerful enough to hold his party together and whip reluctant Democrats into line. Yet at the very time that he called his special session he was faced with a desperate personal crisis. In May he had complained of a sore spot in his mouth, caused—he thought—by his constant cigar smoking. Examining him in June, the White House physician found a growth on the roof of the mouth as large as a twenty-five-cent piece. Laboratory tests showed it to be malignant, and Cleveland was warned that he must have an operation at once. Yet if the President's serious condition should become known, the financial crisis would boil over. And if he should die, the diminutive Populist-influenced Adlai Stevenson would, as his successor, lead the country down the silver path, which would end in a dollar worth only half its former value.

Cleveland did not hesitate. On June 30 he left Washington by train, ostensibly bound for Cape Cod. Once in New York, he left the train and was taken to the Battery, from where he was ferried to a steam yacht, the *Oneida*. A team of surgeons and physicians was aboard waiting for him. Cleveland greeted them, then, standing by the rail, smoked a last cigar and went to bed. Early the next morning the *Oneida* steamed up the East River and through Hell Gate into the waters of Long Island Sound. For the occasion the *Oneida*'s saloon had been turned into an operating room. There, in the becalmed isolation of the sound, the surgeons took over their work. Cleveland, placed in an upright chair to minimize bleeding, received an anesthetic. Two teeth were removed. Then his friend the noted surgeon Dr. Joseph Bryant excised a section of the roof of the President's mouth and from the left antrum cavity scooped a "soft, gray, gelatinous mass"—the deadly carcinoma. Some two hours after it began, the operation was successfully completed.

"My God, Olney, they nearly killed me!" Cleveland later told his Attorney General. But by July 12 he had recovered sufficiently to work on his congressional message, although five days later he had to submit to having the antrum cavity scraped to insure that no malignant cells had been left. Still haggard and miserable, he insisted on returning to Washington two days before the special session in order to exert personally the pressure of his office on recalcitrant congressmen. In his message he announced with uncompromising bluntness:

. . . the operation of the silver purchase law now in force leads in the direction of the entire substitution of silver for gold in the Government Treasury, and . . . this must be followed by the payment of all Government obligations in depreciated silver. . . .

The people of the United States are entitled to a sound and stable currency, and to money recognized as such on every exchange and in every market of the world. Their government has no right to injure them by financial experiments opposed to the policy and practice of other civilized states.

In the House of Representatives the administration floor leader, William L. Wilson of West Virginia, introduced a bill to repeal the Sherman Silver Purchase Act. William Jennings Bryan, in opposition, emerged as the sensation of the debate when on a languid summer afternoon he thrust aside his prepared text and launched into a three-hour defense of bimetallism. Handsome, square-jawed, with a voice that recalled the great orators of the days of Clay and Calhoun, he maintained that there was not a sufficient amount of either gold or silver to stand alone as a standard for the world's currencies.

Both metals were needed. Forcing down the price of silver, Bryan declared, had elevated the price of gold artificially, destroying the 16 to 1 ratio between the prices of gold and silver. Bryan warned:

On the one side stand the corporate interests of the United States, the moneyed interests, aggregated wealth and capital. . . . On the other side stand an unnumbered throng, those who gave to the Democratic party a name and for whom it has assumed to speak. Work-worn and dust-begrimed, they make their mute appeal, and too often find their cry for help beat in vain against the outer walls, while others, less deserving, gain ready access to legislative halls.

On August 28, and for all Bryan's oratory, Wilson's repeal bill passed the House by the decisive vote of 239 to 108. There still remained the higher hurdle of the Senate. Cleveland, forgetting civil service reform for the time

An embarrassed, if good-natured, Chicago Republican hauls the carriage of an exultant Democratic friend in this scene from The Lost Bet—*a lithograph, after a painting by Joseph Klir, which commemorates the Cleveland-Stevenson victory in 1892.*

Cleveland's successful campaign to repeal the Sherman act neither cured the depression nor set at rest the debate over a gold versus a bimetal standard. The Puck *cover above celebrates the 1900 passage of the Currency, or Gold Standard, Act.*

being, brought all the patronage pressure he could muster on reluctant senators. Through September and October debate on the repeal bill continued in the Senate, as bitter as it was long-winded. One of the tougher-larynxed Populists made a fifteen-hour speech. Another silver senator was so overcome by the pathos of his own oratory that he burst into tears. A marathon session of the Senate lasted thirty-eight hours.

As the weeks prolonged into months, many pro-gold Democratic senators became willing to settle for a reduction in the total amount of silver purchased each month rather than outright repeal. But Cleveland would have none of such silver-serving compromises. Pounding the table with his fist at a Cabinet meeting, he announced that he was not prepared to budge an inch. On October 30, the issue at last came to a vote, with 48 senators opting for repeal as against 37 who were opposed. Ailing though he was, Cleveland had won. But William Jennings Bryan warned the victors not to "congratulate yourselves that you have laid away the free coinage of silver in a sepulcher," for the issue would again "lay

aside its grave clothes and its shroud. It will yet rise, and in its rising and its reign will bless mankind."

Despite Cleveland's success in repealing the Sherman act, he foundered in his efforts to alter the McKinley Tariff. A bill introduced by Congressman Wilson of West Virginia proposing a reduction in tariff schedules was so mutilated by lobby-influenced congressmen and senators that by the time it reached the President's desk it had more than six hundred—mostly protectionist—amendments. Denouncing it as a product of "party perfidy and party dishonor," Cleveland allowed it to become law without his signature. One provision of the Wilson bill, much opposed by the Republicans and the Easterners, was for an income tax—the first passed since the Civil War—of 2 per cent on incomes over four thousand dollars a year.

For all Cleveland's hopes, the repeal of the Silver Purchase Act had no effect on a depression that in any case was world-wide and that now with its lowering clouds blotted out the last vestiges of prosperity. By the end of 1893, 642 of the country's banks had closed their doors, one-fourth of its heavy industries was no longer running, and 22,500 miles of railroads were in the hands of receivers. Prosperous farmers saw themselves ruined as corn dropped to thirty-six cents a bushel and cotton to six cents a pound. Revenues fell away, the treasury's gold reserve shrank to sixty million dollars, and as the dismal autumn of 1893 gave way to an even more dismal winter, the government itself seemed on the edge of bankruptcy. To the Populists and the Silver Democrats, Cleveland and gold were to blame.

As the treasury deficit grew, the flight of gold overseas and into hoarders' stockings became faster. During a seventeen-day period in January, 1894, eleven million dollars in gold left the treasury. Cleveland, initially unwilling, finally decided that the only way to maintain a gold reserve was by a new bond issue, and he proposed that fifty million dollars' worth of bonds—bearing 4 per cent interest and redeemable "in coin" after ten years—be sold for gold or for gold certificates. But because of doubts over the legality of the bonds, and because the terms did not specifically guarantee redemption in gold, he and his Secretary of the Treasury, John G. Carlisle, had much difficulty in floating the issue, and only at the last minute was he able to persuade Eastern financiers to take the bonds (on which the holders later lost money).

Meanwhile the Western and Populist clamor for cheap money continued, and Cleveland and Carlisle were denounced as traitors, lickspittles to wealth, and tools of Wall Street. Bending to the silverite pressure, the House and the Senate in early March passed the Bland bill, which allowed the government to coin the silver bullion—some fifty-five million dollars' worth—that had accumulated in the treasury. But even this relatively minor concession seemed to Cleveland the opening silver wedge. In spite of enormous political pressures, he vetoed the bill, calling it a hindrance to the financial recovery that he maintained was now slowly getting under way, and he used his influence to see that a reluctant Congress sustained his veto. With the repeal of the Silver Purchase Act, with the floating of the new bond issue, and with the veto of the Bland bill—all violently attacked in the West and the South—Cleveland's popularity plummeted. For the Populists and the Populist-minded Democrats he became the incarnation of hard times. And as the mid-term elections of 1894 approached, the times continued to grow worse.

The turbulence and despair of that year found a symbol in the protest march on Washington organized and led by a respectable, prosperous Ohio businessman, Jacob S. Coxey. Owner and operator of a stone quarry near Massillon, Coxey was a Greenbacker, and later also a fervent Populist, who believed that "there's nothing wrong with this country that money won't cure." By "money" he meant limitless issues of paper. His recommended cure for the depression was a vast public works program to hire the unemployed at $1.50 a day to construct and improve roads, and to be financed by half a billion dollars in non-interest-bearing bonds. This program he planned to present to Congress in the form of "a petition with boots on," the boots being those of the Commonweal of Christ, the army of unemployed that he was mustering in Massillon. His expedition soon became known more simply as Coxey's Army, with its commander granted the honorific title of General.

On Easter Sunday, 1894, General Coxey set out from Massillon with a hundred of his soldiers, led by a Negro carrying the flag of the Commonweal and by a seven-piece band playing the Commonweal battle hymn:

> We're marching on Washington
> To right the nation's wrongs.

Standard-bearers bore a banner with a likeness of Christ and the motto: "Peace on Earth, Good Will to Men, But Death to Interest on Bonds." Coxey was then forty years old, a frail and most unmilitary general, who peered mildly through gold-rimmed spectacles above a nondescript mustache and wore a staid business suit and a high wing collar. Instead of mounting a steed, he rode in a buggy. More flamboyant was his publicist and second-in-command, a lank-haired former carnival barker and vendor of Kickapoo Indian Blood Remedy, Carl Browne, who wore a cowboy hat and a buckskin jacket with silver half-dollar buttons inscribed "FREE." Adding additional tone to the marchers were a man who called himself The Great Unknown and who was accompanied by a veiled lady calling herself nothing at all; an astrologer; a Cherokee Indian who ate only oatmeal; a trumpet player with the apt name of Windy Oliver; and the author of a pamphlet called *Dogs and Fleas, by One of the Dogs.* The rank and file consisted of ordinary unemployed workers and the usual number of tramps and eccentrics.

Coxey claimed that his marchers were "patriots, not bummers," but he still expected his army to travel on donations. These were forthcoming. Communities provided rations and shelter in jails and public buildings, if only to speed the ragtag along on its way, while many individuals out of charity or sympathy gave food and money to the marchers. By the time Coxey's Army had passed through Homestead, Pennsylvania, it had expanded to six times its original size, and a nervous Congress stayed in special session on April 18 till 6 P.M. to debate the oncoming "red menace." On the march through Maryland, while General Coxey was absent on a side trip, mutiny broke out in the army when The Great Unknown led a faction against Browne, who had caused much resentment not only through his enthusiasm as a disciplinarian but by his habit of spending his nights in the best hotels while the army camped outdoors or on the floors of barns and jails. Only Coxey's quick return and his expulsion of The Great Unknown and the veiled lady rescued Browne from the mutineers.

By the time the Army of the Commonweal was approaching the District of Columbia, the commissioners had issued a manifesto aimed at Coxey, forbidding soliciting of funds within the District, assembling on the Capitol grounds, and obstructing roads and highways. "If they starve in the streets of Washington," Coxey said, "the stench from their ashes will force Congressional relief." On May Day, and despite the police, Coxey's Army marched up Pennsylvania Avenue to the Capitol while thousands of spectators lined the sidewalks. The general and his wife, with their infant son, Legal Tender Coxey, rode in a buggy, which was preceded

Coxey's Army was sometimes called a gang of loafers. But,
protested the army's poet laureate, try finding work, "with
money scarce and business dull, and then see how you feel./
Your shoulder may be willing but you cannot find a wheel.

by his white-robed seventeen-year-old daughter on a cream-colored horse as the goddess of peace. Another mounted goddess of peace, an actress from Philadelphia, was draped in the American flag. Browne rode a gray Percheron stallion. The rank and file carried white peace banners interspersed with signs denouncing plutocrats and proclaiming reincarnation.

Accounts of what happened next differ in many details, but the following was the report of one reliable observer. On reaching the Capitol, Coxey tried to address the crowd from the east steps, but was barred by the police, who refused him permission even to read a written protest. As he handed a copy of his protest to newsmen, his followers surged forward in what was later described as a riot, and a squadron of mounted police charged them. Within five minutes the crowd had dissolved, Browne—pursued by mounted police—had vaulted his Percheron over a low wall, and Coxey, Browne, and another lieutenant, one Christopher Columbus Jones, in a top hat and peppermint-striped coat, found themselves under arrest. Charged with walking on the grass of the Capitol, they were each fined five dollars and sentenced to twenty days in jail. With the loss of its general, Coxey's Army dissolved. A hundred or so members camped over the Maryland line, raiding the local farms for food until the Baltimore police jailed most of them as vagrants. On his release from jail, Coxey returned to Ohio, but remained active in politics. In 1914 he led another march, and in 1932 he was the Farmer-Labor candidate for President. He died in 1951 at the age of ninety-seven.

As the mid-term elections approached, all the signs continued to point to a repudiation of the Democrats. A group of silver-minded Democrats, who called themselves The Wild Horses, broke with Cleveland completely. Ben Tillman, campaigning through South Carolina for the Senate, told his rural audiences: "Send me to Washington and I'll tickle Cleveland's fat ribs with my pitchfork!" The silver agitation that year reached its climax through an itinerant lawyer and journalist, William H. Harvey, whose pamphlet *Coin's Financial School* was perhaps the most influential since Thomas Paine's *Common Sense*. Within a year it had reached half a million readers. For several years Harvey had been editor of a magazine, *Coin*, devoted to the cause of free silver, and so had become known as Coin Harvey. His *Coin's Financial School* was a fictive account of how his hero, "a smooth little financier," had set up a school in the Art Institute of Chicago to instruct capitalists, editors, publishers, and professors in the principles of finance and to solve the paradox of want in the midst of plenty. For Harvey it all boiled down to the scarcity or abundance of money. The repeal of the Silver Purchase Act had brought about a state of affairs where "hungered and half-starved men are banding into armies and marching toward Washington; the cry of distress is heard on every hand . . . riots and strikes prevail throughout the land. . . ." To Coin Harvey the villains were the capitalists, the national and international goldbugs, who had erected a wall of gold between themselves and the people. A new age of silver would level this wall, bringing the prosperity that was being withheld by the few.

Beyond the silver agitation, his waning popularity, and the defections from his party, Cleveland was faced with the most formidable crisis of the year in the Pullman strike of May, 1894. By the 1890's the Pullman Palace Car Company, in addition to its celebrated sleeping cars, was making dining cars and chair cars. Pullman stockholders were receiving an annual 8 per cent dividend, and George Pullman had become one of the great industrialists of his age. In 1880 he had bought a seven-mile-square tract some miles outside Chicago and there he had built the town of Pullman. In comparison with the industrial grime of Chicago, Pullman was a sparkling model town, with cozy brick buildings, paved and shaded streets, landscaped yards, and even an artificial lake beside which Pullman's eighty-piece band gave concerts in the summer. Pullman schools had a longer term than most other schools; there was an evening school for adults and—a great innovation for its day—a kindergarten. Yet there was another side to the garden city with its lake and its schools and its luxurious new library, for Pullman was a self-righteous moralist who knew what was good for others as well as for himself, and who was autocratically determined both that his workers should conform to his views and that his dream city should make money. As a long-term investment, the project had been richly rewarding, for the land for which he had paid eight hundred thousand dollars in 1880 was worth five million dollars twelve years later. But even with this, Pullman was disappointed that his investment paid at most 4.5 per cent annually, in contrast to his stockholders' safe and steady 8 per cent. He stood firm against liquor, loose women, and trade unions, and employed a network of spies within his model town to keep his workers on his designated straight and narrow path and to weed out subversives. The workers paid well for the neatness of Pullman's tree-lined streets, for rents were 25 per cent higher there than in Chicago.

Many, if not most, of Pullman's workers responded to his arbitrary paternalism with smoldering resentment. As one bitter employee put it: "We are born in a Pullman house, fed from the Pullman shop, taught in the Pullman school, catechized in the Pullman church, and when we die we shall be buried in the Pullman cemetery and go to the Pullman hell."

Pullman responded to the 1893 Panic with retrenchment. In July of that year he employed fifty-five hundred workmen, the next May only thirty-three hundred. While actually increasing dividends, he slashed wages by 25 per cent. Rents continued at their old rate. Whether a dweller in the ideal city was at work at reduced wages or out of work altogether made no difference to George Pullman. Rents were a fixed charge.

The winter of 1893–94 was bleak and bitter in the model town. Destitution spread from neat brick house to neat brick house along the network of well-planned streets. Many children lacked shoes to go to school; others had to stay in bed because there was no coal in the house.

Into the desolation of Pullman in the spring of the year came, with his American Railway Union, the energetic, farseeing Eugene Debs, an agitator with a gift of speech that gave him the power to move men. The utopian Debs looked forward to an America of brotherly love from which poverty, violence, and selfishness had vanished. Troubled by the exclusiveness of the existing railroad craft unions, he formed his union to include the unskilled workers scorned by the aristocratic railroad brotherhoods. In the spring of 1894 Debs's union won a savage strike against James Hill's Great Northern Railroad, the first that any union had ever won against a major road. With this startling success behind him, Debs proceeded to organize the Pullman workers, who thronged in desperation to the American Railway Union, and though Debs was against it, insisted on going out on strike immediately. "We struck because we were without hope," a committee of Pullman delegates told the June A.R.U. convention. "We joined the American Railway Union because it gave us a glimmer of hope. . . ."

When committees of strikers came prepared to arbitrate, Pullman's vice president told them that there was nothing to arbitrate. Wages and working conditions were for Pullman, the owner and arbiter, to determine. Debs countered with a boycott whereby switchmen refused to switch Pullman cars onto trains. In turn the General Managers' Association, representing the twenty-four railroads running out of Chicago, challenged the American Railway Union by announcing that switchmen who supported the boycott would be punished. Debs's boycott began on June 26 and at once spread to twenty-seven states and territories. Sixty thousand men walked out the first two days, and the strike spread until twenty railroads were shut down. Debs did his best to avoid any violence, but the situation was an explosive one. General Managers' agents scoured the cities for strikebreakers even as leaders of the brotherhoods denounced the upstart union. Freight traffic in and out of Chicago and to the West was soon paralyzed. In spite of Debs's warnings, turbulent crowds began to hold up trains and make them detach Pullman cars. Newspapers, like the Chicago *Tribune*, blew up such incidents into headlines that claimed the mob to be in control of the city.

Beyond the rights and wrongs of the strike, the obliga-

tion rested on the federal government to see that the mails got through and that the Interstate Commerce Act of 1887, guaranteeing freedom of traffic between states, was enforced. To Attorney General Richard Olney, on whom responsibility for action devolved, Debs's inciting of the men to strike was an interference with the mails and with interstate commerce. Olney could scarcely have been considered an impartial mediator, for not only had he long been an attorney for a number of railroads but he had also been a railroad director and for a time a member of the General Managers' Association. An arbitrary, quick-tempered man, much feared by his subordinates, he was so little in sympathy with the strike that he would have dispatched federal troops to Chicago immediately to clear the tracks. Since Cleveland was bound to take a more moderate view, Olney by a process of maneuvering and misinformation proceeded to lead the President along the strikebreaking path that he wished him to follow. Arguing that the American Railway Union was a combination in restraint of trade

Virtually all pictures of the Pullman strike of 1894 depict the strikers as undisciplined, destroying mobs and the military as stalwart defenders of the peace. This one, no exception, has the cavalry clearing the track through the strikers' lines.

contrary to the Sherman Antitrust Act, he sought an injunction from a sympathetic federal judge against the union and the strikers, on the ground that the strike was "a public nuisance" because of its interference with use of the highways. The injunction turned out to be one of the most sweeping and drastic ever issued, enjoining the strike leaders from so much as talking about the boycott. Railroad workers who quit an interstate job or even those who failed to operate switches were held to be guilty of committing a crime. The Managers' Association hailed the injunction as "a gatling gun on paper." Olney himself felt that it would prove unenforceable, and planned to appeal to the President to send in troops.

Through Olney's machinations—and over the protests of Chicago's Mayor John P. Hopkins and Illinois's prolabor Governor John Peter Altgeld—Cleveland was induced to send infantry, cavalry, and artillery to Chicago to insure the safety of the mail trains. The troops arrived on the Fourth of July. Aiding them were some thirty-six hundred deputy federal marshals—the flotsam of the city—selected for the government by the General Managers' Association. Until the soldiers' arrival, outbreaks of violence had been sporadic, though much exaggerated by the press. But with their coming and the presence of the deputy marshals, violence exploded. A mob of hoodlums and criminals, with very few strikers among them, stopped trains, smashed switches, and burned hundreds of box cars. Six large buildings of the Great White City, which still stood from the Columbian Exposition of the preceding year, went up in flames. Eastern newspapers represented the mob as ruling supreme. On July 7 a mob challenged the soldiers directly, and in that clash seven men were killed outright. The next day Cleveland issued an order forbidding all unlawful assemblies and announced, "There will be no vacillation in the decisive punishment of the guilty."

Two days later, July 10, 1894, Debs and three colleagues were arrested for obstructing the mails, and Debs was later sentenced to six months in jail for having violated the injunction. Pullman still refused to consider arbitration; the strikers, hungry and broken, finally gave up the struggle. Many of them were black-listed in the

This Lynn, Massachusetts, factory worker was photographed in 1895 by Frances B. Johnston. By 1900, when the average employee in manufacturing earned $435 a year, over one million women were working in the manual trades in the United States.

288

Pullman plants, and all those who went back were forced to sign a pledge that they would not join a union. Angry voices were raised in support of the strikers, among them that of the young journalist Finley Peter Dunne, just beginning to develop his alter ego, Mr. Dooley, who attacked Pullman from behind a mask of dialect:

". . . 'tis not th' min [of Pullman] ye mind; 'tis th' women an' childhern. Glory be to Gawd, I can scarce go out f'r a walk f'r pity at seein' th' little wans settin' on th' stoops an' th' women with thim lines in th' face that I seen but wanst befure, an' that in our parish over beyant, whin th' potatoes was all kilt be th' frost an' th' oats rotted with th' dhrivin' rain. . . . Musha, but 'tis a sound to dhrive ye'er heart cold whin a woman sobs an' th' young wans cries, an' both because there's no bread in th' house. . . .

"But what's it all to Pullman? Whin Gawd quarried his heart a happy man was made. He cares no more f'r thim little mat-thers iv life an' death thin I do f'r O'Connor's tab. 'Th' women an' childhern is dyin' iv hunger,' they says. 'Will ye not put out ye'er hand to help thim?' they says. 'Ah, what th' 'ell,' says George. 'What th' 'ell,' he says. 'What th' 'ell,' he says. 'James,' he says, 'a bottle iv champagne an' a piece iv crambree pie. What th' 'ell, what th' 'ell, what th' 'ell.'"

To frightened middle-class Chicagoans and to the conservative press generally, Cleveland's dispatching of troops was a decisive blow against social disorder and anarchy. Mayor Hopkins and Governor Altgeld knew better, but uninformed public opinion outside the union movement backed the President. Labor condemned him bitterly, joining with the Populists and the silverites in their opposition to the President. Cleveland later appointed a commission to investigate the strike, and its fair and tempered report placed the principal blame for the Chicago disturbances on George Pullman and the General Managers' Association.

Yet, though Cleveland's action in the Pullman strike brought him general, if temporary, approval, he found himself increasingly isolated from his party as it fragmented on the silver issue. Instead of improving, times continued to grow worse. For politicians, the handwriting on the wall grew to billboard size as the 1894 elections approached. Former Republican Speaker of the House Tom Reed observed early in the year, "The Democratic mortality will be so great next fall that their dead will be buried in trenches and marked 'unknown.'" Late in the year he added the postscript "till the supply of trenches gives out." The November balloting almost doubled the number of Republicans in the House of

Representatives, for a total of 244 Republicans to 105 Democrats. Populists, still on the upswing, received a million and a half votes—an increase of 42 per cent in two years—and elected six United States senators and seven congressmen.

In the winter following the election, the economy continued downward. Stubbornly determined to maintain the price of gold, Cleveland found himself forced to float a new bond issue. His first issue had sustained the treasury for ten months, the second, which he had called for in November, 1894, for only ten weeks. With the necessity for a third bond issue immediate, and the fate of the gold standard in the balance, the President and the Secretary of the Treasury, John G. Carlisle, were compelled to turn to the Eastern financiers J. P. Morgan and August Belmont for a large loan. These two banking interests, with the overseas cooperation of the Rothschilds, took over the bond issue and pegged the price of gold. Morgan and Belmont had brought needed assistance to their government, but they had struck a hard bargain. Outraged Populists were convinced anew that Cleveland had allied himself with the plutocracy at the expense of ordinary people, and many maintained that Cleveland and Carlisle had been suborned by Morgan and the Rothschilds and other international financiers. To such feelings of suspicion and resentment was added the weight of the Supreme Court's decision in May, 1895, striking down the income tax provision of the Wilson bill. Unemployed might tramp the streets, the farmer might freeze among his unsold crops, but the Morgans and the Belmonts and the Carnegies, for all their wealth, were to pay no taxes for the protection they enjoyed. William Jennings Bryan, who had already denounced the bond issue as a bribe, declared that the Court had taken the side of the wealthy against the poor.

Cleveland in his last two years in office found himself in the isolation that Johnson, Hayes, and Arthur had known at the end of their terms. Only a diminishing number of Gold Democrats and a few Mugwumps remained loyal to him. Members of Congress rarely visited the White House. "I have been dreadfully forlorn these many months, and sorely perplexed and tried," he wrote in the spring of 1895 to his ambassador to England, Thomas F. Bayard. "Think of it! Not a man in the Senate with whom I can be on terms of absolute confidence. . . . Mrs. Cleveland and the babies are well. God be praised for that! I often think that if things should go wrong at that end of the house, I should abandon the ship."

The effect of the Morgan-Belmont loan lasted almost a year. The loan engendered such bitter criticism, however, that when a fourth bond issue became necessary, Cleveland determined that it would have to be by public subscription. In agitating against any further private deals, Pulitzer, in the January 4, 1896, issue of his New York *World*, used the phrase "Robber Barons" to accompany a cartoon showing Morgan and his associates as pirates demanding ransom from Uncle Sam.

By the time of this fourth and final bond issue the world supply of gold was increasing even as United States redeemable paper currency decreased, and the inflationary pressures at last seemed checked. However, the improved financial situation had no effect on the silver movement, which was now sweeping the Democratic party like a religious revival, with *Coin's Financial School* as the new gospel. Even Republicans were not wholly immune, while in state after state the Demo-

The portrait of J. P. Morgan was made around the turn of the century by a photographer now unknown. Edward Steichen, who also photographed the testy Morgan, said that facing his gaze was like facing the headlights of an oncoming train.

cratic party organization was taken over by the Silver Democrats. Secretary of the Treasury Carlisle, speaking in his home town of Covington, Kentucky, was showered with rotten eggs. More and more party leaders were turning their backs on Cleveland.

With the advent of the presidential election year of 1896, Silver, with a capital S, had become the one glittering issue beside which all other issues grew dim. General Weaver and Ignatius Donnelly and other Populist leaders felt that this time they could win by focusing on the money question alone, by forming a united front with Silver Democrats and Western Republicans. Silver kings, solicitous of their vast mining interests, remained discreetly in the background while opening their pocketbooks to the Populists. The struggle of silver against gold became a class struggle, the struggle of the debtor against the creditor, country against city. All the silver movement lacked now was a leader, a Moses.

The Republicans had their leader found for them in the person of the former congressman and present governor of Ohio, William McKinley, a man of imposing mien and impeccable party regularity, a politician's politician. William Allen White, the young Kansas journalist, described him as having a "statesman's face, unwrinkled, unperturbed: a face without vision but without guile . . . the mask of a kindly, dull gentleman . . . a cast most typical to represent American politics; on the whole decent, on the whole dumb, and rarely reaching above the least common multiple of the popular intelligence. . . . He walked among men like a bronze statue . . . determinedly looking for his pedestal." The man who found McKinley, at least for the convention of 1896, was the Republican boss of Cleveland Mark Hanna, whose long devotion to the Ohio governor was the most disinterested act of his life. "I love McKinley!" he once remarked. "He is the best man I ever knew." Eighteen months before the convention, Hanna began organizing a McKinley band wagon, openly proclaiming him the people's choice while secretly buying up every available delegate from the rotten boroughs of the South. In the depression spring of 1896 he plastered the billboards of the country with posters hailing "McKinley: The Advance Agent of Prosperity." By the time of the June convention in St. Louis, and despite the opposition of bosses Platt and Quay, Hanna had cornered enough delegates to make McKinley's nomination on the first ballot certain. But such acceptance was not granted to the platform, which declared uncompromisingly for the gold standard. McKinley had earlier shown bimetallic waverings. Hanna's own gold sentiments coincided with those of the platform, although astutely he let the Eastern financiers believe they had forced his hand. The Republicans from the Silver West, demanding the coinage of silver at the 16 to 1 ratio and hoping at least for a gesture toward bimetallism, were outraged. Just prior to the nominating speeches, Senator Henry Teller of Colorado, followed by some thirty silverite delegates, stalked down the convention hall's main aisle and out the door.

When the Democrats met in Chicago three weeks after the Republicans, it was clear that Cleveland's battle for the gold standard had already been lost. The elderly Silver Dick Bland, for all his age, seemed the likeliest candidate. Cleveland's former Secretary of the Navy, William C. Whitney, as the leader of the Gold Democrats, had ordered a special "Gold Train" to take him and like-minded Democrats from New York to Chicago. But his group was dismayed when on its arrival at the station it was met by a hostile crowd displaying silver badges. The very atmosphere of the streets seemed wildly radical. "The sceptre of political power has passed from the strong, certain hands of the East to the feverish, headstrong mob of the West and South," editorialized the New York *World*.

That the sceptre had passed was explicit in the Democratic platform, which condemned the gold standard not only as un-American but anti-American. Calling upon "that spirit . . . which proclaimed our political independence in 1776 and won in the war of the Revolution," the platform demanded "the free and unlimited coinage of both silver and gold at the present legal ratio of sixteen to one." Silver coinage at this ratio would have cut the value of the dollar by a third. But Democratic emotions were not to be constrained by reason. Tillman denounced Cleveland from the platform as a "tool of Wall Street" and suggested that he be impeached. Defenders of the gold standard attempted to answer, but their words fell on angry and resentful ears. The key moment of the convention—possibly the most dramatic moment in the history of American conventions—came when William Jennings Bryan rose to speak. Still relatively obscure, at least in the East, he had at the age of thirty-six matured his youthful gift of oratory. In a full mellow voice that reached to every corner of the hall, he began his famous Cross of Gold Speech, which throbbed with the rhythms of the King James Bible. Again and again he was interrupted by crashes of applause as he eloquently defended the little man against the great. He concluded:

Having behind us the producing masses of this nation and the world, supported by the commercial interests, the laboring interests and the toilers everywhere, we will answer their demand for a gold standard by saying to them: You shall not press down upon the brow of labor this crown of thorns, you shall not crucify mankind upon a cross of gold.

The twenty thousand delegates present were too hypnotized to respond. "When I finished my speech, I went to my seat in a silence that was really painful," Bryan recalled afterward. "When I neared my seat, somebody near me raised a shout, and the next thing I was picked up—and bedlam broke loose!" Edgar Lee Masters recorded the electric moment: "The delegates arose and marched for an hour, shouting, weeping, rejoicing. They lifted this orator upon their shoulders and carried him as if he had been a god. At last a man!"

Bland still managed to keep his delegates in line for three ballots, but, on the fourth, cries of "Bryan! Bryan!" echoed through the hall like a barbaric chant. On the fifth ballot it was all over, a Bryan landslide.

The Populists, in an anticlimactic convention, adopted Bryan as their candidate but drew the line at his running mate, the wealthy shipbuilder Arthur Sewall, preferring their own Tom Watson. Teller's Silver Republicans also backed Bryan, while the Gold Democrats—now calling themselves the National Democratic party—seceded to hold their own minuscule national convention in Indianapolis and name their own candidate. The campaign that followed, the "battle of the standards," picked up velocity with each passing week. In Bryan the inflationists had at last found their Moses, who would lead them to the promised land of cheap money and prosperity. Shallow in his eloquence, ignorant of economic consequences, Bryan nevertheless in his emotional fervor touched the heart of the common man—the farmer and workman, to say nothing of the radicals, failures, cranks, and misfits who flocked to hear him repeat his variations on the Cross of Gold Speech. If the election had been held in the summer, the thirty-six-year-old Boy Orator of the Platte, as Bryan was now being called, would have swept the country. But in the four months until November much could be done, and Hanna, as McKinley's campaign manager, was the man to do it.

Hanna's designation as chairman of the Republican National Committee typified the period's politics: the businessman in government running things like a private enterprise and dedicated to serving the needs of business—particularly his own. A man with an inanimate round face and animate dark eyes, he, to his hurt, found himself caricatured grossly and unforgettably by Homer Davenport of the New York *Journal* as the ruthless, bloated capitalist, with the dollar sign branded on his thumb and woven into his clothes. It was an unjust portrait, as Davenport himself would later admit, for Hanna was not money-hungry. In a sense he was not even power-hungry, for he had become one of the great capitalists of the country more by instinct than intention. An ironmaster of Cleveland and the Great Lakes, he had picked up property the way a jay picks up bright objects—Cleveland's bankrupt opera house, a bank, mines, the Cleveland *Herald*. Yet as an employer he was fair and open, paying top wages. Practical business considerations brought him into politics. For instance, when he purchased a broken-down street railway line, he found that he needed transit franchises to expand and improve his line, and these were controlled by the Cleveland city council. Faced with the dilemma of bribing councilmen or going out of business, Hanna bribed. To gain his ends he kept on bribing.

While Bryan scoured the country, visiting twenty-seven states, appealing to the people at every crossroad, Hanna prepared his countermeasures against the appeal of free silver and cheap money. He saw to it that banks, corporations, and industrialists contributed generously to the McKinley campaign fund. At least three and a half million dollars were raised, a large part of it in New York. Never had so much money been spent on a presidential election. Hanna conducted the first modern political advertising campaign, selling his candidate to the public like soap or tobacco. From his headquarters in Chicago he sent out fourteen hundred trained speakers and hundreds more went out from New York; he distributed more than two hundred million circulars. He coined the slogan "A full dinner pail," and in a dozen languages he explained to the people what inflation really would mean for them.

While Bryan journeyed, McKinley stayed at home in his angular gingerbread house in Canton, Ohio, in what came to be known as the Front Porch Campaign. Instead of going to the people, he had the people—with the help of free tickets and cheap excursion rates—come to him. They came by the thousands, trampling the lawn and flower beds into mud, and pressing forward to the peril of the front porch itself. From time to time McKinley appeared in all his amiable frock-coated dignity, made

Free trade might be economically sensible in the long run, but it was difficult for politicians seeking election to ignore the immediate needs of the voters. This 1896 campaign poster made out free trade to be not simply unsound but unpatriotic as well.

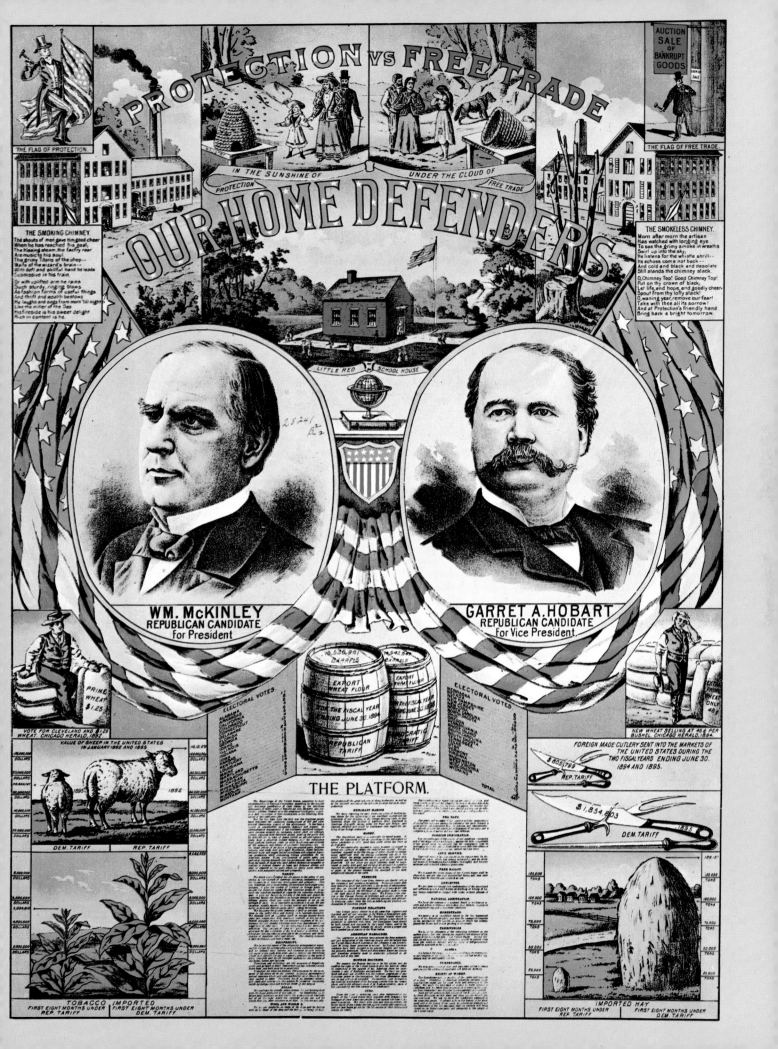

PROTECTION vs FREE TRADE

THE FLAG OF PROTECTION.

THE FLAG OF FREE TRADE.

IN THE SUNSHINE OF PROTECTION

UNDER THE CLOUD OF FREE TRADE

OUR HOME DEFENDERS

THE SMOKING CHIMNEY.

THE SMOKELESS CHIMNEY.
Morn after morn the artisan
Has watched with longing eye
To see the grimy smoke in wreaths
Swirl up into the sky,
He listens for the whistle shrill—
Its echoes come not back—
And cold and black and desolate
Still stands the chimney slack.

O, Chimney Top! Good Chimney Top!
Put on thy crown of black,
Let life and hope, and goodly cheer
Spout from thy lofty stack!
O, waning year, remove our fear!
Take with thee all its sorrow!
And at Protection's friendly hand
Bring back a bright tomorrow.

LITTLE RED SCHOOL HOUSE

WM. McKINLEY
REPUBLICAN CANDIDATE
for President

GARRET A. HOBART
REPUBLICAN CANDIDATE
for Vice President.

PRIME WHEAT $1.25

VOTE FOR CLEVELAND AND $1.25
WHEAT. CHICAGO HERALD, 1892

NEW WHEAT SELLING AT 40¢ PER
BUSHEL. CHICAGO HERALD, 1894.

ELECTORAL VOTES

EXPORT WHEAT FLOUR FOR THE FISCAL YEAR ENDING JUNE 30. 1894.

EXPORT WHEAT FLOUR FOR THE FISCAL YEAR ENDING JUNE 30, 1896.

REPUBLICAN TARIFF

DEMOCRATIC TARIFF

ELECTORAL VOTES

TOTAL

VALUE OF SHEEP IN THE UNITED STATES
IN JANUARY 1892 AND 1895.

FOREIGN MADE CUTLERY SENT INTO THE MARKETS OF
THE UNITED STATES DURING THE
TWO FISCAL YEARS ENDING JUNE 30.
1894 AND 1895.

$805,799 REP. TARIFF

$1,854,603 DEM. TARIFF

1895

1895

1892

DEM. TARIFF   REP. TARIFF

THE PLATFORM.

MERCHANT MARINE

THE NAVY

MONEY

FOREIGN IMMIGRATION

CIVIL SERVICE

FREE BALLOT

PENSIONS

NATIONAL ARBITRATION

FOREIGN RELATIONS

MONROE DOCTRINE

ARMENIAN MASSACRES

TERRITORIES

ALASKA

TEMPERANCE

RIGHTS OF MEN

RECIPROCITY

CUBA

TOBACCO
FIRST EIGHT MONTHS UNDER
REP. TARIFF

IMPORTED
FIRST EIGHT MONTHS UNDER
DEM. TARIFF

IMPORTED HAY
FIRST EIGHT MONTHS UNDER
REP TARIFF

FIRST EIGHT MONTHS UNDER
DEM. TARIFF

AUCTION SALE OF BANKRUPT GOODS

his brief set speeches, delivered himself of a few melliffluous truisms, and shook a thousand hands. "Good money never made times hard," he told his admiring audiences. By mid-October it was clear to Mark Hanna, who conducted continuing public-opinion polls, that promotion and advertising were winning the day, that for all Bryan's oratory the odds were now on McKinley. And so it proved on the first Tuesday in November. Even after adding his 200,000 Populist votes to his 6,300,000 Democratic votes, Bryan was still 600,000 behind McKinley's total of 7,100,000. Bryan carried the Solid South and the Western silver states, but the industrial North and the Middle West, with California and Oregon, went for McKinley. The National Democrats polled a mere 134,000 votes, only a few thousand more than the Prohibitionist candidate received. After sending the customary telegram of congratulations to his successful rival, Bryan reassured his supporters: "In the face of an enemy rejoicing in its victory, let the roll be called for the next engagement. I urge all friends of bimetallism to renew their allegiance to the cause. If we are right, as I believe we are, we shall yet triumph."

With increasing quantities of gold being mined in the Klondike, South Africa, and Australia during McKinley's first term, and with much-improved methods of extracting gold from ore coming into use in the United States, the gold base of the currency was able to expand. The Treasury increased its supply of notes. As gold itself began to prove inflationary, for the first time since the Civil War the decline in the price level was checked, and the issue of bimetallism seemed on the way to solving itself. Cleveland's second term had been shadowed by depression, and—as is usually the case—he as President became the scapegoat. McKinley's time in office, though one of internal prosperity, would be shadowed by foreign affairs.

In the usual reaction to the end of a major conflict, Americans after the Civil War had been eager to get back to what President Harding would in the next century define as "normalcy." Whatever else the term might mean, it embraced a rapid scaling down of the nation's armed forces. From the world's largest and most formidable modern fighting force, the United States Army soon found itself with a mere twenty-five thousand men—little more than a skeleton organization of cavalry and infantry detachments scattered in forts and engaged in policing the Western Indians. While the Army dwindled to a corporal's guard, the Navy was succumbing to "rot, rust and obsolescence." Five years after the peace the fleet had been reduced from seven hundred vessels to two hundred, of which only fifty-two were in commission. Under Grant's Secretary of the Navy, the New Jersey lawyer George M. Robeson, the department was riddled with graft. Robeson himself left office in 1877 with an unaccountable fortune.

Not until 1883 was a bill passed by Congress providing for the construction of three steel ships. Meanwhile the older officers, men like the old sea dog Admiral David D. Porter, head of the Board of Inspection, carried on as best they could with the minuscule Navy. In 1871 occurred the almost forgotten Korean War, when Rear Admiral John Rodgers landed a punitive expedition of six hundred and fifty sailors and marines from his Asiatic Squadron of two steam gunboats and four smaller vessels to "chastise hostile Koreans" after they had fired on an American trading vessel and murdered the crew. Three Americans and three hundred and fifty Koreans were killed in the action.

Though the term "Manifest Destiny" had been coined in 1845, expansionism fell from popular favor in the years just after the Civil War despite the imperialistic efforts of Secretary of State Seward. Blaine, as Secretary of State under Garfield and Harrison, did his best to revive the flagging idea. He foresaw a day when the United States would annex Cuba and Puerto Rico, and a much nearer day when his country would take over Hawaii as an outpost for the defense of American Oriental trade. He hoped to modify the Clayton-Bulwer Treaty with England to secure an American-controlled canal across the Isthmus of Panama. Blaine faced a crisis in the first days of the Harrison administration in 1889. The new imperial Germany had forced a confrontation with the United States when Chancellor Bismarck had sent the battleship *Deutschland* with three smaller warships to Samoa, long coveted by Germany as a coaling station. President Cleveland had responded to the challenge by dispatching the remodeled wooden sloop the U.S.S. *Vandalia* and two wooden frigates to Samoa. War between the United States and Germany seemed imminent. But on March 15–16, 1889, two weeks after Cleveland had left office, the confrontation—fortunately for the Americans—was broken off by a hurricane that smashed both fleets, leaving the wrecked vessels—as Robert Louis Stevenson, then living on Samoa, noted— "as schoolboys' caps tossed on a shelf." Later in the year, in the calmer atmosphere of Berlin, the United

ALL: UNDERWOOD & UNDERWOOD

William Jennings Bryan—lawyer, editor, politician, Chautauqua circuiteer, and great spellbinder—speaks at the Jamestown (Virginia) Exposition in 1908. That year Bryan made his third race for the Presidency and, for the third time, lost.

States, England, and Germany negotiated a treaty setting up a tripartite protectorate over the Samoan Islands. But the embarrassing weakness of the United States squadron displayed at Samoa at last persuaded Congress to modernize and rebuild the Navy.

In 1891 the United States again tottered on the edge of war after a group of sailors from the U.S.S. *Baltimore*, on shore leave in Valparaiso, Chile, had been set upon by a mob. Two sailors were killed and seventeen injured. Many Americans clamored enthusiastically for war. The hot-tempered Harrison demanded "prompt and full reparations" for the insult "to the uniform of

United States sailors," and when that was not immediately forthcoming, sent what amounted to a war message to Congress. Blaine finally managed to calm the President and the matter was eventually settled by a Chilean apology and offer to pay damages.

By the end of the eighteenth century American trade with China was already brisk, and the Stars and Stripes familiar to Chinese ports. With the Treaty of Wanghia in 1844 the China trade expanded rapidly. The Hawaiian Islands became an important way station on the route to the Orient, and their importance increased after Commodore Perry opened the kingdom of Japan in 1854. Even before the Civil War there was a movement to annex Hawaii. Missionaries settled on the islands, and their more practical descendants turned to sugar growing and became the islands' dominant social and economic group. By a reciprocity treaty in 1875, Hawaiian sugar was admitted duty-free to the United States.

295

When the McKinley Tariff of 1890 discontinued this favorable arrangement, Hawaiian-American sugar growers agitated for annexation. The following year Hawaii's indolent, easygoing King Kalakaua died and was succeeded by the energetic Queen Liliuokalani, who pressed for "Hawaii for the Hawaiians." Fearful of this nationalistic threat, the American settlers, with the encouragement of the American minister to Hawaii, staged a coup. Aided by one hundred and fifty marines from the cruiser *Boston*, then conveniently in Honolulu, they deposed Liliuokalani, set up their own government, and sent a delegation to Washington requesting annexation. In the administration's closing days, the Secretary of State negotiated a treaty with the new Hawaiian government and sent it to the Senate for approval, but before it could be acted on, Cleveland had become President.

Cleveland, opposed to expansionism both personally and in the "unbroken American tradition," ordered the treaty of annexation withdrawn. Liliuokalani was supported overwhelmingly by the natives, and he would

have preferred to see her back on her throne, but since the insurgent planters were by this time too firmly entrenched to be overthrown, Cleveland felt he could not intervene further.

Latin-American diplomats were relieved to see Cleveland once more installed in the White House. Neither in Hawaii nor in a fugitive incident in Nicaragua would he take the stand demanded of him by the bellicose expansionists. But near the end of his term he came close to leading his country into war against England in a crisis over Venezuela. A long dispute over the boundary between Venezuela and British Guiana had grown sharper after gold was discovered in the disputed area in the 1880's. Cleveland, seeking a popular issue and at the same time feeling that he was defending a weak neighbor against an overbearing enemy, ordered Secretary of State Richard Olney—Cleveland had moved him to that office from his former post of Attorney General in 1895— to send a near ultimatum to the British demanding that the dispute be submitted to arbitration. Since a certain

296

John La Farge painted this water color in Samoa during a tour he took with Henry Adams in 1890–91—just after the Berlin Conference had coped with the island's status. On their trip the two old friends visited Hawaii and the South Seas.

amount of anti-British feeling was always present in the United States and American feelings had recently been ruffled by disagreements about fishing rights off Canada and seal hunting in the Bering Sea, Cleveland's friends felt he had everything to gain by exploiting the Venezuela issue. "Turn this Venezuela question up or down, North, South, East or West," one of them told him, "and it is a winner."

Although the American note threatened war, the British government chose to ignore it for some months. When Lord Salisbury, the British prime minister and foreign secretary, finally replied, his answer was icily supercilious, a refusal even to consider arbitrating Venezuela's "exaggerated pretensions." In December, 1895, an angry Cleveland asked Congress for authority to appoint a commission to determine the correct boundary between the two countries, adding that the United States would resist "by every means in its power" any attempt by Britain to seize territory rightfully belonging to Venezuela. "Every means" implied even war. But clearer heads in England saw the futility of a confrontation with the United States over a few hundred square miles of jungle, particularly in the light of the growing challenge of the new Germany and with troubles threatening in South Africa. To fight with the United States, Her Majesty's colonial secretary observed, "would be an absurdity as well as a crime." His observation was a prelude to a second British answer, agreeing to arbitrate, which turned away American wrath.

After due consideration an arbitration committee awarded most of the disputed area to the British. Yet Cleveland, in his assertion of the American right to intervene in the hemisphere, demonstrated unconsciously the expansionist spirit that was increasingly coming to dominate all the great nations of the West, to be summed up within the decade by Rudyard Kipling's stirring claptrap:

> Take up the White Man's burden—
>   Send forth the best ye breed—
> Go bind your sons to exile
>   To serve your captives' need;

Few indeed were capable of Mr. Dooley's derisive clarity when he suggested, "Take up th' white man's burden an' hand it to th' coons." In 1885 the historian John Fiske, in an article in *Harper's New Monthly Magazine*, revived the phrase Manifest Destiny. An evolutionist since his undergraduate days, Fiske saw the Anglo-Saxon race as moving toward a world hegemony in which English would be the universal tongue. Fiske found his views absorbed largely by the younger generation of political figures, men like Henry Cabot Lodge of Massachusetts and Theodore Roosevelt. Lodge felt in his expansionist bones that his country must expand from the Rio Grande to the Arctic Ocean, build a trans-Isthmian canal, control Hawaii, and maintain American influence in the Caribbean since "the great nations were rapidly absorbing for their future expansion and their present defense all the waste places of the earth" and the United States as a great nation "must not fall out of the line of march."

Manifest Destiny found a more tempered and realistic exponent in the scholarly head of the newly established Naval War College, Captain Alfred Thayer Mahan. His *The Influence of Sea Power Upon History 1660–1783*, which was first published in 1890, became one of the most influential books of the age, enduring long after the decline of the myth of Anglo-Saxon superiority. To his land-minded countrymen with their decrepit little Navy, Mahan hammered home his doctrine of the omnipotence of sea power. In sea power he found the key to history; without its protecting arm no nation could become strong, prosperous in peace and invulnerable in war. What was required for national greatness was a merchant marine, a navy capable of defending it, and strategically located bases all over the world. Mahan demanded for his country a modern fleet, an Isthmian canal, bases in the Caribbean, and the annexation of Hawaii as a prelude to a more extensive colonial empire, which must in the end face the challenge of the Orient— the challenge that the Kaiser, in more melodramatic terms, would call the Yellow Peril. Congressman Henry Cabot Lodge of Massachusetts, elected to the Senate in 1893, echoed Mahan in persistently advocating a modern and expanded navy. "Sea Power," he liked to repeat, "is essential to the greatness of every splendid people."

By the time McKinley was installed in the White House, the Navy was growing in strength and size, and the idea of an American empire on which the sun never set was taking firmer root. Continental expansion had come to an end with the closing of the frontier, the completion of essential railroads, and the consolidation of industry. "The nation is made—its mode of action is determined," Princeton's Professor Woodrow Wilson observed in 1897, then asked, "Where do we go from here?" The answer given by disciples of Mahan, like

OVERLEAF: *Though it looks like a painting of an illuminated Venice, the scene shown here is at the Grand Columbian Exposition, held in Chicago in 1893. In the center is the Administration Building, which was designed by Richard M. Hunt.*

Senator Lodge and the bellicose Theodore Roosevelt, was "overseas."

The first clean-shaven President since Johnson, McKinley exuded a courtliness that echoed the federalist era. Deftly he balanced patronage with personalities, as politically adroit in his appointments as he was suave in his rejections. In Ohio the President moved skillfully between the Foraker and Hanna factions, backing the election of his friend and sponsor Mark Hanna to the Senate, yet offending Fire Alarm Joe as little as possible. With equal deftness he moved among the New York factions, keeping Boss Platt in his place while at the same time setting at his disposal that most juicy of political plums, the collectorship of the Port of New York. For Secretary of the Navy, McKinley had chosen his friend John D. Long, a Harvard-educated lawyer who had been three times governor of Massachusetts before moving on to Congress. Gentle, a scholar, Long was hypersensitive, always trembling on the edge of a breakdown—nervous prostration, as they then called it. The only favor Senator Henry Cabot Lodge had to ask of the new President was that his young friend Theodore Roosevelt, then police commissioner of New York City, become assistant secretary of the Navy. Even though Roosevelt was a regular Republican, scornful of Mugwumps and reformers, he was equally scornful of the Platts and their cohorts, and he was a vociferous expansionist. McKinley wondered uneasily if Roosevelt harbored any "preconceived plans," but finally agreed to the appointment. Though scarcely an expansionist, McKinley favored annexing Hawaii, although as a politician he realized that the necessary two-thirds majority in the Senate would not be obtainable in 1897. Beyond that, as he announced in his inaugural address, "we want no wars of conquest; we must avoid the temptation of territorial aggression."

Prosperity was blunting the force of both the silver and the tariff issues. The President postponed the question of an international bimetallic currency, but in the summer of 1897 he did request a new protective tariff. Yet the archprotectionist was himself coming to question the doctrine of high protection, shifting slowly but certainly to the belief that foreign trade could become almost as important as domestic trade. The Republican-sponsored Dingley tariff act, which he requested, would give the President much leeway in arranging tariff concessions with other countries. If the tariff and monetary issues seemed more readily solvable than McKinley had

Word of a gold strike in the Klondike started a rush from the United States in 1897; in the next three years 100,000 people headed north by a variety of difficult routes. Shown in the E. A. Hegg photo is Chilkoot Pass on the Alaska border.

expected, the one problem that faced him like a baying dog that would not be quieted was that of Cuba.

Ever since Jefferson's day, Americans, including Jefferson himself, had mulled over the idea of annexing Cuba. The Democrats before the Civil War wanted it as an additional slave state and until 1860 regularly included annexation in their party platform. Polk had tried to buy the island. In 1851 a "liberty" invasion army, made up of adventurers, including a number of Americans, left New Orleans (under General Narciso

300

López) for an unsuccessful attempt to overthrow the Spanish colonial government. In 1868 a ten-year insurrection broke out on the island, more an affair of dissident generals than a popular uprising. In 1873 a Spanish gunboat near Jamaica captured the *Virginius*, a vessel of dubious status but flying the American flag and bound for Cuba with a cargo of guns. When the Spanish authorities executed a number of the crew, including the American captain, press and politicians at once called for war. The Navy was ordered to prepare for combat, only to reveal that there was virtually no Navy. Secretary of State Hamilton Fish was able to smooth matters over while at the same time warning the Spanish colonial government that if the insurrection did not end soon, it might be the duty of the United States to intervene.

The depression of 1893 damaged the cane sugar in-dustry, on which Cuba's whole economy was based, and the Wilson-Gorman Tariff of 1894, by reintroducing duties on Cuban sugar, completed the ruin. Although the insurrection had ended, émigré Cuban groups in the United States continued to plot against the island's colonial government, which, though autocratic and inefficient, could hardly have been considered brutal. In 1891 a young Cuban émigré in New York, José Julián Martí, combined the various exiled dissidents into the Cuban Revolutionary party, and as Cuban economic life deteriorated, began smuggling arms and men to the island. In February, 1895, a small group of insurgents—with Martí still in New York—raised the single-starred flag of independence in a remote section of eastern Cuba. Two weeks later the American steamer *Alliança* of the Columbia Line arrived in New York with the cap-

301

tain's outraged report that his vessel, "flying the American flag, had been fired upon and chased for twenty-five miles by a Spanish gunboat on the high seas." The American reaction, bolstered by expansionist sentiment, was for war. Even members of the Senate's Foreign Relations Committee felt that the time had come to support the Cuban rebels and take over Cuba.

By April, 1895, the Spanish government had sent to Cuba, as captain general, Martínez Campos, the commander who had earlier brought the ten-year insurrection to an end. Martí, joining the insurgents on the island, was killed in an ambush and was succeeded by the austere and uncompromising, though elderly, Máximo Gómez. Too astute to confront the Spanish regulars directly, Gómez engaged in partisan warfare. Ordinary Americans, uninformed about even the generalities of

Hispanic politics, saw Gómez as a Cuban Washington attempting to throw off the shackles of royalty and colonialism. American businessmen developed certain doubts after Gómez gave orders that all sugar plantations—including those that were American-owned—"shall be totally destroyed," but among the masses enthusiasm for the Cuban "patriots," encouraged by the sensational press, ran high. As the smoke rose over the plantations, so close to Havana by the beginning of 1896 that it could be seen from the city, the Spanish government took harsher measures to put down the spreading insurrection, and able General Valeriano Weyler y Nicolau was sent from Madrid to replace Campos.

Theodore Roosevelt told his friend Senator Lodge in 1895 that the country needed another war, "something to think about which isn't material gain." It was a per-

When the Maine *blew up (above)* Hearst's Journal *immediately blamed the disaster on Spain and demanded war. However, so personally involved a witness as the* Maine's *commander, Captain Charles D. Sigsbee, asked that America be calm.*

vasive opinion, made the more so by the truculent nationalism that expansionist sentiments brought in their wake, and abetted by the flamboyant captains of journalism Hearst and Pulitzer. Whatever else the Cuban rebels did or did not do, they succeeded in maintaining an efficient propaganda service both in the United States and in Havana, where American correspondents, excluded from the fighting areas, gathered in convenient bars to concoct stories of engagements never fought and atrocities so appalling that they darkened the American headlines for days. The shelling of Havana by nonexistent insurgent artillery and details of its capture were even reported.

Weyler, a conscientious professional who was making notable progress in putting down the rebellion, was portrayed by the circulation-avid Hearst and Pulitzer as Butcher Weyler, whose troops wantonly outraged and slaughtered women, killed children, poisoned wells, and fed prisoners to the sharks. Something, Americans felt, would have to be done about Cuba. The Republican platform of 1896 proclaimed a "deep and abiding interest [in] the heroic battles of the Cuban patriots against cruelty and oppression," while the Democrats extended their sympathy to the people of Cuba "in their heroic struggle for liberty and independence." Cleveland felt that a war with Spain would be a pointless disgrace, and he tried privately to persuade the Spanish government to make concessions to the rebel junta—concessions that would then have meant little, since the insurgents had decided to settle for nothing less than independence.

Then in 1897 Cleveland was out and McKinley was in, a Republican President with solid Republican majorities behind him in both houses of Congress. Sharing Cleveland's dislike of war, with little place for expansionism in his sedate nature, McKinley wanted nothing more for his Presidency than peace and a revival of prosperity. But unlike Cleveland, he lacked determination, and in the end events would prove too much for him. Hearst and the sensational press were doing their best to force matters with descriptions of Spanish outrages, concentration camps, and mass starvation in Cuba. When artist Frederic Remington, after several boring months in Havana, telegraphed that things were quiet and that there would be no war, Hearst replied grandly: "You furnish the pictures and I'll furnish the war." Earlier Remington had imaginatively illustrated a dispatch from Richard Harding Davis—later proved to be wrong —that told of Spanish officers on board the American steamship *Olivette* in Havana Harbor stripping a young lady suspected of carrying insurgent dispatches. Hearst piled sensation on sensation. From the naked, nubile dispatch bearer, he moved on to Evangelina Cisneros, whom Americans called the Cuban Joan of Arc, held in a Havana prison for what Hearst claimed—without foundation—was her crime of resistance to attempts on her virtue by Spanish officers. "Enlist the women of America!" Hearst commanded, and the women of America stepped forward in closed virtuous ranks: Mrs. Jefferson Davis; Julia Ward Howe; Mrs. U. S. Grant; Frances Hodgson Burnett, author of *Little Lord Fauntleroy*; and even the mother of President McKinley.

While Hearst was engaged in promoting a war that he would later come proudly to believe was his, the energetic and equally war-minded Assistant Secretary of the Navy Roosevelt was evolving plans for attacking the Philippines and seizing Manila as his contribution to rescuing Cuba from Spanish oppression. Like the German Kaiser, Roosevelt was obsessed with the Yellow Peril and saw such a vaulting step as a means of keeping the Japanese in check.

A sudden change in government in Madrid in September, 1897, seemed to McKinley to offer a hope of a peaceful solution, for a new liberal regime recalled Weyler and offered the Cuban insurgents autonomy, reserving for Spain only matters of defense, foreign relations, and the administration of justice. Backed by American opinion and increasingly hopeful of drawing the United States into the conflict, the insurgents still refused to settle for anything less than complete independence. Meanwhile in Havana, a pro-Spanish mob demonstrated against newspapers accused of reflecting on the honor of the Spanish Army. The American consul general, the former Confederate cavalry commander Fitzhugh Lee, in undue alarm sent a telegram to Washington expressing his fears for the safety of American citizens. McKinley ordered the battleship *Maine* under Captain Charles D. Sigsbee to Havana Harbor in the guise of paying a courtesy call. The *Maine*'s reception by the Spaniards was correct if cool while Havana appeared as peaceful as Washington or New York. Captain Sigsbee and his officers went sightseeing, attended a bullfight, and even received a case of fine sherry from the acting captain general. As Captain Sigsbee sat in his cabin on the overcast and sultry evening of February 15 writing a letter to his wife, he doubtless saw the prospect of war as slighter every day. He signed his letter, addressed it, and was about to seal it. And at that moment the *Maine* exploded. With his hand on the envelope the captain heard a roaring in his ears, felt the floor buckle under him, and saw the lights go out. Then came the rushing of water, the screams of wounded men, bursts of flame, and successive explosions—and Sigsbee knew his ammunition had exploded and that his ship was doomed. Though he, the last to leave the ship, was unhurt, 252 of the 350 officers and men on board were killed or drowned and 8 more mortally injured.

What caused the explosion has never been exactly determined, but there is a strong body of evidence that an internal explosion, possibly in the coal bunkers, set off the forward ammunition magazine and that the *Maine* destroyed herself. Immediately the nearby Spanish cruiser *Alfonso XII* dispatched rescue boats to the scene. The captain general shed tears when he heard the news. All Havana was decked in mourning the following day, and the dead were given a solemn state funeral. Yet even these conciliatory gestures were not enough to silence the war dogs in the United States. Probably nothing could have quieted the cries for war.

The destruction of the *Maine* became for Americans an act of national symbolism, like the siege of the Alamo and the firing on Fort Sumter. To the bellicose expansionists it gave a slogan, Remember the *Maine*! For William Randolph Hearst the *Maine*'s destruction became the work of malevolent Spaniards with a "secret infernal machine," and he offered fifty thousand dollars' reward for the apprehension of the perpetrators. Day after day his *Journal* stirred up the country with huge headlines proclaiming that the *Maine* had been destroyed by treachery or that the Havana population had insulted the memory of the dead American sailors. Any rumors, any gossip, any lies, were good enough material for the *Journal* to belabor the Spaniards. To Hearst, those who still looked for a peaceful solution of the difficulties between the United States and Spain were either traitors or Wall Street moneygrubbers. Secretary of the Navy Long, Senator Hanna, the President himself, anyone who opposed war, felt the weight of Hearst's *Journal*, corroborated by the equally war-minded Pulitzer, whose *World*, to his distress, was now running second in the circulation race.

On March 28 President McKinley handed the report of a naval court of inquiry to Congress, in which the court found that "the *Maine* was destroyed by the explosion of a submarine mine" but declined to specify who was responsible. Hearst had no such hesitancies. Long before the official report, his *Journal* had anticipated that the court would find that "Spanish government officials blew up the *Maine*." "Write to your Congressmen at once," the *Journal* kept urging its readers and even proposed the organizing of a regiment of America's most noted athletes, who "would overawe any Spanish regiment by their mere appearance. They would scorn Krag-Jorgensen and Mauser bullets." *Journal* reporters were sent to interview the mothers of the dead sailors. "How would President McKinley have felt, I wonder," the *Journal* quoted one of the mothers as saying, "if he had a son on the *Maine* murdered as was my little boy?"

McKinley himself was not sure how he felt. "I have been through one war," he told a friend in his distress. "I have seen the dead piled up, and I do not want to see another." But his politician's instinct warned him how damaging it might be to his party if he failed to sustain the country's increasingly restive and pugnacious mood. So he temporized. ". . . no more backbone than a chocolate eclair," the impatient Roosevelt described the President to his friends. From Madrid in April, 1898, the American ambassador informed McKinley that the Spanish government was ready to concede all important United States demands, even to granting an immediate armistice to the Cuban rebels. For Cleveland this would have been good and sufficient grounds for an amicable peace. But the pacific McKinley could not as a politician stand up to the Hearst- and Pulitzer-inspired anger of the masses. The majority of Americans in 1898 wanted war, and McKinley had no wish to find himself in the isolation of Cleveland's last months in the White House. He grew haggard and nervous, and once, talking with a friend about the martial-minded Republican Congress, he shed tears. Finally on April 11 he sent a legalistic, almost humdrum message asking Congress for authority to use the Army and Navy to secure peace and a stable government in Cuba. War was now up to Congress. On April 19 the Senate passed a war resolution by the narrow margin of 42 to 35; the House of Representatives, with more martial fervor, concurred 310 to 6. The next day the President signed the resolution, and for the first time since the Mexican War of 1846 the United States was at war with a foreign power. "Our war," Hearst, talking with his staff, called it. The *Journal* made its own declaration with a four-inch-type headline: "NOW TO AVENGE THE MAINE!"

In the Melting Pot

During the half century that followed the Civil War some twenty-six million persons entered the United States from other countries to become citizens and raise families. America was unique: its society was fluid, self-consciously democratic; it offered considerable living space; and a man could indeed make a new life there. Furthermore, although the flood of foreigners was disturbing to many natives, it was possible for the children of immigrants to make a good start at being absorbed into the community, and for their children virtually to cease to be aliens—if they were white. And whether they were assimilated or not, they enriched the culture with words and ideas and attitudes. The process began for many of them at Ellis Island in New York Harbor. Historian Willard A. Heaps interviewed a number of immigrants many years after their arrival, among them Signora Bianca De Carli, who had come from Genoa in 1913.

"Sir, you cannot understand—only those of us left who passed through the Island can speak of it knowingly. We were impatient but yet patient; we were nervous—how do you say, confused, *agitato?*—because we still were not sure of passing through. A thousand times during the last day or two I put my hands on my passport and papers which I kept wrapped in a handkerchief under the front of my dress. This was just to make sure they were still there.

"One of my companions said, 'Signora, you are very foolish! When you keep your hand inside your dress and on your breast you are telling everyone that your papers and money are there! Maybe a bad person will see. Take your hands away. Nothing can happen now.'

"Now, years later, I know it was very foolish and silly, but we heard so many stories about others who were turned back because their papers were not in order. Everyone asked each other over and over, 'Are your papers in order?' and then we always checked them. No one trusted their pockets even, because this showed where our money was, and crowded together most of the time it would be easy to have our pockets picked.

"One woman had sewed her papers and money (in small bills which she planned to cash in at the Island) into the folds of her seventeen skirts! Yes, seventeen; I know I am right in remembering, and she wore them all. She came from a Hungarian or something province which is no more, and she told me that a woman's wealth was proved by the number of skirts she could wear.

"Well, that afternoon when we could see the land (it was the south shore of Long Island) a steamship man told us all to check our papers, as if we hadn't done this thousands of times, and have everything ready so that it would not be necessary to search through our bags and bundles. He told us to have our money ready to show, which was one of the questions we had answered, including the head tax (I remember it was $4 because we had the $8 set aside in lire) and what we would exchange for railroad tickets if we were going beyond New York.

"Well, this skirt lady I was telling you about started to cry and wail. We finally knew that she thought she would not have time to cut the hundreds of threads which held those little paper monies into her skirts. Another lady had a lot of sewing scissors and a little blade, and so about five of us divided the skirts and we went over every inch of them—they had lots of folds and when spread out were very wide—and put what we found each in a little pile.

"She even had love letters which she wanted to be safe. When she was sure that no one in America cared how many skirts she had, each with its money, she wore only two through the examinations and carried the others in a big bundle!

"Yes, we all trembled because of the strangeness and the confusion and the unknownness. Some were weak from no movement and exercise, and some were sick because of the smells and the unfresh air. But somehow this did not matter because we now knew it was almost over. But I will never forget it!"

Willard A. Heaps
The Story of Ellis Island, 1967

One observer interested in the impact of these millions was H. G. Wells, who had come to America after the turn of the century to gather material for his book on the nation's future. Being a seasoned, well-established reporter, he saw the process at Ellis Island from a viewpoint quite different from that of a newly arrived immigrant. Below are some of his comments.

I visited Ellis Island yesterday. It chanced to be a good day for my purpose. For the first time in its history this filter of immigrant humanity has this week proved inadequate to the demand upon it. It was choked, and half a score of gravid liners were lying uncomfortably up the harbor, replete with twenty thousand or so of crude Americans from Ireland and Poland and Italy and Syria and Finland and Albania; men, women, children, dirt, and bags together. . . .

I made my way with my introduction along white passages and through traps and a maze of metal lattices that did for a while succeed in catching and imprisoning me, to Commissioner Wachorn, in his quiet, green-toned office. There, for a time, I sat judicially and heard him deal methodically, swiftly, sympathetically, with case after case, a string of appeals against the sentences of deportation pronounced in the busy little courts below. First would come one dingy and strangely garbed group of wild-eyed aliens, and then another: Roumanian gypsies, South Italians, Ruthenians, Swedes, each under the intelligent guidance of a uniformed interpreter, and a case would be started, a report made to Washington, and they would drop out again, hopeful or sullen or fearful as the evidence might trend. . . .

Down-stairs we find the courts, and these seen, we traverse long refectories, long aisles of tables, and close-packed dormitories with banks of steel mattresses, tier above tier, and galleries and passages innumerable, perplexing intricacy that slowly grows systematic with the Commissioner's explanations.

Here is a huge, gray, untidy waiting-room, like a big railway-depot room, full of a sinister crowd of miserable people, loafing about or sitting dejectedly, whom America refuses, and here a second and a third such chamber each with its tragic and evil-looking crowd that hates us, and that even ventures to groan and hiss at us a little for our glimpse of its large dirty spectacle of hopeless failure, and here, squalid enough indeed, but still to some degree hopeful, are the appeal cases as yet undecided. In one place, at a bank of ranges, works an army of men cooks, in another spins the big machinery of the Ellis Island laundry, washing blankets, drying blankets, day in and day out, a big clean steamy space of hurry and rotation. Then, I recall a neat apartment lined to the ceiling with little drawers, a card-index of the names and nationalities and significant circum-

Immigrants debark, above, on the southern tip of Manhattan Island, at Castle Garden, where before 1892 their processing took place.

stances of upward of a million and a half of people who have gone on and who are yet liable to recall.

The central hall is the key of this impression. All day long, through an intricate series of metal pens, the long procession files, step by step, bearing bundles and trunks and boxes, past this examiner and that, past the quick, alert medical officers, the tallymen and the clerks. At every point immigrants are being picked out and set aside for further medical examination, for further questions, for the busy little courts; but the main procession satisfies conditions, passes on. It is a daily procession that, with a yard of space to each, would stretch over three miles, that any week in the year would more than equal in numbers that daily procession of the unemployed that is becoming a regular feature of the London winter, that in a year could put a cordon round London or New York of close-marching people, could populate a new Boston, that in a century — What in a century will it all amount to? . . .

On they go, from this pen to that, pen by pen, towards a desk at a little metal wicket — the gate of America. Through this metal wicket drips the immigration stream — all day long, every two or three seconds an immigrant, with a valise or a bundle, passes the little desk and goes on past the well-managed money-changing place, past the carefully organized separating ways that go to this railway or that, past the guiding, protecting officials — into a new world. The great majority are young men and young women, between seventeen and thirty, good, youthful, hopeful, peasant stock. They stand in a long string, waiting to go through that wicket, with bundles, with little tin boxes, with cheap portmanteaus, with odd packages, in pairs, in families, alone, women with children, men with strings of dependents, young couples. All day that string of human beads waits there, jerks forward, waits again; all day and every day, constantly replenished, constantly dropping the end beads through the wicket, till the units mount to hundreds and the hundreds to thousands. . . .

The sketch above and the engraving below are the work of William Allen Rogers. They were done for an article about New York's Jewish quarter that appeared in Harper's Weekly *in the spring of 1890.*

Yes, Ellis Island is quietly immense. It gives one a visible image of one aspect at least of this world-large process of filling and growing and synthesis, which is America.

"Look there!" said the Commissioner, taking me by the arm and pointing, and I saw a monster steamship far away, and already a big bulk looming up the Narrows. "It's the *Kaiser Wilhelm der Grosse*. She's got — I forget the exact figures, but let us say — eight hundred and fifty-three more for us. She'll have to keep them until Friday at the earliest. And there's more behind her, and more strung out all across the Atlantic."

In one record day this month 21,000 immigrants came into the port of New York alone; in one week over 50,000. This year the total will be 1,200,000 souls. . . .

H. G. Wells
The Future in America, 1906

*A*mong the many immigrants who made important contributions to America was Jacob Riis, a Dane who had come ashore in 1870 and by the end of the century was recognized as an authority on the foreign-born and their problems. In

308

his autobiography, first published in The Outlook, *he talked about the immigrant's need to join the American procession instead of just watching it or gravitating into what Riis called the looters' army. Then he described his first major act in the United States.*

So as properly to take my own place in the procession, if not in the army referred to, as I conceived the custom of the country to be, I made it my first business to buy a navy revolver of the largest size, investing in the purchase exactly one-half of my capital. I strapped the weapon on the outside of my coat and strode up Broadway, conscious that I was following the fashion of the country. I knew it upon the authority of a man who had been there before me and had returned, a gold digger in the early days of California; but America was America to us. We knew no distinction of West and East. By rights there ought to have been buffaloes and red Indians charging up and down Broadway. I am sorry to say that it is easier even to-day to make lots of people over there believe that, than that New York is paved, and lighted with electric lights, and quite as civilized as Copenhagen. They will have it that it is in the wilds. I saw none of the signs of this, but I encountered a friendly policeman, who, sizing me and my pistol up, tapped it gently with his club and advised me to leave it home, or I might get robbed of it. This, at first blush, seemed to confirm my apprehensions; but he was a very nice policeman, and took time to explain, seeing that I was very green. And I took his advice and put the revolver away, secretly relieved to get rid of it. It was quite heavy to carry around.

Jacob A. Riis
The Making of an American
The Outlook, March 16, 1901

*P*oor *when they arrived, taken advantage of by employers (when they could find work), the new immigrants crammed into city tenements, six or eight or a dozen to a room. The streets outside thronged with children fighting and playing, with peddlers and pushcarts, with loungers and old folk. Inside, the mattresses cluttered the floors; often cockroaches and other vermin roomed with the tenants, and so did sickness. Ernest Poole wrote about the role tenements played in perpetuating the Great White Plague—tuberculosis.*

Rooms here have held death ready and waiting for years. Up on the third floor, looking down into the court, is a room with two little closets behind it. In one of these a blind Scotchman slept and took the Plague in '94. His wife and his fifteen-year-old son both drank, and the home grew squalid as the tenement itself. He died in the hospital. Only a few months later the Plague fastened again. Slowly his little daughter grew used to the fever, the coughing, the long, sleepless nights. The foul court was her only outlook. At last she, too, died. The mother and son then moved away. But in this room the germs lived on. They might all have been killed in a day by sunlight; they can live two years in darkness. Here in darkness they lived, on grimy walls, in dusty nooks, on dirty floors. Then one year later, in October, a Jew rented this same room. He was taken and died in the summer. The room was rented again in the autumn by a German and his wife. She had the Plague already, and died. Then an Irish family came in. The father was a hard, steady worker, and loved his children. The home this time was winning the fight. But six months later he took the Plague. He died in 1901. This is only the record of one room in seven years.

Ernest Poole
The Plague in Its Stronghold, 1903

For the sake of a chance at a better life, immigrants often gave up much that was of value when they left their native homes. This selection from Jacob Riis indicates some of these lost treasures—familiar sights and friends, sometimes health, even sunlight.

Above, artist B. West Clinedinst depicts a scene once common in the ghetto: people doing work at home.

In a Stanton Street tenement, the other day, I stumbled upon a Polish capmaker's home. There were other capmakers in the house, Russian and Polish, but they simply "lived" there. This one had a home. The fact proclaimed itself the moment the door was opened, in spite of the darkness. The rooms were in the rear, gloomy with the twilight of the tenement, although the day was sunny without, but neat, even cosy. It was early, but the day's chores were evidently done. The teakettle sang on the stove, at which a bright-looking girl of twelve, with a pale but cheery face, and sleeves brushed back to the elbows, was busy poking up the fire. A little boy stood by the window, flattening his nose against the pane and gazing wistfully up among the chimney pots where a piece of blue sky about as big as the kitchen could be made out. I remarked to the mother that they were nice rooms.

"Ah yes," she said, with a weary little smile that struggled bravely with hope long deferred, "but it is hard to make a home here. We would so like to live in the front, but we can't pay the rent."

I knew the front with its unlovely view of the tenement street too well, and I said a good word for the air shaft—yard or court it could not be called, it was too small for that—which rather surprised myself. I had found few virtues enough in it before. The girl at the stove had left off poking the fire. She broke in the moment I finished, with eager enthusiasm: "Why, they have the sun in there. When the door is opened the light comes right in your face."

"Does it never come here?" I asked, and wished I had not done so, as soon as the words were spoken. The child at the window was listening, with his whole hungry little soul in his eyes.

Yes, it did, she said. Once every summer, for a little while, it came over the houses. She knew the month and the exact hour of the day when its rays shone into their home, and just the reach of its slant on the wall. They had lived there six years. In June the sun was due. A haunting fear that the baby would ask how long it was till June—it was February then—took possession of me, and I hastened to change the subject. Warsaw was their old home. They kept a little store there, and were young and happy. Oh, it was a fine city, with parks and squares, and bridges over the beautiful river,—and grass and flowers and birds and soldiers, put in the girl breathlessly. She remembered. But the children kept com-

310

ing, and they went across the sea to give them a better chance. Father made fifteen dollars a week, much money; but there were long seasons when there was no work. She, the mother, was never very well here,—she hadn't any strength; and the baby! She glanced at his grave white face, and took him in her arms. The picture of the two, and of the pale-faced girl longing back to the fields and the sunlight, in their prison of gloom and gray walls, haunts me yet. I have not had the courage to go back since. I recalled the report of an English army surgeon, which I read years ago, on the many more soldiers that died—were killed would be more correct—in barracks into which the sun never shone than in those that were open to the light. It is yet three months to the sun in Stanton Street.

Jacob A. Riis
"The Tenement House Blight"
The Atlantic Monthly, May, 1899

Many of the immigrants only passed through New York, headed for cities farther inland, for the Great Plains, for the gold-mining country. Robert Louis Stevenson followed in their track—from Europe to New York to California—and shared their experiences, which later he reported. Below, in Across the Plains, *he writes about a special train carrying migrants westward.*

The families once housed, we men carried the second car without ceremony by simultaneous assault. I suppose the reader has some notion of an American rail-road-car, that long, narrow wooden box, like a flat-roofed Noah's ark, with a stove and a convenience, one at either end, a passage down the middle, and transverse benches upon either hand. Those destined for emigrants on the Union Pacific are only remarkable for their extreme plainness, nothing but wood entering in any part into their constitution, and for the usual inefficacy of the lamps, which often went out and shed but a dying glimmer even while they burned. The benches are too short for anything but a young child. Where there is scarce elbow-room for two to sit, there will not be space enough for one to lie. Hence the company, or rather, as it appears from certain bills about the Transfer Station, the company's servants, have conceived a plan for the better accommodation of travellers. They prevail on every two to chum together. To each of the chums they sell a board and three square cushions stuffed with straw, and covered with thin cotton. The benches can be made to face each other in pairs, for the backs are reversible. On the approach of night the boards are laid from bench to bench, making a couch wide enough for two, and long enough for a man of the middle height; and the chums lie down side by side upon the cushions with the head to the conductor's van and the feet to the engine. When the train is full, of course this plan is impossible, for there must not be more than one to every bench, neither can it be carried out unless the chums agree. It was to bring about this last condition that our white-haired official now bestirred himself. He made a most active master of ceremonies, introducing likely couples, and even guaranteeing the amiability and honesty of each. The greater the number of happy couples the better for his pocket, for it was he who sold the raw material of the

Dark tenements might sadden, as Riis said (left), but Charles B. Falls's Spring *here implies a darkness of the soul no sun can cure.*

beds. His price for one board and three straw cushions began with two dollars and a half; but before the train left, and, I am sorry to say, long after I had purchased mine, it had fallen to one dollar and a half. . . .

Before the sun was up the stove would be brightly burning; at the first station the natives would come on board with milk and eggs and coffee cakes; and soon from end to end the car would be filled with little parties breakfasting upon the bed-boards. It was the pleasantest hour of the day.

There were meals to be had, however, by the wayside: a breakfast in the morning, a dinner somewhere between eleven and two, and supper from five to eight or nine at night. We had rarely less than twenty minutes for each; and if we had not spent many another twenty minutes waiting for some express upon a side track among miles of desert, we might have taken an hour to each repast and arrived at San Francisco up to time. For haste is not the foible of an emigrant train. It gets through on sufferance, running the gauntlet among its more considerable brethren; should there be a block, it is unhesitatingly sacrificed; and they cannot, in consequence, predict the length of the passage within a day or so. . . .

Hard times bowed them out of the Clyde, and stood to welcome them at Sandy Hook. Where were they to go? Pennsylvania, Maine, Iowa, Kansas? These were not places for immigration, but for emigration, it appeared; not one of them, but I knew a man who had lifted up his heel and left it for an ungrateful country. And it was still westward that they ran. Hunger, you would have thought, came out of the east like the sun, and the evening was made of edible gold. And, meantime, in the car in front of me, were there not half a hundred emigrants from the opposite quarter? Hungry Europe and hungry China, each pouring from their gates in search of provender, had here come face to face. The two waves had met; east and west had alike failed; the whole round world had been prospected and condemned; there was no El Dorado anywhere; and till one could emigrate to the moon, it seemed as well to stay patiently at home. Nor was there wanting another sign, at once more picturesque and more disheartening; for, as we continued to steam westward toward the land of gold, we were continually passing other emigrant trains upon the journey east; and these were as crowded as our own. Had all these return voyagers made a fortune in the mines? Were they all bound for Paris, and to be in Rome by Easter? It would seem not, for, whenever we met them, the passengers ran on the platform and cried to us through the windows, in a kind of wailing chorus, to "come back." On the plains of Nebraska, in the mountains of Wyoming, it was still the same cry, and dismal to my heart, "Come back!" That was what we heard by the way "about the good country we were going to."

Robert Louis Stevenson
Across the Plains, 1892

Paul Frenzeny and Jules Tavernier portrayed immigrants on a railroad journey westward in 1873 and 1874. Here: In the Emigrant Train.

𝓜any, of course, went west not to hit a mineral jack pot but simply to work in factories or to homestead. Wherever they headed, they finally stepped down from the train in an unfamiliar spot. Usually they spoke no English, knew no one, and had spent weeks and months being pushed around and pettily cheated;

they were frightened. The cities might offer them a rough kind of hospitality—a ghetto where a familiar tongue was spoken. But in farm land there was nothing so cozy. The immigrant family moved onto its 160-acre quarter section, often miles from town, and started to cope.

There are few social events in the life of these prairie farmers to enliven the monotony of the long winter evenings; no singing-schools, spelling-schools, debating clubs, or church gatherings. Neighborly calls are infrequent, because of the long distances which separate the farmhouses, and because, too, of the lack of homogeneity of the people. They have no common past to talk about. They were strangers to one another when they arrived in this new land, and their work and ways have not thrown them much together. Often the strangeness is intensified by differences of national origin. There are Swedes, Norwegians, Germans, French Canadians, and perhaps even such peculiar people as Finns and Icelanders, among the settlers, and the Americans come from many different States. It is hard to establish any social bond in such a mixed population, yet one and all need social intercourse, as the thing most essential to pleasant living, after food, fuel, shelter, and clothing. An alarming amount of insanity occurs in the new prairie States among farmers and their wives. In proportion to their numbers, the Scandinavian settlers furnish the largest contingent to the asylums. The reason is not far to seek. These people came from cheery little farm villages. Life in the fatherland was hard and toilsome, but it was not lonesome. Think for a moment how great the change must be from the white-walled, red-roofed village on a Norway fiord, with its church and schoolhouse, its fishing-boats on the blue inlet, and its green mountain walls towering aloft to snow fields, to an isolated cabin on a Dakota prairie, and say if it is any wonder that so many Scandinavians lose their mental balance.

E. V. Smalley
"The Isolation of Life on Prairie Farms"
The Atlantic Monthly, September, 1893

Meanwhile, the flood of new citizens was creating conflicts in the United States. On the one hand, there was the traditional American pride in being the country of the common man—as expressed in a sonnet about the Statue of Liberty whose closing lines are among the best known in American poetry.

Not like the brazen giant of Greek fame,
With conquering limbs astride from land to land;
Here at our sea-washed, sunset gates shall stand
A mighty woman with a torch, whose flame
Is the imprisoned lightning, and her name
Mother of Exiles. From her beacon-hand
Glows world-wide welcome; her mild eyes command
The air-bridged harbor that twin cities frame.
"Keep, ancient lands, your storied pomp!" cries she
With silent lips. "Give me your tired, your poor,

Your huddled masses yearning to breathe free,
The wretched refuse of your teeming shore.
Send these, the homeless, tempest-tost to me,
I lift my lamp beside the golden door!"

Emma Lazarus
"The New Colossus"
The Poems of Emma Lazarus, 1889

On the other hand, all this raw citizenry constantly swarming in through Manhattan was unsettling. Half a million people were entering every year by 1889. Poverty and language helped force them together in the cities, and this in turn intensified the fear that an alien and inimical society was being created within the larger American community. Such a spirit can be sensed in the following selection by Lafcadio Hearn, then writing for the Cincinnati Enquirer. *A gruesome murder had just been committed in that city's "quarter of shambles."*

Sightseers crowd the torch of the Statue of Liberty in the 1880's for a dramatic view of the harbor.

Probably there is no city in America which contains a quarter so hideous as that noisome district of Cincinnati. . . . It is a quarter where the senses of sight and hearing and smell are at once assailed with all the foulnesses of the charnel-house and the shambles. It is the center of all those trades which harden and brutalize the men who engage in them. Its gutters run with ordure and blood; its buildings reek with smells of slaughter and stenches abominable beyond description. An atmosphere heavy with the odors of death and decay and animal filth and steaming nastiness of every description, hangs over it like the sickly smoke of an ancient holocaust. In fact, it has an atmosphere peculiar to itself, whose noisome stagnation is scarcely disturbed on the breeziest days by a clear fresh current of heaven's purer air. Mammoth slaughter-houses, enormous rendering establishments, vast soap and candle factories, immense hog-pens and gigantic tanneries loom up through the miasmatic atmosphere for blocks and blocks in every direction. Narrow alleys, dark and filthy, bordered by sluggish black streams of stinking filth, traverse this quarter in every direction. The main streets here lose their width and straightness in tortuous curves and narrow twists and labyrinthine perplexity — so that the stranger who loses his way in this region of nastiness must wander wildly and long ere he may cease to inhale the ghoulish aroma of stink-factories and the sickening smell of hog-pens fouler than the stables of Augeas. Night-carts, which elsewhere leave far behind them a wake of stench suggestive of epidemics, here may pass through in broad daylight without betraying their presence. Rats propagate undisturbed and grow fat and gigantic among the dung-piles and offal-dumps.

Amid these scenes and smells lives and labors a large and strangely healthy population of brawny butchers, sinewy coopers, muscular tanners — a foreign population, speaking a foreign tongue, and living the life of the Fatherland — broad-shouldered men from Pomerania; tall, fair-haired emigrants from Bohemia; dark, brawny people from Bavaria; rough-featured fellows from the region of the Hartz Mountains; men speaking the strange dialects of strange provinces. They are mostly rough of aspect, rude of manner and ruddy of feature. The greater part of them labor in tanneries, slaughter-houses and soap factories, receiving small salaries upon which an American workman could not support his family, and doing work which Americans instinctively shrink from—slaughtering, quartering, flaying—handling bloody entrails and bloody hides—making slaughter their daily labor, familiarizing themselves with death and agony, and diurnally drenching themselves in blood.

Such occupation destroys the finer sensibilities of men, and more or less brutalizes their natures; while in return it gives them health and strength and brawn beyond the average. The air they breathe is indeed foully odorous, but it is heavily rich with globules of fresh blood and tallow and reeking flesh—healthy for the lungs and veins of the breathers.

Lafcadio Hearn
"The Quarter of Shambles"
The Cincinnati *Enquirer*, November 15, 1874

Immigrants were considered "low" people by and large. Most of them had little education; they did the kind of nasty, menial jobs Hearn talks about above (not necessarily by choice, however: that was where the work was); they accepted low wages. And then, not content with having jobs at any wages, they claimed they were being exploited. They unionized, they went out on strike, they shouted about a revolution of the lower classes. Here again, the foreign-born were a menace to their "betters." At the same time, a disillusioned native aristocracy and a materialistic middle class were disengaging themselves from government. Into the vacuum moved the more enterprising of the new Americans. And that, too, added to the fear of a take-over by an alien rabble.

On a single Chicago hoarding, before the spring election of 1912, the writer saw the political placards of candidates with the following names: Kelly, Cassidy, Slattery, Alschuler, Pfaelzer, Bartzen, Umbach, Andersen, Romano, Knitckoff, Deneen, Hogue, Burres, Short. The humor of calling "Anglo-Saxon" the kind of government these gentlemen will give is obvious. At that time, of the eighteen principal personages in the city government of Chicago, fourteen had Irish names, and three had German names. Of the eleven principal officials in the city government of Boston, nine had Irish names, and of the forty-nine members of the Lower House from the city of Boston, forty were obviously of Hibernian extraction. In San Francisco, the mayor, all the heads of the municipal departments, and ten out of eighteen members on the board of supervisors, bore names reminiscent of the Green Isle. As far back as 1871, of 112 chiefs of police from twenty-two States who attended the national police convention, seventy-seven bore Irish names, and eleven had German names. In 1881, of the chiefs of police in forty-eight cities, thirty-three were clearly Irish, and five were clearly German.

In 1908, on the occasion of a "homecoming" celebration in Boston, a newspaper told how the returning sons of Boston were "greeted by Mayor Fitzgerald and the following members of Congress: O'Connell, Kelihar, Sullivan, and McNary—following in the footsteps of Webster, Sumner, Adams, and Hoar. They

The cartoon of the Irish-American in politics was captioned, "He is taken to a Dimmycratic Matin', and shown the working of the Machine."

were told of the great work as Mayor of the late beloved Patrick Collins. At the City Hall they found the sons of Irish exiles and immigrants administering the affairs of the metropolis of New England. Besides the Mayor, they were greeted by John J. Murphy, Chairman of the board of assessors; Commissioner of Streets Doyle; Commissioner of Baths O'Brien. Mr. Coakley is the head of the Park Department, and Dr. Durgan directs the Health Department. The Chief of the Fire Department is John A. Mullen. Head of the Municipal Printing Plant is Mr. Whelan. Superintendent of the Street Cleaning is Cummings; Superintendent of Sewers Leahy; Superintendent of Buildings is Nolan; City Treasurer, Slattery; Police Commissioner, O'Meara."

Edward A. Ross
"Immigrants in Politics"
The Century Magazine, January, 1914

There were those who insisted that immigration should be severely limited. The writer of the following selection, a leading sociologist, was worried that in the Northeast "the foreign element" was rapidly pushing native Americans out of the urban lower class, which traditionally had a very high birth rate.

The evils, therefore, of immigration, if they are to be called evils, are not temporary. The direct descendants of the people who fought for and founded the Republic, and who gave us a rich heritage of democratic institutions, are being displaced by the Slavic, Balkan, and Mediterranean peoples. This is the fact in the problem of immigration which is of greatest importance. Discussion of the problem should be elevated to a different plane from that which has been taken in the past. It involves too much socially and politically in the world's progress to be ignored or lightly considered. It is a question of babies and birthrates, and whatever decision is made regarding immigration, it is perforce a decision concerning the kind of children that shall be born. The decision for Congress to make consciously and deliberately is simply whether or not it is better for the world that the children of native parents should be born instead of the children of foreign parents. The making of the decision cannot be avoided. It is made now, although unconsciously, and it is a decision against the children of native parents. Immigration, therefore, means that, by permitting free and unlimited entry, we are stimulating the birth-rate both in this country and abroad of Italians, Hungarians, Lithuanians, Ruthenians, Croatians, and Polish, Roumanian, and Russian Jews. This increase means that the places of those who emigrate to this country are filled in a generation, and the misery and oppression, which emigration is supposed to relieve, continue unimproved, while in the United States the peasantry from other countries, degraded by foreign oppression, are supplanting the descendants of the original stock of this country. This is the race-suicide, the annihilation of our native stock, which unlimited immigration forces upon us, none the less powerfully because it is gradually and stealthily done. The native stock of America, possessed of rare advantages, freed by its own efforts from oppression and the miseries of oppression, might have peopled the United States with the seventy millions which now inhabit it. It has not done so for the reason that "we cannot welcome an indefinite number of immigrants to our shores without forbidding the existence of an indefinite number of children of native parents who might have been born."

Immigration presents for our serious consideration a formidable array of dangers. It is unnecessary to summarize the facts and the arguments which have been given. These are the two things which, of all that have been stated, seem the most important: the likelihood of race annihilation and the possible degeneration of even the succeeding American type. It seems unquestionable that the unfittest class of immigrants that have ever come to our shores is increasing yearly in numbers. We may and should be willing to permit our native stock to be annihilated by a superior people; but it is inconceivable that we should knowingly promote, by conscious act, an intermarrying and intermingling of peoples, which will indefinitely lower the standard of American or any other manhood.

Robert Hunter
Poverty, 1904

In a spirit akin to Hunter's (excerpt beginning at left) this depicted "the last Yankee" as "a possible curiosity of the twentieth century."

That ruminative observer Henry James provided something of an answer to Hunter's arguments. Back in the United States after more than a quarter century's residence in England, James visited Ellis Island; he felt it was like having eaten of the tree of knowledge or "seen a ghost in [one's] supposedly safe old house." Other experiences bothered him: Europeans who would have been friendly to him on a meeting in Europe were distinctly chilly as immigrants.

To inquire of these things on the spot, to betray, that is, one's sense of the "chill" of which I have spoken, is of course to hear it admitted, promptly enough, that there is no claim to brotherhood with aliens in the first grossness of their alienism. The material of which they consist is being dressed and prepared, at this stage, for brotherhood, and the consummation, in respect to many of them, will not be, cannot from the nature of the case be, in any lifetime of their own. Their children are another matter—as in fact the children throughout the United States are an immense matter, are almost the greatest matter of all; it is the younger generation who will fully profit, rise to the occasion and enter into the privilege. The machinery is colossal—nothing is more characteristic of the country than the development of this machinery, in the form of the political and social habit, the common school and the newspaper; so that there are always millions of little transformed strangers growing up in regard to whom the idea of intimacy of relation may be as freely cherished as you like. *They* are the stuff of whom brothers and sisters are made, and the making proceeds on a scale that really need leave nothing to desire. All this you take in, with a wondering mind, and in the light of it the great "ethnic" question rises before you on a corresponding scale and with a corresponding majesty. . . .

The process of the mitigation and, still more, of the conversion of the alien goes on . . . not by leaps and bounds or any form of easy magic, but under its own mystic laws and with an outward air of quite declining to be unduly precipitated. How little it may be thought of in New York as a quick business we readily perceive as the effect of merely remembering the vast numbers of their kind that the arriving reinforcements, from whatever ends of the earth, find already in possession of the field. There awaits the disembarked Armenian, for instance, so warm and furnished an Armenian corner that the need of hurrying to get rid of the sense of it must become less and less a pressing preliminary. The corner growing warmer and warmer, it is to be supposed, by rich accretions, he may take his time, more and more, for becoming absorbed in the surrounding element, and he may in fact feel more and more that he can do so on his own conditions. . . . the alien is taking his time, and . . . you go about with him meanwhile, sharing, all respectfully, in his deliberation, waiting on his convenience, watching him at his interesting work. The vast foreign quarters of the city present him as thus engaged in it, and they are curious and portentous and "picturesque" just by reason of their doing so. You recognize in them, freely, those elements that are not elements of swift convertibility, and you lose yourself in the wonder of what becomes, as it were, of the obstinate, the unconverted residuum. . . .

Who and what is an alien, when it comes to that, in a country peopled from the first under the jealous eye of history? — peopled, that is, by migrations at once extremely recent, perfectly traceable and urgently required. They are still, it would appear, urgently required — if we look about far enough for the urgency; though of that truth such a scene as New York may well make one doubt. Which is the American, by these scant measures? — which is *not* the alien, over a large part of the country at least, and where does one put a finger on the dividing line, or, for that matter, "spot" and identify any particular phase of the conversion, any one of its successive moments? . . .

The great fact about [the observer's alien copassengers in the electric cars] was that, foreign as they might be, newly inducted as they might be, they were *at home*, really more at home, at the end of their few weeks or months or their year or two, than they had ever in their lives been before. . . . There are many different ways, certainly, in which obscure fighters of the battle of life may look, under new high lights, queer and crude and unwrought; but the striking thing, precisely, in the crepuscular, tunnel-like avenues that the "Elevated" overarches . . . the striking thing, and the beguiling, was always the manner in which figure after figure and face after face already betrayed the common consequence and action of their whereabouts. Face after face, unmistakably, was "low" — particularly in the men, squared all solidly in their new security and portability, their vague but growing sense of many unprecedented things; and as signs of the reinforcing of a large local conception of manners and relations it was difficult to say if they most affected one as promising or as portentous.

The great thing, at any rate, was that they were all together so visibly on the new, the lifted level — that of consciously not being what they *had* been, and that this immediately glazed them over as with some mixture, of indescribable hue and consistency, the wholesale varnish of consecration, that might have been applied, out of a bottomless receptacle, by a huge whitewashing brush. Here, perhaps, was the nearest approach to a seizable step in the evolution of the oncoming citizen, the stage of his no longer being for you — for any complacency of the romantic, or even verily of the fraternizing, sense in you — the foreigner of the quality, of the kind, that he might have been *chez lui*. Whatever he might see himself becoming, he was never to see himself that again, any more than you were ever to see him. He became then, to my vision (which I have called

Indicative of the many new threads being woven into the national fabric was this New York street shrine, sketched in 1906 by Jerome Myers.

fascinated for want of a better description of it), a creature promptly despoiled of those "manners" which were the grace (as I am again reduced to calling it) by which one had best known and, on opportunity, best liked him. He presents himself thus, most of all, to be plain—and not only in New York, but throughout the country—as wonderingly conscious that his manners of the other world, that everything you have there known and praised him for, have been a huge mistake. . . .

Henry James
The American Scene, 1907

What made immigration work for America was the very thing James described —the alien's readiness to be American. The effort that many made in that direction was prodigious; one hopes the anonymous Pole, below, found the help he sought.

I'm in this country four months (from 14 Mai 1913 . . .).

I am polish man. I want be american citizen—and took here first paper in 12 June N 625. But my friends are polish people—I must live with them—I work in the shoes-shop with polish people—I stay all the time with them—at home— in the shop—anywhere.

I want live with american people, but I do not know anybody of american. I go 4 times to teacher and must pay $2 weekly. I wanted take board in english house, but I could not, for I earn only $5 or 6 in a week, and when I pay teacher $2, I have only $4—$3—and now english board house is too dear for me. Better job to get is very hard for me, because I do not speak well english and I cannot understand what they say to me. The teacher teach me—but when I come home —I must speak polish and in the shop also. In this way I can live in your country many years—like my friends—and never speak—write well english—and never be good american citizen. I know here many persons, they live here 10 or moore years, and they are not citizens, they don't speak well english, they don't know geography and history of this country, they don't know constitution of America.— nothing. I don't like be like them I wanted they help me in english—they could not—because they knew nothing. I want go from them away. But where? Not in the country, because I want go in the city, free evening schools and lern. I'm looking for help. If somebody could give me another job between american people, help me live with them and lern english—and could tell me the best way how I can fast lern—it would be very, very good for me. Perhaps you have somebody, here he could help me?

If you can help me, I please you.

I wrote this letter by myself and I know no good—but I hope you will understand whate I mean.

Excuse me,
F. N.
Letter of an anonymous Polish immigrant
Report of the Commission on Immigration on
The Problem of Immigration in Massachusetts, 1914

"ONE FLAG" "ONE COUNTRY"

WM MCKINLEY

THEO. ROOSEVELT

FOR PRESIDENT.

FOR VICE PRESIDENT.

"PROSPERITY AT HOME PRESTIGE ABROAD"

War with Spain

*I*n the strict military sense the Spanish-American War was scarcely more than a badly conducted exercise—at least on land—lasting only three months and twenty-two days. Some two hundred thousand Americans sprang or stumbled to their country's call. Of these, 379 were killed in action and 1,604 wounded. By contrast, almost four thousand soldiers died from fever, from ailments brought on by the appalling sanitary conditions of the Army camps, and—so many volunteers claimed—from food poisoning caused by the "embalmed beef" served the troops for rations. Observing events from his post as ambassador to Great Britain, where distance obscured the worst examples of military mismanagement, Lincoln's former secretary John Hay found it "a splendid little war; begun with the highest motives, carried on with magnificent intelligence and spirit, favored by that fortune which loves the brave." It was too quickly won, too bloodless, for the usual public disillusion to set in and too short even to cause the inflation that almost always accompanies wars. Yet this martial interlude, undertaken with maximum inefficiency and a minimum of justification, was a turning point in the country's history. McKinley, the reluctant, grasped the larger implications of the splendid little war when he later said: "And so it has come to pass that in a few short months we have become a world power; and I know, sitting here in this chair, with what added respect the nations of the world now deal with the United States, and it is vastly different from the conditions I found when I was inaugurated."

Following the war resolution, McKinley called for an army of one hundred and twenty-five thousand volunteers, and the eager and adventurous responded, just as other and more mercenary adventurers at the same time and in almost the same numbers were responding to the Klondike gold rush. In cities and towns across the country young men marched away to the strains of "There'll Be a Hot Time in the Old Town Tonight" while young, damp-eyed women proudly watched them. Nor was it only the young who flocked to the colors. William Jennings Bryan, putting aside political differences, emerged astride a black horse in the blue uniform of the colonel of the Third Nebraska Volunteers. Theodore Roosevelt, convinced that the sword was mightier

They were different in style and attitudes, yet Roosevelt liked his chief, remarking that McKinley—then lying mortally hurt—was the "absolute representative" of the average, hard-working citizen.

than the pen, resigned as assistant secretary of the Navy to organize one of the three cavalry regiments authorized by Congress to be recruited in the West. Officially the unit was commanded by Roosevelt's friend Captain Leonard Wood of the Regular Army—made a colonel for his new post—but it was soon apparent that the First Volunteer Cavalry Regiment was Lieutenant Colonel Roosevelt's own. Wood and Roosevelt prepared a camp at San Antonio, Texas, and appealed to the Territorial governors of Arizona, New Mexico, and Oklahoma for recruits who were "young, good shots, and good riders." Not only cowboys, rangers, Indians, and other Western-ers responded in overwhelming numbers but also so-cially prominent Easterners, including polo players and gentlemen riders from New York's Harvard, Yale, and Princeton clubs. Soon the First Volunteer Cavalry be-came known, and would go down in history, as Roose-velt's Rough Riders.

As a gesture of national conciliation, former Union Ma-jor McKinley appointed as major generals of volunteers two former Confederate commanders, "Fighting Joe" Wheeler and Robert E. Lee's nephew Fitzhugh Lee. When the President's call to arms was issued, there were only twenty-eight thousand men in the Army, and the War Department lacked an effective organization for mobilizing. Most of the regulars were sent on to Tampa, where they came under the command of the three-hundred-pound Brigadier General William R. Shafter. They were to be the nucleus of a force for an invasion of Cuba. As for the volunteers, many of them were sent to hastily and poorly organized tent cities in Georgia, Virginia, Alabama, Florida, and California, on the theory that in those warm states they would become precondi-tioned to Cuban heat. Instead, they soon lost much of the enthusiasm that had led them to enlist and an ap-palling number of them succumbed to disease. The volunteer army was headed by political incompetents; it lacked even such elementary equipment as clothing and boots, and it was armed with ancient Springfield rifles using smoke-producing black powder.

While the old Army was just beginning to flounder into new life, the new Navy was making history on the other side of the globe. That renewed Navy had had its beginning in 1883, when Congress authorized the first steel vessels, three cruisers. By the beginning of the Spanish-American War the Navy had six battleships, two armored cruisers, ten protected cruisers (deck armor only), and a number of smaller vessels. Assistant Secre-tary of the Navy Roosevelt had come to office hoping for a fight, which he was sure "would be a splendid thing for the Navy." He had considered the possibility of a war with Spain, and he had long-range plans not just for Cuba and Puerto Rico but also for the Philip-pines. The assistant secretary used his influence to have Commodore George Dewey placed in command of the Asiatic Squadron. After the destruction of the *Maine*, Roosevelt, taking advantage of one of Secretary of the Navy John D. Long's many absences, cabled Dewey, then in Hong Kong, to coal his ships and prepare in the event of war to attack the Spanish squadron of Rear Admiral Patricio Montojo y Pasarón in the Philippines.

HARPER'S PICTORIAL HISTORY OF THE WAR WITH SPAIN, 1899

This lithograph of the crew of a five-inch gun at the Battle of Manila Bay was done by Frederick Coffay Yohn. Yohn achieved a reputation as a battle artist who was expert in details. Yet he never in his life actually observed a military engagement.

With professional thoroughness Dewey quickly took care of all supply matters. When he left Hong Kong aboard his flagship *Olympia* just after the declaration of war, his squadron consisted of four protected cruisers, two gunboats, and a revenue cutter. Awaiting him within the shelter of Manila Bay, much too far behind the sentinel islands of Corregidor, Caballo, and El Fraile to get any support from their antiquated guns, lay Admiral Montojo's impotent flotilla of two small protected cruisers and five almost worthless unprotected cruisers. Dewey's ships mounted ten eight-inch guns, twenty-three six-inch, and twenty five-inch. Montojo had only seven 6.3's, four obsolete 5.9's, and twenty 4.7's, while the land batteries defending the bay were old smoothbores. The only hope for the Spaniards lay in closing the port with mines, but Montojo had only fourteen of these and they were useless because they lacked fuses.

From the government in Madrid to the commanders in the field, the Spaniards were possessed by a singular fatalism as war with the United States approached. They had no hope of winning, and their chief concern seemed to be to achieve an honorable defeat. When Montojo learned of Dewey's approach, his first thought was to spare the city of Manila, and he moved his ships to the navy yard six miles from the capital. There he awaited the Americans stoically.

By the time day broke on May 1, Dewey had led his fleet past the Spanish fortifications into Manila Bay. The batteries near the city fired a few times, without result, and the Americans ignored the fire. What followed was more a practice shoot than a battle. Dewey in the *Olympia* approached to within three miles of the Spanish fleet before he gave his famous laconic order: "You may fire when ready, Gridley." Back and forth before the navy yard the American squadron steamed, its gunfire raking the Spanish ships. The Spanish return fire was wildly inaccurate. Both fleets were using black powder, and clouds of smoke billowed across the water, obscuring for several hours the devastating accuracy of the American attack. Montojo's little armada was destroyed, he himself wounded. By eleven o'clock, when the white flag was finally hoisted over the navy yard, the Spaniards had lost 381 men killed or wounded. One overweight American engineer had died of heat prostration.

Not until a week after the battle did the news arrive in the United States, a week of suspense and rumors that Dewey's fleet had suffered heavily. The announcement of the overwhelming American victory electrified the country and made Dewey the hero of the hour. Congress created the rank of Admiral of the Navy for Dewey. Colleges showered him with honorary degrees *in absentia*. Dewey odes and poems flowered in the newspapers. Victor Herbert wrote a triumphal battle song. A song with verses of immortal doggerel, which first appeared in the Topeka *Daily Capital*, echoed from coast to coast:

> O Dewey was the morning
>   Upon the first of May,
> And Dewey was the Admiral
>   Down in Manila Bay;
> And Dewey were the Regent's eyes,
>   "Them" orbs of royal blue!
> And Dewey feel discouraged?
>   I Dew not think we Dew.

This mood of exultation was soon followed by a feeling akin to panic when the main Spanish fleet, under Admiral Pascual Cervera y Topete, which had left the Cape Verde Islands on April 29 headed west, did not turn up in the Caribbean on schedule. Dwellers along the largely unfortified North Atlantic coast besieged Washington with demands for protection. Boston businessmen began transferring the contents of their safety deposit boxes inland. The cause of the alarm consisted of four thinly equipped armored cruisers and three torpedo boats. But this fleet, its size and whereabouts still unknown, seemed an ominous threat to coastal dwellers.

To such as Theodore Roosevelt, the chief threat was that the war might remain purely naval. With Dewey's victory and a blockade of Cuba there might not be any land conflict at all even though on May 8 the President had directed General Nelson A. Miles to organize a seventy-thousand-man army and capture Havana. Plans for a Cuban invasion were made, discarded, remade. "There is no head, no management whatever in the War Department," Roosevelt complained. Yet with Admiral Cervera still on the loose somewhere in the Atlantic, it seemed folly to dispatch an expeditionary force certain to be inferior in numbers to the one hundred and fifty thousand Spanish regulars and forty-six thousand volunteers defending the island. The recently promoted Rear Admiral William T. Sampson, busy blockading Havana, now searched the north coast of Cuba for Cervera's fleet while his former senior and present subordinate Commodore Winfield S. Schley, with the Flying Squadron that belied its name, carried on the hunt in the

versaries would have to travel. To make it even worse for the advancing troops, the American artillery had not yet switched to smokeless powder and revealed its position with every salvo. The Signal Corps had sent up an observation balloon, and this large gas-filled bag, floating overhead and towed along by four men, marked the progress of the Americans along the jungle path. Shrapnel aimed at the balloon showered down on the plodding men, bullets snapped and hummed through the palm trees, and long before the divisions arrived at the open meadow, they had suffered many casualties.

Lawton, meanwhile, moving on El Caney, soon found the fort with its blockhouse a much harder nut to crack than anyone had anticipated. Shafter had thought that it could be reduced in a few minutes. The few minutes stretched to hours; the Spaniards from their solidly entrenched position fought with skill and courage against odds of more than 10 to 1. By the time Lawton's 6,653 men had taken the crest, 441 Americans had been either killed or wounded. While Lawton's division was being punished, the other two divisions were beginning their assault on San Juan Ridge. Unable to see any enemy soldiers or even the enemy's position as they pushed along the jungle road, they heard the roar of their own batteries behind them as a heavier counterpoint to the Spanish shrapnel. "The front had burst out with a roar like a brushfire," correspondent and novelist Stephen Crane wrote. "The noise of the rifle bullets broke in their faces like the noise of so many lamp-chimneys or sped overhead in a swift cruel spitting. And at the front the battle-sound, as if it were simply music, was beginning to swell and swell until the volleys rolled like a surf." The men of New York's Seventy-first Regiment, who had been put in the front—green volunteers with the telltale black-powder ammunition and led by incompetent political officers—refused to go forward. Roosevelt—now in command of his regiment, for Colonel Wood had been transferred to other duties—with his Rough Riders, passed them contemptuously while the feckless infantry, lying in the underbrush, attempted to cheer him.

Across San Juan River the rest of the vanguard assembled at the edge of the meadow with Fort San Juan Hill looming above. During ten minutes of waiting a quarter of the Sixth Infantry became casualties. Under the fire from above, the position became untenable, and the order finally came to take the heights at all hazards.

Wheeler's cavalry ranged directly in front of Kettle Hill, the most advanced Spanish position. While waiting for the order to attack, Roosevelt spurred his horse ahead conspicuously, and when the bugle sounded, he gestured forward imperiously. Up the hill the Rough Riders swarmed, mixed inextricably with troopers of the Ninth and Tenth Cavalry, both colored regiments. Whether the Rough Rider colonel was the first to attain the top of the hill, no one could say for certain afterward, but certainly he was the most visible of the ridge's conquerors. His charge, he felt later, was an act worthy of the Congressional Medal of Honor.

Gathered in triumph on the top of Kettle Hill, though still under fire from the high ground in front of them, the Rough Riders saw the main attack surge and then crawl up toward Fort San Juan Hill. Richard Harding Davis watched the Sixth and Sixteenth Infantry start up the slope. Fortunately for the crawling figures, the Spanish fire was too high to be very lethal. Davis wrote:

They had no glittering bayonets, they were not massed in regular array. There were a few men in advance, bunched together, and creeping up a steep, sunny hill, the tops of which roared and flashed with flame. . . . Behind these first few, spreading out like a fan, were single lines of men, slipping and scrambling in the smooth grass. . . . It was much more wonderful than any swinging charge could have been. They walked to greet death at every step, many of them, as they advanced, sinking suddenly or pitching forward and disappearing in the high grass, but the others waded on, stubbornly, forming a thin blue line that kept creeping higher and higher. . . . the crests of the hills crackled and burst in amazed roars, and rippled with waves of tiny flame. But the blue line crept steadily up and on, and then, near the top, the broken fragments gathered together in a sudden burst of speed, the Spaniards appeared for a moment outlined against the sky and poised for instant flight, fired a last volley and fled before the swift-moving wave that leaped and sprang up after them.

Before the Americans lay the city of Santiago. Yet the moment of triumph was scarcely one to savor. The exhausted troops had only a thin line of men on the hill, and they were not at all sure they could hold their position. Neither was the ailing Shafter, in the face of his heavy casualties, his ammunition and supply problems, and possible Spanish counterattack. Even the buoyant Roosevelt would write two days later, as the Fifth Corps dug in on the San Juan slopes, that "we are within measurable distance of a terrible military disaster." The morning of July 3 Shafter felt the defenses of Santiago were still too strong for him to deal with and was considering drawing his army back five miles to reorganize and refit. At the same time he sent a message to the Spanish commander demanding the city's surrender and threatening otherwise to shell it.

The real decision came that same day at sea, where the battleships *Oregon, Iowa, Indiana,* and *Texas,* the cruiser *Brooklyn,* and the armed yachts *Vixen* and *Gloucester* lay anchored in a blockading arc before Santiago Harbor. Admiral Sampson, expecting no naval developments, had sailed early that morning aboard the *New York* to Siboney to confer with Shafter and had sent the *Massachusetts* to Guantánamo for refueling. The Sunday morning calm left the water like glass. Sailors in their white uniforms were preparing for divine services;

officers were relaxing in their cabins with postbreakfast cigars. Suddenly a signal gun rang out and the astonished sailors looking at the placid gap of water between the Morro heights and Socapa Hill saw the flagship of Admiral Cervera, the cruiser *Infanta María Teresa,* steaming down the channel with the red and gold battle flags of Spain fluttering from her masts. The Spanish fleet was coming out at last.

The *María Teresa* was followed by the three armored cruisers *Vizcaya, Cristóbal Colón,* and *Almirante Oquendo,* with the destroyers *Furor* and *Plutón* bringing up the rear. "The Spanish ships came out as gaily as brides to the altar," Captain John Philip of the *Texas* wrote. It took several minutes for the surprised Ameri-

The huge General Shafter, above, had won the Medal of Honor in the Civil War. Like many of his troops he was afflicted by illness in Cuba, and he was the target, too, of blame for mismanagement—much of which rightly belonged to Washington.

can fleet to get under way, and by that time the Spanish ships had slipped by. In passing, the *María Teresa* fired a salvo at the American fleet, which like most subsequent Spanish shells fell short.

Cervera, in obeying orders from Madrid to sail, knew that he was doomed. Earlier he had told deaf ears across the ocean that "the absolutely certain result will be the ruin of each and all of the ships and the death of the greater part of their crews." Under the best conditions his ships would have been no match for the Americans, and they were at their worst, with barnacle-fouled bottoms and defective ammunition. Just possibly the Spanish admiral might have escaped at night. He knew that in daylight his fleet would almost certainly die. Like hounds after a hare, the American ships sped in the wake of the Spaniards, with Commodore Schley in the *Brooklyn* in command in the temporary absence of Admiral Sampson. All four Spanish cruisers fired with persistent ineffectiveness. The *María Teresa*, bearing the brunt of the American attack, was the first to go. Her wooden decks ablaze, her water mains ruptured, her ammunition exploding, she headed for shore, to be beached and abandoned six miles west of her starting point. Next to succumb in the unequal contest was the *Oquendo*, blazing fore and aft and her interior a furnace when she reached the beach. The two destroyers perished quickly, torn to pieces by concentrated shell fire. Not until noon did Schley's squadron overtake the *Vizcaya*, but then, pounded by the *Brooklyn*, *Oregon*, and *Iowa*, she too burst into flames and was run onto the beach, where she exploded. One of her last stray shells decapitated a seaman on the deck of the *Brooklyn*—the sole American death. The *Cristóbal Colón*, the fastest Spanish ship, might have escaped, but by midafternoon, running out of high-quality coal, her speed slackened, and as the *Oregon* neared, she turned toward the shore. The Americans held their fire while the Spanish commander beached his ship, hauled down his colors, and waited quietly in his cabin until he was taken prisoner. In the destruction of their fleet, the Spaniards lost 323 men with 151 wounded.

Admiral Sampson, racing in the *New York* to catch up

Heroism and victory in the tropics (San Juan Hill left) had grisly accompaniments. Roosevelt remarked on flocks of rapacious vultures and on the land crabs, some "almost as big as rabbits," that collected in "gruesome rings round the fallen."

329

with the running fight, reached his fleet half an hour after the end of hostilities, to be greeted by Schley's signal from the *Brooklyn*: "We have gained a great victory." Sampson's testy reply was: "Report your casualties." His subsequent messages did not even mention Schley: "The fleet under my command," he informed Washington, "offers the nation as a Fourth of July present the whole of Cervera's fleet."

There were the bits and pieces to pick up, "the outlying things," as Senator Lodge called them, but after Cervera's defeat it was as clear to the Spaniards as to the Americans that the war was over. Shafter, who to Roosevelt's disgust took the pedestrian view that negotiations were better than heroics, devoted the next two weeks to successfully persuading General José Toral to surrender Santiago. The city fell on July 17. Eight days later General Miles with three thousand troops landed in Puerto Rico against almost no opposition.

By the peace terms agreed to on August 12, Puerto Rico and Guam were to be ceded to the United States. Spain was to renounce all sovereignty over Cuba. There were many Americans eager to annex Cuba, but they

In the naval battle off Santiago (above) a converted yacht, the Gloucester, *doughtily took on two Spanish destroyers by herself before she was joined in the attack by the battleship* Indiana; *that part of the action evidently inspired this lithograph.*

with forty-seven
and seven Popu
"we are going t
Bryan stood out
response to the
have no subjects
stand, believing
other islands we
but trouble, for w
and from which
Bryan lobbied
Democratic and
result that it pas
In the weeks
yellow fever, ty
through the ran
typhoid and dys
in the United St
as had died by
soldiers wanted
ground level ev
denouncing the
Secretary Alger,
voices was that
States by mid-A
his Rough Ride
Montauk Point,
Roosevelt, wl
Cuba that the n
a meeting with
agreement. Pla
candidate to of
publican state
Erie Canal. The
Platt's concern
Roosevelt was
taste for Blaine
the wilderness,
Platt wanted
would not "ma
tauk Point wer
ing he had tak
vitation had n
Colonel's amb
Roosevelt ar
heroes of the
quickly with h
would remain

were forestalled by an amendment that Senator Henry M. Teller of Colorado had attached to the resolution under which the nation had gone to war. The Teller Amendment disclaimed "any disposition or intention to exercise sovereignty, jurisdiction or control" over Cuba, and was an obstacle difficult for even the most fervid expansionists to surmount. The Philippines were another matter, to be dealt with in formal peace talks in Paris in October. The Spaniards still held a forlorn hope of retaining these, their last island possession, but American public opinion, primed by Hearst and prodded by Lodge, was all for taking them. Though no expansionist at heart, McKinley finally decided to send troops to the Philippines to occupy all the islands, pending further developments. Already in a burst of war-engendered enthusiasm Congress had voted on July 6 to annex Hawaii—which had no connection with Spain.

Long before the war's outbreak, General Emilio Aguinaldo, a sharp-eyed, resolute Filipino, had become the leader of an insurrection against Spanish control of the Philippines. At the onset of hostilities between Spain and the United States, Aguinaldo had cooperated with the Americans, while proclaiming himself the dictator-president of a revolutionary Philippine republic. But Aguinaldo's views became increasingly distasteful to American expansionists, and the arrival of large numbers of American troops made it clear to Aguinaldo that the United States government, far from supporting a Philippine republic, had come to consider the islands the spoils of a successful war. While annexation was still being debated in the Senate, he renewed his insurrection. For the next three years American soldiers would battle Filipino insurgents, suffering more casualties than they had in the entire Cuban campaign in a guerrilla war that was more costly, bloody, and far more bestial.

Among the occupying forces in Cuba, heroes and villains were soon switching roles, as they had done in the Philippines. Soon after hostilities had ended, American and Spanish soldiers were fraternizing and expressing mutual contempt for the insurgents, who, in the opinion of Shafter's divisional commander General Samuel B. M. Young, whose view was typical, were "a lot of degenerates, absolutely devoid of honor or gratitude. They are no more capable of self-government than the savages of Africa." With the approbation of upper-class Cubans, Leonard Wood—now a major general—became governor of Santiago and later, military governor of Cuba. Many felt, as did Wood, that Cuba's

despoiled condition and America's economic and strategic interest in the island made annexation the best solution. Nevertheless, with the protection of the Teller Amendment, Cuba by 1902 was to attain independence in handling her internal affairs, though the United States retained a strong voice in her foreign affairs by the Platt Amendment of March 2, 1901, under which the Cuban government was to make no treaty compromising its independence. By other clauses of the Platt Amendment the United States government continued to occupy naval bases on Cuban soil and also reserved the right to intervene to maintain a government able to protect life, property, and individual liberty.

When American and Spanish negotiators met in Paris on October 1, 1898, the only real issue was the Philippines. McKinley by then had decided that the islands could not be turned back to Spain nor could they be allowed to fall to Germany or Japan; but since they were unfit for self-government—though Aguinaldo might feel otherwise—"there was nothing left for us to do but to . . . educate the Filipinos, and uplift and civilize and Christianize them . . ." whether they liked it or not. The United States offered Spain twenty million dollars as a settlement, and the Spaniards, having no alternative, reluctantly agreed. But the peace treaty still faced the hurdle of the United States Senate, with 60 votes needed for the required two-thirds majority. As Senator Lodge of the Foreign Relations Committee realized, it would be a touch-and-go vote, for in spite of America's quick victory, there remained a substantial antiexpansionist minority in the country, diverse but voluble in its opposition: idealists, like columnist Finley Peter Dunne and President Charles W. Eliot of Harvard; political figures, like Cleveland and Schurz; eccentric industrialists, like Carnegie; racists, like Pitchfork Ben Tillman, who wanted no more dark-skinned Americans; labor leaders, like the American Federation of Labor's President Samuel Gompers, who feared the competition of Filipino laborers for American jobs.

When the Senate met to take action on the treaty, a firm minority of senators had already decided to save the people from themselves by blocking its passage. "It seems impossible," the indignant Theodore Roosevelt wrote, "that men of ordinary patriotism can contemplate such an outrage upon the country." Yet the leader of the opposition was the venerable Senator George F. Hoar of Massachusetts, one of the last surviving founders of the Republican party, and the composition of the Senate,

the Democrats as was McKinley of the Republicans. At the Democratic convention in Kansas City, under a banner reading "The Flag of the Republic forever; of an Empire never!" he was nominated by acclaim, with Cleveland's former Vice President Adlai Stevenson as his running mate. The Populists, much diminished by the McKinley prosperity, again nominated Bryan, as did the Silver Republicans and the Anti-Imperialist League. The Democratic platform proclaimed imperialism as "the paramount issue of the campaign," and Bryan still held stubbornly to his old demand of a 16–1 coinage of silver. But the currency issue, which had burned so brightly four years earlier, flickered only dimly. With the increase in the supply of gold, a silver monetary system no longer seemed the solution to the world's ills, and the Republicans could boast that a gold standard and a protective tariff had brought back prosperity. As for imperialism, Americans two years after the war had come to accept an American empire as an accomplished and laudable fact, and even the Democrats were not prepared to denounce the annexation of Hawaii and the acquisition of Puerto Rico. When Bryan charged that McKinley and the Republicans had violated American principles by subjugating millions of defenseless people, McKinley replied that his administration had not subjugated them but liberated them "from the yoke of imperialism."

An issue of far more immediate concern was that of the trusts, and here the Republicans and Democrats diverged most sharply. Never had it been more apparent than under McKinley that the Republican party was the party of big business, of the moneyed interests. Railroads disregarded the Interstate Commerce Act as easily as corporations disregarded the Sherman act, with no sign of disapproval from the White House. As the campaign wore on, Bryan, campaigning in twenty-four states and making some six hundred speeches, turned his Messianic zeal more and more from denouncing imperialism to denouncing the trusts. Bryan's appeal was still potent to the dispossessed and discontented, the Populists, the agrarians, the large unions of the American Federation of Labor. By mid-campaign Roosevelt was seized with the frightened feeling that the majority of Americans might be Bryanites, "all the lunatics, all the idiots, all the knaves, all the cowards, and all the honest people who are slow-witted." McKinley belatedly spoke out against the trusts in veiled words, while Roosevelt proceeded to attack them without any

veil at all. The President thought it beneath the dignity of his office to campaign, and the chief burden of campaigning fell on the Rough Rider. He felt himself equal to it. His energy was as great as, his voice as loud as, and his personality even more magnetic than, the aging Boy Orator's. Stump speaking with spread-eagle fervor, extolling the unstained flag, and painting lurid pictures of the "fearful misery, fearful disaster" a Democratic victory would bring, Roosevelt was willing to travel as far and as fast as Bryan. "I am strong as a bull moose," he hoarsely told reporters, with his easy gift for striking off a phrase.

As summer gave way to fall, the Bryan campaign faltered, and to the Republicans McKinley's re-election seemed more and more a certainty. A wit in New York's Union League Club offered odds of 16 to 1 on a McKinley victory. The odds were hardly exaggerated. Not since Grant's second election had the Republicans scored such a triumph. McKinley's 292 electoral votes

Civilization lines up against the barbarians in this magazine cover of 1900, after the Boxer Rebellion. Note the weapons of the opposing sides. Americans were becoming increasingly conscious of what would come to be called the Yellow Peril.

included Populist Kansas and even Bryan's Nebraska. To conservatives generally, social unrest seemed stilled. The business community was exultant. Wall Street opened with a bull market. Yet McKinley accepted the returns in a sober, almost sad mood. "It has to me no personal phase," he told the guests at a Union League banquet in Philadelphia. He was more concerned with the policies of his next four years: the reciprocity treaties that he, the former protectionist, had set his heart on; the long-talked-of Panama canal; just and orderly government of Spain's former possessions; a generous settlement with China; and support of the Permanent Court of International Arbitration at The Hague, which he felt was "the noblest forum for the settlement of international disputes."

Even before the election, Hanna, his own health failing, had grown increasingly uneasy over the President's safety. In Europe Empress Elizabeth of Austria and King Humbert of Italy had both been assassinated by anarchists, Humbert by an agent sent by an anarchist group in Paterson, New Jersey. An informer had produced a memorandum for the Secret Service to show that Queen Victoria, the President of the United States, and the Kaiser were also on the list. On learning this, Hanna saw to it that a Secret Service agent was assigned to be constantly with the President. McKinley himself was stoically indifferent to any danger. His chief private concern was to be back in his own home in Canton for the summer months, from July through September, the long quiet interlude with his ailing wife to be broken only by a visit in September to the National Encampment of the Grand Army of the Republic in Cleveland. He had also agreed to visit the Pan-American Exposition in Buffalo, New York, on his way to Cleveland, to deliver an important speech, and he further agreed that the day after his speech he would attend a public reception at the exposition's Temple of Music. Concerned with McKinley's safety, his secretary, George Courtelyou, twice had the reception eliminated from the program, but each time McKinley insisted on having it replaced. "No one would wish to hurt me," he explained to his secretary. Courtelyou, masking his uneasiness, ordered additional Secret Service guards and police to be on hand.

On September 5, 1901, McKinley arrived in Buffalo with his wife, who was much improved by the weeks in Canton. Fifty thousand persons gathered to hear his long-considered speech, in which, in his mellow voice, he reiterated his fundamental belief that "isolation is no longer possible or desirable. . . . God and man have linked the nations together. . . . The period of exclusiveness is past." That evening he visited the exposition, where he saw a water ballet and a display of fireworks, which reached its climax in his illuminated portrait and the blazing inscription: "Welcome to McKinley, Chief of Our Nation."

The next day there was a leisurely tour of Niagara Falls and then at four o'clock the public reception at the Temple of Music, a building as ornate as a wedding cake, decorated inside with potted palms and bay trees. By noon the crowd had begun to gather in the hot sunshine, waiting for the temple's closed doors to open. Somewhere in the crowd, inconspicuous enough to pass unobserved, stood twenty-eight-year-old Leon Czolgosz, the hate-warped son of Polish immigrants. Slender, clean-shaven, wearing a neat black suit, he looked like a millworker or mechanic in his Sunday best, which was not far wrong, for until three years earlier he had worked in a wire mill. There he had become attracted to anarchism and the doctrine that all rulers were enemies of the people and that the people had the right to kill them. He approached various anarchist groups, but his obviously unstable nature made him suspect to them. At the end of August he had come to Buffalo, rented a two-dollar-a-week room, bought a revolver, and resolved to kill the President.

At four o'clock the doors of the temple swung open and the crowd pressed forward. The President was flanked by guards, and palms and a large American flag stood beside and behind him. An orchestra was playing a Bach sonata. The apprehensive Courtelyou had arranged for extra Secret Service men to be present as well as the exposition police, Buffalo detectives, and a squad of soldiers. Yet none of these noticed Czolgosz in the double line as he advanced, the revolver in his right hand concealed by a handkerchief with which he occasionally dabbed his forehead.

As McKinley reached out with mechanical amiability, the young man with the handkerchief-wrapped hand struck the President's extended hand aside. Two shots rang out, two small black holes appeared in the handkerchief, and then there was a moment of stunned silence. McKinley, motionless, stared with contempt for the instant until the guards fell on Czolgosz in fury. "Don't let them hurt him," the President said as they helped him to a chair.

One bullet had grazed the President's ribs without penetrating his body, but the other had gone through the stomach, the pancreas, and one kidney. For a few days the doctors issued optimistic bulletins, but by the week's end gangrene had set in and it was clear even to McKinley himself that he was dying. "It is useless, gentlemen," he told the doctors assembled in his bedroom. "I think we ought to have prayer." Early on the morning of September 14 he died.

During the President's last agony the country seemed united in its sympathy and affection for the dying man. And following this unifying affection came a wave of vindictive anger, the belief that Czolgosz was only one of a group of conspirators. Anarchists all over the country were rounded up as possible conspirators.

In McKinley's death most Americans felt a sharp sense of personal loss. When the news flashed over the wires from Buffalo, bells across the nation tolled all the rest of the night. And in the six days of mourning that followed, with crepe-shrouded buildings and newspapers with black borders, there was fear as well as grief, a sighing in the wind as the President's funeral train passed.

Roosevelt was mountain climbing when the news finally reached him that the President had had a relapse. A mad drive over mountain roads took him to a station where a special train waited, and there he learned that McKinley had died. On arriving in Buffalo, Roosevelt took the oath of office in the library of the house where McKinley's body still lay. At forty-two years of age the twenty-sixth President of the United States was by far the youngest President the country had had. All the Presidents since Lincoln had worn Union blue in the Civil War except Cleveland, who had stayed home to support his family so that his two brothers could serve. Major McKinley was the last Civil War soldier to occupy the White House. His passing marked the passing of the Boys in Blue as a political force. No one would ever again wave the bloody shirt in Congress. Time and the Spanish-American War had closed the old breach between North and South. New times, new issues, new men, new conflicts, were waiting with the new century, which in America dated far more from Roosevelt's arrival than it did from New Year's Day, 1900, when the twentieth century had begun.

With the Roosevelts, the White House itself came alive after the years in which the downstairs had come to resemble the lobby of a New York hotel. Instead of the hush of the McKinleys, the old Mansion now echoed with shouts and young laughter. Roosevelt had brought a family with him as boisterously energetic as himself: his seventeen-year-old daughter, Alice, who would shortly shock Washington by smoking cigarettes in public; and the daughter and four young sons of his second marriage.

So overwhelming was Roosevelt's personality that it tended to dwarf his accomplishments. One remembers him today more for what he was than for what he did. Henry Adams, who had to learn to like him, described him as showing "more than any other living man . . . the singular primitive quality that belongs to the ultimate in matter . . . *he was pure act.*" In much of his exuberance he managed to be pure adolescent. On his forty-sixth birthday his friend Elihu Root congratulated him: "You have made a very good start in life and your friends have hopes for you when you grow up."

As a family the Roosevelts were as close to an aristocracy as America, or at least New York, had produced, and Theodore was born to wealth and assured position. He was also born with a keen, inquiring mind and an assertive temperament. What was lacking was the strength of body to go with the rest, for he was a puny, asthmatic child with defective vision. His curiosity about the world was unending. When he was scarcely out of childhood, he began a natural history museum in his bedroom, and in his adolescent years thought of becoming a naturalist or zoologist.

The turning point in Roosevelt's life came when he was thirteen and had been sent alone to Moosehead Lake in Maine. During the journey he found himself in a coach with two husky boys of his own age, who responded to his friendly overtures by teasing him. When he lost his temper and tried to fight, they easily held him at arm's length. In his humiliation, he had to face the fact that he was a weakling. "Having become quickly and bitterly conscious that I did not have the natural prowess to hold my own," he wrote later, "I decided I would try to supply its place by training." Back in New York, he spent a large part of each day in a gymnasium his father had built for him. By the time he entered Harvard, he was a capable boxer. In the days when wealthy undergraduates aspired to no more than a passing grade, Roosevelt worked hard, disputed with his professors, and ran where others walked. In his senior year he was elected to Phi Beta Kappa. Yet he found time to attend the fashionable Boston dances, and he was proud of his membership in Porcellian, Harvard's most exclusive

McKinley's body is borne up the steps of the Capitol during the state funeral. In the South news of his death spawned a blues song. "Czolgosz, Czolgosz, you done him wrong," went one verse, "Shot po' McKinley when he was walking along. . . ."

club, so proud of it that he mentioned it in later years to such crowned heads as Edward VII and Kaiser Wilhelm. When he was appointed lieutenant colonel of the Rough Riders, he ordered his uniform from New York's rather exclusive Brooks Brothers. After San Juan Hill, he openly asserted his right to the Congressional Medal of Honor.

Though he was assured a high position through birth, he carried in him some inner insecurity, which punctuated the restless virility of his public life with periods of acute depression. The word "gentleman" came just a little too readily to his lips, his fists clenched just a little too quickly. Some disturbing memory would always remain with him of that small, defenseless boy in the coach.

While still at Harvard Roosevelt met seventeen-year-old Alice Lee, a fair-haired girl of great charm and

Theodore Roosevelt, the soul of enthusiastically applied energy, believed in participatory democracy every bit as much as he believed in himself: ". . . the man who wishes to do good in his community," he said, "must go into active political life."

beauty, who would become his wife four months after his graduation and die in childbirth three years later. After his honeymoon he began studying law at Columbia and while at law school became the successful candidate for assemblyman from one of the few safely Republican New York City districts. At first the patrician newcomer to Albany was looked on as a comic figure, but before his second term had ended he had made a name for himself in the assembly. He represented the reform element in his party, so much so that for a time his name was linked with that of the Democratic governor, Grover Cleveland, a conservative of much the same cut. Assemblyman Roosevelt was more concerned with public honesty than with social issues. An act to limit streetcar operators to a twelve-hour day seemed to him socialist.

After his wife's death in 1884 he was a member of the New York delegation to the Republican National Convention, which nominated Blaine. Although he regarded the Plumed Knight with contempt, he was not ready to join the Mugwump walkout. After the convention he abandoned the East for the Dakota Badlands, where he had bought a cattle ranch. Now, in that jagged country, he found release in physical activity. As a rancher he dressed, or overdressed, the cowboy part, with a sombrero, silver spurs, and a fringed buckskin shirt, but he achieved some peace of spirit on the empty plains. In the fall of 1886 he returned to New York, where the Republican party, lacking any well-known candidate, drafted him to run for mayor in a year when the most celebrated candidate in a three-way race was the reformer and single-tax advocate Henry George. Roosevelt came in a poor third, his political career apparently at an end.

After the election, he went to London, where on December 2, 1886, he married his childhood playmate Edith Carow. On returning to the United States in the spring he hurried to the Badlands, but his career as a rancher was ended. The brutal winter of 1886–87 had killed most of his livestock, and he eventually sold his ranch at a loss. With his bride he retreated to Sagamore Hill, the house he had built at Oyster Bay, Long Island, where his family had so often summered. "I'm a literary feller, not a politician, nowadays," he told Columbia's Brander Matthews. At Sagamore Hill, between periods of hiking, hunting, and playing, he wrote two Western books, a hasty and somewhat superficial biography of Gouverneur Morris, and a history of New York. Harrison's defeat of Cleveland offered the rusticated Roosevelt a modest re-entry into public life with his appointment as United States civil service commissioner, a job that no one else wanted. The commission was stagnant, the way Harrison preferred it. Roosevelt, to whom stagnation was anathema, shook the commission up from top to bottom. The six years that Roosevelt spent in Washington as civil service commissioner, though frustrating politically, were personally happy ones. He was never invited to the White House by Harrison, who had been alienated by Roosevelt's zeal, but to his small house off

Connecticut Avenue came Henry Adams, William Howard Taft, Speaker of the House Thomas B. Reed, as well as literary figures, including Kipling and Richard Harding Davis. This interlude ended in 1895, when Roosevelt was appointed to the Board of Police Commissioners by New York's reform mayor, William L. Strong. With the same zest and boundless energy he had given to the Civil Service Commission, he proceeded to shake the city's police department from its embedded graft and corruption. "I am fighting vile crime and hideous vice," he announced. It was an Augean task, and in the end he would have to acknowledge that he was no Hercules. But the job intrigued him far more than had civil service. He liked to prowl the streets evenings searching out police derelictions by himself. If the commissioner spotted a patrolman having a glass of beer in a saloon, he did not hesitate to collar him personally. Papers across the country took note of the zealous crime fighter, calling him one of the most interesting men in public life and even mentioning him as a possible 1896 presidential candidate. Yet the way of a reformer can be hard. Roosevelt's letter-of-the-law insistence on closing the saloons on Sunday made enemies of the workingmen. Platt and Tammany were as one in their opposition to his reformist zeal. Even Mayor Strong grew weary of his appointee's drum-beating enthusiasm. Roosevelt was happy to move to Washington as assistant secretary of the Navy after the Republican restoration ushered in by McKinley.

For the middle classes the beginning of the twentieth century was an era of renewed prosperity as America, having paid the inevitable human price for industrialism, moved toward a consumer economy. There were a variety and abundance of inexpensive goods, which could be found in any hardware or dry-goods or clothing store. Streetcar lines spread out like fans from the cities to create suburbs. Men became more mobile as factories mass-produced safety bicycles. In 1900 there were only eight thousand automobiles registered in the entire country. Five years later President Woodrow Wilson of Princeton was deploring the advent of the auto on the grounds that it was "a picture of arrogance of wealth" that spread socialist feeling. And even as Wilson expressed his dissenting views on the motor age, Henry Ford was already building his first cars. The year that Roosevelt was sworn in, the Wright brothers, Orville and Wilbur, were launching gliders at Kitty Hawk and planning and scheming to make them self-propelled. The telephone was becoming common in city offices and even in homes, and in the same Roosevelt year, Guglielmo Marconi, in Newfoundland, by using a kite aerial, had caught wireless signals from England. Electricity was coming into its own as a source of power. In home and office it replaced gas for lighting.

Mergers and consolidations multiplied at an accelerated rate in the business world. In January, 1901, Andrew Carnegie sold out his steel interests to J. P. Morgan, and the first billion-dollar corporation, United States Steel, came into existence. Unrestrained by income taxes, the rich grew richer in a kind of geometric progression. Nearly seven-eighths of America's wealth was owned by 1 per cent of its families. The way of life of the new-rich continued as crudely conspicuous as before, and American heiresses, to the disgust of Theodore Roosevelt, were veiling their commercial origins by marrying titled Europeans. But there were signs that a reaction was brewing. The Bradley Martins, whose sixteen-year-old daughter had married Lord Craven, spent $369,200 on a ball in the depression winter of 1896–97 "to give an impetus to trade." The ensuing publicity, plus the city's doubling of their tax assessment, drove them permanently overseas to England. Lesser extravaganzas still formed the autumnal pattern of the Gilded Age. Cornelius K. G. Billings gave a dinner on horseback at Sherry's. Rudolf Guggenheimer borrowed nightingales from the zoo for one of his parties at the Waldorf. Harry Lehr, who had become Mrs. Stuyvesant Fish's jester, arranged a Newport dinner to meet a Prince del Drago, who turned out to be a monkey. The climax, at least in public reaction, came in 1905 with the Louis XV masked ball given by James Hazen Hyde, the young Frenchified inheritor of controlling interest in the Equitable Life Assurance Society, at the rumored cost of two hundred thousand dollars. Everyone, in the New York–Newport sense of the word, was there, from Mrs. Potter Palmer with her diamond dog collar and her diamond breastplate to the young Franklin D. Roosevelt. The *World* played it up with indignation, intimating that the money for Hyde's extravagances came from the pockets of Equitable policyholders. The scandal grew so great that Hyde followed the Bradley Martins overseas.

Even if Hyde's party had not cost all of the two hundred thousand dollars his detractors reproached him with, it was given at a time when a factory worker earned five hundred dollars a year. Nor was the worker's sorry lot merely financial. Working conditions were close to primitive and industrial accidents common. Child labor was a complacently accepted fact. Twenty per cent of all boys between ten and fifteen and ten per cent of all girls were employed in the factories or in the fields. President Charles W. Eliot, in turning Harvard from a college to a university, had transformed collegiate education in the United States, but it was still for the very few. For most young Americans education ended with a diploma from grammar school.

In 1880 the New York reporter Jacob Riis had published his study of the slums, *How the Other Half Lives*, a book that had quickened the social conscience of the young patrician Theodore Roosevelt by laying bare the cancerous poverty and the degradation of life in the alleys, in the noisome tenements, and in the mean streets. To the festering warrens newcomers from overseas flocked, exploitable and exploited, following the generation-old way of the Irish in the famine years. Such swarms of aliens were changing the ethnic pattern of America. The tide of immigration was shifting from northern to southern and eastern Europe. The newer immigrants were for the most part Slav or Italian peasants or Jews driven from Russia by persecution. In 1907 the tide reached its height with 1,285,000 newcomers. Long before then the nativist anti-Catholic American Protective Association had agitated against the indiscriminate admission of aliens, but this agitation grew more focused with the founding of the Immigration Restriction League, whose efforts would lead eventually to the establishment in 1921 of a quota system based on national origins of immigrants.

As is customary when a President succeeds to office by death, Roosevelt announced that his predecessor's policies would be his own, and for a time it almost seemed that he meant to continue McKinley's program. His first message to Congress was windy rather than startling. He asked for a Department of Commerce and Labor to guard workmen's rights and investigate corporate earnings, for limiting immigration to the fit, a stronger Navy, a canal—site unspecified—between Atlantic and Pacific, and subsidies for American ships. Financiers breathed easier. The first real uproar he created was in October, when he invited the Negro educator Booker T. Washington to dinner at the White House. Southern reaction was violent. The Memphis *Scimitar* called Roosevelt's action of inviting a "nigger" to the White House "the most damnable outrage ever."

Domestically Roosevelt was soon to show his hand in

his prosecution of the Northern Securities Company for violation of the Sherman Antitrust Act and in his settlement of the coal strike of 1902. The Northern Securities Company had emerged as a compromise after the struggle between the Union Pacific's Edward H. Harriman on one side and James J. Hill of the Great Northern Railroad and J. P. Morgan on the other for control of the Northern Pacific Railroad. The new company, controlled jointly by the Harriman-Hill interests, was to consolidate the Northern Pacific and Great Northern into a single railroad system and then bring the Chicago, Burlington and Quincy into the combine.

The Sherman act had been considered a dead letter until Roosevelt reactivated it. Two years after Roosevelt initiated action, the Supreme Court ordered the Northern Securities Company dissolved. But it was not so much from the result as from the bringing of the action that there arose the image of Roosevelt as the defender of the people against the predatory commercial interests, for the trend toward consolidation was in the end not greatly affected by the Northern Securities case nor by the two dozen other antitrust suits brought by Roosevelt's Attorney General against the beef, oil, and tobacco combinations. But the public thought of Roosevelt as

A golf tournament is in progress at the Chevy Chase Club, near Washington, in the 1902 water color by William T. Smedley. Such scenes indicated a new mode in Washington society—where much government business was, as usual, carried on.

OVERLEAF: *The period was remarkable for the amount of its advertising—in magazines and on posters. These samples, all from about the same time, illustrate a transition in style from an explicit, if comic, hard sell to gentler sophistication.*

"UP AND GOING"
"EXCELSIOR" GINGER ALE
MADE BY
JOHN KLEE, DAYTON, O.
JOSEPH R. PEEBLES' SONS,
SOLE AGENTS,
CINCINNATI, O.
EXCELSIOR
EXCELSIOR
EXCELSIOR
EXCELSIOR
DRINK "EXCELSIOR" GINGER.
JOHN KLEE.
EXCELSIOR
GINGER ALE.
JOHN KLEE.
EXCELSIOR
GINGER ALE.

"THE FAMOUS DUKES"

HIGH GRADE
SMOKING TOBACCO

VICTOR BICYCLES

OVERMAN WHEEL CO.

the dynamic trust buster hotly pursuing "malefactors of great wealth."

"I have always been fond," said Roosevelt, "of the West African proverb 'Speak softly and carry a big stick.'" With him there was usually more Big Stick than soft speech, so much so that it became a cartoonists' prop. The President showed how deftly he could wield it in the coal strike that had run from May to October, 1902, and was threatening to shut down industries and freeze the cities in the coming winter. Conditions in the coal fields were among the most wretched in the country, and the miners' demands for a wage increase seemed more than justified. But the spokesman for the operators, George F. Baer of the Philadelphia and Reading Coal and Iron Company, refused the demands and refused even to consult with John Mitchell of the United Mine Workers, maintaining that labor was best protected "by the Christian men to whom God in his infinite wisdom has given the control of the property interests of this country. . . ." Roosevelt forced a settlement by threatening to send federal troops to seize the mines. Capitulating, the operators agreed to an arbitration committee but refused to consider a labor member on the committee. They did agree, however, to accept an "eminent sociologist," and under this definition Roosevelt appointed the labor leader E. E. Clark. The commission awarded the miners a 10 per cent wage increase and ordered the correction of several other abuses but denied recognition to the United Mine Workers.

Roosevelt's most obvious use of his Big Stick in his first term was in foreign affairs. His Corollary to the Monroe Doctrine was developed after Venezuela and the Dominican Republic had both defaulted their debts to European nationals. He maintained that if foreign nations were not permitted under the Monroe Doctrine to intervene in this hemisphere, the United States must then exercise "an international police power" in the case of any government's "chronic wrongdoing." As a practical application of this corollary, Roosevelt had the customs service of the Dominican Republic seized and operated by the United States.

But the most spectacular and enduring of Roosevelt's actions in his first term was his acquisition of the Panama Canal Zone as a prelude to the start of the trans-Isthmian canal talked of since the Clayton-Bulwer Treaty of 1850. The 1901 Hay-Pauncefote Treaty, abrogating the Clayton-Bulwer agreement, opened the way to undisputed American control of any such canal. Nicaragua had been considered for a possible route, but a commission appointed by McKinley had recommended the Panamanian route as technically superior, and Roosevelt settled on that. Having bought out the claims of a French company that had tried and failed to dig a canal, the United States government offered ten million dollars to Colombia, of which Panama was then a province, plus an annual rental for the canal route. When the Colombian senate attempted to hold up the United States for more money, Roosevelt dispatched a cruiser to Panama, where dissidents were revolting against Colombia, and quickly came to an agreement with the rebels. Within hours the President recognized the new Republic of Panama and almost as quickly negotiated a treaty by which the United States guaranteed the independence of the new republic and for the terms rejected by Colombia was granted in perpetuity a zone ten miles wide across the Isthmus. The long-talked-of canal could now be a fact. However dubious Roosevelt's action in obtaining the Canal Zone, he never ceased feeling pride in what he had done. "I took the Canal," he boasted years later, "and let Congress debate."

Roosevelt at the end of his first term could claim to be the most popular man in the country. An active, provocative figure, he got up at six and exercised violently, he boxed, he took obstacle walks, he rode one hundred miles on horseback—to give an example to the Army, for whom he advocated such rides as well as fifty-mile hikes. He read two books a day, he entertained the pugilist John L. Sullivan, he "discovered" writers, among them the poet Edwin Arlington Robinson and the naturalist W. H. Hudson, he used his Big Stick on recalcitrant industrialists, and what he felt his country needed he took. Everything he and his family did was a newsman's delight. "Teddy" became a household word —would even become the name of a stuffed toy animal after the President on a hunting trip had refused to shoot a bear cub. Yet, as the election of 1904 neared, he was full of gloomy forebodings both as to his nomination and his election. He need not have been concerned. The Democrats, wearied of losing with the Boy Orator, had picked the gold-conservative New York Judge Alton B. Parker as their candidate. Roosevelt overwhelmed him by 2,500,000 votes while snatching Missouri from the Solid South and amassing 336 electoral votes to Parker's 140. The night before his inauguration the President-elect told a few close friends: "Tomorrow I shall come into my office in my own right. Then watch out for me!"

Horseless Carriage Days

Nothing has changed the face of the United States as fast as the creature shown above and its proliferating brothers. Since Henry Clay's time, men with national vision had campaigned for a federal highway system and had been put off by localist resistance. But in 1916, two decades or so after the commercial automobile appeared on American roads, Congress passed the Federal Aid Road Act. The auto spurred the rapid growth of suburbia. Because of it, a host of industries boomed—for example, glass and rubber and petroleum and steel. Isolated farm families were suddenly a part of the community, and Americans who previously had seen little of their own states now might see quite a lot of their country. Fewer each year would display the utter provincialism of that storied Boston lady—a holdout—who, having driven all the way out to California, said she had got there "by way of Dedham"—a suburb of Boston.

The driver of the Great Western appears to be getting at least a horse chuckle as his car sits smoking by a Vermont bridge.

The photograph was taken in 1910. This particular make of car, built from 1908 to 1916, was one of many with short histories.

The hazards facing early motorists were manifold. Roads, for instance, were usually unpaved, unbridged, and uneven. One Ohio route, a driver noted in 1907, "was full of great holes, the depth of which could not be ascertained until the car plunged right into them." Urbanites quickly discovered a problem that has not yet been solved: at right, New York's Fifth Avenue in 1905.

The motorcars purchased in such salons as Smith and Mabley's in New York (left, 1905) were not, at first, often driven by ladies. True, the distaff side helped make electric autos quite popular for a while, and the first American woman licensed to drive won that right in 1899. But until the electric starter removed the crank and much of the danger from driving gas buggies, ladies usually rode as passengers, dressed as above to shield themselves from dust and weather. But when they began taking the wheel in numbers, both skirts and hair styles were shortened.

Exhaust smoke drifts up the track just before the start of the first auto race ever held at the Indianapolis Speedway, in 1909.

Racing was crucial to the young motorcar industry, for it provided both a demanding test of new ideas and valuable publicity.

*Autos could go almost anywhere, given decent traction. At left, a Cadillac is
driven up the steps of a county government building in Michigan in 1902.
Like racing, such stunts sold cars. And so did acceptance by the aristocracy;
above, an embowered electric car races genteelly at a Newport fete in 1899.*

America Enters the Twentieth Century

*A*s Roosevelt took office for the second time, the conviction was growing in him of something he had long suspected, that the rich and powerful in the land were often too stupid and shortsighted for their own and for the country's good. Already he had changed much, and he meant to change much more. He gave himself a term in which to do it. Washington's precedent of two full terms in office was a tradition that no one would dare challenge for another thirty-five years. But there still remained the question of whether a Vice President succeeding to the Presidency should count his initial partial term as a full term. Roosevelt, approaching his first elective term, intended to settle this question for himself and for the future by his public pronouncement:

On the fourth of March next I shall have served three and a half years, and this . . . constitutes my first term. The wise custom which limits the President to two terms regards the substance and not the form. Under no circumstances will I be a candidate for or accept another nomination.

Later he would tell a friend, as he pointed to his wrist: "I would cut my hand off right there if I could recall that written statement!"

Roosevelt's new term would make him not only the most dynamically popular President since Andrew Jackson but the most conspicuous public figure in the world. His popularity would survive a panic and a depression. In 1905, at the beginning of his second term, there was even talk in the South of nominating him in 1908 to run on the Democratic ticket when he became free again. At that time there was earnest discussion of a new party made up of Roosevelt Republicans and Bryan Democrats. Roosevelt would never lose his distaste for the man he described as "a kindly, well-meaning soul, but . . . cheap and shallow," but in the end he would find himself adopting most of the Bryan program in regard to trusts, railroad regulation, pure food laws, and so on, and he would be forced to turn to the insurgent Republicans and the Democrats for needed support. The paradox of Roosevelt was that, at heart a traditionalist and conservative, he was led to more radical ground by the Republican reactionaries, who would have sunk the party in the bog of their intransigence.

The end to American innocence began in a spirit both naïve and bouncy—"It's a grand old flag, it's a high-flying flag." Childe Hassam's painting is of a city street in the rain on Flag Day, 1917.

359

Among the newcomers to the Senate in 1905 was the former governor of Wisconsin Robert M. La Follette, who while governor had been the leader in reviving the old Populist agitation for regulation and control of the railroads. Farmers and small shippers were again up in arms against the railroads' brazen system of rate discrimination, for which the Interstate Commerce Act of 1887 had proved an ineffective remedy. Scarcely more effective had been the Elkins Act of 1903 forbidding rebates. Roosevelt, beginning his second term, saw railroad regulation as his first major legislative objective, one for which he was willing to sacrifice a hoped-for tariff revision.

With general sentiment so against the railroads, even the politicians were viewing them with less benevolence. Introduced January 4, 1906, the Roosevelt-sponsored Hepburn Bill easily passed the House of Representatives. But in the Senate the Republican floor leader and member of the Interstate Commerce Committee, the archconservative Nelson W. Aldrich of Rhode Island,

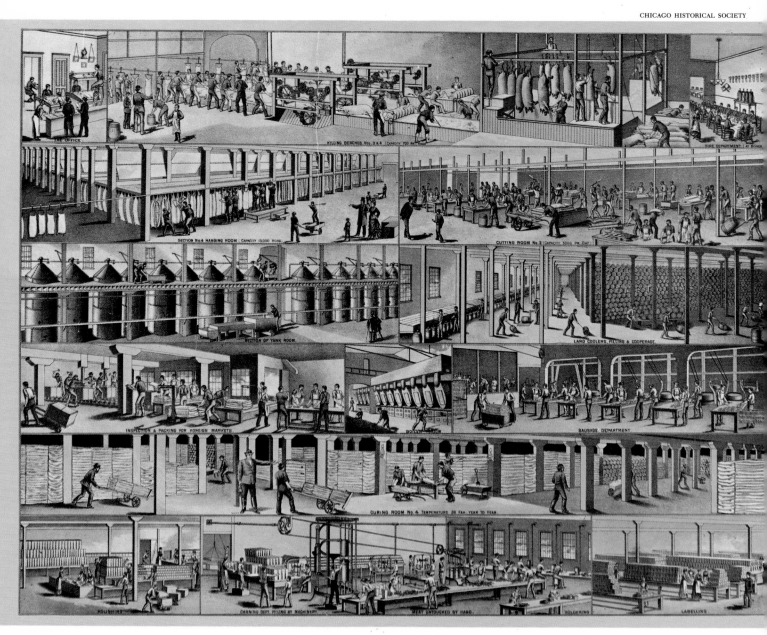

The Interior View of a Modern First Class Pork Packing & Canning Establishment of the United States of America *in about 1880 presented an image of cleanliness that was quite out of keeping with the actual conditions in the meat industry.*

effectively blocked it. The little support that Roosevelt could obtain for the measure came from the outnumbered Democrats and the few dissident Republicans grouped around La Follette. Aldrich sardonically disavowed the administration measure, turning its sponsorship over to the ranking Democratic committee member, none other than rabble-rousing, Roosevelt-hating Pitchfork Ben Tillman.

Roosevelt, who could be a ruthless politician in support of his own ends, made private overtures to Tillman. But when Tillman and La Follette demanded a more radical bill than Roosevelt felt would be acceptable to the moderate Republicans, the President abandoned his temporary allies, then succeeded in creating a climate of opinion so favorable to himself and the bill that the Senate passed the Hepburn Bill overwhelmingly. It was a great personal victory for the President, a demonstration that despite leaders like Aldrich he could transform the Republican party into an instrument of reform.

The new act strengthened the Interstate Commerce Commission greatly, giving it power to enforce its rulings on interstate freight and passenger rates and other aspects of transportation between states. What Tillman and La Follette had demanded, and what the commission did not get, was the power to appraise the property of the railroads as a basis for determining rates. Tillman was forced to admit that if Roosevelt had not brought the matter of railroad rates to the public's attention so insistently, there would not have been any bill at all.

"The heart of Roosevelt's method was to inspire headlines," was newspaperman Mark Sullivan's explanation for the ubiquitous sense of the President's presence in the land. Whenever Roosevelt embraced an issue, the effect was like a clap of thunder. Sometimes in his enthusiasm he went off on tangents. He was absurd at times, as in his tub thumping for simplified spelling, trivial, as in his open quarrel with his ambassador to Austria-Hungary and the latter's wife over the suggested appointment of an American cardinal, ridiculous, as in his attack on Jack London and other lesser animal writers as "nature fakers." But in the larger issues Roosevelt was on target, usually with a bull's eye.

Samuel S. McClure with his magazine was the real trail blazer for much of Roosevelt reform, for it was in the pages of *McClure's Magazine* that the exposés of the greedy and immoral practices of business and government first appeared. Ida M. Tarbell's carefully documented story of the Standard Oil Company appeared in *McClure's* in 1902, followed by Lincoln Steffens' series on municipal corruption — beginning with "Tweed Days in St. Louis" — Ray Stannard Baker's "The Railroad on Trial," and similar articles on patent medicines and adulterated foods. These articles were being imitated by other writers in other magazines with a zeal and at times an exaggeration that would finally, in an angry speech, bring forth Roosevelt's intemperate but apt term "muckraker."

Long before Roosevelt had turned his mind to such things, a group of reformers headed by the chief chemist of the Department of Agriculture, Dr. Harvey Wiley, had been trying to mobilize support for a federal law to prevent the adulteration and misbranding of food, drinks, and drugs. Roosevelt had briefly recommended a pure food and drug bill in his annual message of December, 1905, but was too engrossed with his railroad legislation to concern himself further with it. Then a pure food bill, sponsored by Senator Weldon Heyburn of Idaho and Senator Porter J. McCumber of North Dakota and long bottled up in committee, finally passed the Senate but would have died in the House if it had not been for the publication in February, 1906, of Upton Sinclair's exposure of the meat-packing industry, *The Jungle*. What Sinclair had intended was a socialist novel. What he achieved, in a few incidental pages about the festering filth of the Chicago stockyards, was a national nausea. Mr. Dooley, after reading Sinclair's book, announced that he had been unable "to ate annything more nourishin' thin a cucumber in a week," and he advised: "If ye want to rayjooce ye'er butcher's bills buy 'The Jungle.'"

Roosevelt was so aroused by Sinclair's book that he not only wrote the author but appointed Commissioner of Labor Charles P. Neill and a veteran social worker, James B. Reynolds, to investigate stockyard conditions. The Neill-Reynolds report more than confirmed every allegation in Sinclair's novel. Roosevelt at first was willing to suppress the facts if the packers would agree to government inspection of every process in their plants. When they refused, on what they considered constitutional grounds, and lobbied against a meat inspection rider to an agricultural appropriations bill, he released the first part of the report. The result was as notable as the initial effect of *The Jungle*. Demands for meat products dropped in some cases to less than half; overseas orders faded away. The packers now demanded the government inspection they had claimed unconstitu-

Early in the morning of April 18, 1906, San Franciscans awoke to the shudder of an earthquake. Fires started and in three days burned four square miles of the city. Above, in a photograph by Arnold Genthe, the view down Sacramento Street.

tional as the only means of marketing their products. With slight alterations the meat inspection amendment was hurried through Congress, carrying Heyburn's pure food bill in its wake.

Roosevelt saw himself as walking a progressive middle way between the reactionary Aldrich and his industrialist supporters on one hand and the antibusiness bias of the Bryans and La Follettes on the other. His speech attacking the muckrakers was an attempt to define that middle way, for in it he had made a sharp distinction between fortunes "gained as an incident to performing great services to the community . . . and

those gained in evil fashion by keeping just within the limits of mere law-honesty." And he had added that "no amount of charity in spending [ill-won] fortunes in any way compensates for misconduct in making them." He also found himself coming to the conclusion that huge fortunes, no matter how acquired, should not be passed on intact. From his muckraker speech to the end of his second term, he would repeatedly ask Congress for a steeply graduated inheritance tax, not for the sake of revenue but as a matter of social justice.

For all his quickening conscience as a domestic reformer, Roosevelt was to be remembered more in his second term for his handling of foreign affairs. He took up with easy confidence the role of international statesman. The President of 1905 had much matured from the jingo of 1898, the 1900 denouncer of the Clayton-Bulwer Treaty, the expansionist indifferent to Latin-American sensibilities. He had come to the realization that his

country was irrevocably a world power, that the affairs of Europe and Asia were interrelated and that both were of concern to the United States. In his first months in the White House he had been pleased to watch the Russians expand in the Far East, but the Russian government's flouting of the American Open Door doctrine by refusing to withdraw its troops from Manchuria soon gave him sobering second thoughts. Thereafter he began to look with more benevolence on Japan, a land whose virtues of military discipline and industrial energy he found increasingly attractive as he soured on Russia.

By the time Roosevelt took office for his second term the Russians and the Japanese had been at war for more than a year. After defeating China in 1895, Japan had established Korea as a nominally independent state within the Japanese sphere of influence. But the Russians, solidly occupying Manchuria, showed increasing signs of being ready to push into Korea. To conciliate the colossus of the north the Japanese were willing to give Russia a free hand in Manchuria in exchange for their own freedom of action in Korea. Such a reciprocal arrangement was not to the taste of the Russian expansionists. Faced with a rejection of what it considered most reasonable terms, the Japanese government "gave a last and earnest warning," then in February, 1904, launched a full-scale surprise attack. For all its bluster and size, the Russian giant soon proved pitifully vulnerable. Admiral Togo easily demolished the Russian Pacific Ocean squadron. By the spring of 1905 the Japanese, having been brilliantly successful on land as well as sea, were in firm control of Korea and much of Manchuria. But the Russians still refused to consider any concessions, and Czar Nicholas in a last desperate gamble ordered his European fleet to the Far East to attack Togo. The gamble failed wretchedly, and the Japanese admiral virtually annihilated the last Russian fleet.

363

With their navy triumphant and their armies victorious but overextended, the Japanese were eager now for peace and asked Roosevelt as a friendly neutral to mediate. Demoralized by their defeats, the Russians were at last willing to accept Roosevelt's good offices and to consider Japanese proposals. All during the summer of 1905 Roosevelt with deftness, discretion, and unwonted tact maneuvered to bring the two powers to the conference table. Finally in August, Russian representatives, led by the towering Count Sergei Witte, met the diminutive Japanese envoys, Ambassador Kogoro Takahira and Baron Jutaro Komura, aboard the presidential yacht *Mayflower*, anchored in Oyster Bay. Prickly matters of precedence at once arose, touching national pride. Who should sit on the President's right? Should the first formal toast be to the Czar or to the Mikado? Roosevelt found the solution by serving his guests a buffet luncheon. When everyone was served, he raised his wine glass. "Gentlemen," he said, "I propose a toast to which there will be no answer and which I ask you to drink in silence, standing." He then drank "to the welfare and prosperity of the sovereigns and peoples of the two great nations, whose representatives have met one another on this ship. It is," he concluded, "my most earnest hope and prayer, in the interest . . . of all mankind that a just and lasting peace may speedily be concluded among them." The atmosphere so warmed that on leaving, the Japanese and Russian envoys shook hands cordially with one another.

Roosevelt staked his reputation on the negotiations that followed at Portsmouth, New Hampshire, seeing as his goal the preservation of the balance of power between the two countries. Japan demanded a cash indemnity plus Sakhalin Island; the Russians refused to grant either. And so the days passed with the negotiations at a standstill. Finally, after Roosevelt had privately appealed to the Mikado, the Japanese reluctantly yielded on indemnity and indicated they would settle for half the island. The peace terms were a triumph for the American President. The United States ambassador to Russia felt that the lives of a quarter of a million soldiers had been saved. Congratulations came from all over the world. "This," said the aged Pope Pius X, "is the happiest moment of my life."

Even before the Treaty of Portsmouth was signed, another crisis had developed in Morocco over the Open Door, one of those that would lead to the final crisis of 1914. France, backed by England—in return for French acquiescence in the British domination of Egypt—claimed control over Morocco. The saber-rattling Kaiser demanded equal rights in Morocco and threatened war if this was denied his country. Again the American President was considered by both sides as sufficiently impartial to act as a mediator. After a peace conference that opened in Algeciras, Spain, in January, 1906, came to a stop in deadlock, Roosevelt took over, and by skillfully playing on the Kaiser's vanity, was able to gain German acceptance of a compromise that had already been accepted by the French. For his successful efforts at preserving the peace of the world the American President received the Nobel Peace Prize of 1906, but isolationists in the United States resented the web of entangling alliances that they saw him preoccupied in weaving.

Whenever Roosevelt felt American interests were more directly concerned, he could still show his old belligerence. Chinese nationalists, responding to America's renewal of the Chinese exclusion act of 1883, replied in July, 1905, first with a boycott of American goods and later with street demonstrations, in which an American admiral was mobbed and Alice Roosevelt—on a Far Eastern tour—insulted. In irate reply the President in early 1906 sent the battleship *Oregon* to the China coast and threatened to follow it with an expeditionary force. The weak and harassed emperor was forced to issue an edict condemning expressions of antiforeign sentiments. Only half a year after Roosevelt had dealt so arbitrarily overseas with the Chinese, he was faced at home with the problem of anti-Japanese agitation on the Pacific Coast. Such agitation, much promoted by the labor unions in their hostility toward Japanese laborers, caused the San Francisco Board of Education to segregate the ninety-three Japanese, Korean, and Chinese pupils in its public schools. The Japanese people were outraged. Uneasy about what an unfriendly Japan might signify for the Philippines and Hawaii, the President sought to placate Japanese opinion by sending his infectiously good-natured Secretary of War, William Howard Taft, on a tour of Japan to reassure Japanese leaders and at the same time to appeal to ordinary people by his genial overweight presence. Taft was very popular in Japan, where he was already well-known from a previous visit. This time he was, as he wrote home, "feted all over the place." In private talks with high officials he managed to reach a Gentleman's Agreement, by which both countries agreed to restrict emigration to approved types, which practically speaking meant an end to the emigration of Japanese laborers to California.

Roosevelt intended to convey another message—and one of a different kind—to Japan in 1907 when he ordered the American battle fleet on a round-the-world cruise to demonstrate the new formidability of American naval might. Foreign observers thought that the cruise might incite Japan to hostile action and that Admiral Togo might strike from ambush, destroying the rash Americans as he had the Russians. Many American naval officers believed that war was possible, and feeling in the United States Navy ran high against the Japanese.

The Great White Fleet of sixteen gleaming battleships with glittering gilt bows raised anchor at Hampton Roads on December 16 under the command of Rear Admiral "Fighting Bob" Evans. Down the coast of South America it sailed, through the Strait of Magellan, up the coast to California, and then across the Pacific. Roosevelt in his *Autobiography* considered the eye-catching, if minatory, fourteen-month cruise "the most important service that I rendered to peace," although its less obvious effect may well have been to spur the Japanese to greater efforts in building up their navy. But the reception given the American fleet from Rio de Janeiro and Callao, Peru, to Honolulu, Sydney, and Yokohama was one prolonged and exuberant festival. South American countries vied with each other in hospitality, ready to take offense if the fleet did not call at each of their chief ports. Far from showing enmity, the Japanese treated the fleet's arrival as an extended holiday, with parties, banquets, balls, and parades. A Yokohama daily published a "Fleet Banzai Number." The Chinese government took umbrage when only half the American battleships visited its shores. It explained to its people that the rest of the ships had been lost in a typhoon. President Roosevelt had only thirteen days left in office when the Great White Fleet, a little grimy but still tolerably white, arrived home.

The last half of Roosevelt's term had been shadowed by a business depression culminating in the financial panic of October, 1907. In March the depression was heralded by an abrupt drop in the stock market, followed by a slowing down of industry. Many business leaders turned against Roosevelt as "our chief panic-maker." Roosevelt, challenging his critics, explained the depression as mainly "due to matters not particularly confined to the United States and to matters wholly un-

T. R. took with a grain of salt the praise he won by the Russo-Japanese peace. He saw it as just one step that enhanced America's status; his next, he knew, might not be as popular.

connected with any government action." He laid most of the blame on the "ruthless and determined men" who were trying to discredit him and reverse his forward policies, "malefactors of great wealth," whom he would deal with in good time.

The October Panic, though impelled by the depression, was a currency panic brought about by rash speculation, overdrawn credit, and the lack of any national banking system. Across the country there were runs on banks. The most spectacular was the one that helped bring on the failure of New York's Knickerbocker Trust Company. There thousands of fearful depositors clogged the street in front of the marble-columned façade to withdraw their savings. That the Panic lasted only a few weeks was due chiefly to J. Pierpont Morgan, who, though ailing and in semiretirement, came to New York from Richmond to take measures to confront the crisis. Financial leaders, as well as Secretary of the Treasury

George Courtelyou, deferred to his judgment, and for once Roosevelt—who admitted he was no expert in financial affairs—was willing to let another man assume command, even a man of whom he basically disapproved. During those crisis weeks Morgan became the virtual financial dictator of the United States, and though his decisions—as they always did—reflected self-interest, he, with his enormous resources, experience, and confidence, accomplished what no one else in the country could then have done. Yet, though Morgan succeeded in stemming the Panic, the depression itself dragged on into the 1908 presidential election year.

Roosevelt in his love of the outdoors had instinctively been a conservationist even before the term came into general use. Presidents before him had given only occasional thought to the preservation of the national heritage of water and wilderness. Typical of the politicians' attitude was that of crusty Joseph G. "Uncle Joe" Cannon, who, when chairman of the House Appropriations Committee, proclaimed that there should be "not one cent for scenery."

Conservation did not become a central issue for Roosevelt until his second term. His interest in it arose from his friendship with Gifford Pinchot, the farseeing

The Great White Fleet, greeted by boatloads of sightseers, here steams through the Golden Gate. Roosevelt sent the ships off without enough money in the Navy's budget to bring them home, forcing Congress to raise the money or strand the fleet.

chief forester of the Department of Agriculture's Forest Service, an office to which Pinchot had been named in 1898. Pinchot, with his brother, founded Yale's Pinchot School of Forestry in 1900. He often tried to impress his conservation views on his friend. When Roosevelt was in the White House, Pinchot became a member of the intimate group the President called his Tennis Cabinet. From 1905, constantly advised by Pinchot, Roosevelt moved aggressively toward conservation of natural resources, and before he left the Presidency, he had created national parks at Crater Lake in Oregon, in Murray County in Oklahoma, at Wind Cave in South Dakota, at Sully Hill in North Dakota, and at Mesa Verde in Colorado—as many as all his predecessors together had established. He had also proclaimed sixteen national monuments under the National Monuments Act of 1906 and established fifty-one wildlife refuges. He had fought to preserve the scenic integrity of Niagara Falls, the Grand Canyon, Crater Lake, the Petrified Forest, the Blue Ridge Mountains, and dozens of other spectacular areas that he considered the people's heritage.

Early in his first administration he had backed the Democratic-sponsored Newlands bill, a reclamation measure that created thirty irrigation projects affecting three million arid acres. When anticonservationists attached a rider to an agricultural appropriations bill specifying that no forest reserve should thereafter be set aside within the six states of Oregon, Washington, Idaho, Montana, Colorado, and Wyoming, Roosevelt, before signing the bill, hastily proclaimed twenty-one new forest reserves comprising some sixteen million acres in the six states. Later he wrote gleefully that "the opponents of the forest service turned handsprings in their wrath. . . ." In June, 1908, he established the Federal Commission on the Conservation of Natural Resources, headed by Pinchot, and a month earlier he had called a governors' conference to impress the Roosevelt-Pinchot conservation program and philosophy on state governments.

Roosevelt believed he could do anything not specifically forbidden by the Constitution. "I don't think that any harm comes from the concentration of power in one man's hands," he remarked, "provided the holder does not keep it for more than a certain, definite time, and then returns to the people from whom he sprang." But much of what Roosevelt would have done for what he saw as the common welfare was thwarted by the old-guard Republicans; in much he was forced to compromise with a Congress whose vision lagged far behind his. "Sir," Uncle Joe Cannon had once replied to a progressive questioner, "the function of the Federal government is to afford protection to life, liberty, and property. When that is done, then let every tub stand on its own bottom, let every citizen 'root hog or die'!"

Although forty-three antitrust proceedings were initiated in his terms, Roosevelt shifted in his attitude to the corporations as he came to feel that the age was unavoidably one of combinations and that regulation rather than dissolution would prove the ultimate solution to abuses by big business. But he also felt that big unionism was the necessary counterbalance to big business. He was the first President to make the White House accessible to labor leaders, the first to support the eight-hour day and workmen's compensation measures.

By his own hasty words disavowing a third term, Roosevelt had ruled himself out as a candidate in 1908, but he could at least hand-pick his successor, someone who would continue the task of transforming the Republican party from that of Foraker and Aldrich and Uncle Joe Cannon into the party of his own vigorous hopes and beliefs. His first choice would have been his Secretary of State after Hay's death, Elihu Root. Root was a lawyer with a precise mathematical mind who as McKinley's Secretary of War had shaken up the ossified War Department, then—still as Secretary of War—made his mark by his fair dealings with the Philippines, Puerto Rico, and Cuba. Roosevelt remarked that if he had the powers of a dictator he would make Root President and Taft Chief Justice. But Root, as one of the most sought-after corporation lawyers in the country was not a politically feasible candidate. Taft remained, the loyal, trusted, and subordinate friend who, Roosevelt convinced himself, would make an equally loyal, trusted, and subordinate President to continue the Rooseveltian policies.

The power and the glory of the Presidency held little appeal for the portly Secretary of War, who had always coveted the position of Chief Justice of the United States. "It is the comfort and dignity and power without worry that I like," Chief Justice Taft would later admit after he had attained his goal. Of a respected Cincinnati family, a graduate of Yale and of Cincinnati Law School, Taft at the age of twenty-nine had been appointed to the Ohio superior court by Governor Foraker for devious political reasons. Three years later President Harrison made him solicitor general, and in 1892 he received an appointment as a federal judge. On the bench he established a high reputation among lawyers. In 1899 he was even considered for president of Yale. He stepped into the national picture when he reluctantly resigned his judgeship to become McKinley's first civil governor of the Philippines. So earnestly did he take his responsibilities that he refused his cherished appointment to the Supreme Court when Roosevelt twice offered him a place in 1902. The President was able to persuade him to become Secretary of War only because Taft felt that in that post he could still exercise his moral obligation to oversee Philippine affairs. In 1906 Roosevelt for the third time offered to appoint him to a vacancy on the Supreme Court, with a promise to make him Chief Justice if the opportunity arose. Taft hesitated for three months, but was finally persuaded to decline by his ambitious wife and his half brother, both of whom were far more eager to see him in the White House than in the robes of a Supreme Court justice.

When Roosevelt had finally determined on Taft as his successor, he proceeded to use all his political skills and influence, all the powers of patronage, all the weight of the federal machine, for the paradoxical purpose of defeating himself. What he feared at the convention was a stampede in his favor, and he instructed Senator Lodge, the permanent chairman, to be sure that it did not happen. But it almost did happen. When Lodge in his opening speech to the convention referred to Roosevelt as "the best abused and the most popular man in the United States," delegates jumped to their feet shouting and cheering while hats and handkerchiefs waved in the balconies, and from the floor there came the steady chant of "Four four four years more!" Forty-nine minutes the demonstration lasted, and but for Lodge's firm checkrein the convention would have bolted for Roosevelt. The Taft demonstration, when his name was presented, lasted only half an hour despite all the efforts to make it as impressive as possible. Nevertheless Taft was overwhelmingly nominated on the first ballot with an enthusiasm that seemed almost genuine.

The Democrats, having fared so badly with the conservative Alton B. Parker four years before, turned again to their perennial candidate, William Jennings Bryan. To prove that they could outdemonstrate the Republicans, the Democrats cheered and shouted for eighty-seven minutes following Bryan's nomination. But this year Roosevelt had pre-empted most of the old Bryan stand-bys by his own espousal of inheritance and income taxes and corporation control; and the Democratic demands for repudiation of the Gentleman's Agreement with Japan and for immediate Philippine independence were hardly issues to stir the voters. Taft in his acceptance speech, on which Roosevelt had collaborated, declared: "Mr. Roosevelt led the way to practical reform. My chief function shall be to complete and perfect...."

The Republican candidate spent a wretched four months campaigning while Roosevelt continued to guide, prod, and encourage him. Fatigued, disgruntled by ridicule, troubled by Fundamentalist attacks on his Unitarianism, Taft would have much preferred to stay home in summer somnolence. "Poor old boy!" Roosevelt wrote him from Oyster Bay in mid-July. "Of course you are not enjoying the campaign. I wish you had some of my bad temper. It is at times a real aid to enjoyment."

For all Taft's halfhearted campaigning, his election was assured. But although he received 321 electoral votes to Bryan's 162, his popular majority was only half what Roosevelt's had been four years before, and there were ominous undercurrents of unrest in the West, where a number of Democratic governors had been elected. Eugene Debs, running for the third time as a Socialist, received 420,000 votes, about the same number he had received four years before. Tom Watson, the candidate of the die-hard Populists, received a mere 29,000, a quarter of his total in 1904.

On the last day of 1908 Roosevelt scribbled a note to his successor: "Ha! Ha! *You* are making up your Cabinet. *I* in a light-hearted way have spent the morning testing rifles for my African trip. Life has compensations!" The African hunting trip, he wrote a friend, "is my last chance for . . . a 'great adventure,'" unless another war should break out. He hoped there would be no war, but if it should come, he would "certainly try to raise a brigade, and if possible a division, of cavalry . . . such as . . . my regiment ten years ago."

There is no one point at which one can say that the rift between Roosevelt and Taft began. Roosevelt invited the President-elect to spend the night before his inauguration in the White House, and Taft, accepting, replied: "People have attempted to represent that you and I were in some way at odds during this last three months, whereas you and I know that there has not been the slightest difference between us. . . ." Yet the differences were there, subtle, indicated whisperingly in Taft's reshuffle of Roosevelt's Cabinet or in an off-

The good-humored Taft was universally loved and admired in every office but the Presidency—which he hadn't wanted much anyway and in which he had to succeed the pyrotechnic Roosevelt. Above is a cartoon drawn when he was Secretary of War.

"Never," the New York *Sun* recorded of Taft's inauguration, "did any man come into the Presidency before with such universal good will." The good will would be brief. Thrust upward by the ambitions of his wife and his brother Charles, the good-natured Taft at first found it difficult to realize his own elevation, and to his wife's annoyance, still referred to Roosevelt as President.

Taft's accomplishments in office were solid—some felt they were as solid as Roosevelt's—but he left the White House the most abused and discredited President since Andrew Johnson. During Taft's administration his Attorney General brought many more suits against violations of the Sherman Antitrust Act than had been filed during Roosevelt's more colorful period of trust busting. Taft's Commission on Efficiency and Economy became the precursor of Harding's Bureau of the Budget, and his reforms in administrative spending saved the government millions. The Publicity Act, which he sponsored, made public the lists of contributors to congressional election campaigns. By Executive Order he placed eight thousand assistant postmasters under civil service. He proposed a constitutional amendment to legalize a general income tax, and this, ratified by the states, became in February, 1913, the Sixteenth Amendment to the Constitution. Three months later the Sixteenth Amendment was followed by the ratification of the Seventeenth—repeatedly rejected by the Senate—providing for the direct election of United States senators. Congress during Taft's administration also passed a parcel post act, established the Federal Children's Bureau to deal with the problems of child labor, provided for an eight-hour day on government projects, and established postal savings for depositors wary of savings banks.

Taft's record in foreign affairs was less impressive. When he used the phrase "substituting dollars for bullets" to describe his efforts to bring a stable prosperity to South American countries through infusions of private American capital, his concept became popularly known as Dollar Diplomacy. Dollar Diplomacy's principal effect was to shore up corrupt governments and to breed lasting resentments through such direct United States interventions as the sending of troops to Nicaragua in 1912. Taft's announcement that the Panama Canal when finished would be open to free passage by American ships aroused anger in Europe since under the Hay-Pauncefote Treaty all nations were to be charged the same tolls. His attempts to work out a reciprocal tariff re-

hand remark of Nellie Taft's. Mark Sullivan, dropping in at the White House to see Roosevelt the afternoon before the Taft inauguration, asked him in confidence how he really thought the new President would make out. "He's all right," Roosevelt told him, "he means well and he'll do his best. But he's weak. They'll get around him."

Inauguration Day was ushered in by a snowstorm and biting cold. So bitter was the weather that for the first time since 1833 the actual oath taking was held in the Senate Chamber. As ex-President Roosevelt left the Capitol, he remarked, "I knew there would be a blizzard when I went out."

369

Vaudeville, having been cleaned up for the family trade, was in its heyday. "Real two-a-day vaude-ville," said one observer, "was a personalized business. . . . No microphones got in the way." Above, in a water color by Charles Demuth, two singers render the sentimental "Many Brave Hearts Are Asleep in the Deep." At right, William J. Glackens' painting Hammerstein's Roof Garden.

duction agreement with Canada, though passed by Congress, foundered following his own inept remark about Canada's parting of the ways with the mother country and the vociferation of the Democratic House leader, Champ Clark, that he hoped to see the Stars and Stripes "float over every square foot of the British North American possessions clear to the North Pole."

One of Taft's most cherished hopes on coming to the Presidency was to make some decisive move for the cause of world peace; one of his greatest disappointments was that he failed. He opened negotiations with England and France to expand existing arbitration treaties so that the three nations would submit "all questions determinable by the principles of law and equity" to the international court at The Hague even

when these concerned matters of "vital interest and national honor." Both the French and British governments agreed to such treaties, but when these were submitted to the United States Senate, they were so mutilated by amendments that Taft refused to sign them.

To a public that had delighted in Roosevelt's inexhaustible energy, his portly successor, who took naps in the afternoon and occasionally dozed off in public, was an anticlimax. Mark Sullivan aptly described him as "a placid man in a restless time." With his advent to office, the fissures in the Republican party grew more and more apparent.

Populism, dead in name, was finding new substance in the insurgent Republicans of the rural West, who continued the old Populist and Granger resentments against

That he was "making the dirt fly" on the Panama Canal route was Roosevelt's boast, but he had help—from Army doctors who combated yellow fever and from the engineer George W. Goethals. Above, Jonas Lie's oil of troublesome Culebra Cut.

the moneyed East, the trusts, the industrialists with their tariff wall, the old guard leadership of Aldrich and Cannon. In 1908 the insurgents—all from the predominantly Republican states of the West and grouped around Wisconsin's La Follette—made up about a dozen of the 92 senators. In the House, out of 386 congressmen, there were about 30 insurgents.

Taft and the insurgents quickly came to a parting of the ways after Taft, in accordance with the 1908 party platform, had called a special session of Congress in the spring of 1909 to consider the tariff. The last tariff measure, the Dingley bill of 1897, had revised the tariff upward. Since then the cost of living had risen, and most people expected that the revision promised in the Republican platform would be a lowering of rates. But when a bill introduced into the House by Sereno E. Payne, chairman of the Ways and Means Committee, reached the Senate, Aldrich eliminated most gestures toward tariff reduction and removed altogether a provision for an inheritance tax. Insurgent Republican senators joined the Democrats in a bitter fight against the ensuing Payne-Aldrich bill. The highhanded Aldrich was able to hold the old guard senators firm and force his bill through without any concessions to the Westerners, but he was unable to ward off the mounting public resentment outside the Capitol. Through all the acrimonious summer Taft remained silent, but when the bill finally passed, he signed it willingly. When six weeks later the President in a speech at Winona, Minnesota, described the tariff bill as the best that "the Republican party has ever passed, and therefore the best that has been passed at all," he threw the Western states into a sustained uproar. Taft's break with the progressive wing of his party was now final.

Whatever President Taft did or said seemed to have awkward repercussions. He was troubled by his unpopularity and troubled as well by his wife's health—for Nellie had suffered a stroke from which she would never wholly recover. Insurgency was in the air. In March, 1910, thirty insurgent Republican congressmen combined with their Democratic colleagues to reduce the power of the despot of the House of Representatives, Speaker Uncle Joe Cannon, who by his absolute control of committee membership had been for so long a virtual dictator. The insurgent-Democratic combination also drastically revised, much to the President's anger, a railroad bill written by Taft's Attorney General. By the end of 1909 one could sense Taft's popularity dropping like quicksilver in a barometer before a storm.

Theodore Roosevelt was now a private citizen, although nothing that he would ever do again could be private. On March 23, 1909, accompanied by his twenty-year-old son, Kermit, he sailed from Hoboken on his long-anticipated African safari, carrying with him in his vast luggage three rifles, nine pairs of glasses, and a gold-mounted rabbit's foot, which John L. Sullivan had given him. *Scribner's* had agreed to pay him fifty thousand dollars for an account of his year in Africa.

The Rough Rider in Africa was almost as much news as he had been in Cuba. In the adolescent fiction that this was a scientific expedition, he and Kermit shot three thousand animals in the course of their year. Stuffed, their carcasses would oversupply the National Museum; their mounted heads would grace the Harvard Union and the living room of Sagamore Hill.

Returning by way of Europe, he became the vogue of royalty, visiting the kings of Italy, Norway, and Belgium, Queen Wilhelmina of the Netherlands, and the crown princes of Sweden and Denmark. Aged Emperor Franz Joseph of Austria-Hungary tendered him a banquet; in Rome he got into a first-rate row with the Pope over papal conditions for an audience; while being made a Freeman of the City of London, he took the occasion to advise the British on their Egyptian policy; and he was his country's representative at Edward VII's state funeral. ". . . you are the only private citizen who has ever joined the Emperor in reviewing the troops of Germany," Kaiser Wilhelm told him as the two, on horseback, watched the Guards regiments goose-step past. Later, the Kaiser sent him photographs of the occasion, one of them inscribed: "When we shake hands we shake the world."

Just before Roosevelt sailed home from Southampton on June 10, he received a letter from Taft. "It is now a year and three months since I assumed office," the President wrote, "and I have had a hard time—I do not know that I have had harder luck than other Presidents, but I do know that thus far I have succeeded far less than have others." The former President, on arriving in New York, was welcomed like a returning hero. A naval parade steamed down the harbor to meet his ship. The mayor greeted him at the dock. And to shouts and cheers, the echo of foghorns and the shrill of whistles, the Rough Rider found himself home again.

Roosevelt soon announced that as country squire and contributing editor of *The Outlook* he wanted "to close up like a native oyster." Yet within two weeks of his return he was conferring with Pinchot and with Robert La Follette, who declared that Colonel Roosevelt was not only the greatest living American but that he was in fighting trim. On the last day of June the former President called on the President at his summer home in Beverly, Massachusetts, but the two men were obviously ill at ease and did not see each other alone.

In August Roosevelt left Oyster Bay in a special car provided by *The Outlook*, ostensibly to attend the Frontier Day Celebration at Cheyenne, Wyoming, but actually to make a speaking tour that would take him five thousand miles through sixteen states. Throughout the West he was acclaimed by a crowd of sunburned, plain people at every whistle stop. At Osawatomie, Kansas, he made one of the most meaningful addresses of his career, foreshadowing the whole Progressive movement as he proclaimed a New Nationalism and used his enduring phrase "the square deal" to describe his program. The square deal he defined as not only fair play under the present rules but "having those rules changed so as to work for a more substantial equality of opportunity and reward." He called for control of the political activities of corporations, an expert commission to draw up a tariff, graduated income and inheritance taxes, stringent conservation measures, workmen's compensation laws, and federal regulation of the labor of women and children. "The New Nationalism," he told the Kansans, "puts the national need before sectional or personal advantage."

In his speechmaking he scarcely mentioned Taft. Taft, much offended, wrote to his half brother: "[Roosevelt] allows himself to fall into a style that makes one think he considers himself still the President of the United States. In most of these speeches he has utterly ignored me. . . . He is at the head of the Insurgents, and for the time being the Insurgents are at the top of the wave. . . ."

Though Roosevelt was to make several more speaking tours for his disunited party, he knew that with Taft in the White House, the Republicans were due for a defeat. The voting public was in an insurgent mood, not so much *for* the Democrats as *against* the Republicans, and the mid-term election results were even more one-sided than predicted. In the old House of Representatives the Republicans had had 219 seats to the Democrats' 172. In the new House elected in 1910 the Democrats outnumbered the Republicans 228 to 161. Taft's and

Roosevelt's states, Ohio and New York, with twenty-four others, acquired Democratic governors, while in New Jersey the Democrats elected as the reform governor Woodrow Wilson, the president of Princeton University.

For a year, until November 17, 1911, Roosevelt remained in semiretreat at Sagamore Hill. Three times during that period he met briefly with Taft in an atmosphere of strained cordiality. When there was a threat of war with Mexico early in 1911, the old Rough Rider asked for and received Taft's permission to raise and command a cavalry division in case of hostilities. Yet privately Taft remarked to friends that if they were to remove Roosevelt's skull, they would find "1912" written in his brain.

Roosevelt's break with Taft came in October, 1911, as a belated aftermath of the Panic of 1907. During 1907 the tottering brokerage firm of Moore and Schley had held a large block of Tennessee Coal and Iron Company stock, whose value had fallen to less than the amount of the bank loans for which the stock was the collateral. To save the banks and stem the panic, J. P. Morgan and his United States Steel Corporation associates Judge Elbert H. Gary and Henry Frick agreed to buy Tennessee Coal and Iron at about double the market value of the shares. Even at that price the company was a bargain, and they knew it. Since its acquisition might be considered a violation of the Sherman Antitrust Act, Gary and Frick went to Washington to consult with the President. With less than complete candor they explained to him that though their buying of Tennessee Coal and Iron would do United States Steel little good, it "would be of great benefit to financial conditions, and would probably save further failure of important business concerns." Roosevelt, after consulting with Secretary of State Root, told them that the government had no objection to the transaction.

The decision was to haunt Roosevelt. His opponents maintained that either he had been a dupe or he had sold out to the steel interests for past or future favors. What was his dismay to learn four years after the event that Taft's Attorney General had brought a dissolution suit against the United States Steel Corporation, charging that it was a monopoly, in part because of the purchase of the Tennessee Coal and Iron Company. He alleged that Roosevelt had been misled by Frick and Gary. There was no malice toward Roosevelt in the Attorney General's action. This was just another enforcement of the Sherman act, but to Roosevelt it was

Suffragettes, marching on Washington in 1913, pause before the Elizabeth, New Jersey, Elks Club. Such marches, picketing at the White House, and noisy demonstrations, which occasionally ended in arrests, at last won the ladies the vote in 1920.

an impugning of his honor and his intelligence. He denounced the Attorney General's action, denying that he had been misled and criticizing such indiscriminate antitrust suits. "... nothing ... is gained," he wrote, "by breaking up a huge industrial organization which *has not offended otherwise than by its size*," and he accused Taft of "unintelligent toryism."

Roosevelt's blast at Taft was like a trumpet calling the faithful to Sagamore Hill. Those who obeyed the summons called themselves progressives, a comprehensive term to include Rough Riders, Western insurgents, Eastern reformers, farmers, labor leaders, conservationists, authors, forward-looking business leaders, idealists, college professors, and the chronically discontent. A progressive conference held by Senator James R. Garfield—son of the President—Pinchot, and Toledo's Boss Walter Brown at Columbus, Ohio, early in 1912 demanded the nomination for President of "Robert M. La Follette or Theodore Roosevelt, or any other Progressive Republican." After the shaggy-maned La Follette collapsed in February while on a barnstorming tour, seven Republican governors appealed to Roosevelt to come out for the Presidency. Two days later Taft denounced the progressives as "political emotionalists or neurotics." Roosevelt replied with asperity. Questioned by a reporter as to his intention, he struck off a fresh phrase destined to endure as an American cliché. "My hat," he said, "is in the ring."

Taft, his ordinarily good-natured bulk quivering with anger, denounced his old friend as a "flatterer," "demagogue," "egoist," and "bolter." Roosevelt, his jaws snapping in rebuttal, accused Taft of being "boss-controlled," a "standpatter," "disloyal to every canon of ordinary decency," and worse.

When the Republican convention met in Chicago in June, some 200 of the 1,078 delegates were challenged. Ruling on the disputed delegates, the Taft-controlled National Committee, under the chairmanship of one Victor Rosewater, held eligibility hearings behind closed doors. Through those doors emerged muffled cries of "liar" and "robber" as the committee automatically made each ruling in Taft's favor. Roosevelt adherents from their headquarters proclaimed their frustration in press releases of somewhat excessive vituperation.

The Taftites had achieved firm control of the convention. After a bitter fight, Root the regular was ensconced as chairman and thereafter kept the vociferous minority tightly bottled up. At each Root ruling there were de-

risive shouts from the gallery of "Toot! Toot!" and some Roosevelt supporters rubbed pieces of sandpaper together to imitate the sound of the engine of a steam roller. When Ohio's regular of regulars, former Lieutenant Governor Warren Harding, appeared on the platform to place Taft's name in nomination, he was howled down, and as he tried to make himself heard, several fist fights broke out on the floor.

Roosevelt ordered his supporters not to go through the useless motion of voting, and after Taft had been nominated, the faction stalked out of the hall. "I am feeling as strong as a bull moose," Roosevelt had said, reviving his phrase of 1900 as he arrived in Chicago. His followers quickly seized on the name for their third party, and the Bull Moose held their meeting a mile away, where Roosevelt in a fiery speech promised to be the Progressive candidate if they would nominate him at a regular Progressive convention.

The gathering of the new Progressive party in Chicago was a highly enthusiastic one. Square-faced Hiram Johnson, shortly to be named Roosevelt's running mate, marshaled his California delegation into the convention hall under a banner that read:

> I want to be a Bull Moose
> And with the Bull Moose stand,
> With Antlers on my forehead
> And a Big Stick in my hand.

Oblivious of the incongruity, the Jewish lawyer and diplomat Oscar Straus led the New York delegation down the aisle singing "Onward Christian Soldiers," which, with "The Battle Hymn of the Republic," was to become the Bull Moose anthem.

While the Republicans were preparing to cut one anothers' throats, the Democrats after forty-six ballots nominated New Jersey's reform governor, Woodrow Wilson, over the initial favorite, Speaker of the House Champ Clark. Freed finally from their obsession with Bryan and his Cross of Gold, the Democrats adopted a platform that much resembled that of the Progressives. The New Freedom, Wilson called his program.

For all their hymn-singing fervor, the Progressives were only a minority, and Roosevelt should have known, if he did not, that the Bull Moose movement made Wilson's election inevitable. In mid-October, when the former President was about to make a speech in Milwaukee, a fanatic shot at him almost point-blank with a pistol. The bullet, most of its velocity spent by passing through his overcoat, a spectacles case, and the folded manuscript of his speech, lodged in his lung. Though pallid from shock, Roosevelt insisted on going on. "I will make this speech or die," he said. "It is one thing or the other." The dramatic gesture won him the sympathy of the entire country and might have come close to electing him if the election had been held at that time. But the election was three weeks away, the wound not serious, and in two weeks Roosevelt was again his rugged Bull Moose self. Wilson won as expected, a minority President with 6,286,214 popular votes to 4,126,020 for Roosevelt and 3,483,922 for Taft, while Socialist Eugene Debs trailed with just under 1,000,000. Taft won the electoral votes of only two states. As for Roosevelt, even in losing he had scored an impressive triumph in his challenge to the entrenched regulars with their powers of patronage. In 1916 the Bull Moose would do even better, a friend calling at Sagamore Hill suggested hopefully. "I thought you were a better politician," said Roosevelt. "The fight is over. We are beaten. There is only one thing to do and that is to go back to the Republican Party. You can't hold a party like the Progressive Party together . . . there are no loaves and fishes."

As Taft rode down Pennsylvania Avenue with Wilson on Inauguration Day, 1913, his pleasure in leaving the White House was as evident as Wilson's satisfaction in assuming office. Self-assured to the point of didacticism, Wilson looked the academic that he was. He was born in 1856, and so his early memories were of the bitter years of war and Reconstruction in Georgia, where his father had been a Presbyterian clergyman in Augusta. He first attended a small denominational college in North Carolina, and at the age of nineteen entered Princeton. On graduating, he went on to the University of Virginia Law School, but his health, which had never been robust, soon failed. Studying at home, he passed his Georgia bar examinations and practiced briefly in Atlanta before entering the Johns Hopkins graduate school. Two years later he made himself known academically with *Congressional Government*, which argued that the United States government would be better off reorganized along the lines of the British Cabinet system. He spent three years as associate professor at Bryn Mawr and two more at Wesleyan University in Connecticut before he returned to Princeton as professor of jurisprudence and political economy. Three times in the next decade he refused the presidency of the University of Virginia. Then in 1902 he attained his academic goal when Princeton's board of trustees elected him president. By 1910 he had wearied of the bickering of the academic community and was glad to turn to politics. Nominated in 1910 as the respectable candidate of the Democratic bosses, he soon showed his complete independence of them and made a distinguished mark as a progressive governor. Yet he regarded the governorship as "the mere preliminary of a plan to nominate me in 1912 for the Presidency."

In a more reserved way than Roosevelt, Wilson had the quality of leadership that drew men to him. His weakness was his pride. He felt that he had been elected not only by the people but by destiny. His inherited

A new combination in travel is illustrated here by William Harmden Foster's Catching the Limited *of 1910. Near the station ahead is a field big enough for a landing, and there the daring young traveler will be deposited in time to make his train.*

The birth pangs of a new age in America are displayed in this group of paintings done in the second decade of the twentieth century: a growing urban society is becoming dehumanized, distorted, fragmented. Above is Joseph Stella's Brooklyn Bridge; *top right,* The Factory *by Preston Dickinson; and at right, John Marin's* Movement, Fifth Avenue.

Calvinist self-righteousness made him unable to see any point of view but his own, unable to compromise.

Wilson at the very beginning of his term as President, on April 7, called a special session of Congress to launch his New Freedom. He delivered his message in person, the first President to do so since John Adams. The message dealt with the tariff. On June 23 he addressed Congress again about banking and currency reform. With the Democrats controlling both branches of Congress, he was able to push through the Underwood tariff bill, the first major downward revision of the tariff in sixty-five years. To compensate for the lost revenue an income tax was introduced — legalized by the passage of the Sixteenth Amendment. Wilson and his advisers spent six months evolving a banking and currency bill, and in December the President signed the bill, which created the Federal Reserve System. The New Freedom also created the Federal Trade Commission and obtained passage of the Clayton Antitrust Act. Beyond this Wilson, with his Southern states' rights inheritance, was not prepared to go. He refused in 1914 to endorse a federal child-labor law because he felt it an unconstitutional

Wilson delivers his war message, above. Later that day, said his private secretary Joe Tumulty, "after dwelling upon the tragedies inseparable from war, President Wilson let his head fall on the cabinet table and sobbed as if he had been a child."

interference with the rights of the states, though two years later he did sign such a bill. He would not support woman suffrage. And in the nascent field of civil rights he was a reactionary, sanctioning segregation in federal employment and making no objection when Southern postmasters and Treasury officials removed Negro employees of the federal government.

For Wilson, intent on implementing his New Freedom, foreign affairs were of negligible concern. By the summer of 1914 he had a confident sense of approaching his goal. Yet in the sunny American landscape of that long summer there were dark patches, outlined by such things as the steady rise of the Socialist vote and the belligerent activities of the Industrial Workers of the World—more migrant than industrial. But such grim happenings as the Lawrence, Massachusetts, textile-workers' strike of 1912 and the Paterson silkworkers' strike of 1913, children working from dawn to dusk in Southern textile mills, immigrant newcomers rotting in the slums, tragedies like the death of 146 workers, most of them young girls, in New York's Triangle Waist Company fire in 1911, were imperfections that men of good will could sense were in the process of correction. That summer of 1914 the first vessels passed through the Panama Canal. Airplane flights were becoming common-place. Nickelodeons were showing Pearl White in the movie serial *The Perils of Pauline.* When on Sunday, June 28, far across the Atlantic, Archduke Francis Ferdinand of Austria-Hungary and his morganatic wife were assassinated in Sarajevo, it caused only a momentary flurry in the American press. Few in the United States had paid much attention to the archduke, and fewer still had heard of Sarajevo.

Ambassador to Germany James W. Gerard found Berlin in mid-July "as quiet as a grave." But the ripples from the event at Sarajevo would soon engulf the world. The feverish activities of the chancelleries at July's end, Austria's ultimatum, the mobilizations and counter-mobilizations ordered in Vienna, Petrograd, Berlin, and Paris, seemed a make-believe crisis. At least in America, rumors of war continued to sound in disbelieving ears. Then war came: England, France, and Russia allied against the Central Powers of Germany and Austria-Hungary, soon joined by Bulgaria and Turkey.

Fifty years later, one middle-aged American recalled how he at the age of four in a quiet suburb of Boston had heard the news of the outbreak of World War I. "One of my first cohesive memories," he wrote, "is of a hot August afternoon in 1914, a walk just wetted by a hose and smelling faintly of lime as warm damp concrete does, and my father in a stiff straw hat coming up the steps carrying the evening paper. Although I could not read, I was struck by the huge black lettering of the headlines, and for the first time I heard the word War! 'It will only last six weeks,' my father said." So it seemed in August, 1914, a brief war that—whoever was the victor—would be over well before the winter.

Wilson regarded the war as "a distant event, terrible and tragic, but one which did not concern us closely in the political sense." On August 19 he issued a proclamation urging his countrymen to be "impartial in thought as well as in action . . . . neutral in fact as well as in name." Germany's invasion of Belgium was the event that turned many Americans from their neutrality. Also, except for German-American and Irish-American minorities, Americans had a feeling of kinship with Great Britain, a nation that despite all past differences shared with the United States a common language, literature, and law. Month by month opinion swung over in favor of England and France and—remotely—Russia and against Germany, Austria-Hungary, and Turkey. The war, too, was proving a bonanza for American industries, providing them with a cashbox interest as well as an emotional allegiance. Theoretically, neutral America was ready to supply all buyers. Practically, its market was restricted to the Allies, since the Royal Navy barred matériel or munitions from reaching the Central Powers. In their consuming struggle the Allies could use all that American industry could produce. Suddenly enriched, American manufacturers did not concern themselves too much with abstractions about the freedom of the seas. Nor did the public, influenced as it was by French and British propaganda efforts, which were far defter than the Teutonic countereffforts.

England's blockade of the seas was of no concern to the Kaiser's government so long as the German generals expected to wage what would later be known as a blitzkrieg. But when the First Battle of the Marne in September, 1914, stopped the German advances and brought a bloody stalemate with no end in sight, the Germans fought the blockade with their devastating new weapon, the U-boat, or submarine. America's right as a neutral to trade with all belligerents was first challenged by the British, who claimed a necessity beyond international law to search American ships on the high seas and to confiscate goods presumably destined for the enemy.

Wilson protested many times against these "illegal" practices, but did nothing more. Against the Germans he was far more adamant. Under the old rules of war, a raider was required, in stopping a merchantman, to inspect its papers and cargo, and before sinking it, give the crew and passengers time to get away in lifeboats. For the fragile U-boats, vulnerable even to small-caliber deck guns, such a procedure was impossible. German submarine captains followed what they considered the law of necessity by launching their torpedoes without warning from below the surface regardless of the consequences to their victims. Wilson continued to warn the Germans that he would hold them accountable for any loss of American life or property resulting from violations of neutral rights.

On May 7, 1915, the queen of Britain's Cunard Line, the *Lusitania*, was torpedoed and sunk by a U-boat off Ireland, with the loss of nearly 1,200 lives, including 128 Americans. Not for years would Americans know that the *Lusitania* carried munitions, nor did they at the time question the discretion of their countrymen who were traveling on a belligerent vessel through a war zone. To them the issue seemed much simpler. The Germans had wantonly destroyed a passenger ship with women and children aboard.

At the war's outset Roosevelt had approved of Wilson's neutrality course, and even the invasion of Belgium had not changed his opinion. But the sinking of the *Lusitania* was for him "murder on the high seas," and he announced that he was "sick at heart" over the actions of Wilson and his pacifist Secretary of State, William Jennings Bryan, whose response to the sinking was another series of notes to the German government. Wilson eventually obtained an apology from the German government and a promise to cease attacks on passenger vessels. Nevertheless sinkings continued, culminating in the torpedoing of the French cross-Channel steamer *Sussex* with injury to several Americans in March, 1916. The President dispatched the stiffest of his notes to Berlin, and the Kaiser agreed at last to stop sinking even merchantmen without warning.

The presidential election of 1916 was shadowed by the conflict overseas. Wilson with his slogan "He kept us out of war" was just able to defeat the Republican "bearded iceberg," Associate Justice of the United States Charles Evans Hughes. Roosevelt, already in uniform in his own mind's eye, had refused the nomination proffered him by the last-gasp Progressives.

Yet even by election time Wilson sensed that he could not uphold his pledge to keep the country out of war. His chances seemed better in December, when the Kaiser made the startling offer to enter peace negotiations rather than "to continue the war to the bitter end," and Wilson asked both sides to declare their terms. But the German government refused to make a definite statement, and the Allied terms were much harder than Germany could accept. Struggling now, as it felt, for its life, the German government announced that on February 1 it would resume unrestricted submarine warfare.

For the anguished Wilson the announcement was a prelude to war. On February 3 he appeared before Congress to announce that he had broken off diplomatic relations with Germany, though he still insisted that this did not mean war. About two weeks before this, the Germans had committed an unrealistic act of folly by proposing to the Mexican government—only recently invaded by an American expeditionary force—that in case of war it should join in military action against the United States to restore the lost Mexican territories of Texas, New Mexico, and Arizona. The code message, sent by the German Foreign Minister Arthur Zimmermann, was intercepted by British Naval Intelligence and was forwarded to Washington late in February. When the contents of the Zimmermann note were made public in the United States, war appeared certain. As if to underline its inevitability, U-boats on March 18 sank three American merchantmen. Wilson, feeling that there was no longer any alternative, called a special session of Congress for the evening of April 2 "to receive a communication by the Executive on grave questions of national policy."

A warm rain was falling on that evening of the second of April as the President's limousine, escorted by a detachment of cavalry, came out of the White House drive at 8:20 and turned down Pennsylvania Avenue toward the Capitol. Thousands of citizens, many carrying small flags, stood on the curbs to watch the little procession pass. With a rhythmic clatter of hoofs the cavalrymen rode down the wide avenue, their ponchos glistening in the wet, sparks of light glancing from their drawn sabers. Behind them came the single limousine with the President in the back seat. The ride took approximately ten minutes, and at 8:30 the President faced a joint session of Congress to ask for the declaration that would not only put the United States into a foreign war but would forever mean an end to the nation's time of innocence.

Twilight on Elm Street

"It was confidence, not happiness, that made the great difference between then and now," said Henry Seidel Canby of America in the 1890's. For that decade and the next—particularly in the cities—the confidence held against a rush of change. "The outside world" meant almost all the planet and was very far away. Most of the intrusions into the center of one's life, the home, were of the neighborhood and so were virtually extensions of the home. It was an era of parades, civilians in their old uniforms marching with the high school bands. War was a noble and romantic enterprise. But many in those bands and lining the streets would soon discover otherwise, for bitter war in Europe and radios and automobiles would shortly cast evening shadows over a comfortable way of life.

A fine old elm tree overarches the dusty street and shades the gingerbread house behind it from the summer sun at midday.

The photograph, taken about 1907 by a cameraman now unknown, is of North Avenue in Fishkill, New York, on the Hudson River.

The thespians above were caught in the act around 1915. Chansonetta Stanley Emmons, sister of the twin Stanley brothers (of Steamer fame), photographed the patriotic quartet below. At right, a Main Street parade during the Cooperstown, New York, 1907 centennial.

*Whether one was swimming off the dock or carving initials in
a tree's bark or crocheting or reading or walking by the sea,*

these things took place in an atmosphere of calm and stability—an atmosphere soon to be disturbed, soon nearly gone.

Acknowledgments

The Editors appreciate the generous assistance provided by many individuals and institutions during the preparation of this book. They especially wish to thank the following:

State of Alabama, Department of Archives and History: Milo Howard
American Automobile Association, Washington, D.C.: J. K. Aldous, Mrs. Sue Williams
American Geographical Society, New York City
Automobile Manufacturers Association: Mrs. Bernice Huffman
Bancroft Library, University of California, Berkeley: Mrs. Alma Compton
Mr. and Mrs. William Battey, Greenwich, Connecticut
Brooklyn Museum: Arlene Jacobowitz, Mrs. Dorothy Weiss
Brown Brothers, New York City
Mr. August Busch, Jr., St. Louis
Butler Institute of American Art, Youngstown, Ohio
Chicago Historical Society: Mrs. Mary F. Rhymer, John Trés
Geoffrey Clements, New York City
State Historical Society of Colorado: Mrs. Kathleen Pierson
Community Service Society, New York City
Cooper-Hewitt Museum of Design, Smithsonian Institution, New York City
Culver Pictures, New York City: Robert Jackson
Mrs. James Dabbs, Mayesville, South Carolina
Denver Public Library: Mrs. Alys Freeze
Detroit Institute of Arts: Mrs. Nina Sperando, Mrs. Patricia Godfrey
Detroit Public Library: James Bradley
Mr. and Mrs. J. H. Douglas, Greenwich, Connecticut
Edison National Historic Site, Orange, New Jersey: Norman Speiden, Kathleen McGuirk
Mr. and Mrs. Henry N. Flynt, Deerfield, Massachusetts
Free Library of Philadelphia: Robert Looney, Mary Cattie
Frick Art Reference Library, New York City
Edgar William and Bernice Chrysler Garbisch Collection, New York City: Clifford Shaeffer
George Eastman House, Rochester: Thomas Barrow, Mrs. Ann McCabe
Mr. and Mrs. Paul Gilbert, Kings Point, New York
Gilcrease Institute of American History and Art, Tulsa: Paul Rossi, Mrs. Elaine Proctor
Mrs. Harold Grehan, New Orleans
Mr. and Mrs. Will Hippen, Jr., San Diego
Kansas State Historical Society: Robert Richmond
Kennedy Galleries, New York City
Felix H. Kuntz, New Orleans
Lester Levy, Pikesville, Maryland
Library of Congress, Washington, D.C.: Virginia Daiker, Mrs. Renata Shaw, Milton Kaplan, Leroy Bellamy
McCord Museum, McGill University, Montreal: Stanley Triggs
Massillon Museum, Massillon, Ohio: Albert Hise
Metropolitan Museum of Art, New York City: Mrs. Margaret Nolan, Harriet Cooper
Mr. and Mrs. J. William Middendorf II Collection, New York City: Wendy Shadwell
Missouri Historical Society: Mrs. Ruth Field
Museum of the City of New York: A. K. Baragwanath, C. Larue
Museum of Fine Arts, Boston: Stephanie Loeb, Laura Lucky
Museum of Modern Art, New York City
National Broadcasting Company, New York City: Dan Jones
Nebraska State Historical Society: Myrtle Berry
New Britain Museum of American Art, New Britain, Connecticut: Mrs. Lois Ice
New-York Historical Society: Wilson Duprey, Nancy Hale, Martin Leifer
New York Public Library: Elizabeth Roth, Dr. Gerald McDonald, Jerome Weidman, Laddie Sager
New York State Historical Association, Cooperstown
Ohio Historical Society
Old Print Shop, New York City: Robert Harley
Philadelphia Museum of Art
Mrs. C. J. Post, Bayside, New York
Preservation Society of Newport County, Newport, Rhode Island
Santa Barbara Museum of Art: Goldthwaite Dorr III
C. R. Smith, New York City

Smith College Museum of Art, Northampton, Massachusetts: Mrs. Anna Kennick
Smithsonian Institution, Washington, D.C.
South Carolina Historical Society: Mrs. Mary Prior, Helen McCormick
State Education Department, Office of State History, Albany, New York: Dr. John Still
Tennessee State Library and Archives: Kendall Cram
Toledo Museum, Toledo, Ohio: Mrs. Thomas Bentley
United States Naval Academy, Annapolis
Valentine Museum, Richmond, Virginia: Mrs. Stuart Gibson
Wadsworth Atheneum, Hartford, Connecticut: Elva McCormick
White House Historical Association, Washington, D.C.
Whitney Museum of American Art, New York City
General L. Kemper Williams, New Orleans
Wisconsin Historical Society: Paul Vanderbilt
Yale University Art Gallery, New Haven: Mrs. Heather Nary

The Editors also make grateful acknowledgment for permission to use material from the following works:

The American Magazine, November, 1917, "This Wonderful, Beautiful and Incalculably Interesting Earth!" by David Grayson. Copyright © 1917 by The Crowell Publishing Company, Springfield, Ohio. The excerpt on page 146 reprinted by permission of Crowell Collier and MacMillan, Inc.
The Century Magazine, January, 1914, "Immigrants in Politics" by Edward A. Ross. Copyright © 1913 by The Century Co. The excerpt on pages 315–16 reprinted by permission of Appleton-Century-Crofts, Educational Division, Meredith Corporation
"The Code" from *Complete Poems of Robert Frost*. Copyright 1930, 1939 by Holt, Rinehart and Winston, Inc. Copyright © 1958 by Robert Frost. Copyright © 1967 by Lesley Frost Ballantine. The excerpt from "The Code" on pages 150–52 reprinted by permission of Holt, Rinehart and Winston, Inc.
Hayes, The Diary of a President 1875–1881 edited by T. Harry Williams. Copyright © 1964 by T. Harry Williams. Published 1964 by David McKay Company, Inc., New York. The excerpt from Hayes's diary on pages 77–78 reprinted by permission of David McKay Company, Inc.
House Report No. 2300, *Report of the Commission on Immigration on The Problem of Immigration in Massachusetts*. The letter from a Polish immigrant on page 319 reprinted by permission of Mr. Henry Weaver, Counsel for the Commissioner of Administration and Finance of the Commonwealth of Massachusetts
The Reconstruction, A Documentary History of the South After the War 1865–1877 edited by James P. Shenton. Copyright © 1963 by G. P. Putnam's Sons. The letter to Hon. George W. Boutwell on pages 76–77 reprinted by permission of G. P. Putnam's Sons
Reconstruction, The Battle for Democracy 1865–1876 by James S. Allen, First New World Paperback Edition, 1963. Copyright © 1937 by International Publishers Co., Inc. The quote from the Fairfield *Herald* on page 66 reprinted by permission of International Publishers Co., Inc.
The Sod House by Cass G. Barns, M.D. Copyright © 1930 by Cass G. Barns, M.D. The excerpt on pages 157–58 reprinted by permission of Miss Viola F. Barnes
Sod-House Days by Howard Ruede, edited by John Ise. Copyright © 1937 by Columbia University Press, New York. Published 1937 by Columbia University Press, New York. The description of a sod house on pages 156–57 reprinted by permission of Columbia University Press
The Story of Ellis Island by Willard A. Heaps. Copyright © 1967 by Willard A. Heaps. The interview on pages 306–7 reprinted by permission of The Seabury Press
A Vanished World by Anne Gertrude Sneller. Copyright © 1964 by Syracuse University Press, Syracuse, New York. The excerpts on pages 148–49 and 152–53 reprinted by permission of Syracuse University Press
Williamstown Branch by R. L. Duffus. Copyright © 1958 by R. L. Duffus. The excerpt on pages 153–54 reprinted by permission of W. W. Norton & Company, Inc.

Index

A

ABOLITIONISTS, 20
ABRAHAM LINCOLN, FORT, 128–29
ADAMS, CHARLES F., 64, 174
ADAMS, HENRY, 58, 67–68, 82, 95, 172, 182, 251, 338, 341
ADAMS, JOHN Q., 20
ADE, GEORGE, 187
ADVERTISING, 183, 185, 343
AGRICULTURAL WHEEL, 244
AGUINALDO, GEN. EMILIO, 331
AIRPLANES, 377, 381. *See also* Wright, Orville and Wilbur
AKERMAN, AMOS T., 62
ALABAMA: 124, 245, 322; during Reconstruction, 18, 40, 49, 75–76, 85
ALABAMA CLAIMS, 63
ALASKA, 43, 45
ALCORN, JAMES L., 50
ALDRICH, NELSON W., 205, 251, 360–61, 362, 367, 373
ALDRICH, THOMAS B., 183
ALGECIRAS CONFERENCE, 364
ALGER, HORATIO, 163, 172–73
ALGER, RUSSELL A., 223, 224, 324, 333
ALLIANÇA (steamship), 301
ALLISON, WILLIAM B., 223
ALMIRANTE OQUENDO (cruiser), 327, 329
ALTGELD, JOHN P., 217, 288, 289
AMALGAMATED ASSOCIATION OF IRON AND STEEL WORKERS OF AMERICA, 265–66
AMERICAN COMMONWEALTH, 47–48
AMERICAN FEDERATION OF LABOR, 266, 331, 336
AMERICAN MAGAZINE, 146
AMERICAN PROTECTIVE ASSOCIATION, 342
AMERICAN RAILWAY UNION, 286–87
AMES, GEN. ADELBERT, 50, 63, 86
AMES, OAKES, 82, 142, 200
AMES, OLIVER, 142

ANDREWS, SAMUEL, 164
ANSHUTZ, THOMAS, 162
ANTHONY, SUSAN B., 47
ANTI-IMPERIALIST LEAGUE, 336
ANTIMASONRY, 19, 20
APACHES, 127, 132–34
APPLEBY, JOHN F., 139
ARAPAHOES, 124, 125, 127
ARBEITER-ZEITUNG, 216
ARCHITECTURE, 178–81
ARGOSY, 185
ARKANSAS, 18, 30, 40, 72, 84, 85, 124
ARMY, U.S.: 15, 30, 31, 32, 42, 99, 105, 241, 294; grand review, 16, 21; Indian wars, 124, 125–29, 132–34; Spanish-American War, 321–22, 324–27, 333
ARMY APPROPRIATION ACT, 30
ARTHUR, CHESTER A.: 181, 207; description and early career, 102, 204; as President, 204–7, 215; as Vice Pres., 200, 201
ASHLEY, JAMES M., 33
ASTOR, JOHN JACOB, 178, 212
ASTOR, MRS. WILLIAM, 178
ATCHISON, TOPEKA AND SANTA FE RAILROAD, 229
ATLANTA, GA., 11, 15, 42
ATLANTIC AND GREAT WESTERN RAILROAD, 167
ATLANTIC AND PACIFIC TELEGRAPH CO., 134
ATLANTIC MONTHLY, 183, 311
AUTOMOBILES, 341, 347–57
AVERY, WILLIAM, 91

B

BABCOCK, ORVILLE E., 59, 63, 83, 91–92
BADEAU, GEN. ADAM, 56, 68
BAER, GEORGE F., 346
BÁEZ, BUENAVENTURA, 59
BAKER, RAY STANNARD, 146, 361
BALTIMORE, MD., 27, 64

BALTIMORE (cruiser), 295
BALTIMORE AND OHIO RAILROAD, 105, 141, 142
BANNOCKS, 132
BARBED WIRE, 139
BARNS, CASS G., 157–58
BARTHOLDI, FRÉDÉRIC A., 180
BASEBALL, 187, 189
BASKETBALL, 187, 194
BAXTER, ELISHA, 84
BAYARD, THOMAS F., 208, 211, 290
BEACH, ALFRED E., 140
BEALS, JESSIE T., 272
BEAUREGARD, GEN. PIERRE G. T., 100
BECKER, JOSEPH, 227
BEECHER, HENRY WARD, 28, 211
BELKNAP, WILLIAM W., 94, 129
BELL, ALEXANDER G., 138–39
BELMONT, AUGUST, 279, 290
BENNETT, JAMES G., 28, 185
BENTEEN, CAPT. FREDERICK, 129
BERKMAN, ALEXANDER, 266
BESSEMER, HENRY, 161
BICYCLES, 210, 341
BIERSTADT, ALBERT, 60
BIG FOOT, 133
BILLINGS, CORNELIUS K. G., 342
BILLION DOLLAR CONGRESS, 251
BINGHAM, GEORGE C., 182
BITTERROOT MOUNTAINS, 132
BLACK, JAMES CONQUEST CROSS, 258
BLACK AND TAN CONVENTION, 27
BLACK CODES, 18–19, 26, 66
BLACK FRIDAY (September 24, 1869), 57–58
BLACK HILLS, 121
BLACK KETTLE, 125
BLACKFEET, 124
BLAINE, JAMES G.: 29, 84, 92, 94–95, 100, 221; description and early career, 92; election of 1880, 199–200; election of 1884, 207, 208, 211–12, 214, 341; election of 1888, 223, 224; Mulligan letters, 93, 207; as Sec. of State, 201, 205, 207, 251,

253, 259, 294; and tariff, 221, 241
BLAIR, GEN. FRANCIS P., 39
BLAND, "SILVER DICK," 106, 280, 291
BLAND BILL, 283
BLAND-ALLISON ACT, 242
BLASHFIELD, E. H., 241
BOOTH, JOHN WILKES, 17, 33
BOSTON, MASS.: 85, 174; architecture, 179, 180; immigrants, 315–16; newspapers, 185, 208
BOURBONS, 100
BOUTWELL, GEORGE S., 55–58, 63, 76
BOXER REBELLION, 334, 336
BOXING, 192
BOZEMAN TRAIL, 125–26
BRADLEY, JOSEPH P., 99
BRADY, MATTHEW, 16
BRAGG, GEN. BRAXTON, 13
BRECKINRIDGE, JOHN C., 13, 31
BREWER, FRANCIS B., 163, 164
BRISTOW, BENJAMIN H., 90–91, 92, 94, 95
BROOKE, R. N., 40
BROOKLYN (cruiser), 327, 329, 330
BROOKLYN BRIDGE, 180–81, 230, 378
BROOKS, JAMES, 82
BROWN, B. GRATZ, 64
BROWN, JOHN G., 52, 89
BROWNE, CARL, 283
BROWNLOW, WILLIAM G., 26, 27, 63
BRUCE, BLANCHE K., 47, 50
BRUSH, CHARLES F., 138
BRYAN, WILLIAM JENNINGS: 290, 321, 333, 359, 382; Cross of Gold Speech, 291–92; description; election of 1896, 292, 294; election of 1900, 335–36; election of 1908, 295, 368; and repeal of Sherman Silver Purchase Act, 280, 281, 282
BRYCE, LORD JAMES, 47–48, 187
BUELL, GEN. DON CARLOS, 13
BUFFALO, N. Y., 206, 209, 210, 212, 337
BUFFALO: slaughter of, 127–28, 228–29
BURCHARD, SAMUEL D., 212, 214
BURKE, MAJ. E. A., 100
BURNHAM, DANIEL, 181
BUTLER, BENJAMIN: 15, 27, 28, 51, 55, 62, 85, 87, 206, 211; description, 9–10, 14; election of 1884, 208, 212, 214; and Grant, 38, 58, 62; and impeachment of Johnson, 9, 11, 34–35, 42; and Reconstruction, 63; and "salary grab," 83
BUTTERFIELD, GEN. DANIEL, 57, 58

C

CABLE, GEORGE W., 78–79, 183
CALIFORNIA, 101, 123, 142, 143, 242, 322
CAMERON, JAMES D., 208
CAMERON, SIMON, 42, 55, 58
CAMMACK, ADDISON, 215
CAMPOS, MARTÍNEZ, 302
CANADA, 63, 369, 372. *See also* Fenians
CANBY, HENRY S., 383
CANNON, JOSEPH G., 93, 366, 367, 373
CARLISLE, JOHN G., 282, 290, 291
CARLOTA, EMPRESS, 43
CARNEGIE, ANDREW, 162–63, 172, 221, 233–35, 237, 266, 331, 342
CARPETBAGGERS, 26–27, 100
CARRINGTON, COL. HENRY B., 126
CARY, WILLIAM, 151
CASEY, JAMES F., 86, 87
CASSATT, MARY, 218
CENTENNIAL, UNITED STATES, 94, 97, 196–97, 229
CENTRAL PACIFIC RAILROAD, 106, 142–44, 227
CENTURY MAGAZINE, 316
CERVERA Y TOPETE, ADM. PASCUAL, 323–24, 327, 329
C. F. SMITH, FORT, 126
CHAMBERLAIN, DANIEL HENRY, 100
CHAMBERLAIN, JOHN, 58
CHAMPNEY, J. W., 89
CHANDLER, ZACHARIAH, 58, 98
CHAPMAN, F. A., 81
CHARLESTON, S. C., 15
CHASE, SALMON P., 9, 11, 20, 31, 35, 39, 41
CHATTANOOGA, BATTLE OF, 42
CHEROKEES, 124
CHEYENNES, 124, 125, 126–27, 128
CHICAGO, ILL.: 28, 38, 64, 85, 179, 180, 199, 216, 234, 288, 315; description, 235–37
CHICAGO, BURLINGTON AND QUINCY RAILROAD, 343
CHICKASAWS, 124
CHILE, 295
CHINA, 101, 106, 295, 333–34, 337, 364. *See also* Immigration
CHIVINGTON, COL. JOHN M., 125
CHOCTAWS, 124
CHRISTY, HOWARD C., 325
CHURCH, SANFORD, 39
CINCINNATI, O., 64, 254, 314
CISNEROS, EVANGELINA, 303
CIVIL RIGHTS ACT, 25, 26
CIVIL SERVICE, 64, 77,

104–5, 204–5, 215, 251, 259, 369
CIVIL WAR, 13, 14
CLAGUE, RICHARD, 32
CLARK, CHAMP, 372, 376
CLARK, E. E., 346
CLARK, MAURICE, 166
CLARKSON, JAMES S., 251, 259
CLAYTON ANTITRUST ACT, 380
CLAYTON-BULWER TREATY, 294, 346, 362
CLEARWATER, BATTLE OF, 132
CLEMENS, SAMUEL. *See* Mark Twain
CLEVELAND, GROVER: 208, 223, 259, 303, 331, 335, 338; description and early career, 208–9, 210–11; election of 1892, 264–65, 266; as gov. of N. Y., 181, 206, 208, 211, 341; illness, 280; marriage, 216; as President, 215–17, 220–24, 262, 266, 279–91, 294–97
CLEVELAND, O., 28, 166
CLEVELAND AND PITTSBURGH RAILROAD, 142
CLINEDINST, B. WEST, 310
COBB, TY, 189
COCKRAN, BOURKE, 262
CODY, "BUFFALO BILL," 212
COIN'S FINANCIAL SCHOOL, 285–86, 290
COLFAX, SCHUYLER, 39, 64, 82, 84
COLMAN, NORMAN J., 242
COLOMBIA, 346
COLORADO, 106, 120, 125, 128, 367
COLORED FARMERS' NATIONAL ALLIANCE AND COOPERATIVE UNION, 244
COMANCHES, 124, 127, 128
COMMERCE AND LABOR, DEPARTMENT OF, 342
COMMISSION ON EFFICIENCY AND ECONOMY, 369
COMMONWEAL OF CHRIST, 283
COMSTOCK LODE, 120–21
CONKLING, ROSCOE: 55, 58, 92, 95, 100, 199–200, 204, 205–6, 208, 211, 223; description, 102; and New York Custom House, 62, 102, 104–5, 201
CONNECTICUT, 92, 214
CONSERVATION, 366–67
CONSTITUTION, U.S.: 54–55; Thirteenth Amendment, 18; Fourteenth Amendment, 25, 28, 30, 40, 63, 100, 252; Fifteenth Amendment, 46–47, 55, 62, 252; Sixteenth Amendment, 369; Seventeenth Amendment, 369
CONVENTION OF LIBERAL COLORED REPUBLICANS, 64
CONVENTION OF SOLDIERS AND SAILORS, 38

COOKE, HENRY, 87
COOKE, JAY, 46, 84
COOPER, PETER, 98, 106
COPPERHEADS, 18, 27, 28, 64
CORBETT, JAMES J., 192
CORBIN, ABEL R., 56–58
CORNELL, ALONZO, 102, 205–6, 211
COSMOPOLITAN, 183
COTTON, 44, 282
COURTELYOU, GEORGE, 337, 365
COX, JACOB D., 55, 62
COXEY, JACOB S., 283–85
CRANE, STEPHEN, 326
CRAZY HORSE, 127, 128, 129, 132
CREDIT AND FINANCE CORPORATION, 142
CRÉDIT MOBILIER, 82–83, 200
CREEKS, 124
CRISTÓBAL COLÓN (cruiser), 327, 329
CROCKER, CHARLES, 142, 143
CROKER, RICHARD, 211, 264, 265, 333
CROOK, GEN. GEORGE, 128–29, 132–34
CROWS, 124
CUBA: 55, 294; revolution, 300–301, 302–3; Spanish-American War, 322, 323–30, 331
CURRENCY. *See* Money
CURRENCY ACT, 282
CURRY, JOHN STEUART, 242
CURTIS, CYRUS, 183, 185
CURTIS, EDWARD, 112
CURTIS, GEORGE W., 208, 224
CUSTER, LT. COL. GEORGE A., 27, 127, 128–29
CUSTOM HOUSE RING, 86
CZOLGOSZ, LEON, 337, 338

D

DAIQUIRÍ, CUBA, 324
DALY, JOSEPH F., 333
DANA, CHARLES A., 185, 208, 212
DARTMOUTH COLLEGE, 19
DARWIN, CHARLES, 68, 172
DAVIS, DAVID, 99
DAVIS, JEFFERSON, 12, 15, 64
DAVIS, RICHARD H., 303, 324, 326, 341
DAVIS, THEODORE R., 167
DEAN, MARY, 146–47, 148
DEBS, EUGENE, 286–88, 368, 377
DEERE, JOHN, 139
DEGAS, EDGAR, 44
DELAWARE, 34, 214

DEMOCRATIC PARTY: 10, 13, 17, 19, 28, 29, 62, 85, 106, 206, 303; in 1868, 38–40; in 1872, 64; in 1876, 98–99; in 1880, 200; in 1888, 221, 223; revival in South, 62–63, 85; and silver, 285, 291–92
DEMUTH, CHARLES, 370
DENT, FRED, 91
DEPENDENT PENSION BILL, 221
DEPEW, CHAUNCEY, 194, 223, 224, 251
DESERT LAND ACT, 123
DETROIT TIGERS, 189
DEVENS, R. M., 227
DEWEY, ADM. GEORGE, 322–23, 333, 334
DICKINSON, PRESTON, 378
DODGE, RICHARD IRVING, 228–29
DODGE, FORT, 228–29
DOLLAR DIPLOMACY, 369
DOMINICAN REPUBLIC, 59, 63, 346
DONAGHY, JOHN, 245
DONELSON, FORT, 13, 42
DONNELLY, IGNATIUS, 246, 254, 255, 291
DOOLEY, MR. See Dunne, Finley Peter
DORSEY, STEPHEN, 204
DOUGLASS, FREDERICK, 27, 47
DOYLE, H. S., 258
DRAKE, EDWIN L., 163–64
DREW, DANIEL, 38, 141
DREW, GEORGE F., 100
DUFFUS, R. L., 153–54
DUNN, HARVEY, 119
DUNNE, FINLEY PETER, 237, 289, 331, 361
DURANT, THOMAS C., 142, 144

E

EADS, JAMES, 90
EAKINS, THOMAS, 182
ECONOMIC CONDITIONS: postwar, 54, 55–56, 72, 173; after Panic of 1873, 85, 105, 174; in 1880's, 106, 207; in 1890's, 267, 279, 282, 300; Western, 242–43. See also Panics, Money, Treasury, National Debt
EDISON, THOMAS, 134, 136–38
EDMUNDS, GEORGE F., 207, 208
EDUCATION, PUBLIC, 50, 94, 148–49, 157
EDWARD VII, KING, 340, 373
EIFFEL, GUSTAVE, 180
EIGHT-HOUR DAY, 216, 367, 369
EL CANEY, BATTLE OF, 325–26
ELECTIONS: 1864, 13;

1866, 28; 1868, 41; 1872, 64; 1874, 85; 1876, 77–78; 1880, 200; 1884, 211–12, 214; 1888, 224, 250; 1892, 266; 1896, 294; 1900, 336–37; 1904, 346; 1908, 368; 1912, 382
ELECTORAL COMMISSION, 99
ELECTORAL COUNT BILL, 99
ELECTRICITY, 134, 136–38, 342
ELIOT, CHARLES W., 331, 342
ELIZABETH, EMPRESS, 337
ELKINS ACT, 360
ELLIS, FORT, 128
ELLIS ISLAND, 306–8, 314
EMMONS, CHANSONETTA, 386
EMPIRE TRANSPORTATION COMPANY, 171
ERIE RAILROAD, 56, 141–42, 167, 174
EVANS, ADM. ROBERT, 365
EVARTS, WILLIAM, 102
EVENING POST, New York, 207, 208, 262
EWING, GEN. THOMAS, 33
EXPANSIONISM, 294–97, 331

F

FABENS, COL. JOSEPH W., 59
FAIRCHILD, CHARLES S., 262
FALLS, CHARLES, 311
FARASYN, EDGARD, 199
FARMING: bonanza farms, 242; farmers' organizations, 243–45; hard times, 85, 241–42, 242–43, 246, 247, 282; life described, 146–47, 150–52, 155–56, 158; progress and inventions, 139–40, 146, 159; in South, 31, 71–72, 243
FARRAGUT, ADM. DAVID G., 27, 182
FEDERAL AID ROAD ACT, 347
FEDERAL CHILDREN'S BUREAU, 369
FEDERAL COMMISSION ON THE CONSERVATION OF NATURAL RESOURCES, 367
FEDERAL RESERVE SYSTEM, 380
FEDERAL TRADE COMMISSION, 380
FEDERATION OF ORGANIZED TRADES AND LABOR UNIONS, 216
FENIANS, 45, 46
FERDINAND MAXIMILIAN, EMPEROR, 43
FESSENDEN, WILLIAM P., 25, 28, 34
FETTERMAN, CAPT. WIL-

LIAM J., 126
FETTERMAN, FORT, 129
FIELD, GEN. JAMES G., 264
FIELDEN, SAMUEL, 216, 217
FISH, HAMILTON, 55, 59, 63, 81, 301
FISH, MRS. STUYVESANT, 342
FISHER, WARREN, 211
FISK, JAMES, 56–58, 141, 175
FISKE, JOHN, 297
FIVE POINTS (New York City), 173
FLAGLER, HENRY M., 166
FLORIDA, 18, 40, 49, 86, 98, 124, 134, 245, 322, 324
FLYING SQUADRON, 323
FOLGER, CHARLES J., 205–6, 211
FOOTBALL, 187, 190–91
FORAKER, JOSEPH B., 223, 224, 300, 367
FORCE BILL: 63; of 1890, 252
FORD, HENRY, 341
FORREST, GEN. NATHAN B., 13, 54, 63
FORUM, 159
FOSTER, WILLIAM H., 377
FRANCE, 180, 181, 333, 364, 372, 381
FRANCIS FERDINAND, ARCHDUKE, 381
FRANZ JOSEPH, EMPEROR, 373
FREEDMEN'S BUREAU, 18, 21, 26, 48, 50
FREEMAN, MARY W., 183
FREEMASONRY, 19
FRÉMONT, GEN. JOHN C., 42, 132, 209
FRENCH, DANIEL C., 182
FRENZENY, PAUL, 312
FRICK, HENRY CLAY, 163, 262, 265–66, 374
FROST, ARTHUR, 182
FROST, ROBERT, 150–52
FUROR (destroyer), 327

G

GALL, 128
GARFIELD, JAMES A.: 28, 93; assassination and death, 201, 204; as congressman, 25, 62, 63, 85, 90; and Crédit Mobilier, 82, 200; description and early career, 200; as President, 200–201, 204
GARFIELD, JAMES R., 376
GARLAND, HAMLIN, 183
GARY, ELBERT H., 374
GARY, JOSEPH E., 217
GENERAL MANAGERS' ASSOCIATION, 287–89
GENTHE, ARNOLD, 362
GENTLEMAN'S AGREEMENT, 364
GEORGE, HENRY, 254, 341
GEORGIA, 11, 14, 18, 30,

40, 63, 72, 101, 245, 258, 322
GERARD, JAMES W., 381
GERMANY, 294, 333, 381–82
GERONIMO, 133–34
GIBBON, COL. JOHN, 128–29, 132
GIBSON, CHARLES DANA, 260, 325
GLACKENS, WILLIAM, 370
GLENNY, ALICE, 185
GLIDDEN, JOSEPH F., 139
GLOUCESTER (yacht), 327, 330
GODKIN, EDWIN L., 183, 207, 237
GOETHALS, GEORGE W., 372
GOGEBIC RANGE, 161
GOLD: crisis of 1869, 56–58; discoveries, 120–21, 300, 321; standard, 106; supply of, 64, 282, 294. See also Silver
GOLD EXCHANGE, 57
GOLF, 187, 343
GÓMEZ, MÁXIMO, 302
GOMPERS, SAMUEL, 331
GORDIGIANI, MICHELE, 89
GOULD, JAY, 56–58, 141–42, 185, 205
GRADY, THOMAS, 211
GRAEFLE, ALBERT, 43
GRAHAM, CHARLES, 161
GRAND ARMY OF THE REPUBLIC, 208, 221, 223, 251, 337
GRAND COLUMBIAN EXPOSITION, 180, 181–82, 288, 297
GRANGER MOVEMENT, 243–44
GRANT, ORVILLE, 91
GRANT, ULYSSES S.: 15, 16, 21, 28; description and early life, 41, 81; election of 1868, 39–41; as former President, 100, 104, 199–200; as general, 13, 27, 32, 33, 37–38, 42; and gold crisis, 56–58; as President, 47, 54–64, 67–68, 78, 81–89; and scandals, 50, 64, 82–83, 86–87, 90–92, 94
GRAYSON, DAVID. See Baker, Ray Stannard
GREAT BRITAIN: 63, 224, 241, 372; and Morocco, 364; and Open Door, 333; and Venezuela, 296–97; in World War I, 381–82
GREAT NORTHERN RAILROAD, 286, 343
GREAT WHITE FLEET, 365, 366
GREELEY, HORACE, 28, 62, 63, 64, 121, 262
GREENBACK-LABOR PARTY, 98, 106, 174, 200, 208
GRESHAM, WALTER Q., 223, 224
GRIMES, JAMES W., 35
GRINNELL, MOSES, 62
GUAM, 330
GUGGENHEIMER, RUDOLF, 342
GUITEAU, CHARLES, 201

H

HABERLE, JOHN, 247
HAGUE COURT. *See* Permanent Court of International Arbitration
HAITI, 59
HALPIN, MARIA, 209-10, 212
HAMLIN, HANNIBAL, 14
HAMPTON, GEN. WADE, 50, 100, 245, 246
HANCOCK, GEN. WINFIELD S., 39, 129, 200
HANNA, MARK, 166, 259, 291, 292, 300, 335, 337
HARDING, WARREN G., 207, 294, 369, 376
HARPER'S NEW MONTHLY MAGAZINE, 183, 297
HARPER'S WEEKLY, 9, 11, 14, 59, 66, 73, 161, 167, 182, 208, 287, 308
HARRIMAN, EDWARD H., 343
HARRIS, JOEL CHANDLER, 183
HARRISON, BENJAMIN: description, 223-24, 247, 250; election of 1892, 259, 264, 266; as President, 250-54, 259, 262, 295, 341, 367
HARRISON, CARTER, 216
HARTE, BRET, 183
HARVEY, WILLIAM H., 285-86
HASSAM, CHILDE, 175, 358
HAVEMEYER, HENRY O., 254
HAWAII, 294, 295-96, 297, 300, 331, 336
HAY, JOHN, 183, 223, 321, 333-34
HAYES, RUTHERFORD B.: 206, 207, 250, 264; as congressman, 20, 25; description and early career, 92, 93; election of 1876, 92, 95, 98-99; as President, 77-78, 99-100, 100-106
HAYMARKET SQUARE RIOT, 216-17, 220
HAY-PAUNCEFOTE TREATY, 346, 369
HEAPS, WILLARD A., 306-7
HEARN, LAFCADIO, 314
HEARST, GEORGE, 121, 185, 251
HEARST, WILLIAM RANDOLPH, 183, 185-86, 302-3, 304, 331
HEGG, E. A., 300
HENDRICKS, THOMAS A., 39, 98
HENRY, EDWARD L., 202, 203
HENRY, FORT, 13, 42
HEPBURN ACT, 360-61
HERALD, New York, 28, 66, 100, 185, 208
HERBERT, VICTOR, 323
HEWITT, ABRAM S., 230-31
HEYBURN, WELDON, 361
HICKOK, WILD BILL, 121
HIGGINSON, COL. THOMAS W., 100

HILL, DAVID, 224, 262
HILL, JAMES J., 144, 162, 215, 286, 343
HOAR, E. ROCKWOOD, 55, 62
HOAR, GEORGE, 85, 331
HOBART, GARRET A., 334
HOBSON, RICHMOND P., 236
HOCKEY, ICE, 187
HOE, RICHARD, 140
HOGG, JAMES, 245
HOMER, WINSLOW, 31, 52, 54, 148, 149, 182
HOMESTAKE MINE, 121
HOMESTEAD STRIKE, 265-66
HOMESTEADS: Homestead Act, 121-22, 123-24; legislation, 12
HOOD, GEN. JOHN B., 13
HOPKINS, JOHN P., 288-89
HOPKINS, MARK, 142
HOUSE OF REPRESENTATIVES, U.S.: 12, 45, 93, 280-81, 304; composition of, 28, 62, 85, 216, 289-90, 373, 374; description, 20, 69; and impeachment of Johnson, 9, 11, 33, 34; and Southern delegates, 20, 50
HOVENDEN, THOMAS, 182
HOWARD, GEN. OLIVER O., 132
HOWE, JULIA WARD, 15, 58
HOWELLS, WILLIAM DEAN, 183, 229-30
HUDSON RIVER RAILROAD, 141
HUGHES, CHARLES EVANS, 382
HUMBERT, KING, 337
HUNT, RICHARD M., 178-80, 297
HUNTER, F. L., 230
HUNTER, ROBERT, 17
HUNTINGTON, COLLIS P., 142, 162, 179, 186
HYDE, JAMES HAZEN, 342

I

IDAHO, 121, 132, 367
ILLINOIS, 27, 28, 101, 106, 206
IMMIGRATION: 19, 85, 134, 173-74, 199; Chinese, 106, 200, 206; description, 306-19, 342; Irish, 174, 315; Japanese, 364
IMMIGRATION RESTRICTION LEAGUE, 342
IMPEACHMENT, ARTICLES OF, 9, 11, 34. *See also* Johnson, Andrew
INCOME TAX, 282, 290, 369, 380
INDEPENDENT NATIONAL PARTY, 106
INDEPENDENT REPUBLICANS. *See* Mugwumps

INDIANA, 27, 101, 154, 200, 214
INDIANA (battleship), 327, 330
INDIANS: 64, 112, 124; Indian wars, 124-34. *See also* specific tribes and battles
INDUSTRIAL BROTHERHOOD, 174
INDUSTRIAL WORKERS OF THE WORLD, 381
INDUSTRY, 134. *See also* specific industries
INFANTA MARÍA TERESA (cruiser), 327
INGERSOLL, ROBERT G., 94
INHERITANCE TAX, 362
IÑIQUEZ, CALIXTO GARCÍA, 324
INTERNATIONAL BUREAU OF AMERICAN REPUBLICS, 253
INTERNATIONAL INDUSTRIAL ASSEMBLY OF NORTH AMERICA, 174
INTERSTATE COMMERCE ACT, 287, 336, 360
INTERSTATE COMMERCE COMMISSION, 220, 361
INVENTIONS, 138-40. *See also* specific inventions
IOWA, 241
IOWA (battleship), 327, 329
IRON, 161-62, 163. *See also* Steel
ISTHMIAN CANAL, 294, 337. *See also* Panama Canal
ITALY, 333

J

JACKSON, ANDREW, 9, 12, 19
JAMES, HENRY, 317-19
JAMES, THOMAS, 201
JAPAN, 295, 333, 363
JEWELL, MARSHALL, 90
JEWETT, SARAH ORNE, 183
JOHNSON, ANDREW: 19, 39, 41, 121, 206; description and early career, 11-12, 13-14; impeachment, 9-11, 31, 33, 34-35, 37; as President, 9-35 *passim*, 42-43, 45-47; and Reconstruction, 18, 21, 25, 29, 33, 66; and Tenure of Office Act, 11, 30-31, 33-34; as Vice Pres., 13, 14
JOHNSON, CLIFTON, 156, 157
JOHNSON, EASTMAN, 24, 52
JOHNSON, HIRAM, 376
JOHNSTON, FRANCIS B., 288
JOHNSTOWN FLOOD, 253
JOINT COMMITTEE ON RECONSTRUCTION, 20, 21, 24, 25
JOSEPH, CHIEF, 132

JOURNAL, New York, 186, 302, 303, 304
JUÁREZ, BENITO, 43
JULIAN, GEORGE W., 40

K

KANSAS, 35, 37, 87, 114, 124, 128, 241, 242, 246
KANSAS PACIFIC RAILROAD, 229
KANSAS-NEBRASKA ACT, 20
KELLEY, OLIVER H., 243
KELLEY, WILLIAM D. ("Pig Iron"), 205
KELLOGG, WILLIAM P., 86
KELLY, JOHN, 208, 211, 214
KELLY, WILLIAM, 161
KENT, GEN. J. FORD, 325
KENTUCKY, 28, 101
KETTLE HILL, CUBA, 326
KING, EDWARD, 71-72, 149-50, 232-33
KINSEY, DARIUS, 122
KIOWAS, 124, 127, 128
KIPLING, RUDYARD, 297, 341
KIRBY-SMITH, GEN. EDMUND, 16
KLIR, JOSEPH, 281
KNIGHTS OF LABOR, NOBLE ORDER OF, 174, 216, 244-45, 255
KNIGHTS OF THE WHITE CAMELLIA, 51, 86
KNOW-NOTHING PARTY, 12, 19, 94
KOMURA, BARON JUTARO, 364
KOREA, 294, 363
KU-KLUX KLAN, 40, 51, 54, 63, 64, 70, 85, 167
KU-KLUX KLAN ACTS, 64
KYNER, JAMES H., 158

L

LABOR: 173-74, 175, 220, 288, 342, 367, 381; child, 342, 369, 380-81; strikes, 105-6, 216, 265-66, 286-89, 346
LADIES' HOME JOURNAL, 183
LADIES' WORLD, 183
LA FARGE, JOHN, 296
LA FOLLETTE, ROBERT M., 360, 361, 373, 374, 376
LAND: distribution, 121-24; speculation in, 121, 122-23, 124
LANE, JOHN, 139
LANE, JOSEPH, 13
LARAMIE, FORT, 125
LAS GUÁSIMAS, BATTLE OF, 325
LATIN AMERICA, 253, 346.

See also specific nations
LAWTON, GEN. HENRY W., 324, 325, 326
LAZARUS, EMMA, 180, 314
LEASE, MARY ELIZABETH, 246–47, 264
LEAVENWORTH, FORT, 124
LEE, FITZHUGH, 303, 322
LEE, GEN. ROBERT E., 14, 16, 42, 49, 55, 68, 69–70
LEHR, HARRY, 342
LEITER, LEVI, 215
LIE, JONAS, 372
LILIUOKALANI, QUEEN, 296
LIMESTONE RIDGE, BATTLE OF, 45
LINCOLN, ABRAHAM: 9, 10, 13, 17, 21, 31, 42, 124, 182; death, 14, 16, 33; as President, 13, 14, 15; and South, 15, 66
LIPPINCOTT'S MAGAZINE, 147, 148
LITERATURE, 182–83
LITTLE BIGHORN, BATTLE OF, 128–29
LITTLE CROW, CHIEF, 124
LITTLE ROCK AND FORT SMITH RAILROAD, 93, 211
LODGE, HENRY CABOT, 208, 251, 297, 300, 330, 331, 332, 368
LOGAN, GEN. JOHN A., 199, 208
LONDON, JACK, 361
LONG, JOHN D., 300
LONG BRANCH, N. J., 54, 56
LONGFELLOW, HENRY W., 183
LOUISIANA: 98, 99, 100, 124; during Reconstruction, 15, 18, 33, 40, 49, 50, 66–67, 72, 86, 100
LOWELL, JAMES R., 183
LOYAL LEAGUES, 51, 54
LUKS, GEORGE, 255
LUSITANIA (steamship), 382
LYNCH, JOHN R., 75
LYON, FORT, 125

M

McALLISTER, WARD, 178, 179
McCLELLAN, GEN. GEORGE B., 42
McCLURE, SAMUEL S., 185, 361
McCLURE'S MAGAZINE, 183, 361
McCORMICK, CYRUS, 139, 162
McCULLOCH, HUGH, 46
McCUMBER, PORTER J., 361
McDONALD, JOHN, 91
McENERY, JOHN, 86
McKIM, CHARLES F., 178
McKINLEY, WILLIAM: 207, 223, 252, 259; death, 337–38; description, 291; elec-

tion of 1896, 292, 294; as President, 237, 300, 304, 321–22, 331, 333–38
McKINLEY TARIFF, 252–53, 262, 279, 282
McLEAN, JOHN R., 186
McPHERSON, EDWARD, 20
MAGAZINES, 183, 185. See also specific titles
MAHAN, CAPT. ALFRED T., 297
MAINE, 28, 40, 212
MAINE (battleship), 303–4
MANIFEST DESTINY, 297
MANILA BAY, BATTLE OF, 322, 323
MARCONI, GUGLIELMO, 342
MARÍA TERESA (cruiser), 329
MARIN, JOHN, 378
MARK TWAIN, 58, 68–69, 78, 120–21, 182, 183, 205, 333
MARRYAT, CAPT. FREDERICK, 175
MARTHA'S VINEYARD, 83
MARTÍ, JOSÉ JULIÁN, 301, 302
MARTIN, BRADLEY, 342
MARYLAND, 28, 105
MASSACHUSETTS, 206
MASSACHUSETTS (battleship), 327
MASTERS, EDGAR LEE, 292
MATTHEWS, BRANDER, 341
MAXIMILIAN. See Ferdinand Maximilian
MAYNARD, HORACE, 20
MEDICINE, 152–53
MEMPHIS RIOT, 27
MENLO PARK, N. J., 137
MERGENTHALER, OTTMAR, 140, 183
MERRITT, EDWIN A., 104
MERRITT, LEWIS H., 161–62
MEXICO, 42–43, 133, 382
MICHIGAN, 27, 28, 161
MIDWAY ISLANDS, 43
MILES, GEN. NELSON A., 128, 132, 133–34, 323, 324, 330
MILITARY RECONSTRUCTION ACT, 29, 32
MINNESOTA, 124, 161–62, 241
MISSISSIPPI: 124; during Reconstruction, 14, 18, 40, 41, 47, 49, 50, 55, 63, 72, 74, 76–77, 86
MISSISSIPPI RIVER, 29
MISSOURI, 27, 42, 62, 63, 64
MITCHELL, JOHN, 346
MOLLY MAGUIRES, 105
MONEY: 46, 55; demand for greenbacks, 39, 85, 106. See also Silver, Gold, Treasury, Economic conditions, Panics
MONROE DOCTRINE, 43, 346
MONTANA, 121, 124, 247, 367
MONTOJO Y PASARÓN, REAR ADM. PATRICIO,

322–23
MORAN, THOMAS, 60
MORGAN, JOHN PIERPONT: 163, 214, 279, 290, 342, 343; and Panic of 1907, 365–66, 374
MOROCCO, 364
MORRILL LAND-GRANT ACT, 122
MORSE, SAMUEL F. B., 134
MORTON, LEVI, 224
MORTON, OLIVER, 58, 92, 94, 95
MOSES, FRANKLIN, JR., 48–49
MOTLEY, JOHN L., 55, 63
MOTT, LUCRETIA, 47
MOUNT, WILLIAM SYDNEY, 182
MUCKRAKERS, 361, 362
MUGWUMPS, 208, 211, 214, 215, 341
MULLIGAN, JAMES, 93
MUNSEY, FRANK A., 185
MUNSEY'S MAGAZINE, 183, 185, 230, 232
MURPHY, THOMAS, 62, 102

N

NAPOLEON III, 42–43
NAST, THOMAS, 11, 14, 45, 56, 59, 64, 167, 207
NATION, THE, 56, 83, 183, 200, 208, 262
NATIONAL DEBT, 56, 64. See also Treasury, United States
NATIONAL DEMOCRATIC PARTY, 292, 294
NATIONAL FARMERS' ALLIANCE. See Northern Alliance
NATIONAL FARMERS' ALLIANCE AND INDUSTRIAL UNION. See Southern Alliance
NATIONAL GEOGRAPHIC MAGAZINE, 183
NATIONAL LABOR UNION, 174
NATIONAL MONUMENTS ACT, 367
NATIONAL UNION CONFERENCE (of 1891), 254
NATIONAL UNION CONVENTION, 26, 27
NATIONAL UNION PARTY, 10, 13, 28
NAVY, U.S.: 15, 30, 43, 342; expansion and modernization, 294–95, 297; Great White Fleet, 365; in Spanish-American War, 322–24, 327, 329–30
NEBRASKA, 106, 114, 124, 241, 242
NEGROES: 15, 18, 31, 50, 258; harassment by whites, 51, 54, 86, 98; during Reconstruction, 21, 40, 48, 50, 64, 66–67, 69–77, 78–79; segre-

gation, 101; suffrage, 15, 18, 25, 29, 30, 33, 39, 40, 41, 50, 86, 100, 266–67
NEILL, CHARLES P., 361
NELSON, T. A. R., 37
NEVADA, 120, 123
"NEW DEPARTURE," 64
NEW JERSEY, 214, 374
NEW MEXICO, 128
NEW ORLEANS, LA.: 10, 27, 32, 33, 44, 67; Second Battle of, 86
NEW YORK: 63, 374; in election of 1880, 200; in election of 1884, 214; in election of 1888, 224; rural life, 148–49
NEW YORK, CITY OF: 27, 46, 98, 136, 141, 227, 334, 341, 350; architecture, 178; blizzard of 1888, 223; description, 21, 95, 173, 231; election of 1884, 211–12, 214; electric lights, 138; immigrants, 309–11; Panic of 1873, 85; society, 175, 178–79; and Tweed Ring, 56
NEW YORK (battleship), 327
NEW YORK AND HARLEM RAILROAD, 141
NEW YORK CENTRAL RAILROAD, 141, 167, 223
NEW YORK CUSTOM HOUSE, 62, 102, 104–5, 201
NEW YORK TIMES, 27, 28, 98, 185, 201, 208, 226–27
NEWLANDS BILL, 367
NEWSPAPERS, 185–86. See also specific newspapers
NEZ PERCÉS, 129, 132
NICARAGUA, 346, 369
NICHOLLS, GEN. FRANCIS TILLOU, 98, 100, 245
NORDHOFF, CHARLES, 66–67, 72–73
NORRIS, FRANK, 235–37, 267
NORTH AMERICAN REVIEW, 235
NORTH CAROLINA, 11, 14, 18, 40, 63, 245
NORTH DAKOTA, 106, 247
NORTHERN ALLIANCE, 244–45
NORTHERN PACIFIC RAILROAD, 84, 85, 242, 262, 343
NORTHERN SECURITIES COMPANY, 343
NOTMAN, WILLIAM, 191

O

OHIO: 27, 101, 374; in 1868 election, 41; in 1880 election, 200; in 1882 election, 206
OIL INDUSTRY, 134, 163, 164, 165, 166–67, 170–71
OIL MEN'S LEAGUE, 167
OKLAHOMA, 127, 134
OLIVER, JAMES, 139
OLNEY, RICHARD, 280, 287–88, 296

OLYMPIA (cruiser), 323
OPEN DOOR POLICY, 333–34, 363
OREGON, 108, 123, 132, 367
OREGON (battleship), 327, 329, 364
OREGON TRAIL, 124, 125
OUTLOOK, THE, 309, 373, 374

P

PACIFIC ASSOCIATES, 142
PACIFIC RAILWAY ACT, 142
PACIFIC RAILWAY COMMISSION, 220
PACKARD, STEPHEN, 86, 99, 100
PAINTING, 52, 182, 218
PALE FACES, 51
PALMER, MRS. POTTER, 342
PANAMA, REPUBLIC OF, 346
PANAMA CANAL, 342, 346, 369, 372, 381. *See also* Isthmian canal
PAN-AMERICAN EXPOSITION (1901), 138, 337
PAN-AMERICAN UNION, 253
PANHANDLE RAILROAD, 140
PANICS: of 1873, 84–85, 243; of 1893, 162, 279–80, 286; of 1907, 365, 374
PARKER, ALTON B., 346, 368
PARSONS, ALBERT R., 216, 217
PATENTS, 134
PATRONS OF HUSBANDRY. *See* Granger Movement
PATTERSON, DAVID, 17
PATTERSON, JAMES W., 82, 143
PATTERSON, JOHN, 48
PAYNE, SERENO E., 373
PAYNE-ALDRICH TARIFF, 373
PENDLETON, GEORGE H., 39, 204
PENFIELD, EDWARD, 185
PENNSYLVANIA: 19, 20, 27, 106, 206, 223; election of 1868, 41; oil deposits in, 163–64
PENNSYLVANIA RAILROAD, 141, 142, 162, 167, 171
PEOPLE'S PARTY. *See* Populists
PERMANENT COURT OF INTERNATIONAL ARBITRATION (Hague Court), 337, 372
PETROLEUM. *See* Oil
PETROLEUM PRODUCERS' UNION, 167, 171
PHILADELPHIA, PA., 27, 175, 227

PHILADELPHIA AND READING COAL AND IRON COMPANY, 346
PHILADELPHIA AND READING RAILROAD, 279
PHILIP, CAPT. JOHN, 327
PHILIP KEARNY, FORT, 126
PHILIPPINE ISLANDS, 237–38, 303, 322–23, 331
PHILLIPS, WENDELL, 24
PHONOGRAPH: invention of, 137
PIERREPONT, EDWARDS, 90, 91
PIKE, JAMES S., 48, 69–71
PILLSBURY, CHARLES A., 140
PINCHOT, GIFFORD, 366–67, 374, 376
PITTSBURGH, PA., 105
PITTSBURGH, FORT WAYNE AND CHICAGO RAILROAD, 142
PLATT, THOMAS C.: 201, 259, 291, 300, 335; and Arthur, 206; and election of 1888, 223, 224; and Harrison, 250, 251; and Hayes, 104; and Roosevelt, 333, 341
PLATT AMENDMENT, 331
PLUTÓN (destroyer), 327
POOLE, ERNEST, 309–10
POPULAR SCIENCE MONTHLY, 183
POPULATION, UNITED STATES, 120
POPULIST MANIFESTO, 255
POPULIST PARTY: 247, 254–55, 258, 262, 280–82, 290, 336, 372–73; election of 1892, 264, 266; election of 1896, 294; origins, 246–47
PORTER, ADM. DAVID D., 294
PORTER, HORACE, 57
PORTSMOUTH, TREATY OF, 364
POTTS, JOHN, 33
POWDERLY, TERENCE V., 174, 216
POWELL, CAPT. JAMES, 126
PRENDERGAST, MAURICE, 279
PRINCE, L. BRADFORD, 104
PRINTING PRESS: improved, 140
PROGRESSIVE PARTY, 374, 376
PROHIBITION MOVEMENT, 214, 259
PROMONTORY SUMMIT, 143, 144
PUBLICITY ACT, 369
PUCK, 201, 208, 217, 282
PUERTO RICO, 294, 322, 330, 336
PULITZER, ALBERT, 186
PULITZER, JOSEPH, 185, 290, 303
PULLMAN, GEORGE M.: invents Pullman car, 140; and Pullman strike, 286
PULLMAN, ILL., 286

PULLMAN STRIKE, 286–89
PURE FOOD AND DRUGS, AGITATION FOR, 361

Q

QUAY, MATTHEW, 223, 224, 251, 259, 291, 335

R

RADICAL REPUBLICANS. *See* Republican party, Radical
RAILROADS: 29, 85, 122, 282, 336; expansion and improvement, 49, 82, 140–44; and industry, 134, 166–67, 170–71; regulation, 220, 243–44, 359–61; strikes, 105–6, 171, 286–89; transcontinental, 142–44, 226–27; travel on, description, 311–12. *See also* specific railroads
RAWLINS, JOHN, 55, 56, 68
RAYMOND, HENRY J., 26, 27
RAYMOND, WILLIAM A., 108
RECONSTRUCTION: corruption during, 48–49, 66–67; description, 24, 25–26, 28–30, 47–51, 55, 66–71, 77–79, 85–86; end of, 78, 85, 99, 100; under Lincoln and Johnson, 15, 18
RECONSTRUCTION ACTS, 29–30. *See also* Military Reconstruction Act
RED CLOUD, CHIEF, 126, 127
RED RIVER WAR, 128
RED SHIRTS, 98
REDNECKS, 101, 245–46
REED, THOMAS B., 251, 252, 289, 341
REID, JOHN C., 98
REID, WHITELAW, 32, 140, 223, 259
REMINGTON, FREDERIC, 182, 303
REMINGTON, PHILO, 140
RENO, MAJ. MARCUS, 129
RENO, FORT, 126
REPUBLICAN PARTY: 20, 29, 35, 37, 85, 101, 106, 206, 223; in 1866, 28; in 1868, 37, 38–39, 40; in 1870, 62, 63, 64; in 1874, 85; in 1876, 94–95, 98; in 1880, 199–200; in 1884, 206, 216; in 1886, 216; in 1892, 259; in 1896, 291, 303; in 1900, 336; Liberal, 17, 27, 62, 92, 94, 372–73, 374; Radical, 9, 10, 15, 17, 20–21, 27, 28, 34–35, 37, 46, 62–63, 66, 73. *See also* Stalwarts
REVELS, HIRAM R., 47, 50

REVENUE ACT OF 1872, 90
REYNOLDS, JAMES B., 361
RHEAD, LOUIS J., 185
RICHARDSON, HENRY H., 179, 180
RICHARDSON, WILLIAM A., 85, 90
RICHMOND, VA., 15, 16, 42
RIIS, JACOB, 268, 275, 308–9, 310–11, 342
RILEY, FORT, 124
RIVERS AND HARBORS BILL, 205
ROBERTSON, WILLIAM H., 201, 204
ROCKEFELLER, JOHN D., 162, 163, 164, 165–66, 172
ROCKEFELLER, WILLIAM, 166
RODGERS, REAR ADM. JOHN, 294
ROEBLING, JOHN, 180–81, 230
ROEBLING, WASHINGTON, 181, 230
ROGERS, FAIRMAN, 255
ROGERS, JOHN, 182
ROGERS, WILLIAM ALLEN, 308
ROOSEVELT, THEODORE: 107, 207, 335–36, 342, 373, 382; as assistant sec. of navy, 300, 303, 304, 322; description and early career, 208, 211, 239, 251, 338, 340–41, 346, 361; expansionist, 297, 300, 302, 331; as gov. of N. Y., 333, 335; as President, 238–39, 338–46, 359–68, 372; as a Progressive, 374, 376–77; and Spanish-American War, 321–26 *passim*, 329, 330, 333
ROOSEVELT, THEODORE, SR., 104
ROOT, ELIHU, 338, 367, 374, 376
ROOT, JOHN W., 181
ROSEBUD CREEK, 129
ROSEWATER, VICTOR, 376
ROSS, EDMUND G., 35, 37
ROSS, EDWARD A., 316
ROUGH RIDERS, 322, 324, 325, 326, 333, 340, 376
ROUSE, HENRY, 164
RUEDE, HOWARD, 156–57
RURAL LIFE, 146–59, 313, 384–85, 386, 388, 389. *See also* Farming
RUSSIA: 333; and Alaska, 43, 45; and Japan, 363–65; and World War I, 381
RUSSO-JAPANESE WAR, 363–64, 365
RYDER, ALBERT P., 182

S

SACKVILLE-WEST, LIONEL, 224
SAINT-GAUDENS, AUGUSTUS, 181, 182
ST. JOHN, JOHN P., 214

ST. LOUIS, MO., 28, 91, 98, 185, 232–33
ST. THOMAS, ISLAND OF, 43
SALTUS, EDGAR, 230, 231, 232
SAMANÁ BAY, 59
SAMOA, 294–95
SAMPSON, ADM. WILLIAM T., 323–24, 327, 330
SANBORN, JOHN B., 87, 90
SANBORN, KATE, 155–56
SAND CREEK MASSACRE, 125
SAN FRANCISCO, CAL., 179, 186, 227, 362
SAN JUAN HILL, BATTLE OF, 325–26, 329
SANTA FE TRAIL, 124
SANTIAGO DE CUBA, 323–24, 325, 326, 327, 330
SARGENT, JOHN SINGER, 182, 218
SATURDAY EVENING POST, 183, 237
SAVANNAH, GA., 11, 15, 42
SAWYER, PHILETUS, 251
SCALAWAGS, 27, 50
SCHLEY, CQMO. WINFIELD S., 323–24, 329, 330
SCHURZ, CARL: 58, 62, 63, 64, 207, 208, 215, 331; as Sec. of the Interior, 101, 102
SCIENTIFIC AMERICAN, 183
SCOTT, ROBERT K., 48
SCOTT, FORT, 124
SCULPTURE, 181–82
SELTZER, OLAF, 129
SEMINOLES, 124
SENATE, U.S.: 14, 15, 24, 25, 45, 59, 104, 304, 369; composition of, 28, 50, 62, 216, 251, 331–32; impeachment of Johnson, 9, 34–35, 37; and Tenure of Office Act, 30, 33, 34, 58
SEWALL, ARTHUR, 292
SEWARD, WILLIAM: 31, 37, 59; as Sec. of State, 27, 42–43, 45, 294
SEWING MACHINE: popularity of, 140
SEYMOUR, HORATIO, 38, 39, 40, 41, 55
SHAFTER, GEN. WILLIAM R., 322, 324, 327, 330, 333
SHELLABARGER, SAMUEL, 29, 30
SHENANDOAH VALLEY, 14
SHEPHERD, ALEXANDER R., 87
SHERIDAN, GEN. PHILIP, 14, 33, 40, 43, 86, 127, 129
SHERMAN, JOHN: as Sec. of the Treasury, 101, 102, 104, 106, 199–200; as senator, 25, 28, 85, 94, 99, 223, 224, 252
SHERMAN, GEN. WILLIAM T., 11, 14, 16, 33, 40, 42, 43, 87, 223
SHERMAN ANTITRUST ACT, 252, 254, 288, 336, 343–44, 369, 374
SHERMAN SILVER PURCHASE ACT, 252, 262, 279, 280–82

SHOTGUN PLAN, 86
SIBLEY, COL. HENRY, 124
SIGSBEE, CAPT. CHARLES D., 303–4
SILLIMAN, BENJAMIN, 163
SILVER MOVEMENT, 106, 242, 252, 262, 279, 282–83, 285–86, 290–92, 336
SIMPSON, "SOCKLESS JERRY," 246
SINCLAIR, UPTON, 361
SINGER, ISAAC, 140
SIOUX, 124, 125, 126–27, 128–29
SITTING BULL, 127, 132, 212
SLAVERY, 13, 18, 19
SMALLEY, EUGENE V., 154–55, 158–59, 313
SMEDLEY, WILLIAM T., 343
SMITH, E. E., 107, 111, 117
SMOKY RIVER TRAIL, 124
SNELLER, ANNE GERTRUDE, 148–49, 152–53
SNELLING, FORT, 124
SOCIAL DARWINISM, 172, 234
SOCIAL LIFE, UPPER CLASS, 174–75, 178–79, 267, 268, 271, 274, 342, 343
SOCIETY OF THE WHITE ROSE, 51
SOUSA, JOHN PHILIP, 216
SOUTH: 10, 124; Democratic return to power in, 85, 100–101; farming and Populism in, 243, 246, 254, 258; during Reconstruction, 14, 17–18, 26, 28, 29–30, 40, 48–51, 62–63, 64, 66–67, 69–77, 78–79, 85–86. *See also* individual states
SOUTH CAROLINA: 98, 100, 246; during Reconstruction, 11–12, 14, 18, 40, 48–49, 50, 63, 66, 69–70, 86
SOUTH DAKOTA, 106, 116, 119, 247
SOUTH IMPROVEMENT COMPANY, 167, 170
SOUTHERN ALLIANCE, 244–45, 254, 258
SOUTHERN PACIFIC RAILROAD, 186
SPAIN: war with. *See* Spanish-American War
SPANISH-AMERICAN WAR, 236, 237–38, 304, 321–30
SPECIE RESUMPTION ACT, 106
SPENCER, HERBERT, 172
SPIES, AUGUST, 216–17
SPORTS. *See* specific sports
SPRAGUE, KATE CHASE, 102
SPRAGUE, WILLIAM, 102
STALWARTS: 58, 92, 100, 211; and Arthur, 205, 206; in campaign of 1872, 64; in campaign of 1880, 199, 200, 201; and civil service reform, 104–5; and Garfield's death, 204; and Reconstruction, 63

tion, 63
STANBERY, HENRY, 34, 37
STANDARD OIL COMPANY, 166–67, 170–71
STANFORD, LELAND, 142, 144
STANTON, EDWIN S.: 20, 39, 47; description and early career, 31–32; as Sec. of War, 11, 15, 31, 32–33
STARIN, JOHN H., 204
STATUE OF LIBERTY, 180, 181, 313, 314
STEEL, 90, 134, 161, 163, 232–33, 265
STEFFENS, LINCOLN, 361
STEICHEN, EDWARD, 290
STELLA, JOSEPH, 378
STEPHENS, ALEXANDER H., 18, 50
STEVENS, JOHN, 126
STEVENS, THADDEUS: 20, 24, 25, 27, 28, 47, 51, 93; description and early career, 19; and impeachment of Johnson, 9, 34–35; and Reconstruction, 19, 20, 29
STEVENSON, ADLAI E., 262, 280, 336
STEVENSON, ROBERT LOUIS, 294, 311–12
STEWART, A. T., 55, 175
STODDARD, RICHARD H., 183
STOECKL, BARON EDWARD DE, 43, 45
STRAUS, ISADOR, 215
STRAUS, OSCAR, 376
STRONG, WILLIAM L., 341
SUGAR TRUST, 254
SULLIVAN, JOHN L., 192, 373
SULLIVAN, LOUIS HENRI, 180
SULLIVAN, MARK, 361, 368–69, 372
SUMNER, CHARLES: 19, 24, 25, 28, 32, 45, 55, 58, 59, 62, 93; description, 15; and Grant, 63, 64; and Reconstruction, 15, 28, 33, 47
SUMNER, GEN. SAMUEL S., 325
SUMNER, WILLIAM G., 224
SUN, New York, 82, 185, 208, 212, 369
SUPREME COURT, UNITED STATES, 14, 101, 290, 343
SUSQUEHANNA RIVER, 196
SUSSEX (steamship), 382
SWANN, THOMAS, 142
SWIFT, GUSTAVUS, 140, 162

T

TAFT, WILLIAM HOWARD: 333, 341, 364; description and early career, 367–68, 369, 372; election of 1908, 368; election of 1912,

377; as President, 369–77
TAKAHIRA, KOGORO, 364
TAMMANY HALL: 38, 39, 62, 262; and Cleveland, 208, 211, 264–65; and Roosevelt, 333, 341
TANNER, JAMES, 251
TARBELL, EDMUND C., 262
TARBELL, IDA M., 170–71, 361
TARIFF: 63–64; and Arthur, 205; and Cleveland, 221, 282; and development of industry, 134; in 1888, 223; and McKinley, 252–53, 300; in 1900, 337; and Taft, 369, 372, 373; and Wilson, 380
TAVERNIER, JULES, 87, 312
TAXES. *See* Income tax, Inheritance tax
TAYLOR, BAYARD, 183
TELEGRAPH: early development, 134
TELEPHONE: invention of, 139
TELLER, HENRY M., 291, 331
TENNESSEE: 12, 13, 26, 101; farming and rural life, 149–50, 245; during Reconstruction, 18, 28, 62–63
TENNESSEE COAL AND IRON COMPANY, 374
TENNIS, 187
TENURE OF OFFICE ACT, 10–11, 30–31, 33–34, 58
TERRY, GEN. ALFRED H., 128, 129
TEXAS: 124, 128; during Reconstruction, 18, 41, 55, 63
TEXAS (battleship), 327
THOMAS, GEN. GEORGE, 33
THOMAS, GEN. LORENZO, 33–34
THOMSON, J. EDGAR, 142
THULSTRUP, THURE DE, 37
THURMAN, ALLEN G., 208, 211, 223
THURSTON, JOHN M., 224
TIFFANY, LOUIS, 204
TILDEN, SAMUEL, 78, 98–99, 208, 335
TILLMAN, BENJAMIN R., 245–46, 262, 285, 331, 361
TILTON, THEODORE, 27
TIMBER AND STONE ACT, 123
TIMBER CULTURE ACT, 123
TORAL, GEN. JOSÉ, 330
TOWNSEND, JAMES M., 163
TRANSPORTATION: in 1875, 95. *See also* Airplanes, Automobiles, Bicycles, Railroads
TREASURY, UNITED STATES: 55, 90; under Arthur, 205; under Cleveland, 221, 279, 282, 290; under Harrison, 251; in 1896, 294
TRIANGLE WAIST COMPANY FIRE, 381
TRIBUNE, New York, 63,

64, 121, 140, 154-55, 185, 204, 223
TRIBUNE AND FARMER, 183
TROWBRIDGE, JOHN, 16
TRUMBULL, LYMAN, 15
TRUSTS: growth of, 171, 254, 342; and Roosevelt, 367
TWEED, WILLIAM M. ("Boss"), 62, 211
TWEED RING, 50, 56, 98
TWO MOON, CHIEF, 128, 129
TYPEWRITER: development of, 140

U

UNDERWOOD TARIFF, 380
UNIFICATION MOVEMENT, 100
UNION LEAGUE, 51
UNION PACIFIC RAILROAD, 82, 93, 142-44, 174, 228, 311, 343
UNITED MINE WORKERS, 346
UNITED STATES MILITARY ACADEMY. *See* West Point
UNITED STATES STEEL CORPORATION, 342, 374
UTAH, 64
UTES, 132

V

VALLANDIGHAM, CLEMENT, 27, 39, 64
VANDERBILT, ALVA (later Mrs. O. H. P. Belmont), 178, 271
VANDERBILT, CORNELIUS, 38, 141, 162, 178, 276
VANDERBILT, MRS. CORNELIUS, III, 268
VANDERBILT, WILLIAM K., 178
VAUDEVILLE, 370
VENEZUELA, 296-97, 346
VERDICT, THE, 170, 255
VERMONT, 19, 40, 212
VETERANS, 205, 221, 223, 251. *See also* Grand Army of the Republic
VICTORIA, QUEEN, 337
VICTORIO, 133
VILAS, WILLIAM F., 215
VILLARD, HENRY, 262, 279
VIRGINIA: 42, 101, 322; during Reconstruction, 14, 18, 41, 55, 62, 85
VIRGINIA CITY, NEV., 120-21, 125
VIRGINIUS (ship), 301
VIXEN (yacht), 327
VIZCAYA (cruiser), 327, 329

W

WADE, BENJAMIN F., 16, 20, 28, 47
WAGON BOX FIGHT, 126
WALKER, GEN. GILBERT C., 62
WALKER, JAMES, 21, 247
WALL STREET, 56, 57, 85, 337
WALLACE, LEW, 183
WANAMAKER, JOHN, 224
WARD, CHARLES C., 104
WARD, SAMUEL, 58, 178
WAREHOUSE ACT, 244
WARMOTH, HENRY CLAY, 49, 86
WARNER, CHARLES DUDLEY, 68-69
WASHINGTON, BOOKER T., 342
WASHINGTON, 123, 247, 367
WASHINGTON, D.C., 9, 58, 67, 68-69, 81, 87, 283, 285
WASHINGTON, TREATY OF, 64
WASHINGTON MONUMENT, 58, 68-69
WATSON, THOMAS, 254, 258, 292, 368
WATSON, THOMAS A. (assistant to Alexander Graham Bell), 139
WATTERSON, HENRY, 99 264
WEAVER, GEN. JAMES B., 106, 200, 258, 264, 291
WEBB, WALTER P., 139
WEBSTER, DANIEL, 9, 15
WEED, THURLOW, 38
WELCKER, JOHN, 58
WELLES, GIDEON, 27, 28, 32, 39, 47, 55
WELLMAN, SAMUEL T., 161
WELLS, H. G., 231, 238-39, 307-8
WELLS, H. H., 62
WELLS, J. MADISON, 99
WEST: description, 107-17, 121, 228-29; farming in, 139, 247; migration to, 106, 120, 121, 311-12. *See also* Farming, Gold, Indians
WEST, WILLIAM, 207
WEST POINT, 40, 41, 67
WEST VIRGINIA, 105
WESTERN UNION TELEGRAPH COMPANY, 134, 136, 137, 144
WESTINGHOUSE, GEORGE, 140-41
WEYLER Y NICOLAU, GEN. VALERIANO, 302-3
WHEELER, GEN. JOSEPH, 322, 324, 325
WHIG PARTY, 12, 19, 100, 101
WHISKEY RING SCANDAL, 91-92
WHISTLER, JAMES M., 182, 218
WHITE, ANDREW D., 207
WHITE, HORACE, 85
WHITE, PEARL, 381

WHITE, WILLIAM ALLEN, 251, 291
WHITE LEAGUE, 51, 86, 98
WHITMAN, WALT, 119, 180
WHITNEY, WILLIAM C., 262, 264, 291
WHITTIER, JOHN GREENLEAF, 183
WILD HORSES, THE, 285
WILEY, DR. HARVEY, 361
WILHELM, KAISER, 337, 340, 364, 373
WILLIAMS, GEORGE H., 90
WILSON, HENRY, 64, 82, 90
WILSON, WILLIAM L., 280, 282
WILSON, WOODROW: 297, 341, 374; description and early career, 377; election of 1912, 376-77; as President, 380-82
WILSON-GORMAN TARIFF, 282, 301
WINDOM, WILLIAM, 199
WITTE, COUNT SERGEI, 364
WOMAN SUFFRAGE, 47, 375, 381
WOMEN'S CHRISTIAN TEMPERANCE UNION, 214, 255
WOOD, FERNANDO, 27
WOOD, GEN. LEONARD, 322, 324, 331
WOOD LAKE, BATTLE OF, 124
WOOL, GEN. JOHN E., 27
WORLD, New York, 26, 41, 185, 215, 290, 291
WORLD WAR I: beginnings of, 381-82
WORMLEY CONFERENCE, 99
WOUNDED KNEE, BATTLE OF, 133
WRIGHT, FRANK LLOYD, 180
WRIGHT, ORVILLE AND WILBUR, 341
WYOMING, 124, 367

Y

YATES, RICHARD, 42
YELLOW PERIL, 297, 303, 336
YELLOWSTONE NATIONAL PARK, 60, 132
YOHN, FREDERICK C., 322
YOSEMITE VALLEY, 60
YOUNG, GEN. SAMUEL B. M., 331

Z

ZIMMERMANN, ARTHUR, 382